0 1 2 3 4 5 6 7 8 9

TEN COUNT

1

t e n   c o u n t   b y   r i h i t o   t a k a r a i

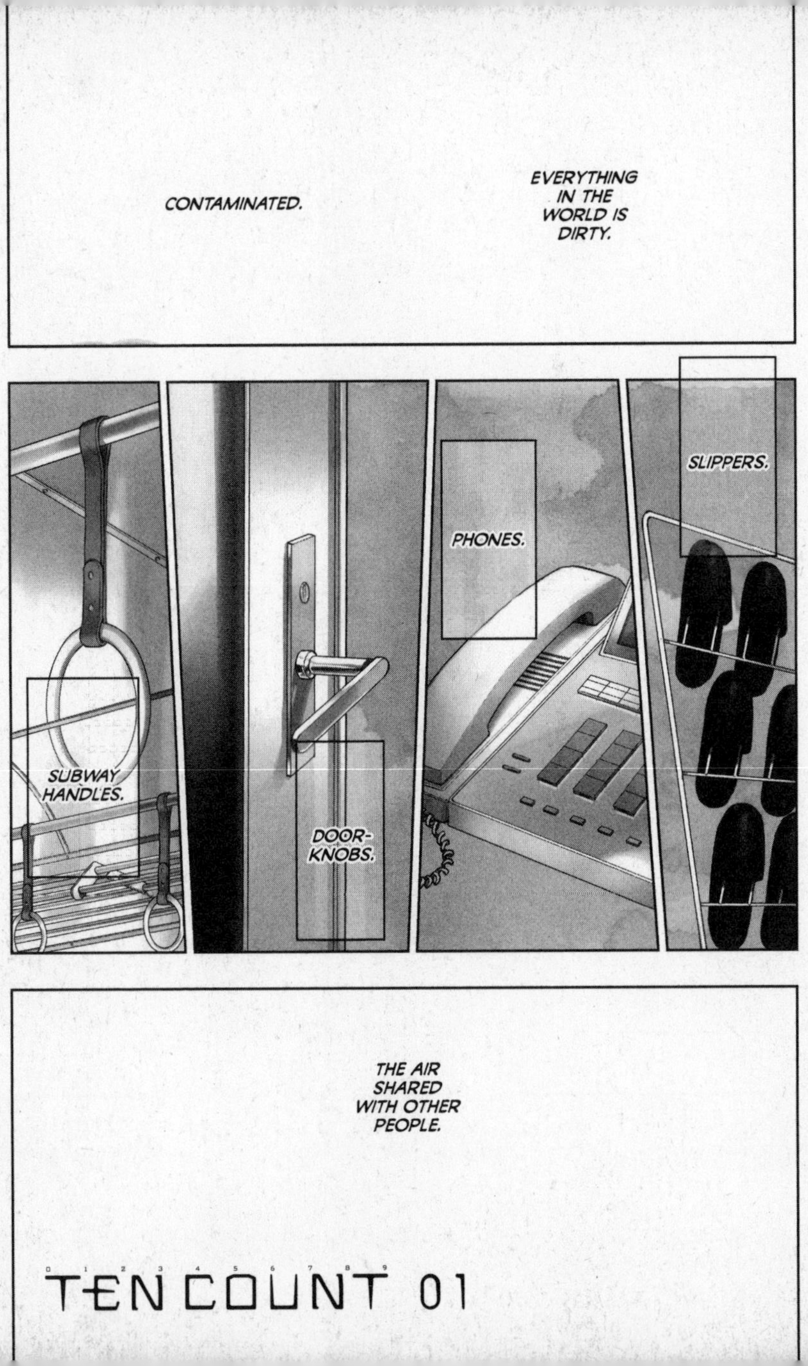
EVERYTHING IN THE WORLD IS DIRTY.
CONTAMINATED.
SLIPPERS.
PHONES.
DOOR-KNOBS.
SUBWAY HANDLES.
THE AIR SHARED WITH OTHER PEOPLE.
0 1 2 3 4 5 6 7 8 9
TEN COUNT 01

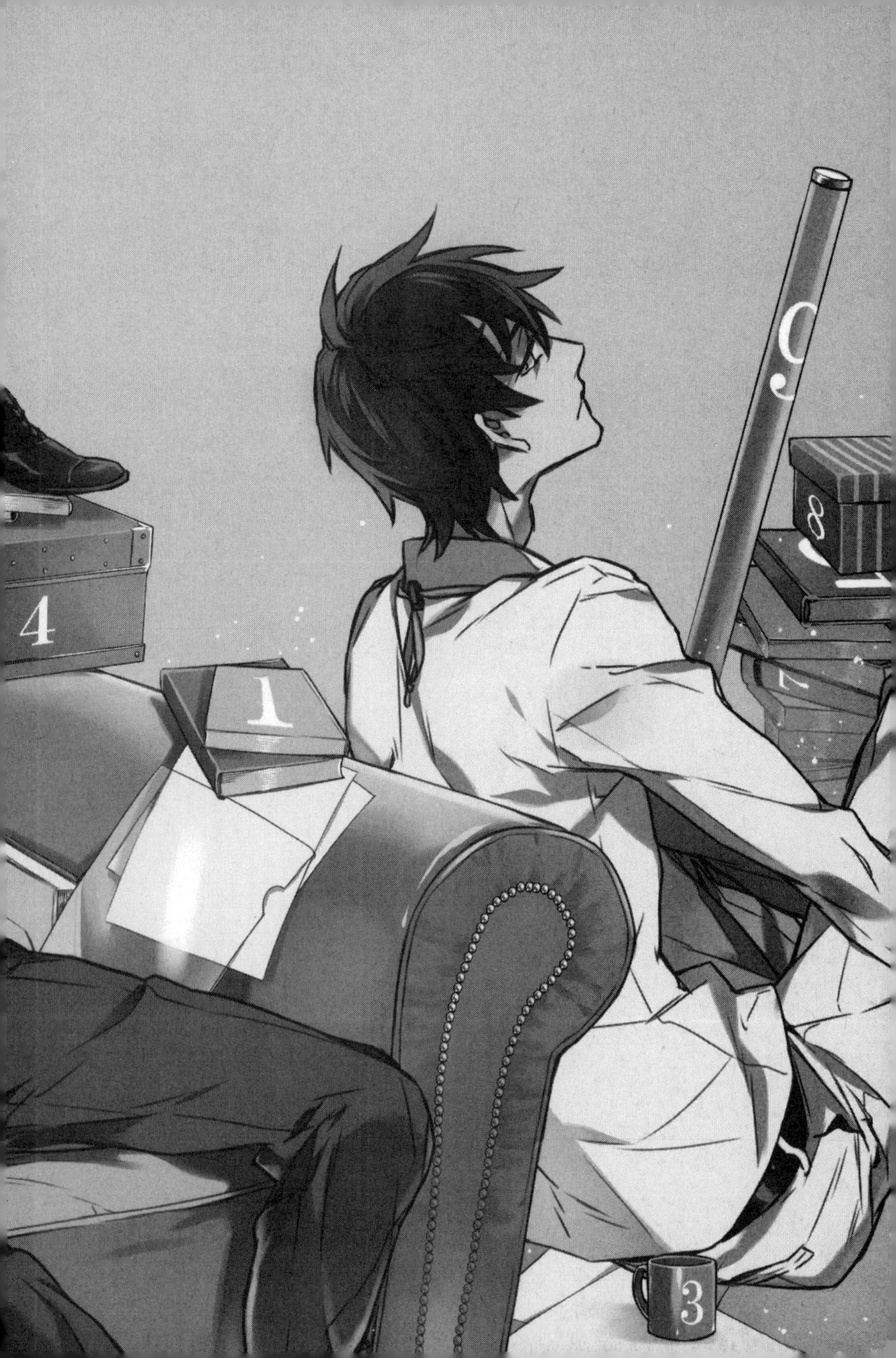
9
8
4
1
3

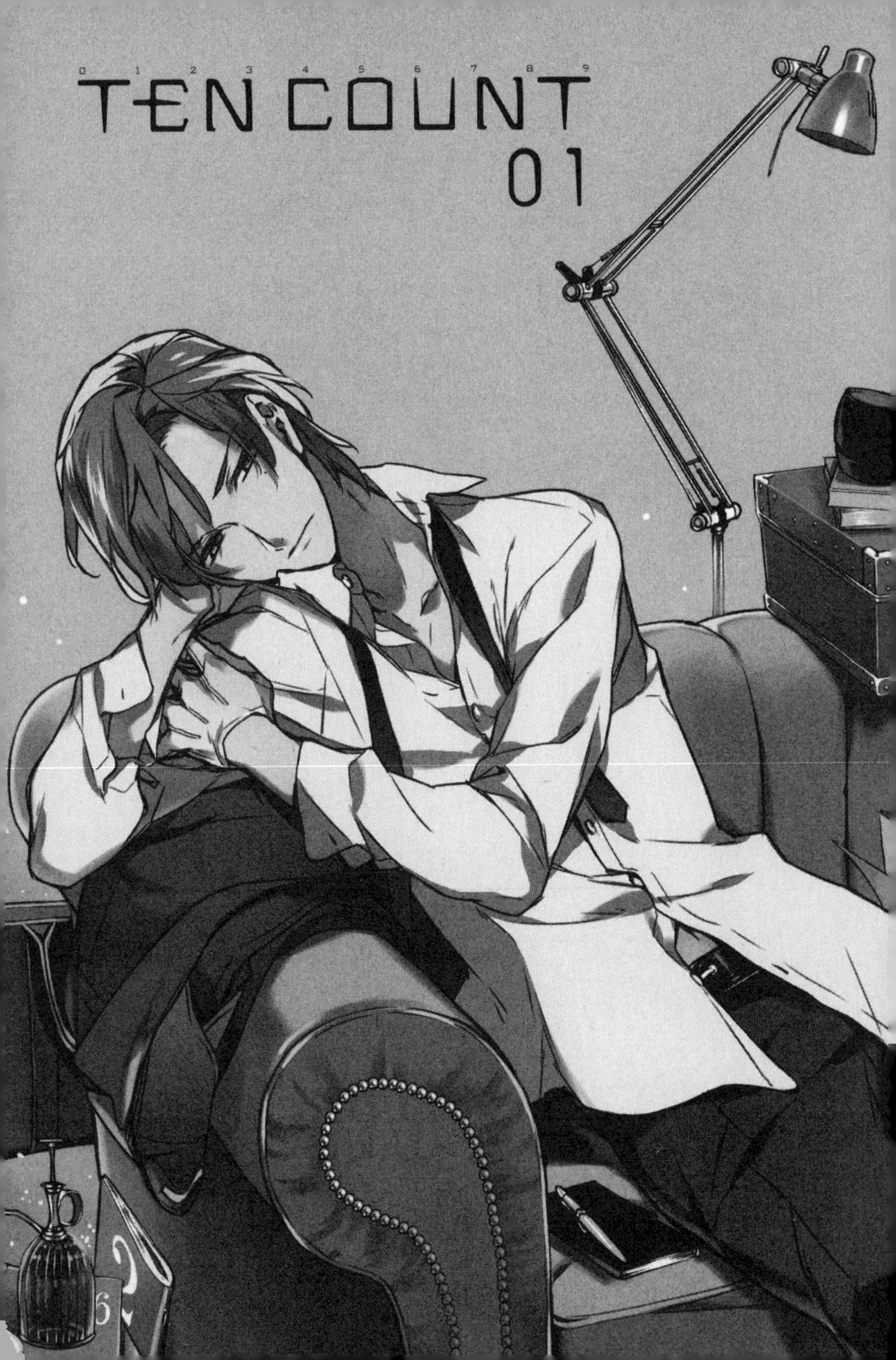
0 1 2 3 4 5 6 7 8 9
TEN COUNT
01

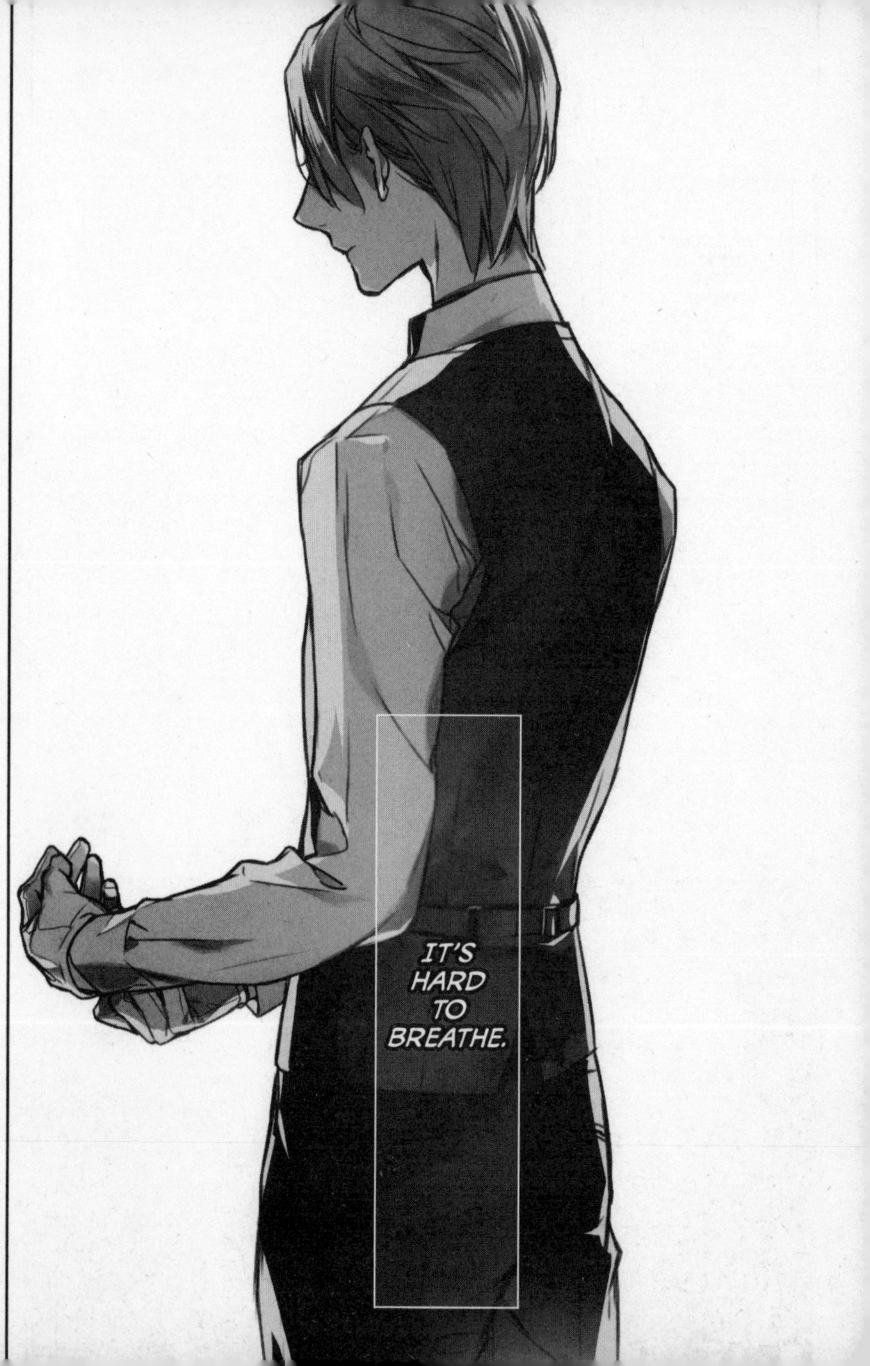
IT'S HARD TO BREATHE.

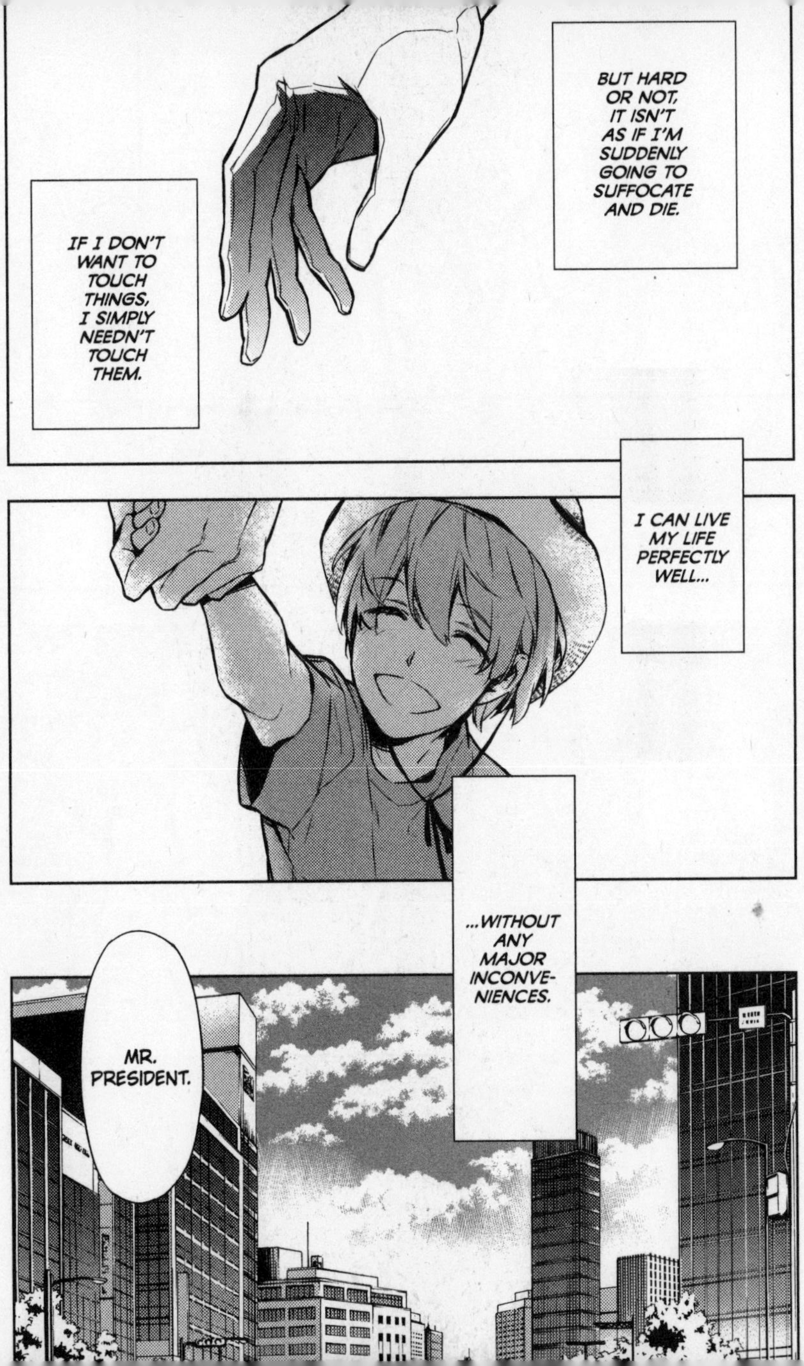
BUT HARD OR NOT, IT ISN'T AS IF I'M SUDDENLY GOING TO SUFFOCATE AND DIE.
IF I DON'T WANT TO TOUCH THINGS, I SIMPLY NEEDN'T TOUCH THEM.
I CAN LIVE MY LIFE PERFECTLY WELL...
...WITHOUT ANY MAJOR INCONVE-NIENCES.
MR. PRESIDENT.

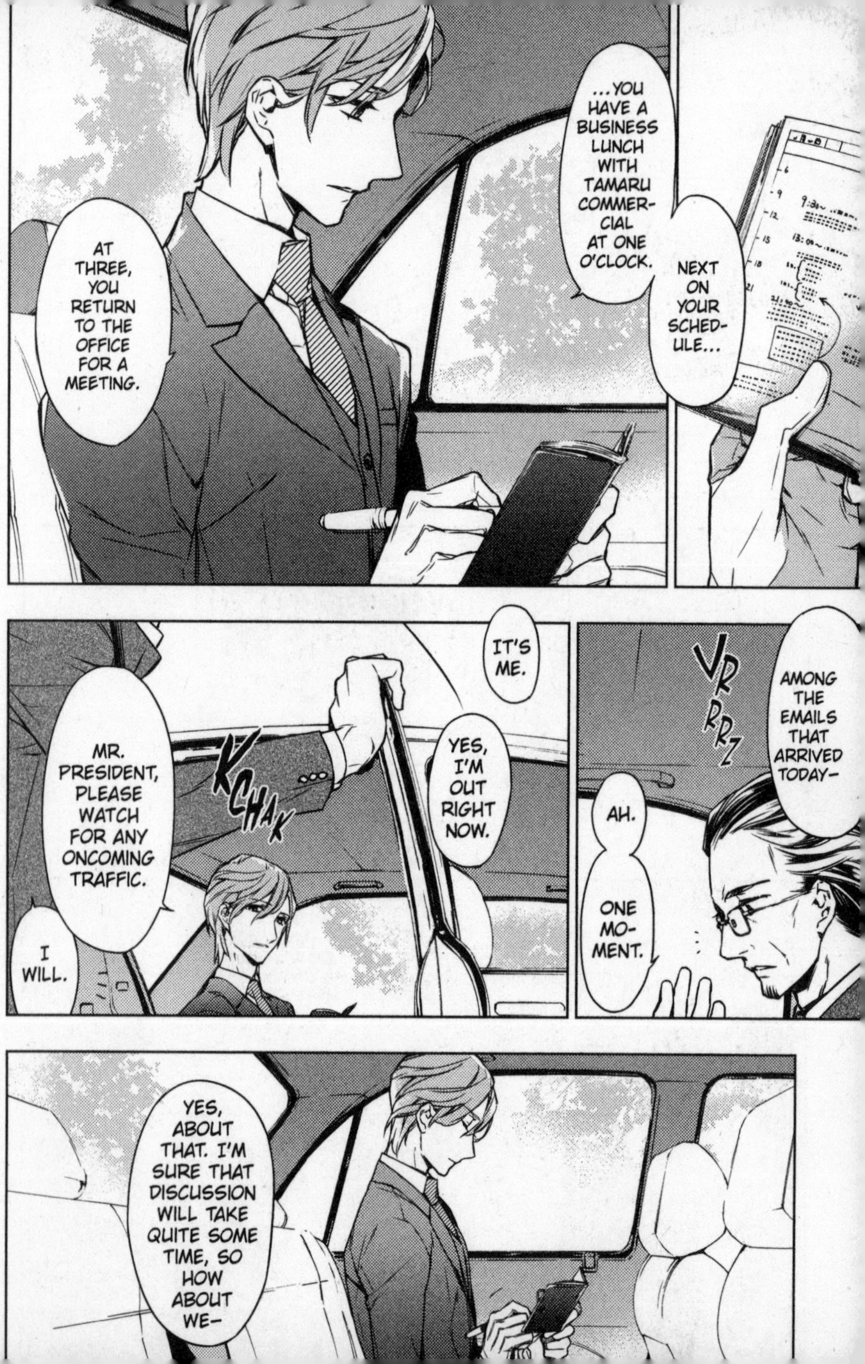
NEXT ON YOUR SCHEDULE...
...YOU HAVE A BUSINESS LUNCH WITH TAMARU COMMERCIAL AT ONE O'CLOCK.
AT THREE, YOU RETURN TO THE OFFICE FOR A MEETING.
VRRRZ
AMONG THE EMAILS THAT ARRIVED TODAY—
AH.
ONE MOMENT.
IT'S ME.
YES, I'M OUT RIGHT NOW.
KCHAK
MR. PRESIDENT, PLEASE WATCH FOR ANY ONCOMING TRAFFIC.
I WILL.
YES, ABOUT THAT. I'M SURE THAT DISCUSSION WILL TAKE QUITE SOME TIME, SO HOW ABOUT WE—

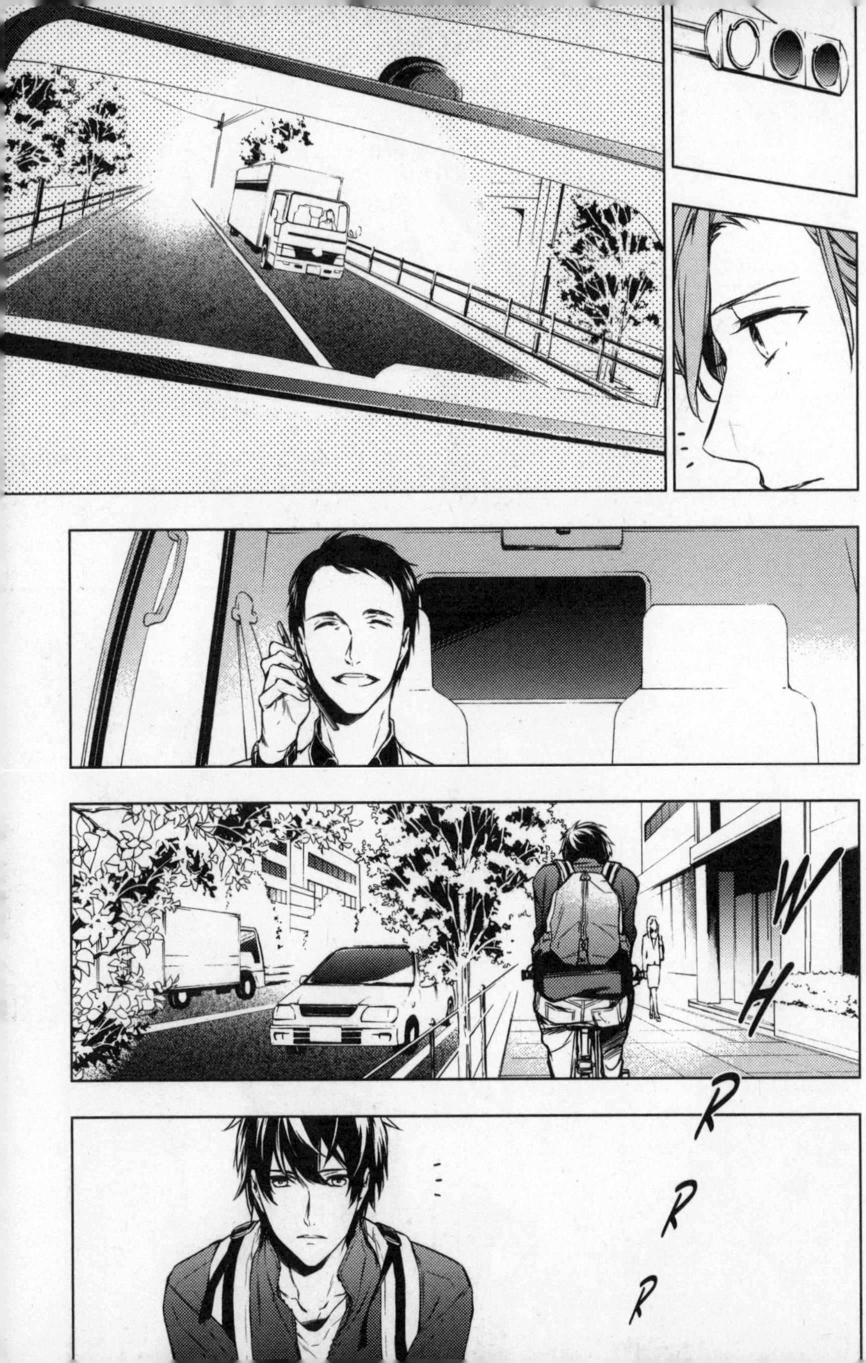
WHRRR

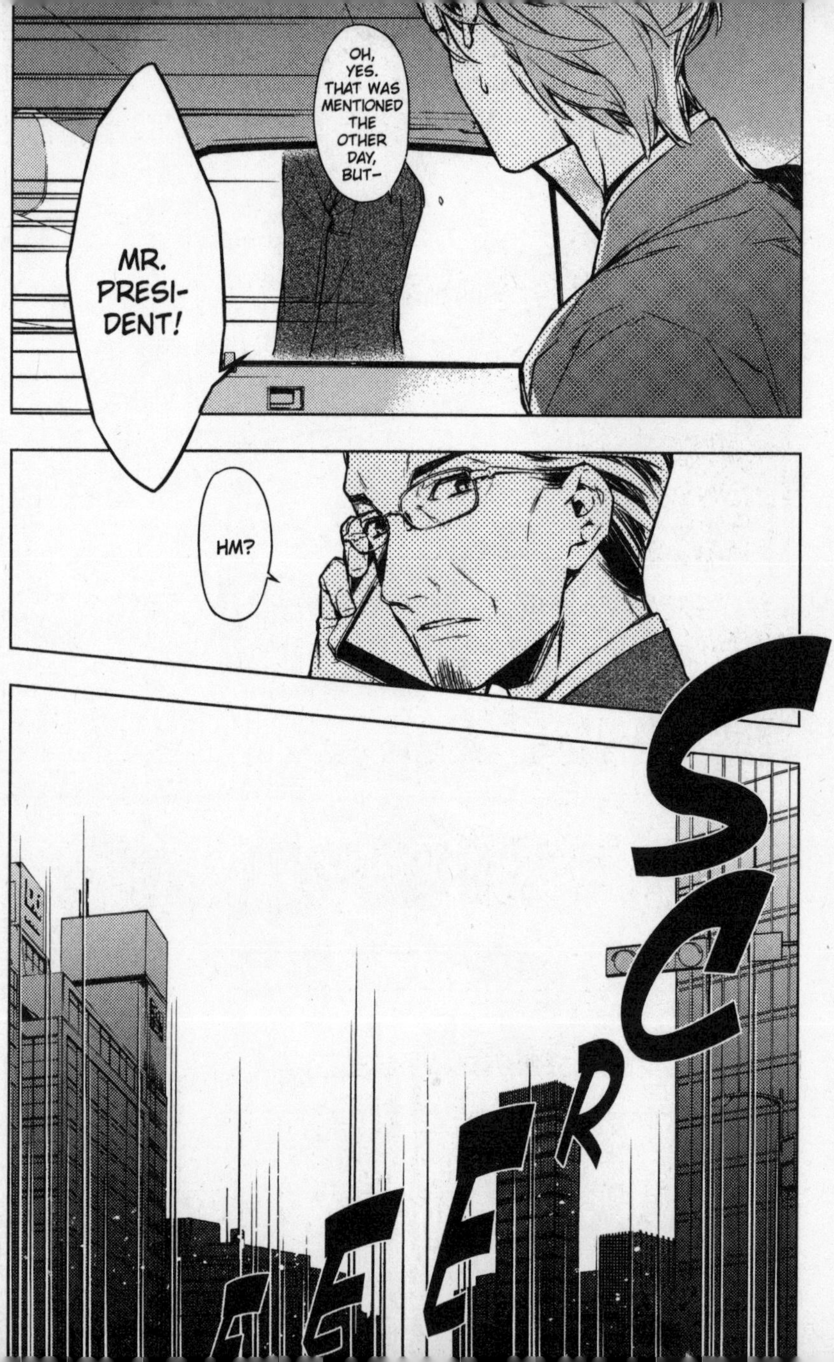
OH, YES. THAT WAS MENTIONED THE OTHER DAY, BUT—
MR. PRESIDENT!
HM?
SCREEEE

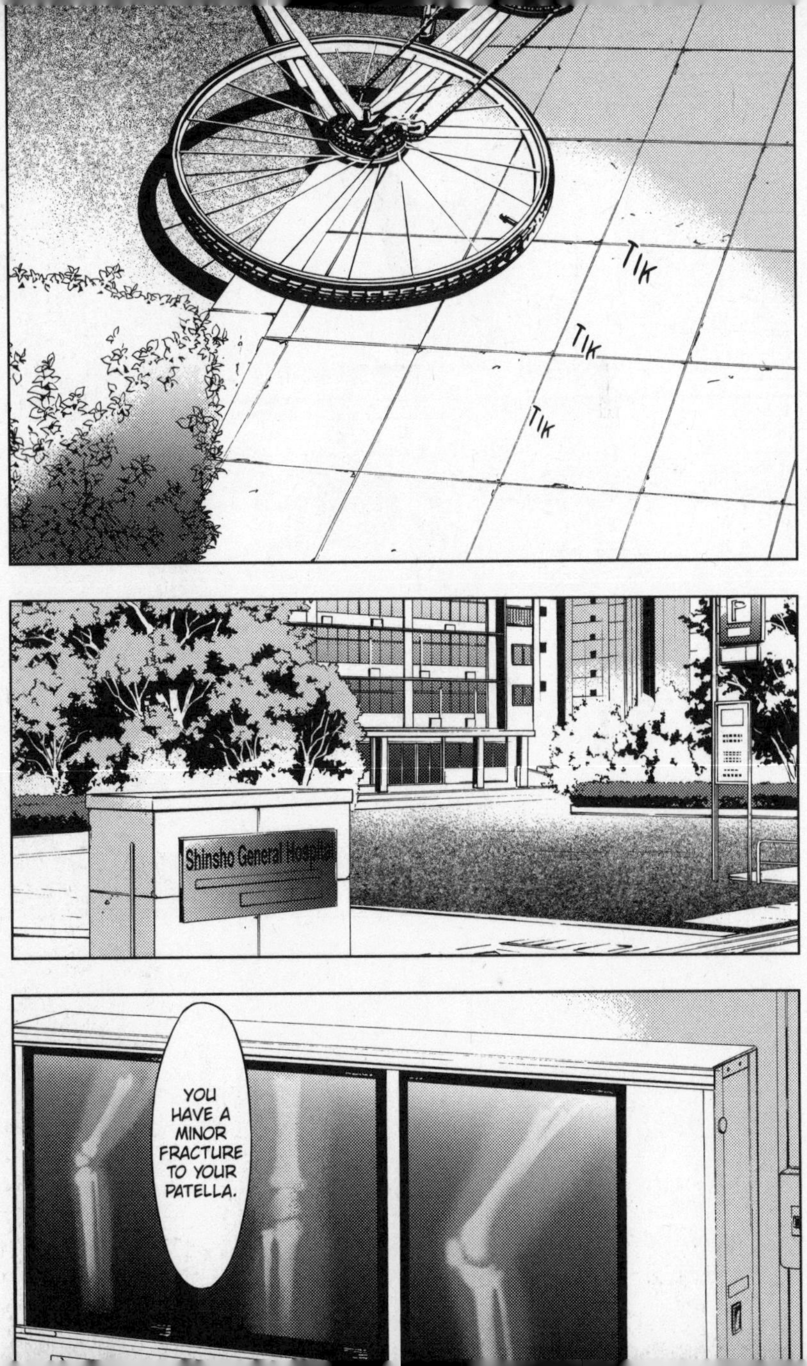
TIK
TIK
TIK
Shinsho General Hospital
YOU HAVE A MINOR FRACTURE TO YOUR PATELLA.

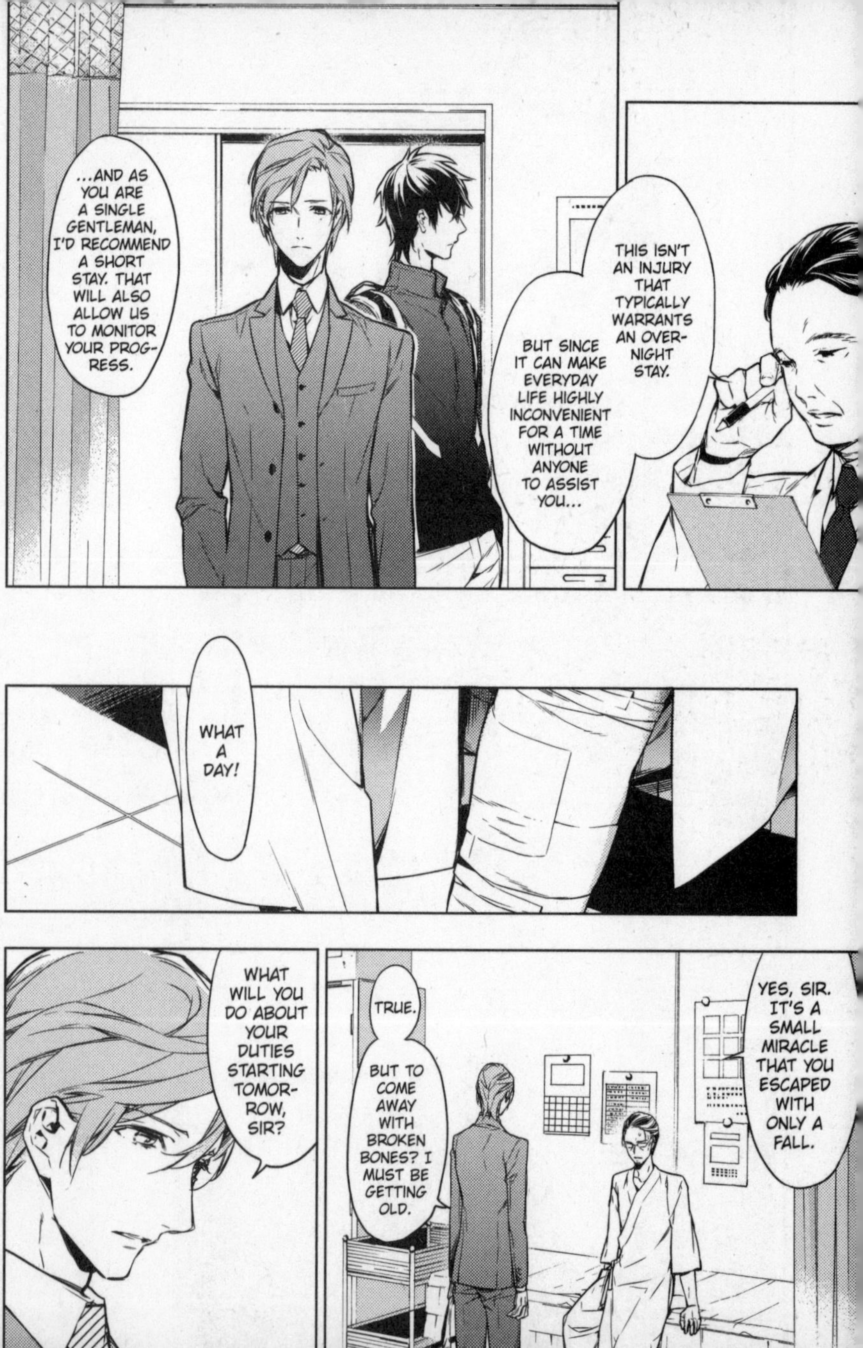
THIS ISN'T AN INJURY THAT TYPICALLY WARRANTS AN OVER-NIGHT STAY.
BUT SINCE IT CAN MAKE EVERYDAY LIFE HIGHLY INCONVENIENT FOR A TIME WITHOUT ANYONE TO ASSIST YOU...
...AND AS YOU ARE A SINGLE GENTLEMAN, I'D RECOMMEND A SHORT STAY. THAT WILL ALSO ALLOW US TO MONITOR YOUR PROG-RESS.
WHAT A DAY!
YES, SIR. IT'S A SMALL MIRACLE THAT YOU ESCAPED WITH ONLY A FALL.
TRUE.
BUT TO COME AWAY WITH BROKEN BONES? I MUST BE GETTING OLD.
WHAT WILL YOU DO ABOUT YOUR DUTIES STARTING TOMOR-ROW, SIR?

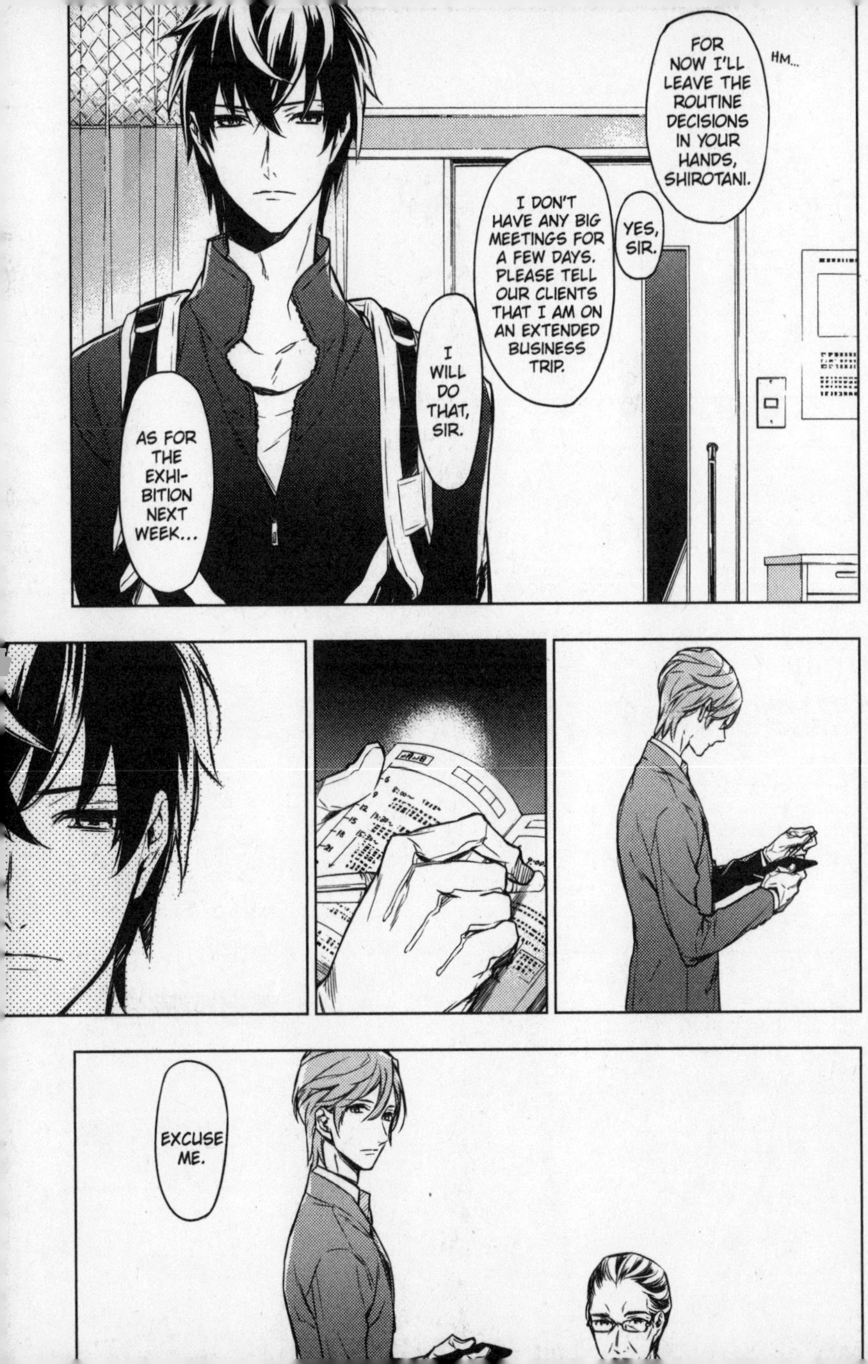
HM...
FOR NOW I'LL LEAVE THE ROUTINE DECISIONS IN YOUR HANDS, SHIROTANI.
YES, SIR.
I DON'T HAVE ANY BIG MEETINGS FOR A FEW DAYS. PLEASE TELL OUR CLIENTS THAT I AM ON AN EXTENDED BUSINESS TRIP.
I WILL DO THAT, SIR.
AS FOR THE EXHIBITION NEXT WEEK...
EXCUSE ME.

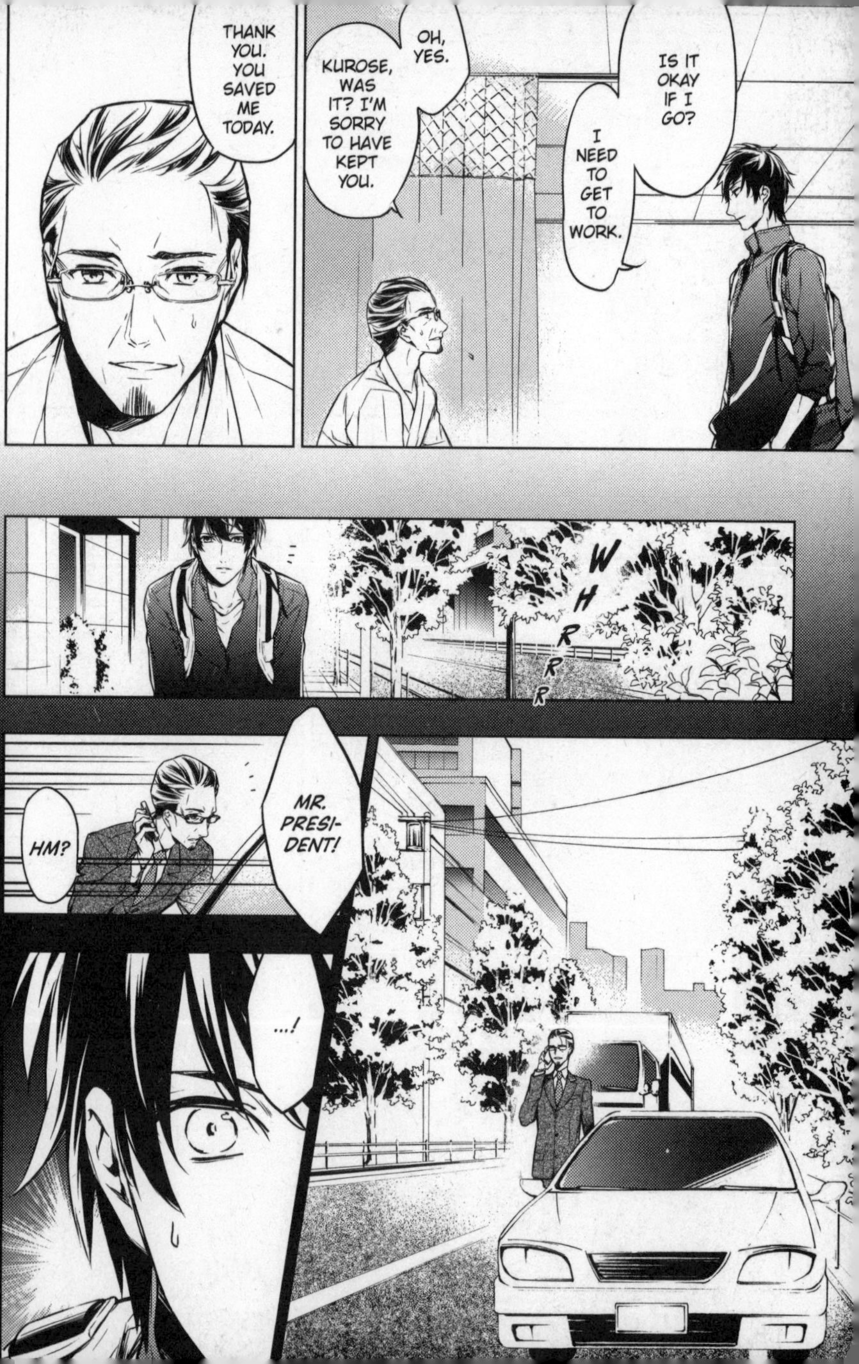
IS IT OKAY IF I GO?
I NEED TO GET TO WORK.
OH, YES.
KUROSE, WAS IT? I'M SORRY TO HAVE KEPT YOU.
THANK YOU. YOU SAVED ME TODAY.
WHRRRR
MR. PRESIDENT!
HM?
...!

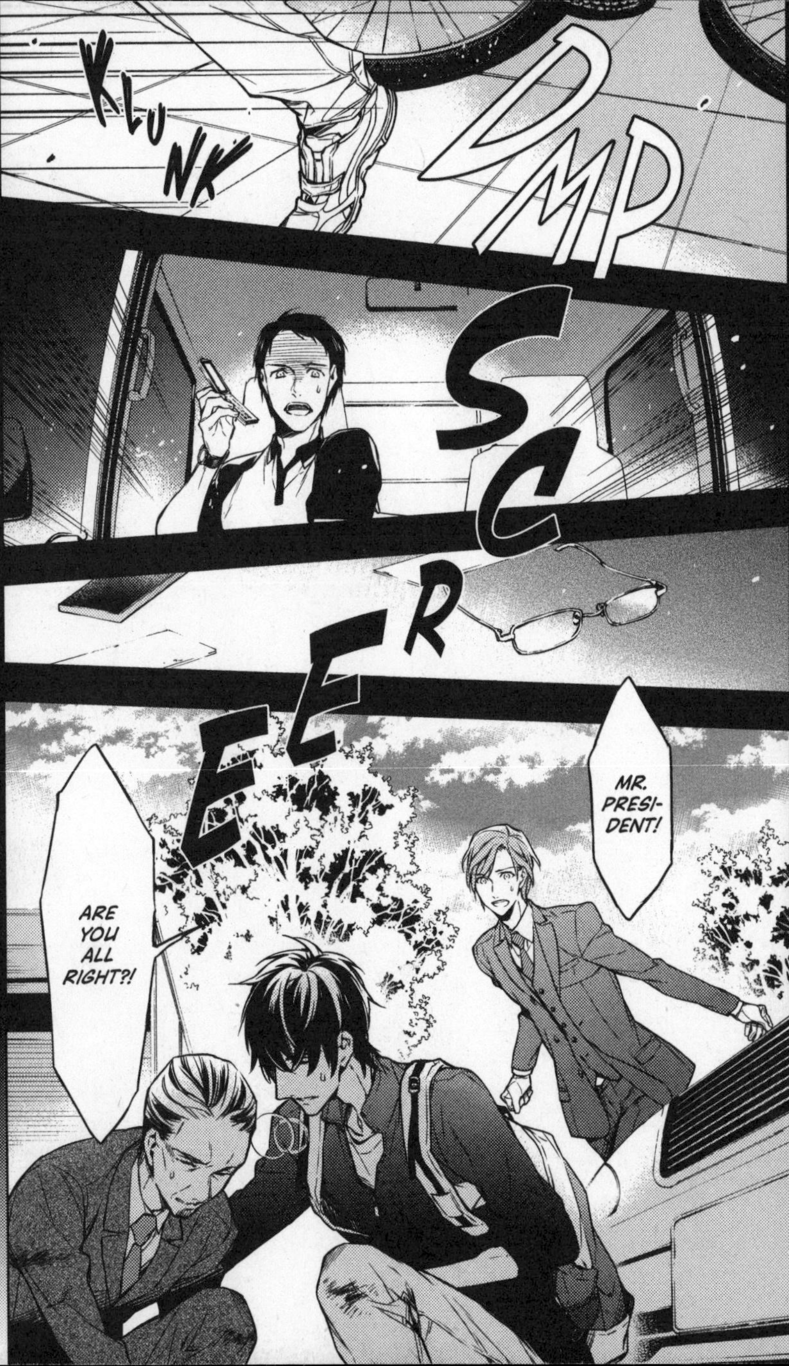
DMP
KLUNK
SCREECH
MR. PRESIDENT!
ARE YOU ALL RIGHT?!

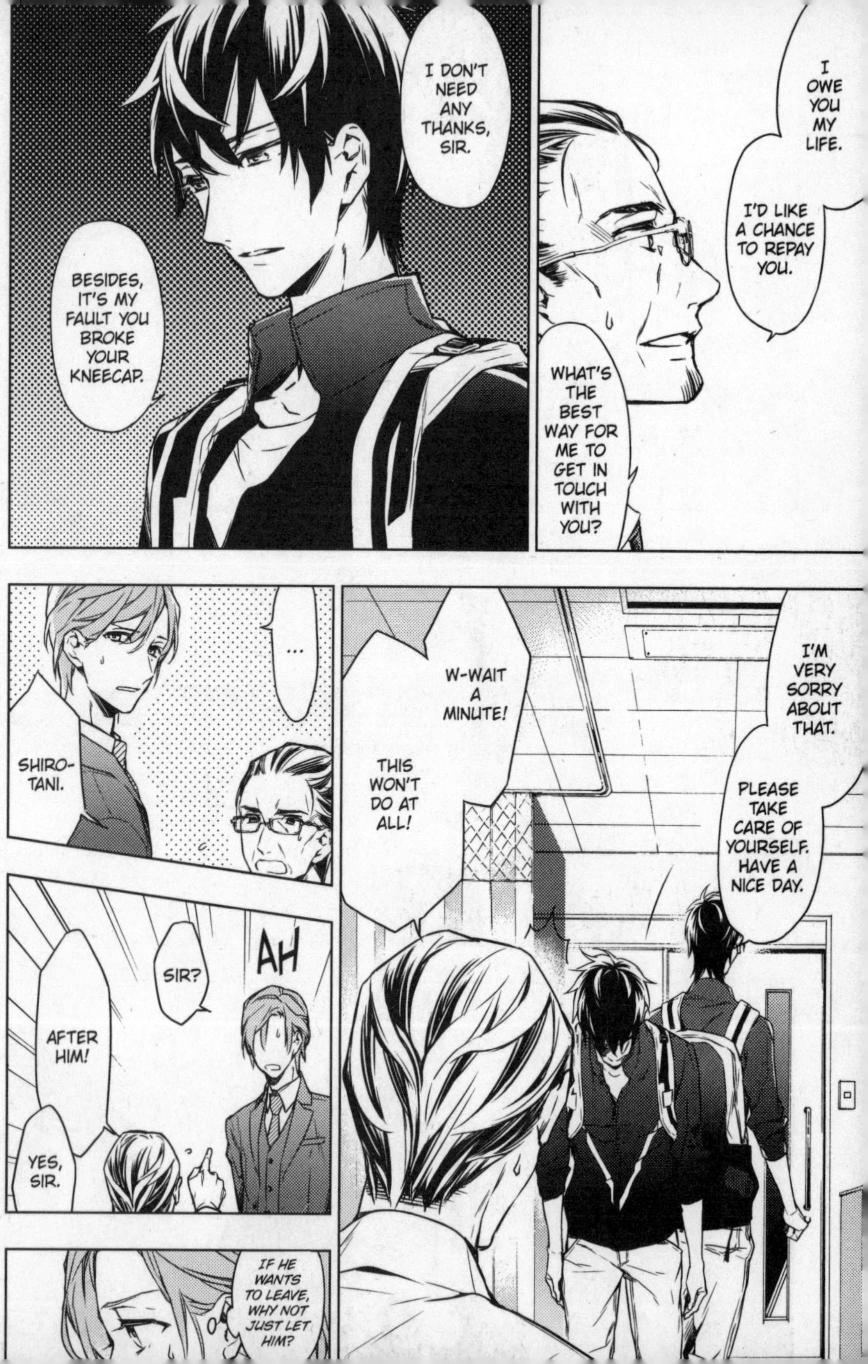
I OWE YOU MY LIFE.
I'D LIKE A CHANCE TO REPAY YOU.
WHAT'S THE BEST WAY FOR ME TO GET IN TOUCH WITH YOU?
I DON'T NEED ANY THANKS, SIR.
BESIDES, IT'S MY FAULT YOU BROKE YOUR KNEECAP.
I'M VERY SORRY ABOUT THAT.
PLEASE TAKE CARE OF YOURSELF. HAVE A NICE DAY.
W-WAIT A MINUTE!
THIS WON'T DO AT ALL!
...
SHIRO-TANI.
AH
SIR?
AFTER HIM!
YES, SIR.
IF HE WANTS TO LEAVE, WHY NOT JUST LET HIM?

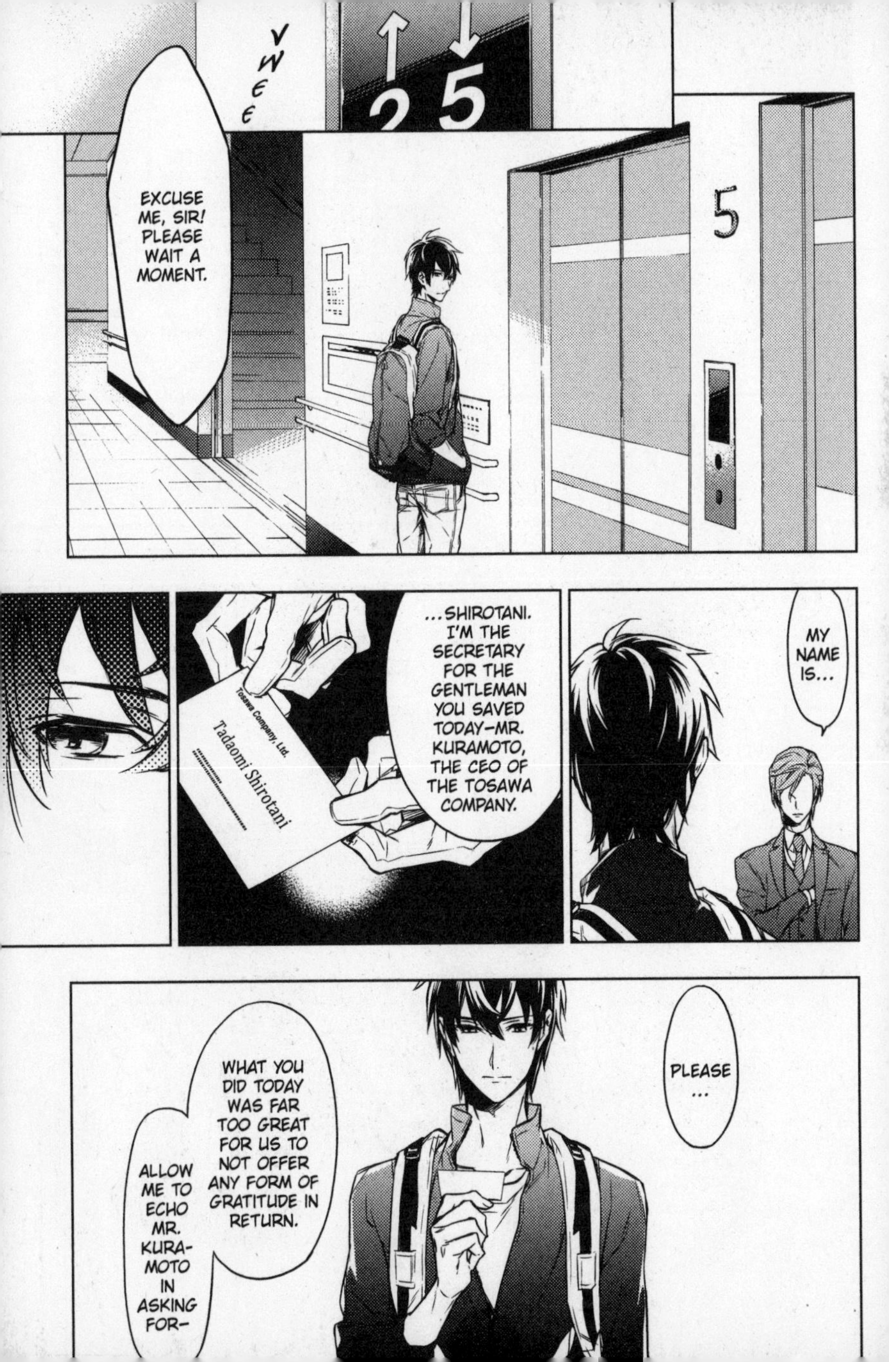
VWEE
EXCUSE ME, SIR! PLEASE WAIT A MOMENT.
MY NAME IS...
...SHIROTANI. I'M THE SECRETARY FOR THE GENTLEMAN YOU SAVED TODAY—MR. KURAMOTO, THE CEO OF THE TOSAWA COMPANY.
Tosawa Company, Ltd.
Tadaomi Shirotani
PLEASE ...
WHAT YOU DID TODAY WAS FAR TOO GREAT FOR US TO NOT OFFER ANY FORM OF GRATITUDE IN RETURN.
ALLOW ME TO ECHO MR. KURAMOTO IN ASKING FOR—

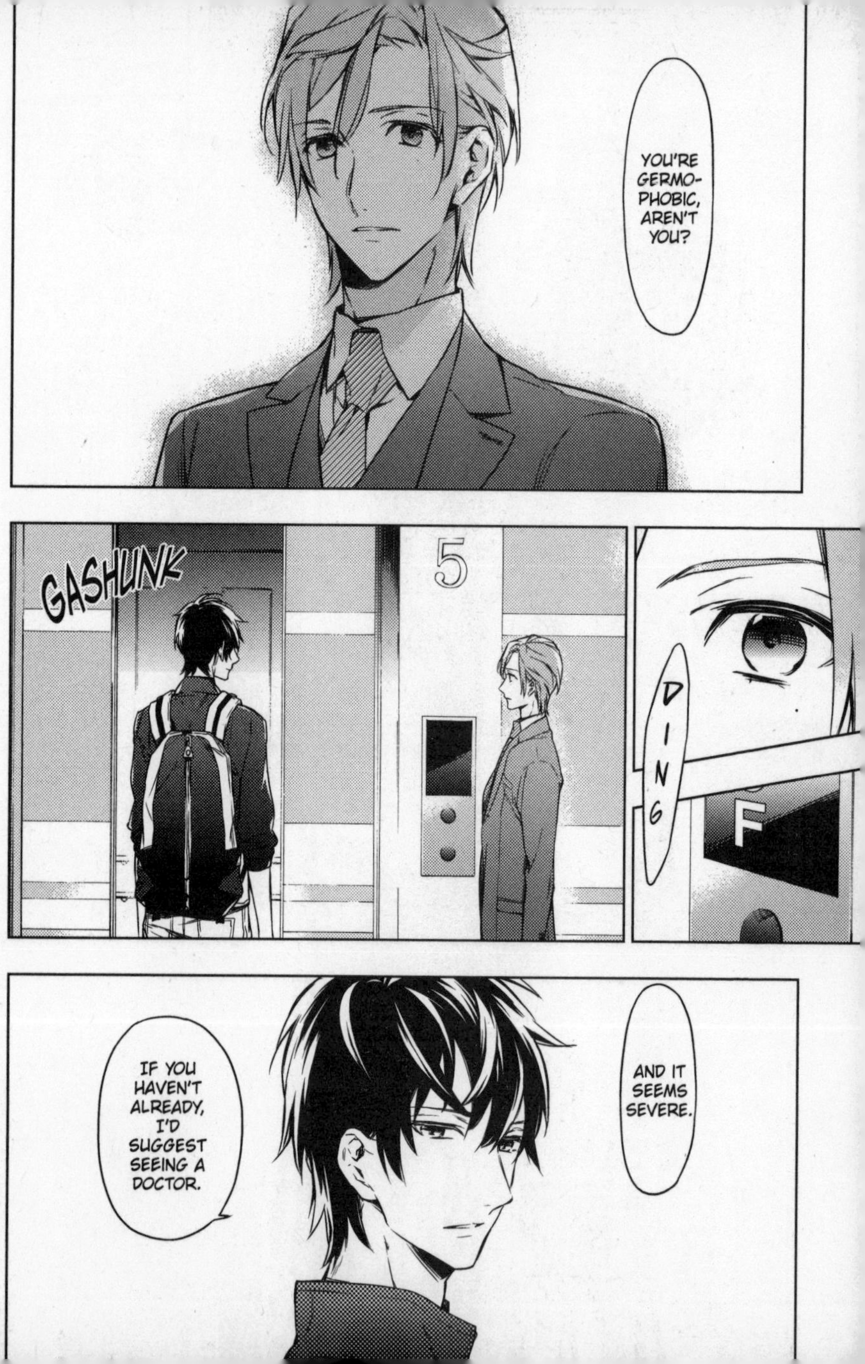
YOU'RE GERMO-PHOBIC, AREN'T YOU?
DING
GASHUNK
5
AND IT SEEMS SEVERE.
IF YOU HAVEN'T ALREADY, I'D SUGGEST SEEING A DOCTOR.

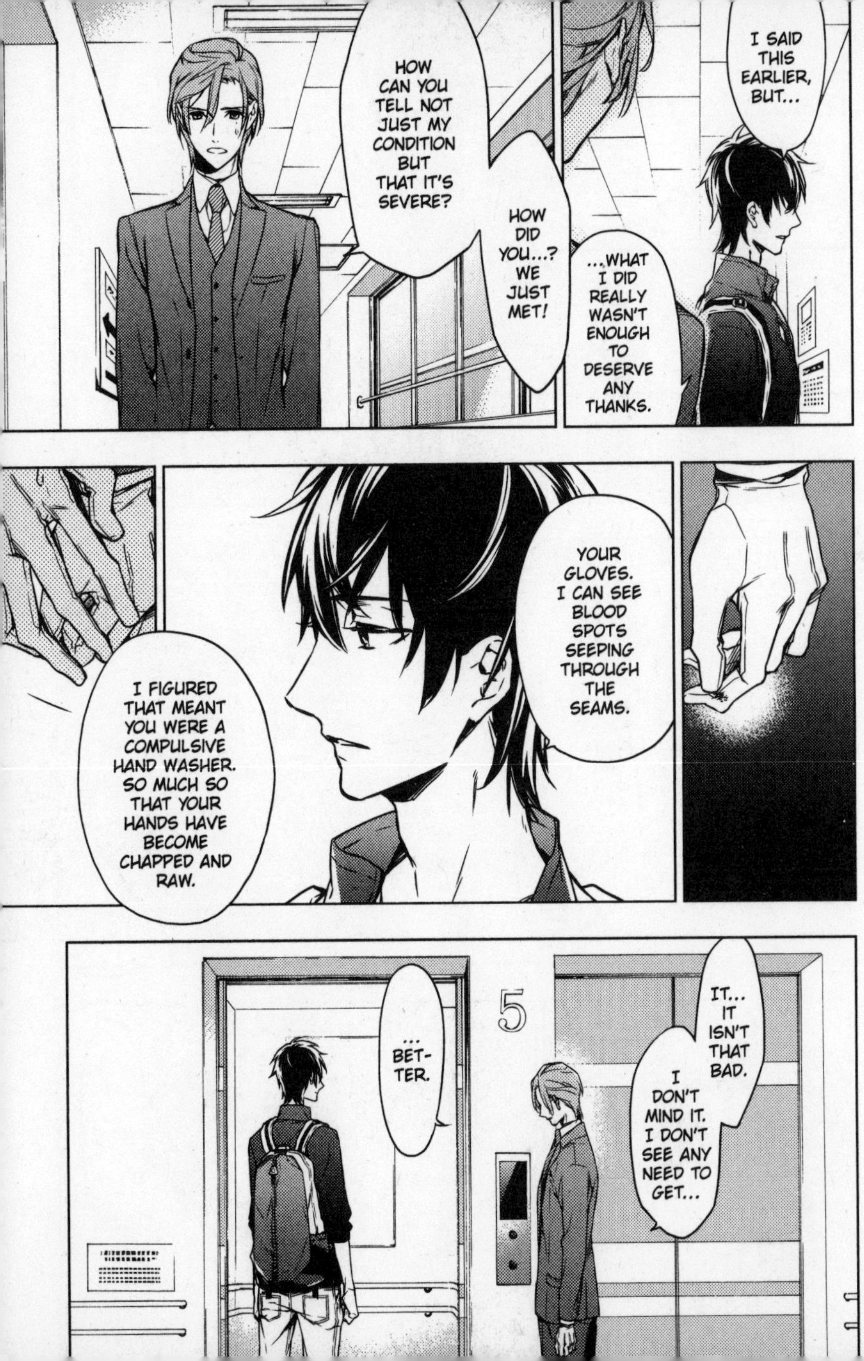
I SAID THIS EARLIER, BUT...
...WHAT I DID REALLY WASN'T ENOUGH TO DESERVE ANY THANKS.
HOW DID YOU...? WE JUST MET!
HOW CAN YOU TELL NOT JUST MY CONDITION BUT THAT IT'S SEVERE?
YOUR GLOVES. I CAN SEE BLOOD SPOTS SEEPING THROUGH THE SEAMS.
I FIGURED THAT MEANT YOU WERE A COMPULSIVE HAND WASHER. SO MUCH SO THAT YOUR HANDS HAVE BECOME CHAPPED AND RAW.
IT... IT ISN'T THAT BAD.
I DON'T MIND IT. I DON'T SEE ANY NEED TO GET...
5
...BET-TER.

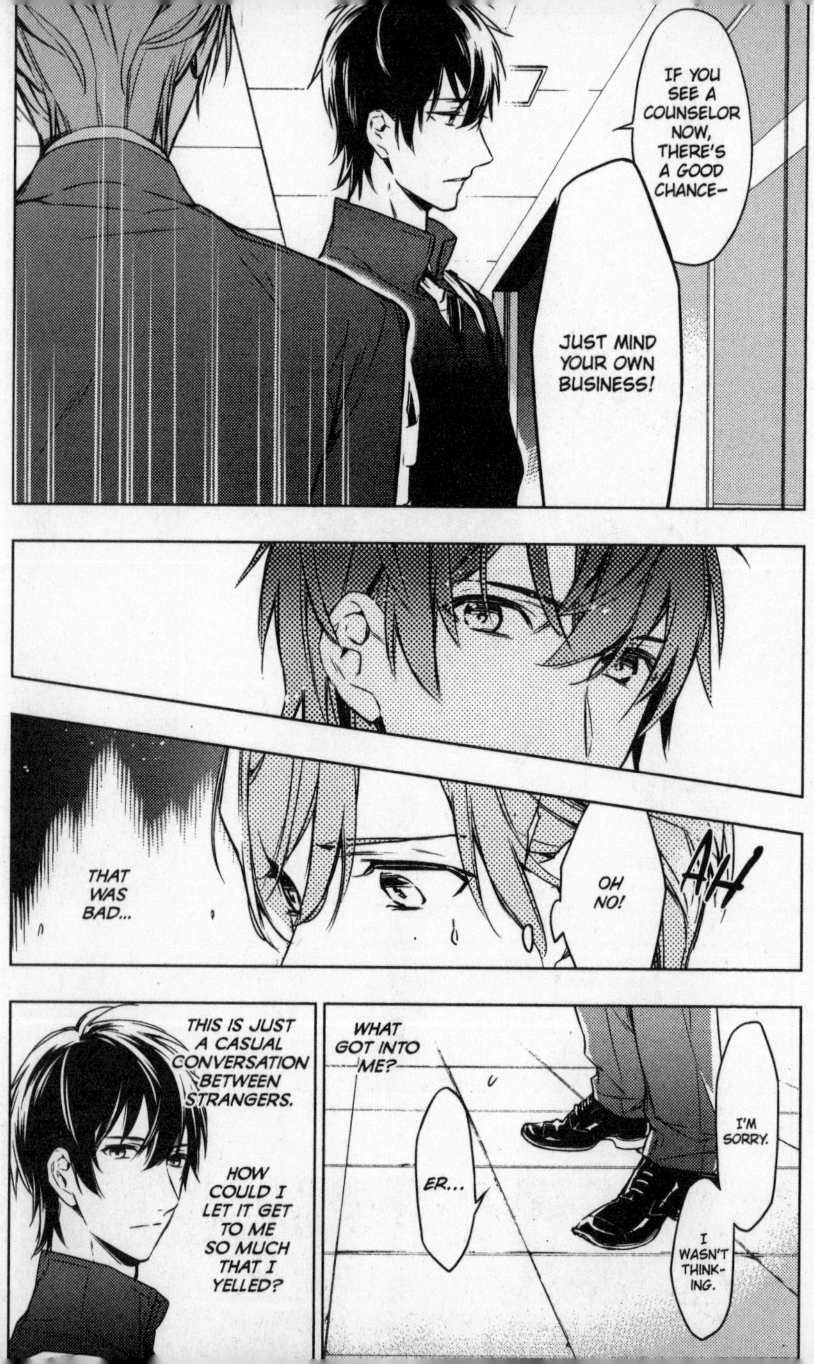
IF YOU SEE A COUNSELOR NOW, THERE'S A GOOD CHANCE—
JUST MIND YOUR OWN BUSINESS!
AH
OH NO!
THAT WAS BAD...
I'M SORRY.
I WASN'T THINKING.
ER...
WHAT GOT INTO ME?
THIS IS JUST A CASUAL CONVERSATION BETWEEN STRANGERS.
HOW COULD I LET IT GET TO ME SO MUCH THAT I YELLED?

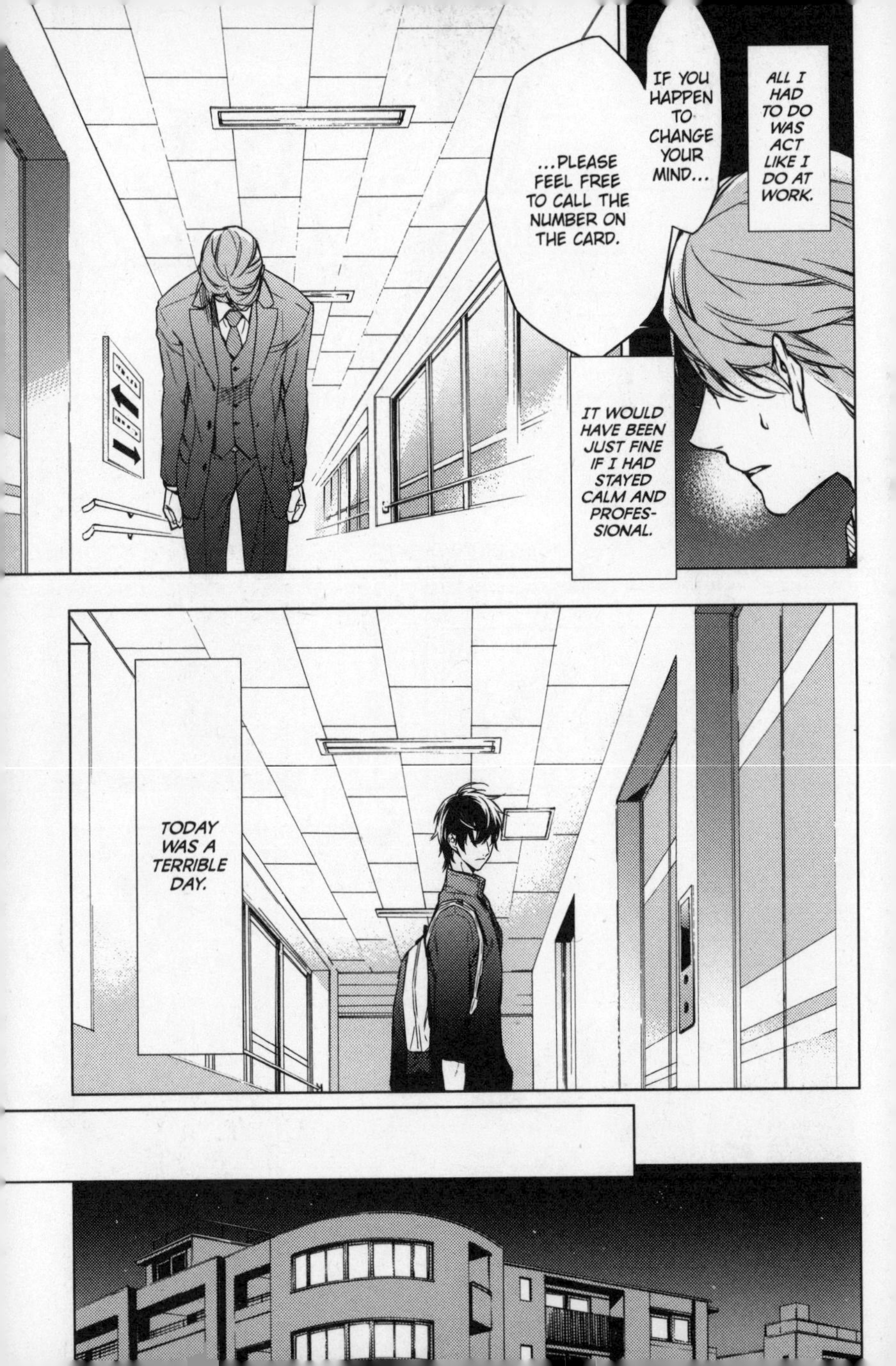
ALL I HAD TO DO WAS ACT LIKE I DO AT WORK.
IF YOU HAPPEN TO CHANGE YOUR MIND...
...PLEASE FEEL FREE TO CALL THE NUMBER ON THE CARD.
IT WOULD HAVE BEEN JUST FINE IF I HAD STAYED CALM AND PROFES-SIONAL.
TODAY WAS A TERRIBLE DAY.

SIGH
...

BTAM

THE DAY IS FINALLY OVER.

SERIOUSLY. STEP OUTSIDE, AND IT'S NOTHING BUT UNPLEASANTNESS AND ANNOYANCES.

FWUF

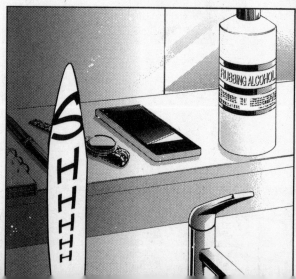

SHHHH

RUBBING ALCOHOL

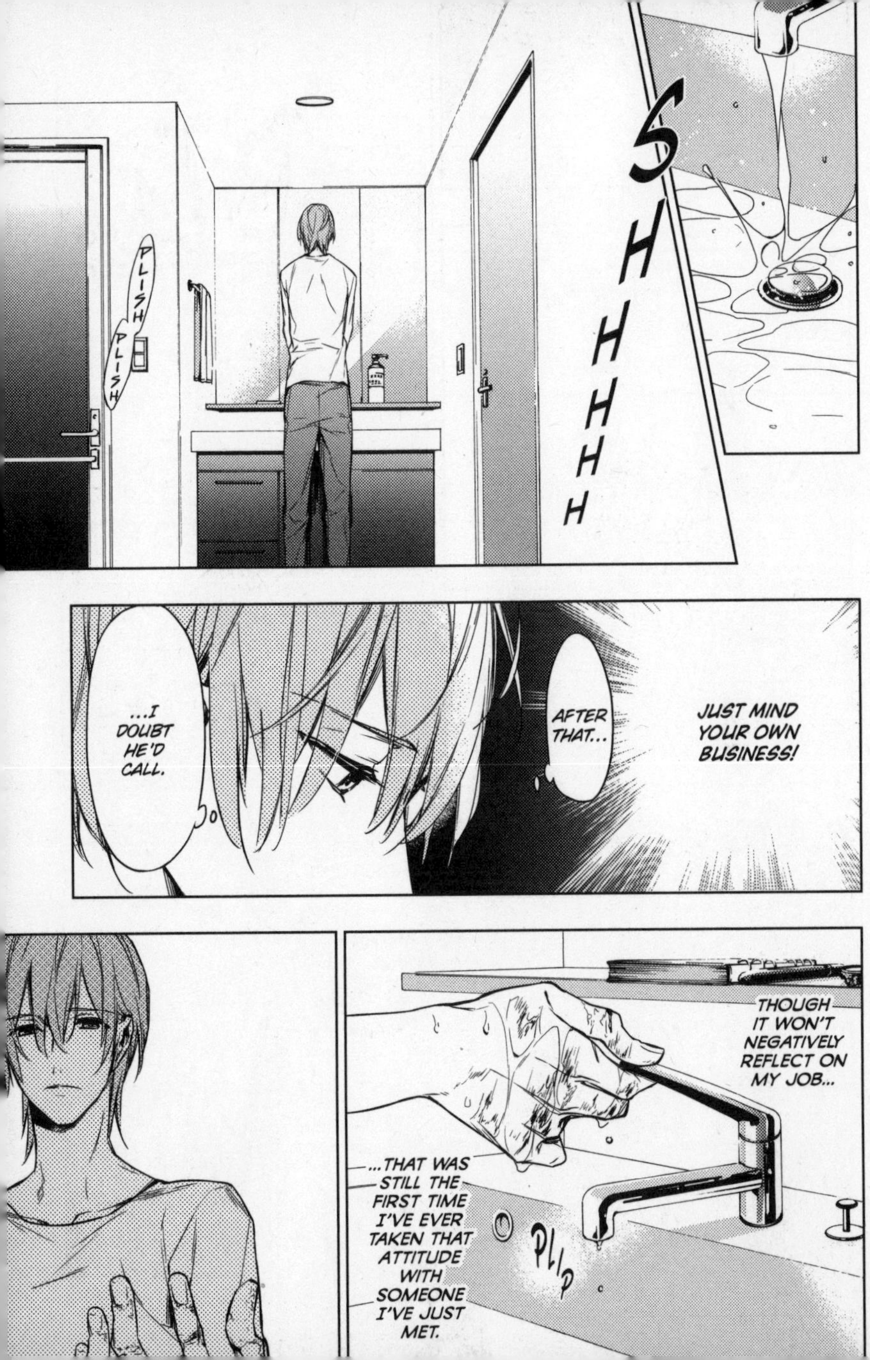
SHHHHHHH
PLISH PLISH
JUST MIND YOUR OWN BUSINESS!
AFTER THAT...
...I DOUBT HE'D CALL.
THOUGH IT WON'T NEGATIVELY REFLECT ON MY JOB...
...THAT WAS STILL THE FIRST TIME I'VE EVER TAKEN THAT ATTITUDE WITH SOMEONE I'VE JUST MET.
PLIP

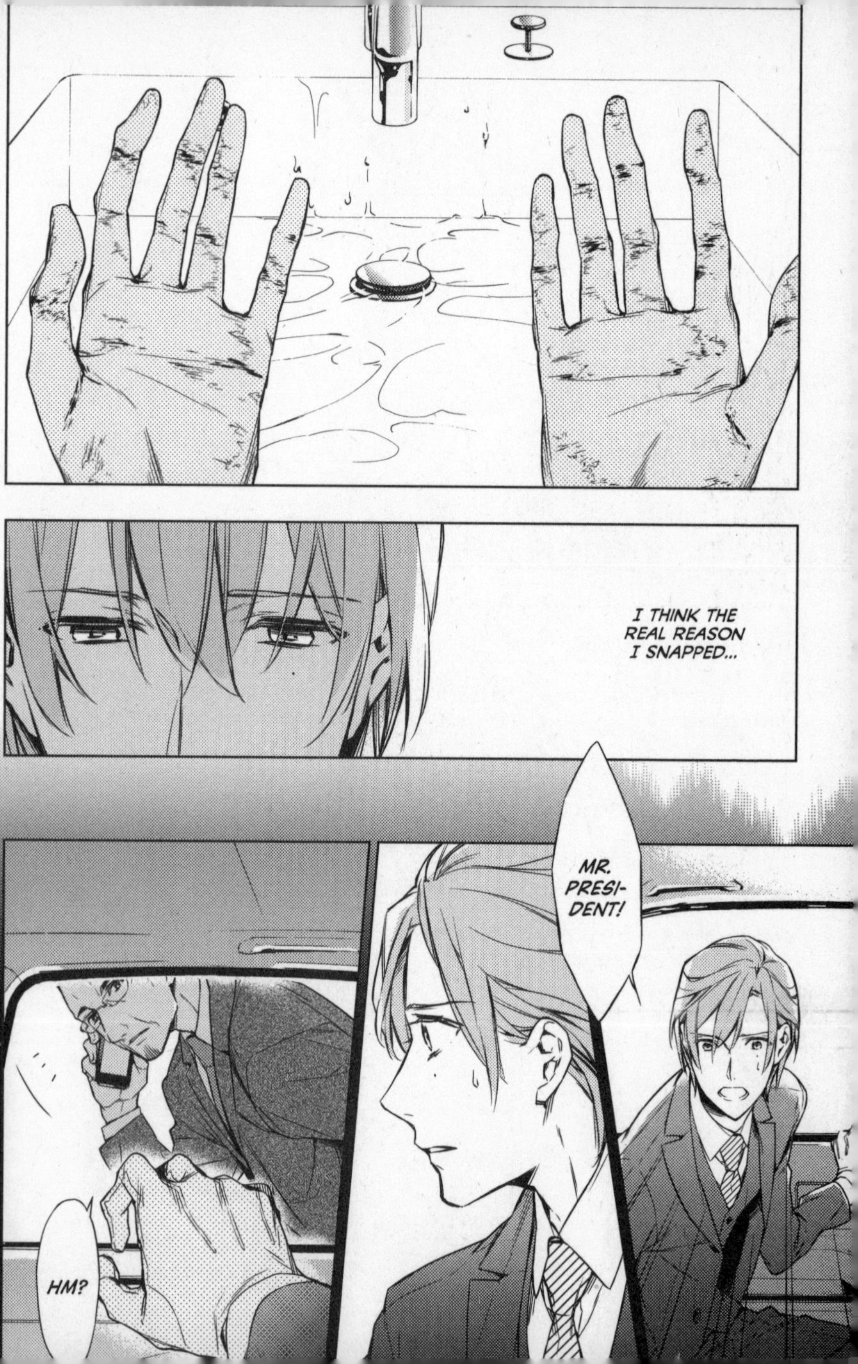
I THINK THE
REAL REASON
I SNAPPED...
MR.
PRESI-
DENT!
HM?

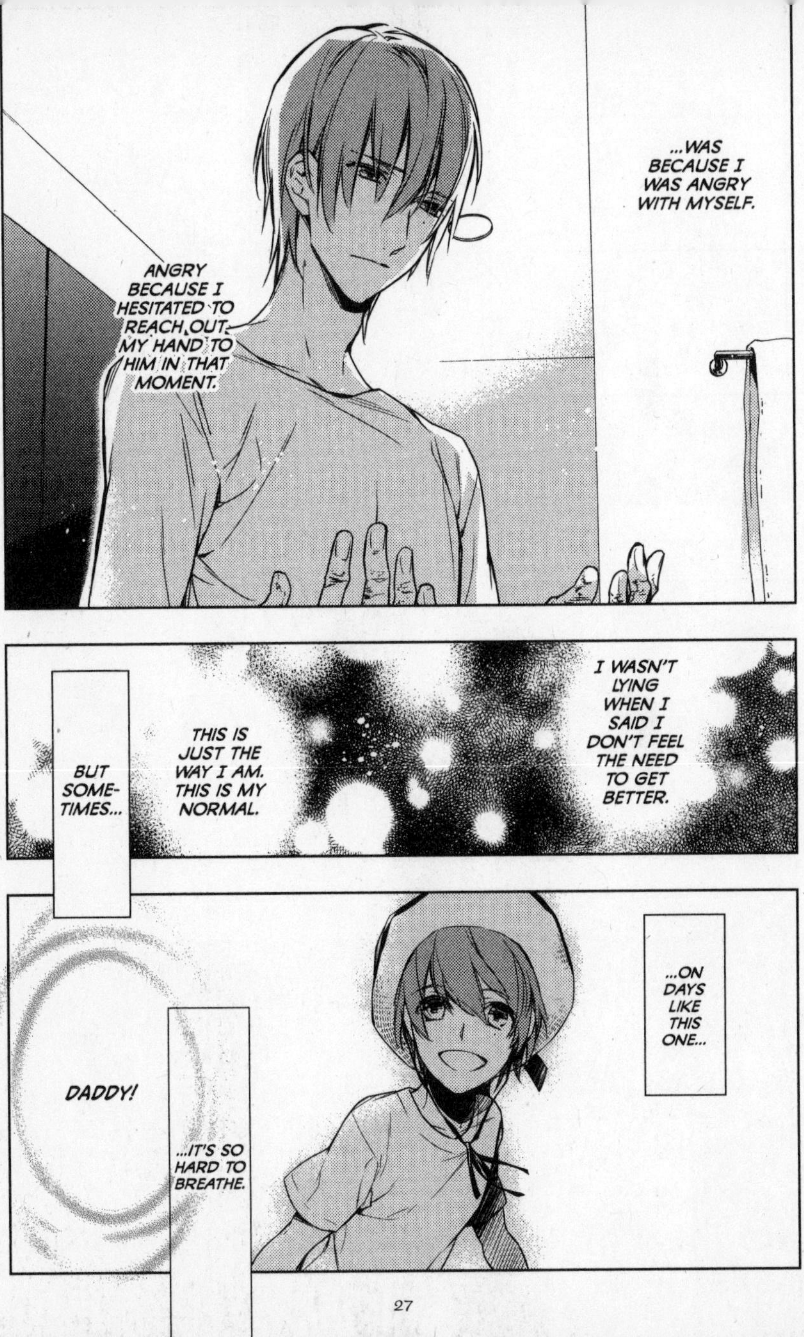
...WAS BECAUSE I WAS ANGRY WITH MYSELF.
ANGRY BECAUSE I HESITATED TO REACH OUT MY HAND TO HIM IN THAT MOMENT.
I WASN'T LYING WHEN I SAID I DON'T FEEL THE NEED TO GET BETTER.
THIS IS JUST THE WAY I AM. THIS IS MY NORMAL.
BUT SOME-TIMES...
...ON DAYS LIKE THIS ONE...
DADDY!
...IT'S SO HARD TO BREATHE.

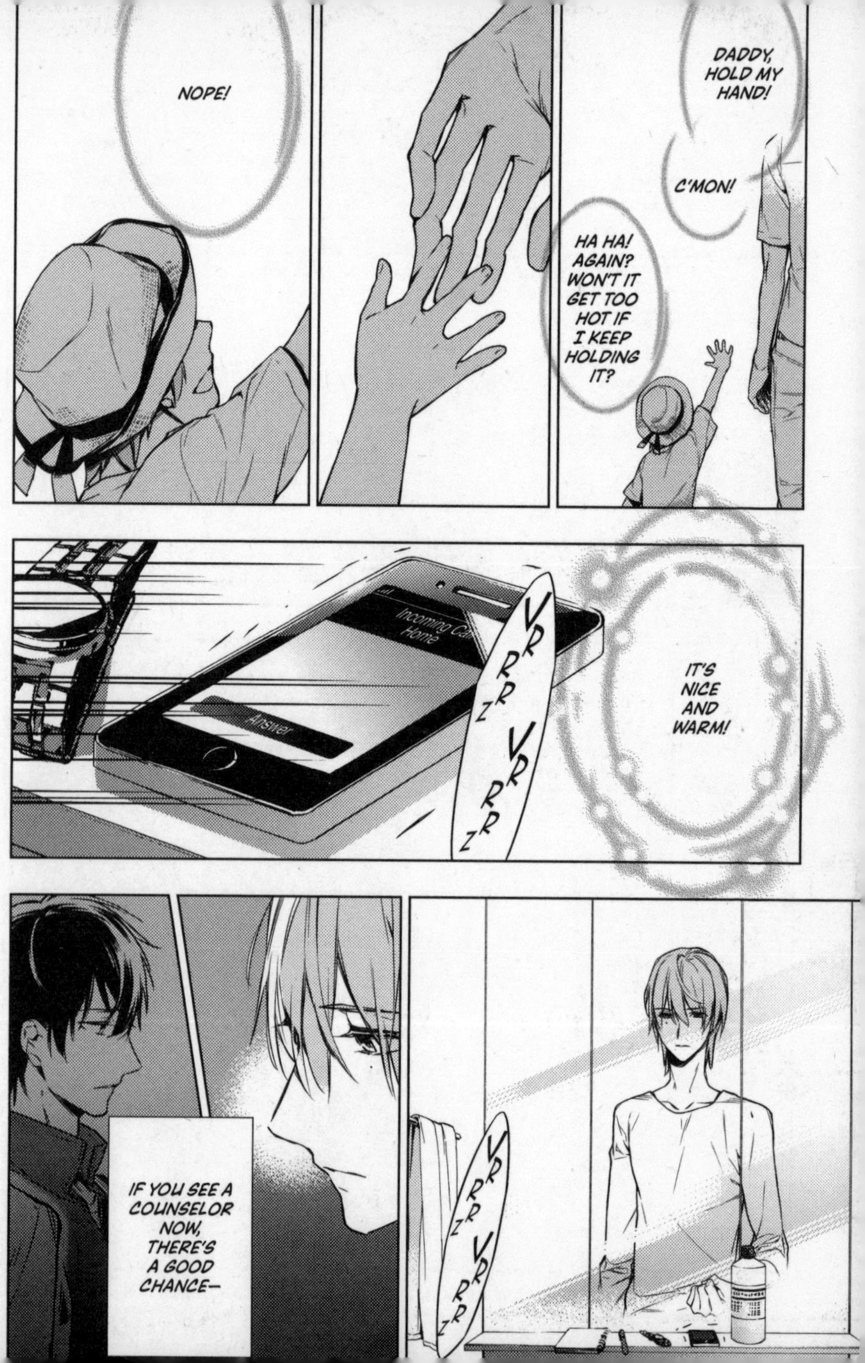
DADDY, HOLD MY HAND!
C'MON!
HA HA! AGAIN? WON'T IT GET TOO HOT IF I KEEP HOLDING IT?
NOPE!
IT'S NICE AND WARM!
Home
Answer
VRRRZ VRRRZ
VRRRZ VRRRZ
IF YOU SEE A COUNSELOR NOW, THERE'S A GOOD CHANCE—

A GOOD
CHANCE
OF
WHAT?

THAT I'LL
FINALLY BE
ABLE TO
BREATHE
EASILY?

...

Shimada Psychiatric
Center

● Practices Available
Psychiatry • Neurology

HOURS	Mo	Tu	We	Th	Fr	Sa
10:00~12:00	○	○	○	○	○	○
15:00~20:00	○	○	○	○	○	△

Open on Fridays on the first and third
weeks of the month only.

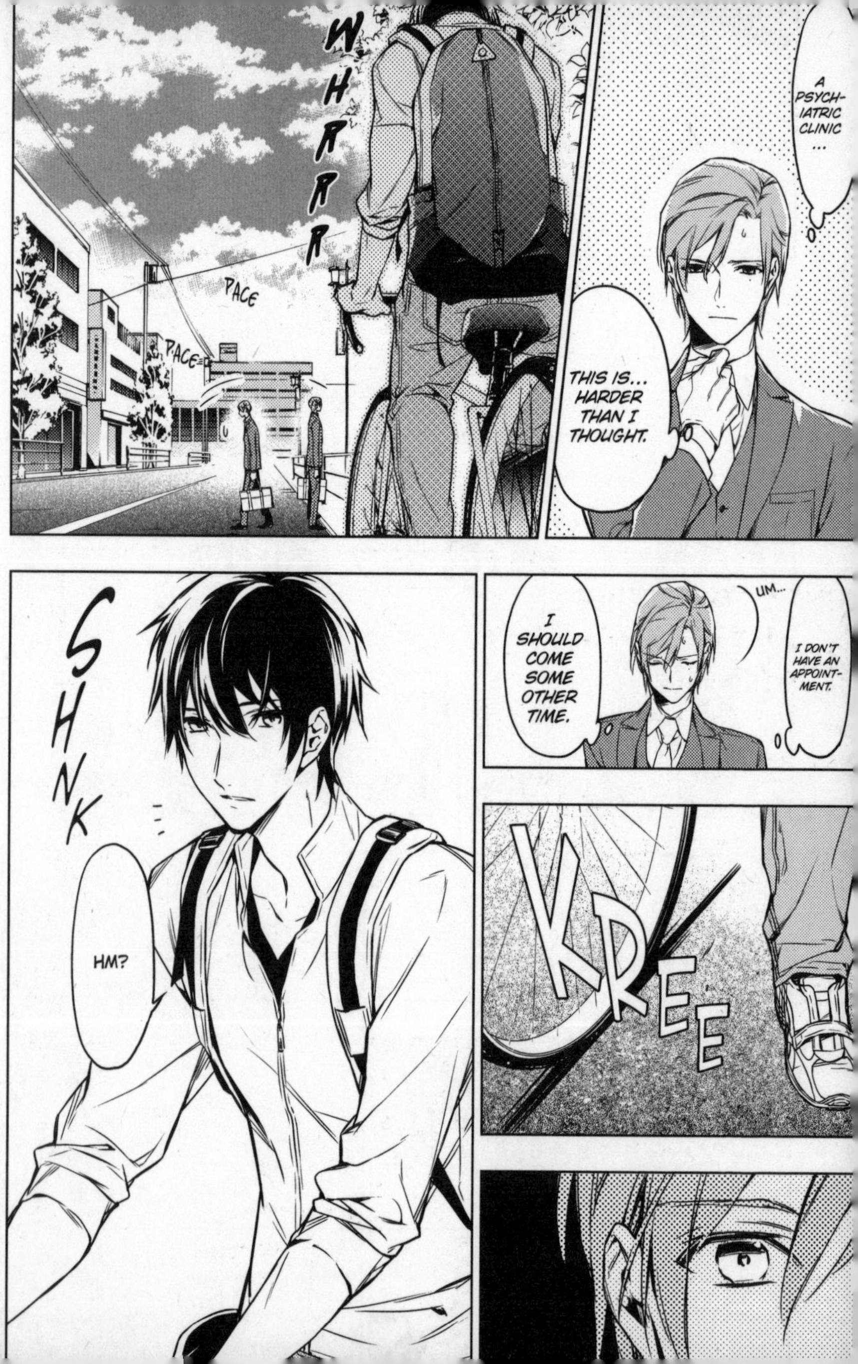
A PSYCHIATRIC CLINIC...
THIS IS... HARDER THAN I THOUGHT.
WHRRRR
PACE
PACE
UM...
I DON'T HAVE AN APPOINTMENT.
I SHOULD COME SOME OTHER TIME.
KREEE
SHNK
HM?

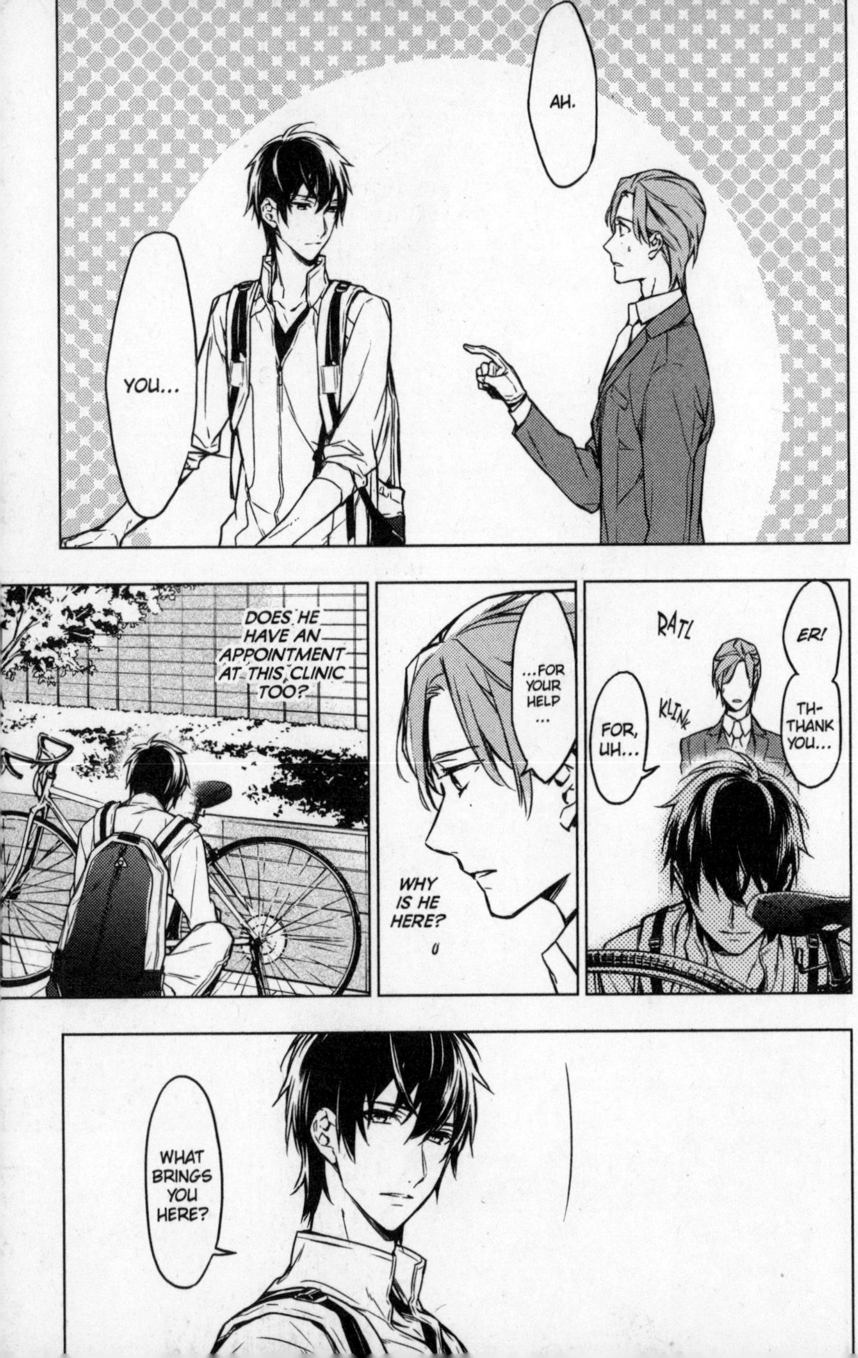
AH.
YOU...
ER!
TH-THANK YOU...
RATL
KLINK
FOR, UH...
...FOR YOUR HELP ...
WHY IS HE HERE?
DOES HE HAVE AN APPOINTMENT AT THIS CLINIC TOO?
WHAT BRINGS YOU HERE?

ARE YOU ALSO COM- ING...

...TO THIS CLINIC FOR SOME KIND OF TREATMENT?

ARE YOU HAVING SECOND THOUGHTS...

...ABOUT YOUR CONDITION?

I WORK HERE. I'M A COUNSELOR.

Shimada Psychiatric Center

● Practices Available ●
Psychiatry • Neurology

ME?

NO.

Shimada Psychiatric Center

Practices Available ●
Psychiatry • Neurology

HOURS	Mo	Tu	We	Th	Fr	Sa	Su
1000~1200	○	○	○	○	/		
1500~2000	○	○	○	○	△		

Open on Fridays on the first and third weeks of the month only.

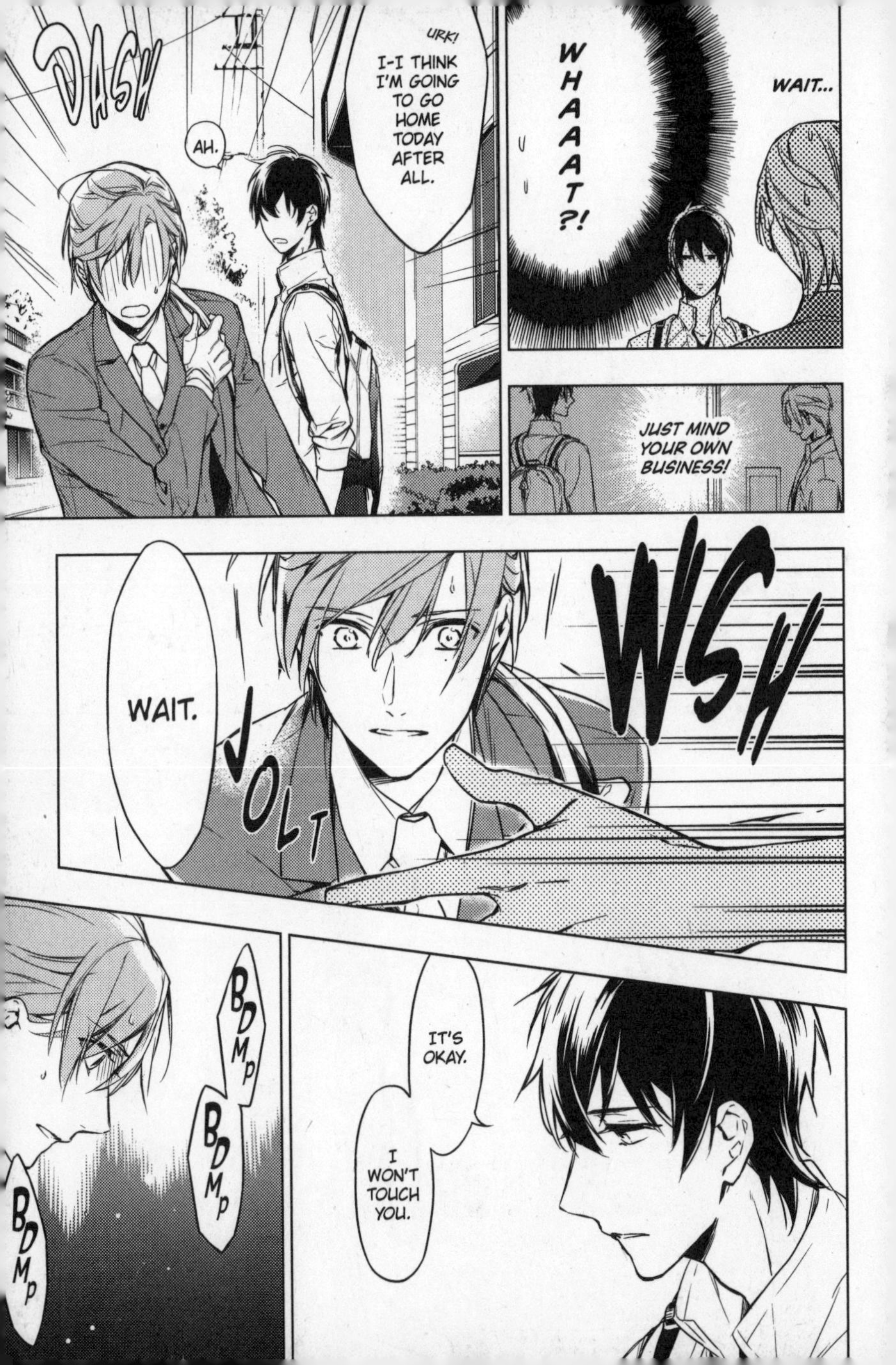
WAIT...
WHAAAAT?!
JUST MIND YOUR OWN BUSINESS!
URK!
I-I THINK I'M GOING TO GO HOME TODAY AFTER ALL.
AH.
DASH
WSH
JOLT
WAIT.
IT'S OKAY.
I WON'T TOUCH YOU.
BDMP
BDMP
BDMP

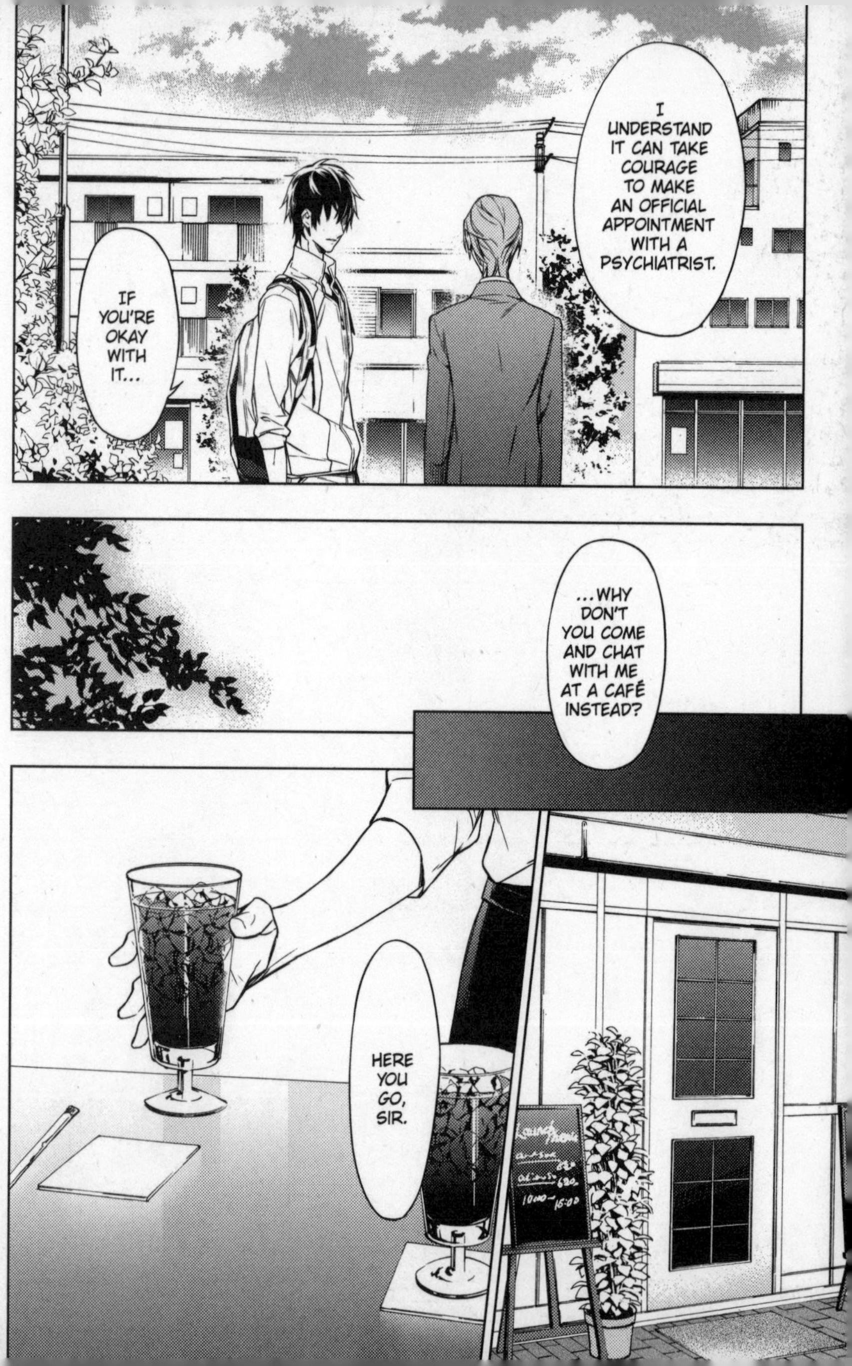
I UNDERSTAND IT CAN TAKE COURAGE TO MAKE AN OFFICIAL APPOINTMENT WITH A PSYCHIATRIST.
IF YOU'RE OKAY WITH IT...
...WHY DON'T YOU COME AND CHAT WITH ME AT A CAFÉ INSTEAD?
HERE YOU GO, SIR.

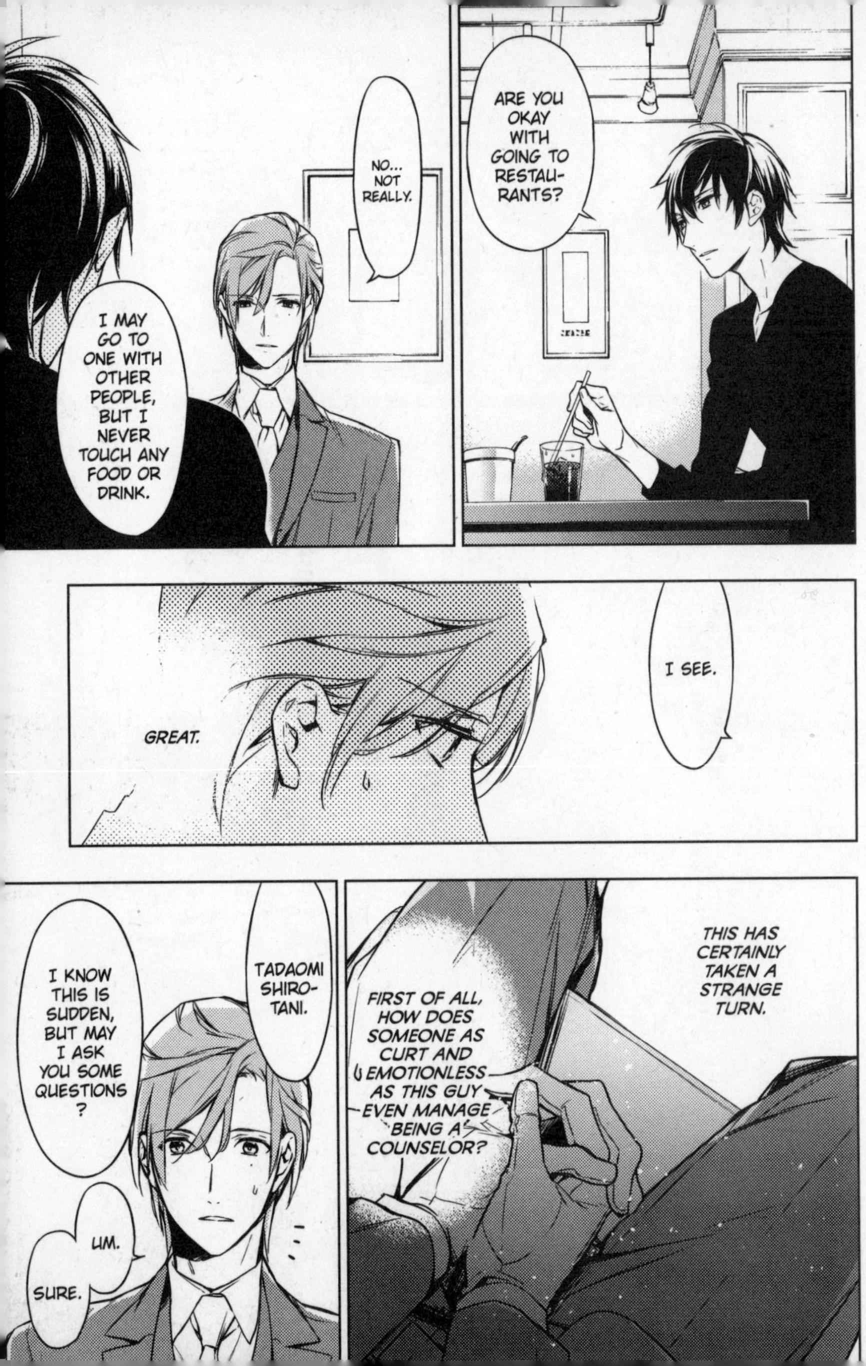
ARE YOU OKAY WITH GOING TO RESTAURANTS?
NO... NOT REALLY.
I MAY GO TO ONE WITH OTHER PEOPLE, BUT I NEVER TOUCH ANY FOOD OR DRINK.
I SEE.
GREAT.
THIS HAS CERTAINLY TAKEN A STRANGE TURN.
FIRST OF ALL, HOW DOES SOMEONE AS CURT AND EMOTIONLESS AS THIS GUY EVEN MANAGE BEING A COUNSELOR?
TADAOMI SHIRO-TANI.
I KNOW THIS IS SUDDEN, BUT MAY I ASK YOU SOME QUESTIONS?
UM.
SURE.

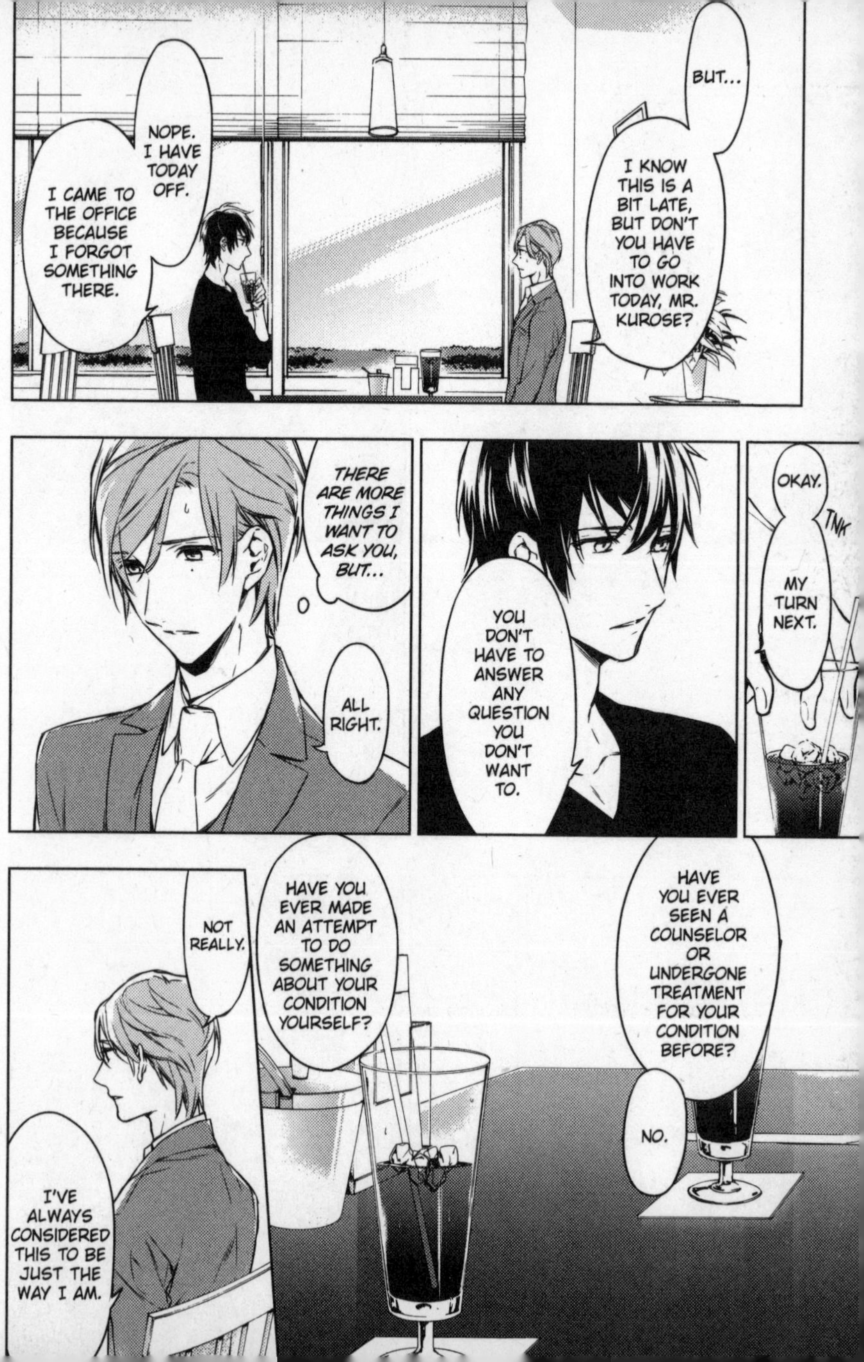
BUT...
I KNOW THIS IS A BIT LATE, BUT DON'T YOU HAVE TO GO INTO WORK TODAY, MR. KUROSE?
NOPE. I HAVE TODAY OFF.
I CAME TO THE OFFICE BECAUSE I FORGOT SOMETHING THERE.
OKAY.
TNK
MY TURN NEXT.
YOU DON'T HAVE TO ANSWER ANY QUESTION YOU DON'T WANT TO.
THERE ARE MORE THINGS I WANT TO ASK YOU, BUT...
ALL RIGHT.
HAVE YOU EVER SEEN A COUNSELOR OR UNDERGONE TREATMENT FOR YOUR CONDITION BEFORE?
NO.
HAVE YOU EVER MADE AN ATTEMPT TO DO SOMETHING ABOUT YOUR CONDITION YOURSELF?
NOT REALLY.
I'VE ALWAYS CONSIDERED THIS TO BE JUST THE WAY I AM.

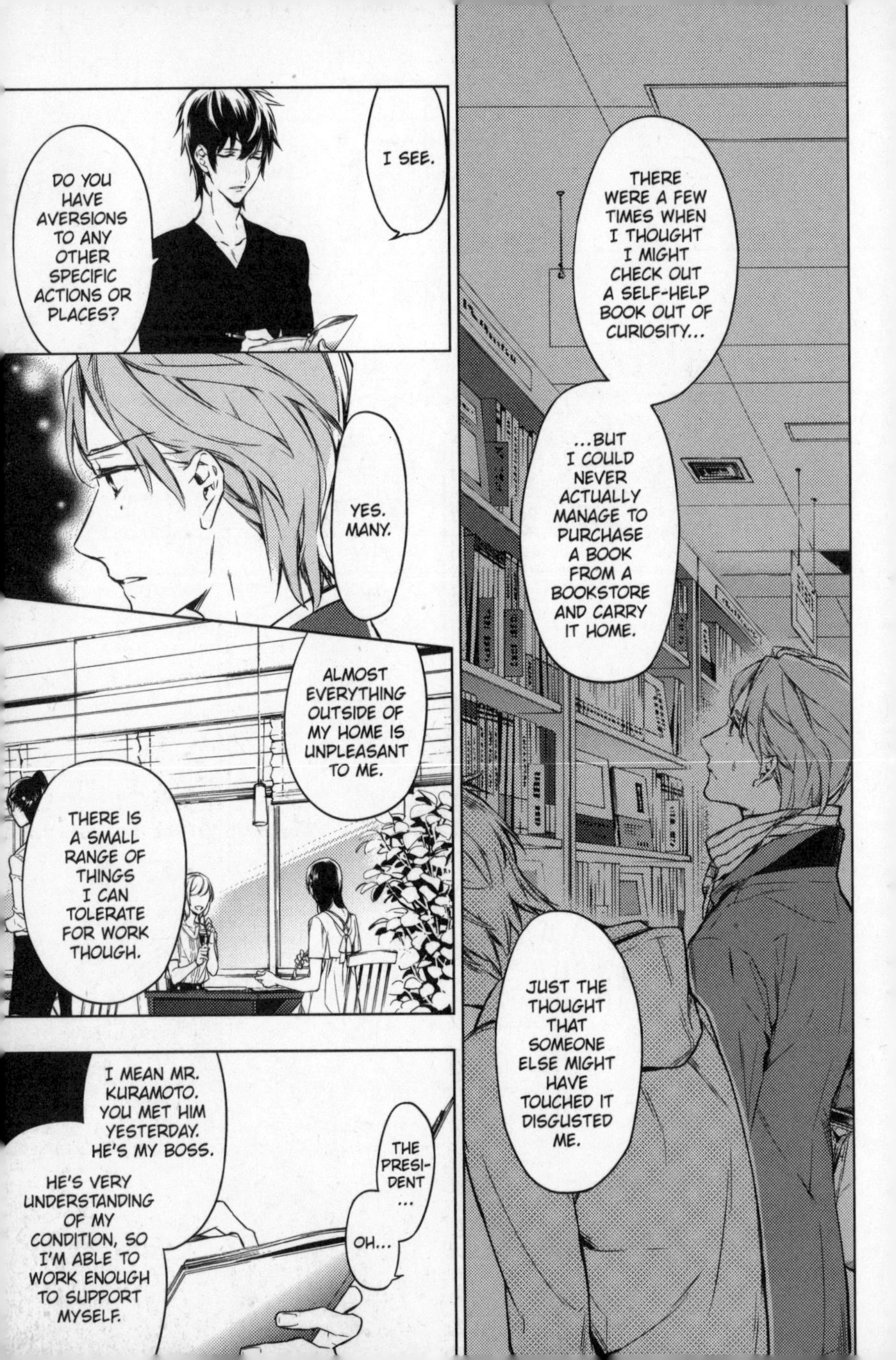
THERE WERE A FEW TIMES WHEN I THOUGHT I MIGHT CHECK OUT A SELF-HELP BOOK OUT OF CURIOSITY...
...BUT I COULD NEVER ACTUALLY MANAGE TO PURCHASE A BOOK FROM A BOOKSTORE AND CARRY IT HOME.
JUST THE THOUGHT THAT SOMEONE ELSE MIGHT HAVE TOUCHED IT DISGUSTED ME.
I SEE.
DO YOU HAVE AVERSIONS TO ANY OTHER SPECIFIC ACTIONS OR PLACES?
YES. MANY.
ALMOST EVERYTHING OUTSIDE OF MY HOME IS UNPLEASANT TO ME.
THERE IS A SMALL RANGE OF THINGS I CAN TOLERATE FOR WORK THOUGH.
I MEAN MR. KURAMOTO. YOU MET HIM YESTERDAY. HE'S MY BOSS.
THE PRESI-DENT...
OH...
HE'S VERY UNDERSTANDING OF MY CONDITION, SO I'M ABLE TO WORK ENOUGH TO SUPPORT MYSELF.

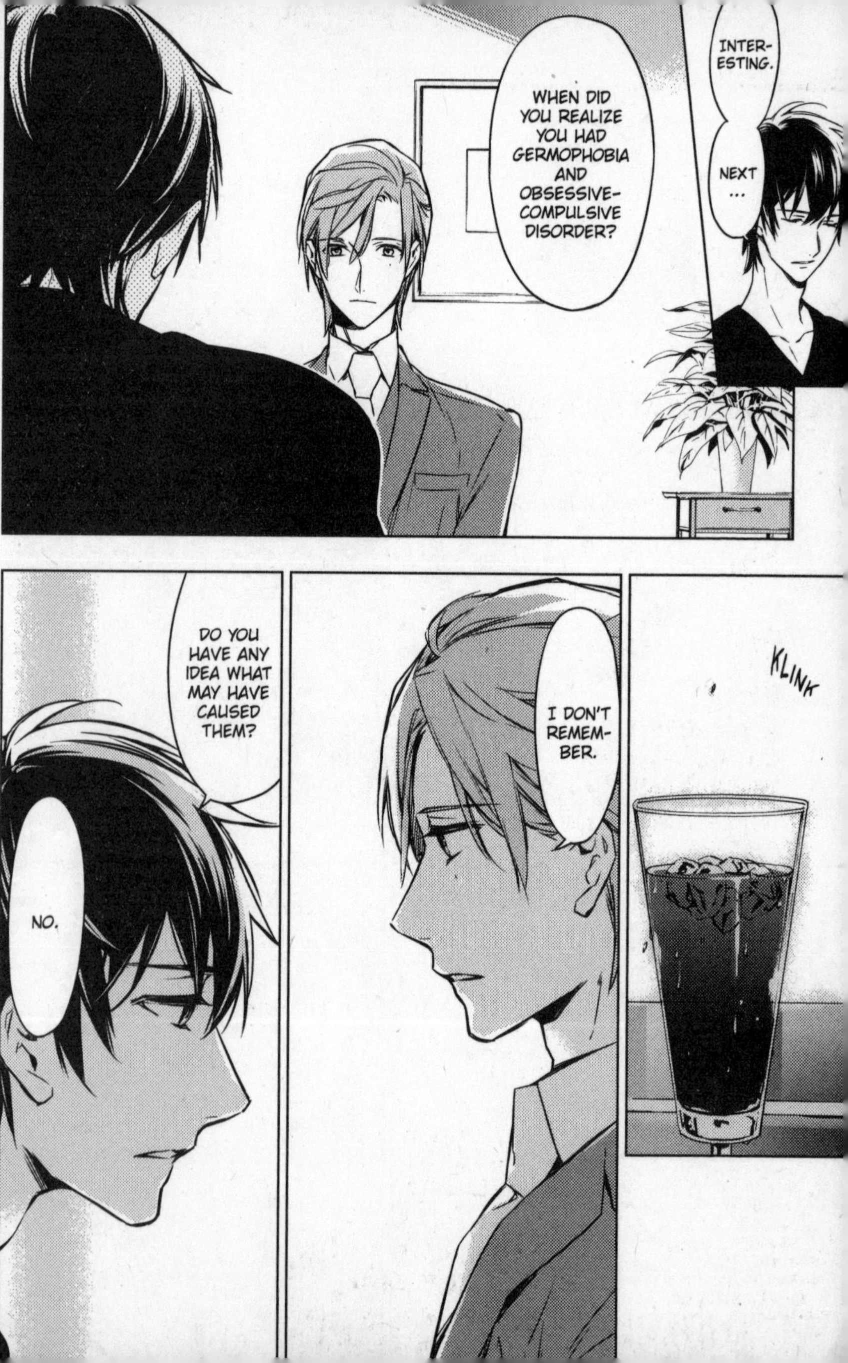
INTER-ESTING.
NEXT...
WHEN DID YOU REALIZE YOU HAD GERMOPHOBIA AND OBSESSIVE-COMPULSIVE DISORDER?
KLINK
I DON'T REMEM-BER.
DO YOU HAVE ANY IDEA WHAT MAY HAVE CAUSED THEM?
NO.

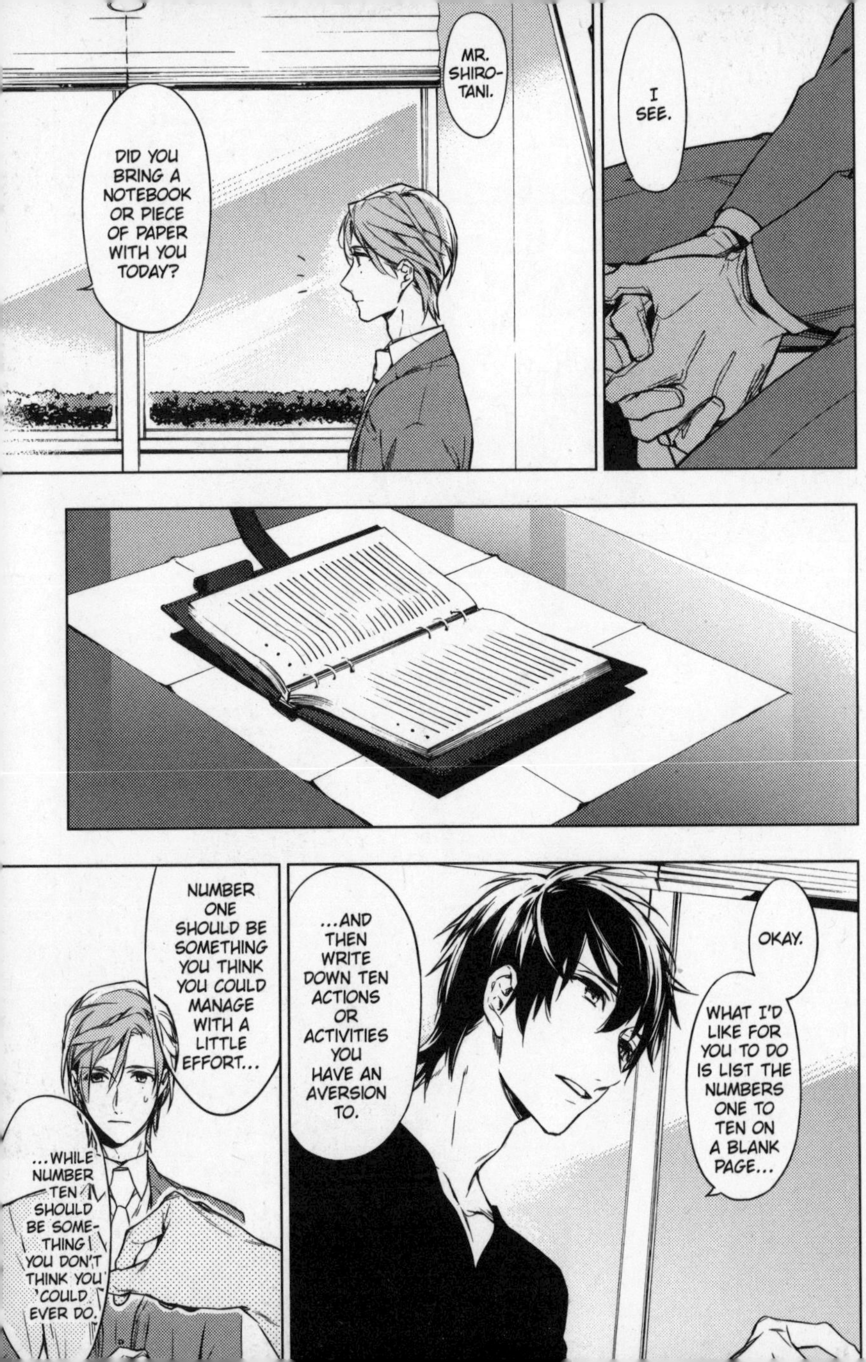
I SEE.
MR. SHIRO-TANI.
DID YOU BRING A NOTEBOOK OR PIECE OF PAPER WITH YOU TODAY?
OKAY.
WHAT I'D LIKE FOR YOU TO DO IS LIST THE NUMBERS ONE TO TEN ON A BLANK PAGE...
...AND THEN WRITE DOWN TEN ACTIONS OR ACTIVITIES YOU HAVE AN AVERSION TO.
NUMBER ONE SHOULD BE SOMETHING YOU THINK YOU COULD MANAGE WITH A LITTLE EFFORT...
...WHILE NUMBER TEN SHOULD BE SOME-THING YOU DON'T THINK YOU COULD EVER DO.

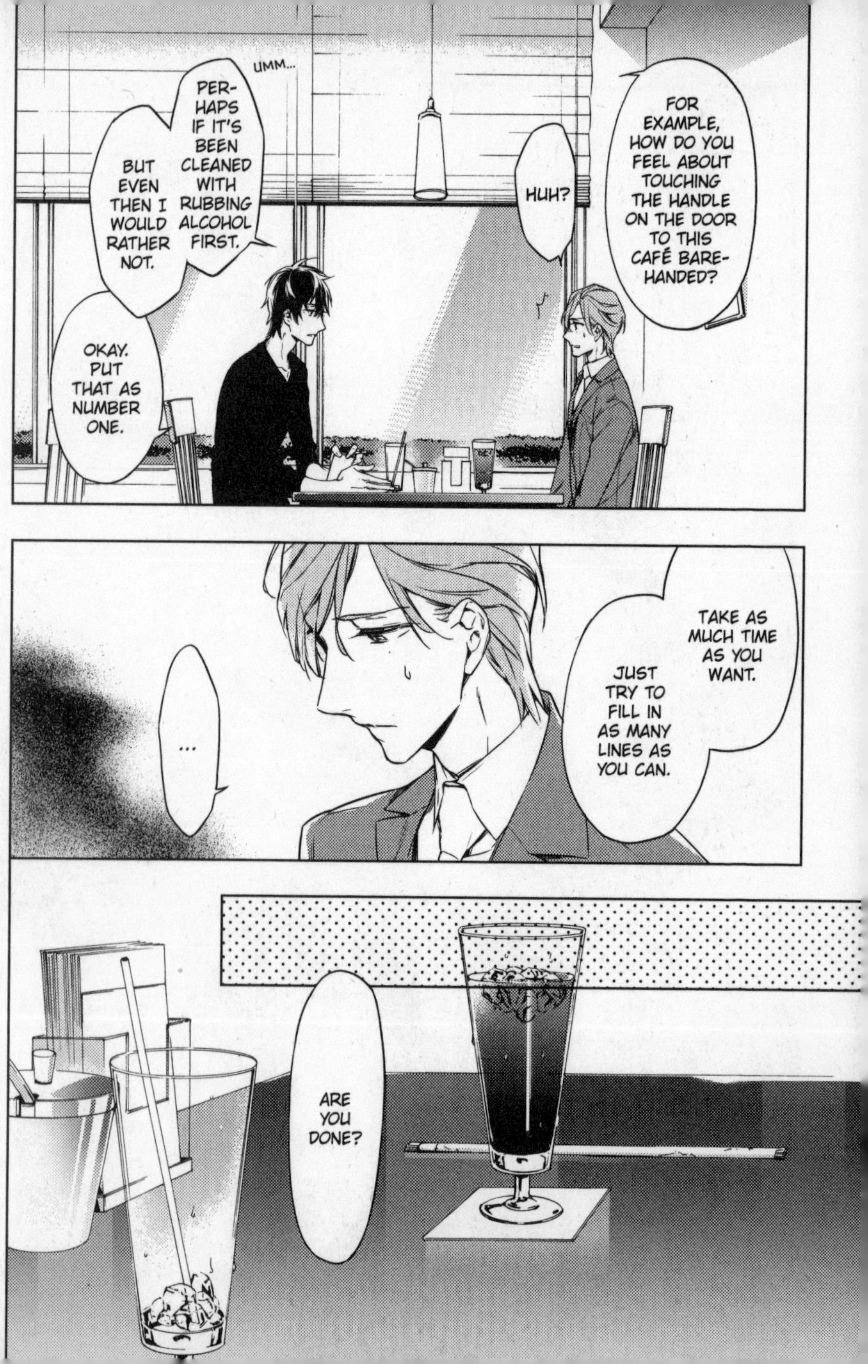
FOR EXAMPLE, HOW DO YOU FEEL ABOUT TOUCHING THE HANDLE ON THE DOOR TO THIS CAFÉ BAREHANDED?
HUH?
UMM...
PERHAPS IF IT'S BEEN CLEANED WITH RUBBING ALCOHOL FIRST.
BUT EVEN THEN I WOULD RATHER NOT.
OKAY. PUT THAT AS NUMBER ONE.
TAKE AS MUCH TIME AS YOU WANT.
JUST TRY TO FILL IN AS MANY LINES AS YOU CAN.
...
ARE YOU DONE?

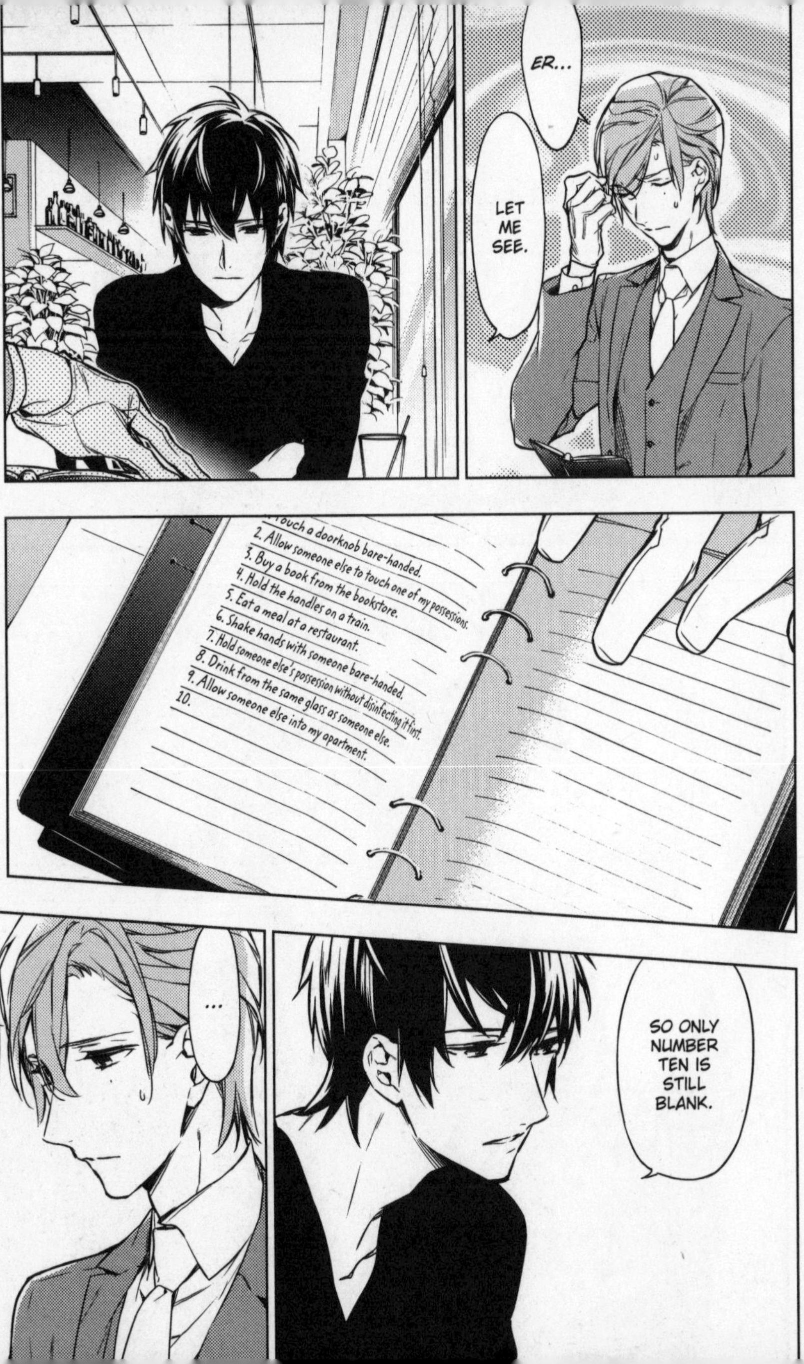
ER...
LET ME SEE.
ouch a doorknob bare-handed.
2. Allow someone else to touch one of my possessions.
3. Buy a book from the bookstore.
4. Hold the handles on a train.
5. Eat a meal at a restaurant.
6. Shake hands with someone bare-handed.
7. Hold someone else's possession without disinfecting it first.
8. Drink from the same glass as someone else.
9. Allow someone else into my apartment.
10.
SO ONLY NUMBER TEN IS STILL BLANK.
...
OH WELL.

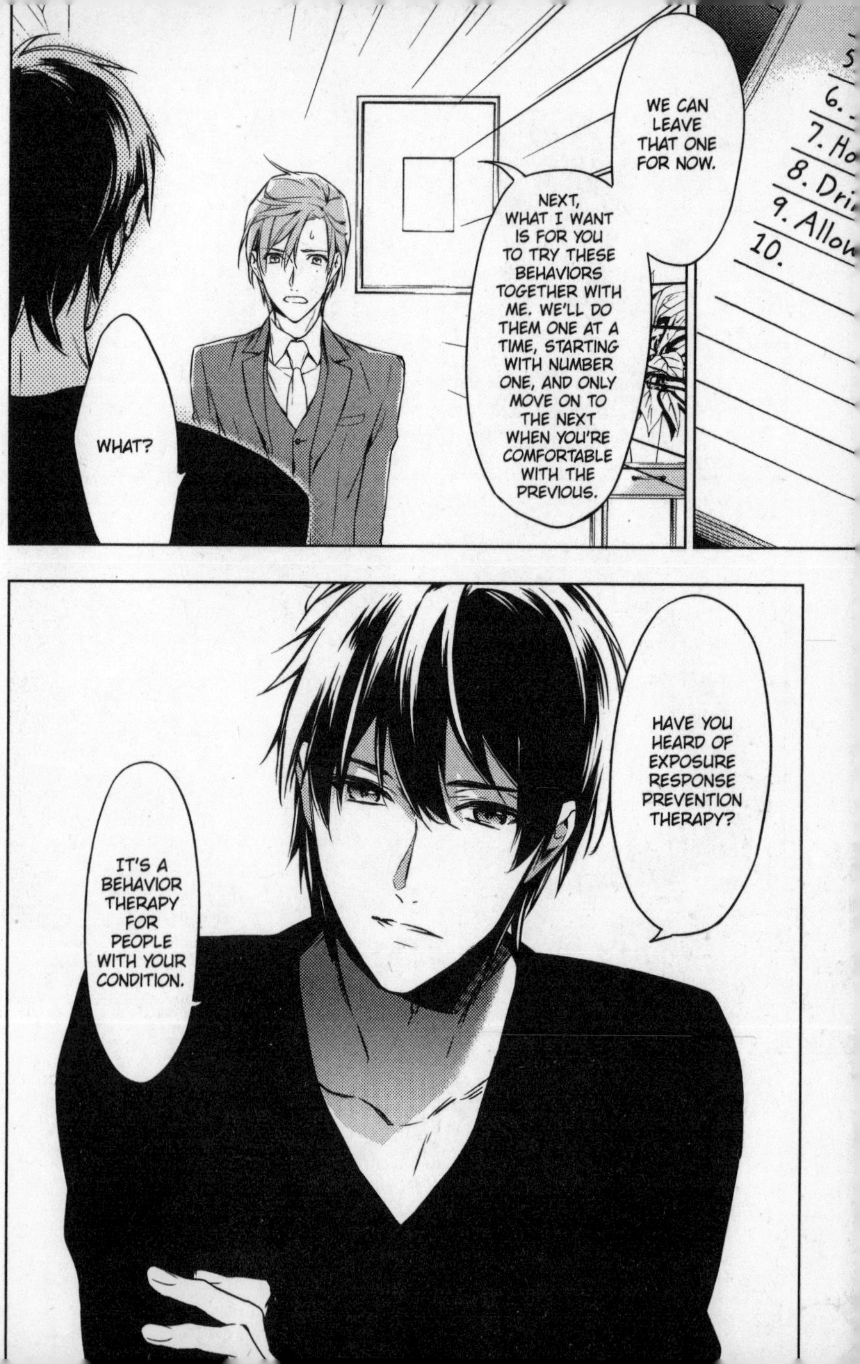
WE CAN LEAVE THAT ONE FOR NOW.
NEXT, WHAT I WANT IS FOR YOU TO TRY THESE BEHAVIORS TOGETHER WITH ME. WE'LL DO THEM ONE AT A TIME, STARTING WITH NUMBER ONE, AND ONLY MOVE ON TO THE NEXT WHEN YOU'RE COMFORTABLE WITH THE PREVIOUS.
WHAT?
HAVE YOU HEARD OF EXPOSURE RESPONSE PREVENTION THERAPY?
IT'S A BEHAVIOR THERAPY FOR PEOPLE WITH YOUR CONDITION.

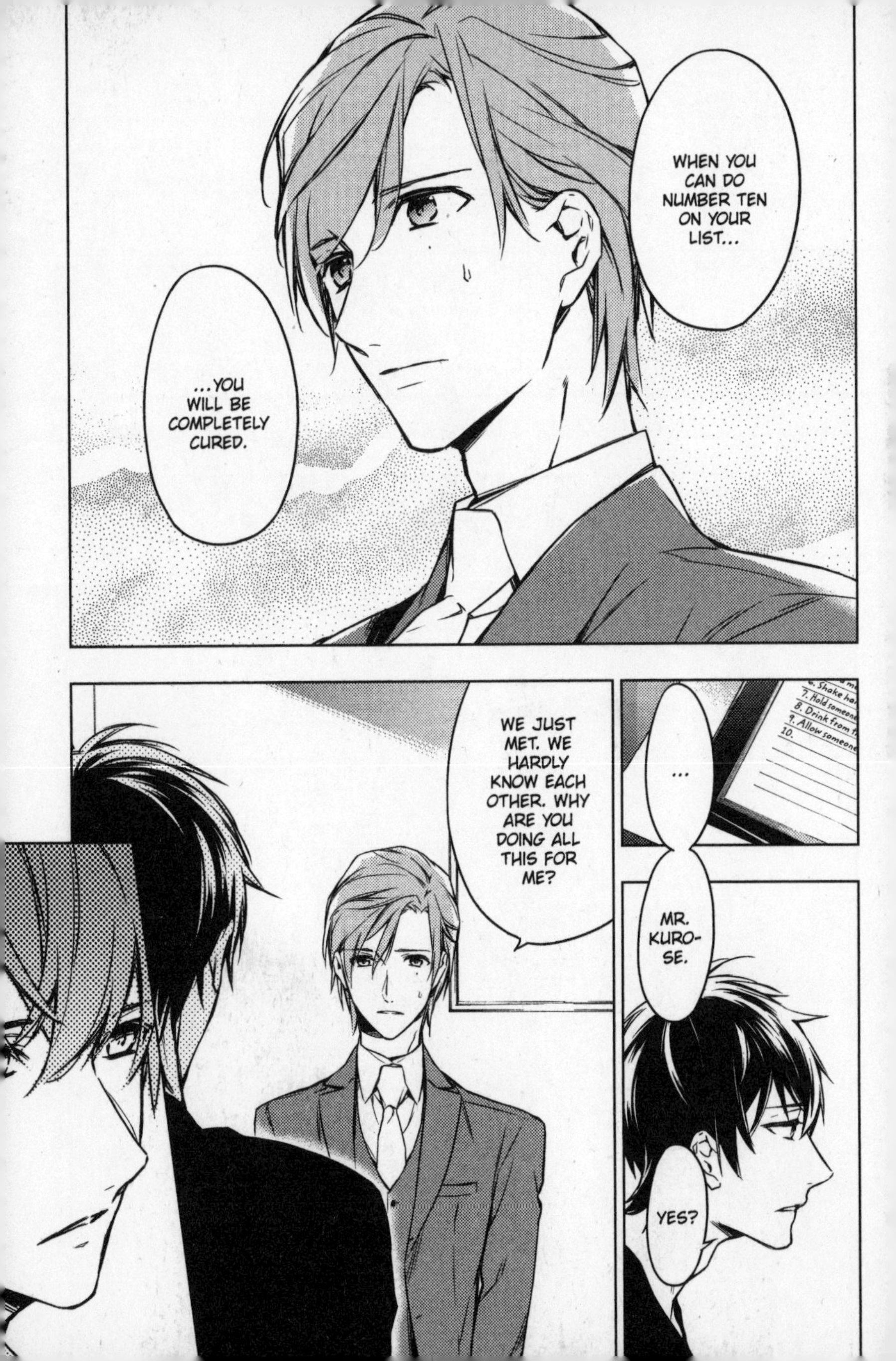

WHEN YOU CAN DO NUMBER TEN ON YOUR LIST...
...YOU WILL BE COMPLETELY CURED.
7. Hold someone
8. Drink from
9. Allow someone
10.
...
MR. KURO-SE.
YES?
WE JUST MET. WE HARDLY KNOW EACH OTHER. WHY ARE YOU DOING ALL THIS FOR ME?

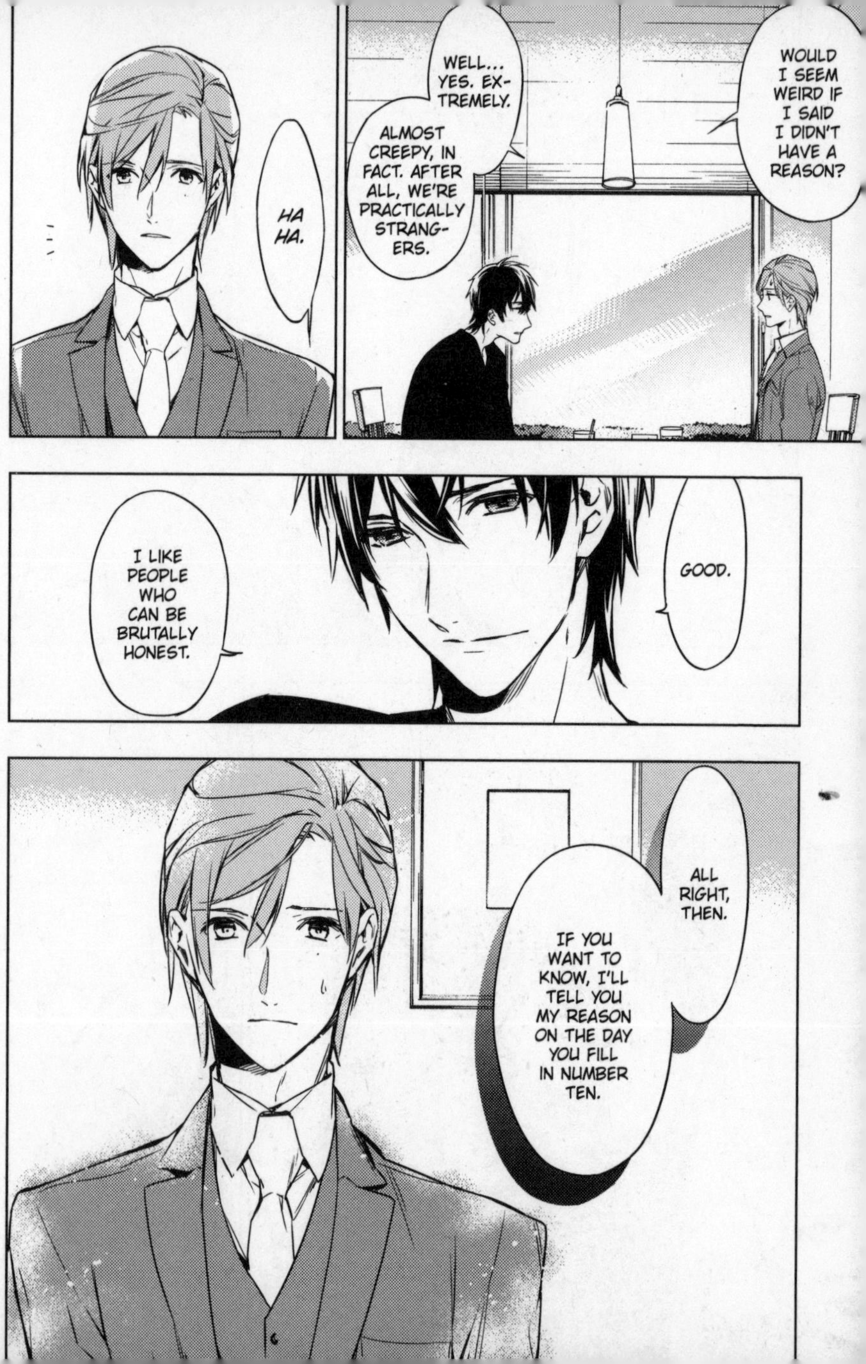
WOULD I SEEM WEIRD IF I SAID I DIDN'T HAVE A REASON?
WELL... YES. EX-TREMELY.
ALMOST CREEPY, IN FACT. AFTER ALL, WE'RE PRACTICALLY STRANG-ERS.
HA HA.
GOOD.
I LIKE PEOPLE WHO CAN BE BRUTALLY HONEST.
ALL RIGHT, THEN.
IF YOU WANT TO KNOW, I'LL TELL YOU MY REASON ON THE DAY YOU FILL IN NUMBER TEN.

TEN COUNT 02

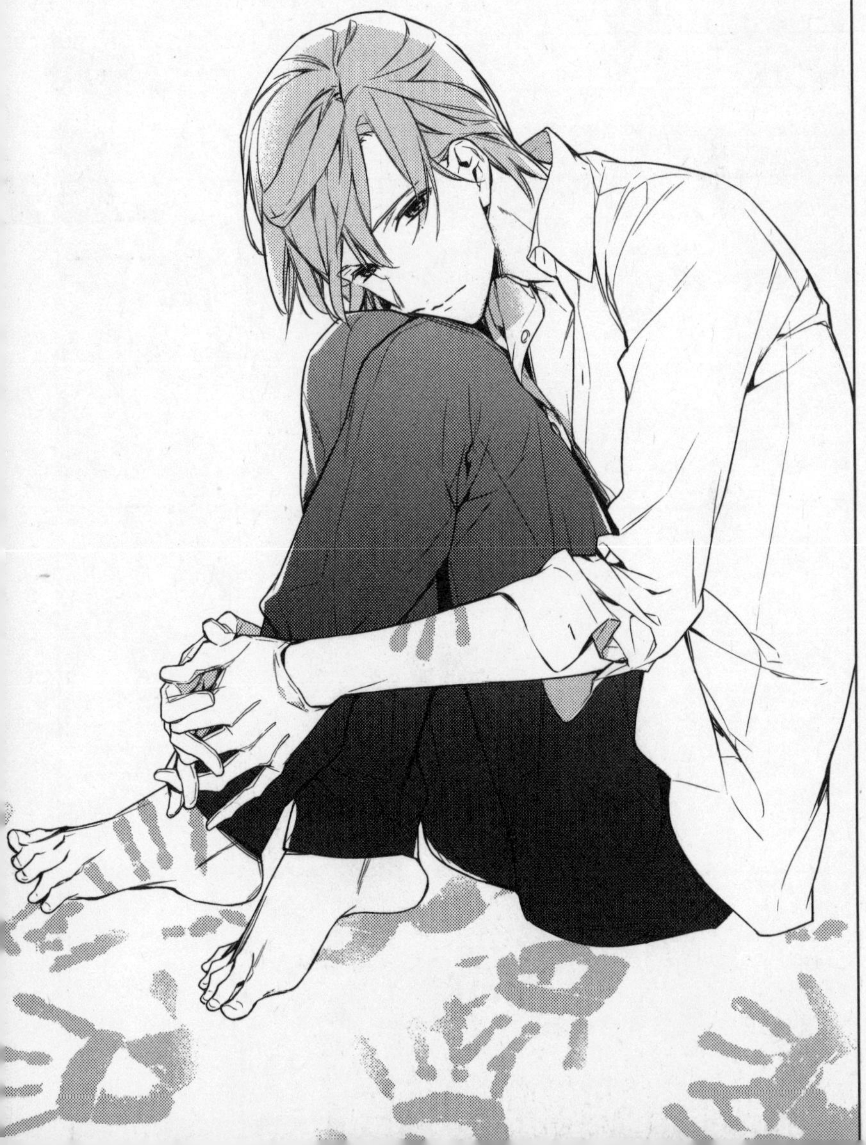

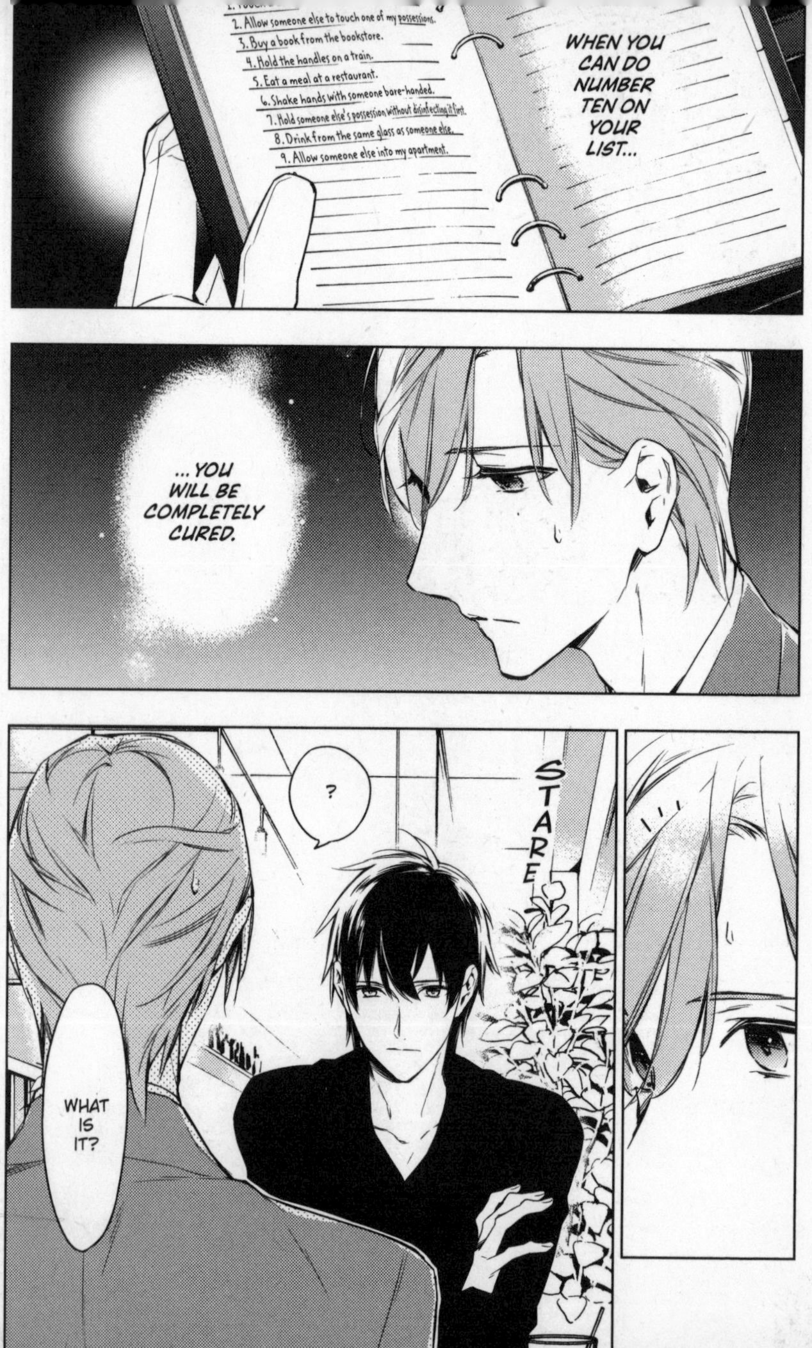
WHEN YOU CAN DO NUMBER TEN ON YOUR LIST...
2. Allow someone else to touch one of my possessions.
3. Buy a book from the bookstore.
4. Hold the handles on a train.
5. Eat a meal at a restaurant.
6. Shake hands with someone bare-handed.
7. Hold someone else's possession without disinfecting it first.
8. Drink from the same glass as someone else.
9. Allow someone else into my apartment.
...YOU WILL BE COMPLETELY CURED.
STARE
?
WHAT IS IT?

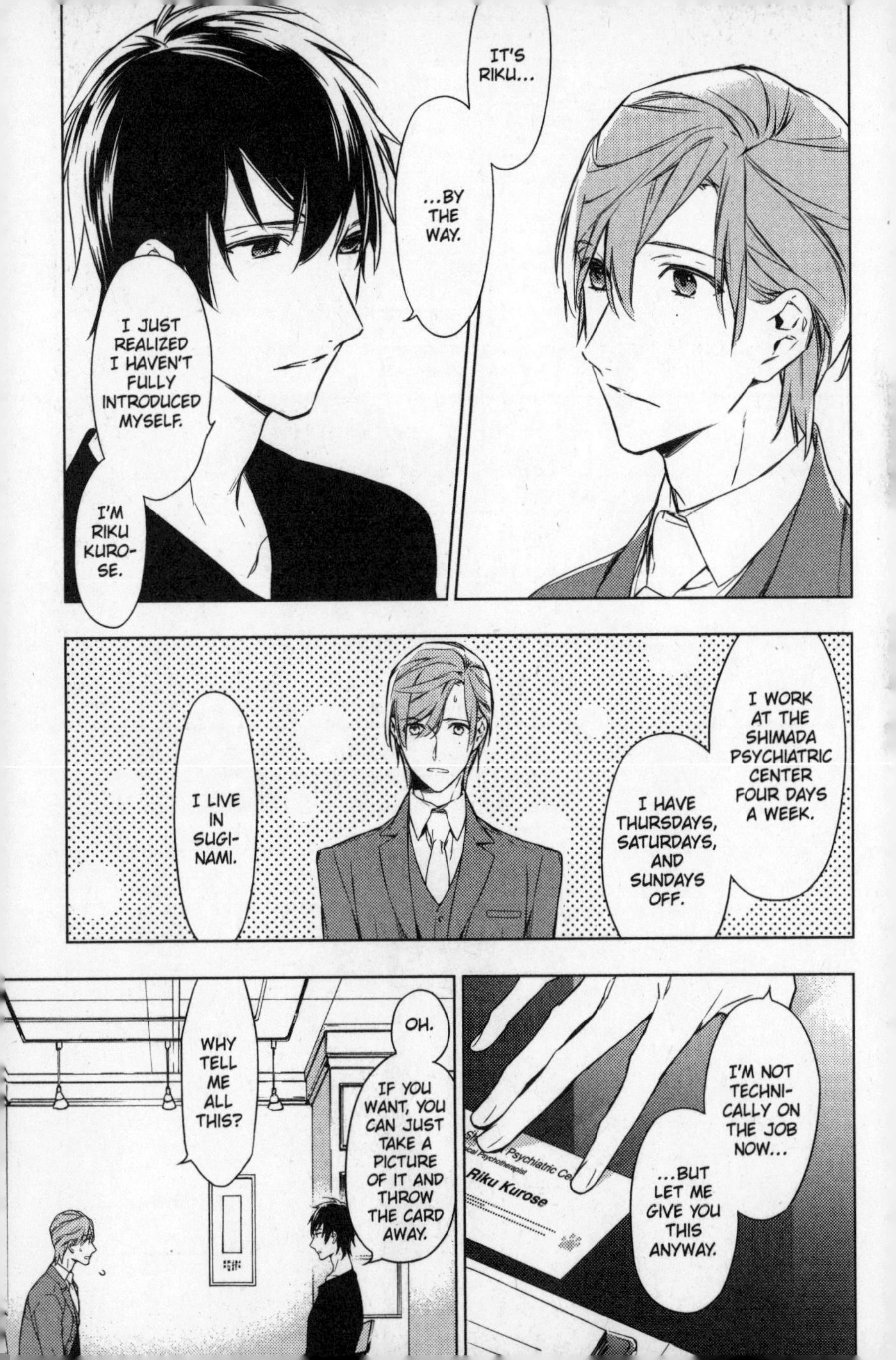
IT'S RIKU...
...BY THE WAY.
I JUST REALIZED I HAVEN'T FULLY INTRODUCED MYSELF.
I'M RIKU KUROSE.
I WORK AT THE SHIMADA PSYCHIATRIC CENTER FOUR DAYS A WEEK.
I HAVE THURSDAYS, SATURDAYS, AND SUNDAYS OFF.
I LIVE IN SUGINAMI.
I'M NOT TECHNICALLY ON THE JOB NOW...
...BUT LET ME GIVE YOU THIS ANYWAY.
Riku Kurose
OH.
IF YOU WANT, YOU CAN JUST TAKE A PICTURE OF IT AND THROW THE CARD AWAY.
WHY TELL ME ALL THIS?

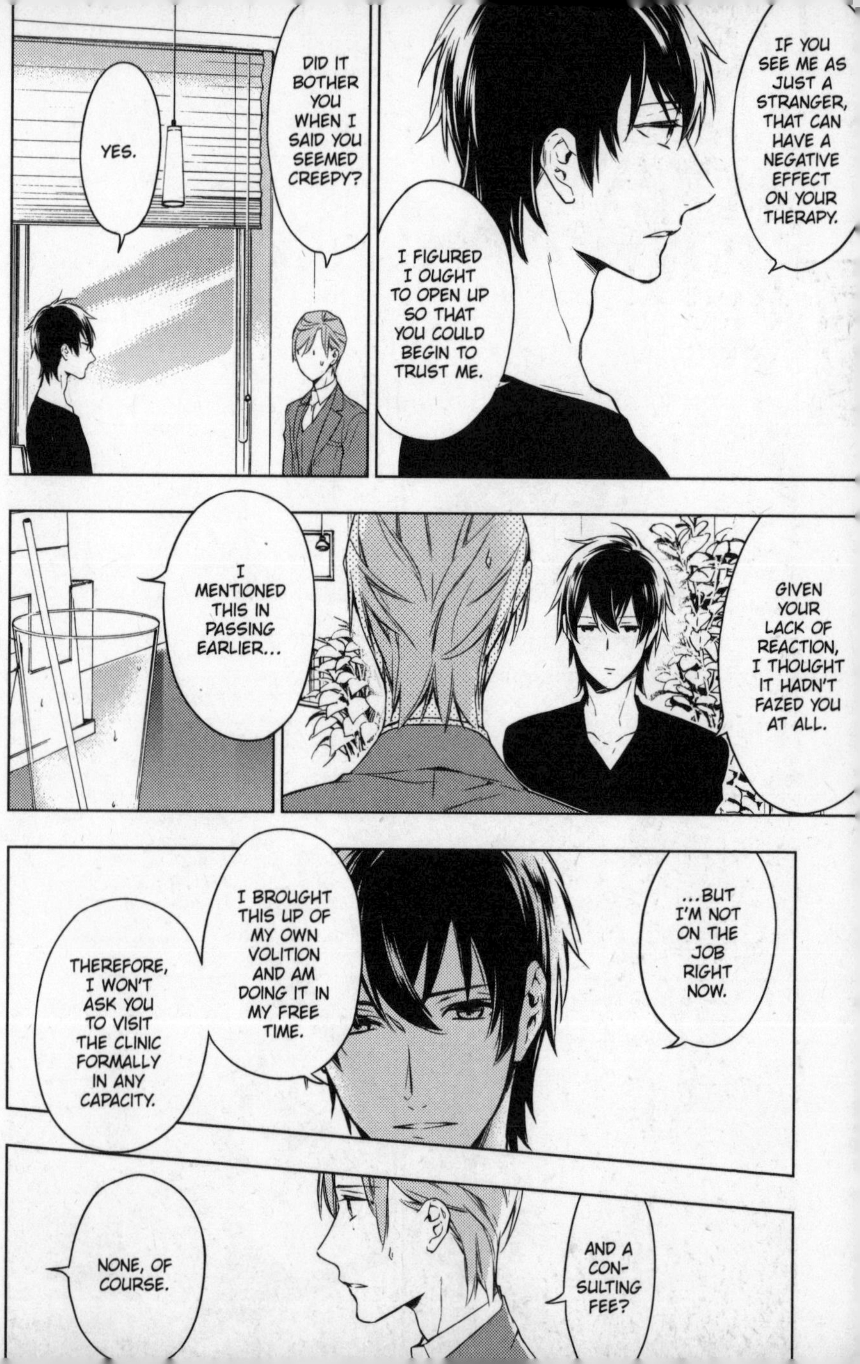
IF YOU SEE ME AS JUST A STRANGER, THAT CAN HAVE A NEGATIVE EFFECT ON YOUR THERAPY.
I FIGURED I OUGHT TO OPEN UP SO THAT YOU COULD BEGIN TO TRUST ME.
DID IT BOTHER YOU WHEN I SAID YOU SEEMED CREEPY?
YES.
GIVEN YOUR LACK OF REACTION, I THOUGHT IT HADN'T FAZED YOU AT ALL.
I MENTIONED THIS IN PASSING EARLIER...
...BUT I'M NOT ON THE JOB RIGHT NOW.
I BROUGHT THIS UP OF MY OWN VOLITION AND AM DOING IT IN MY FREE TIME.
THEREFORE, I WON'T ASK YOU TO VISIT THE CLINIC FORMALLY IN ANY CAPACITY.
AND A CON-SULTING FEE?
NONE, OF COURSE.

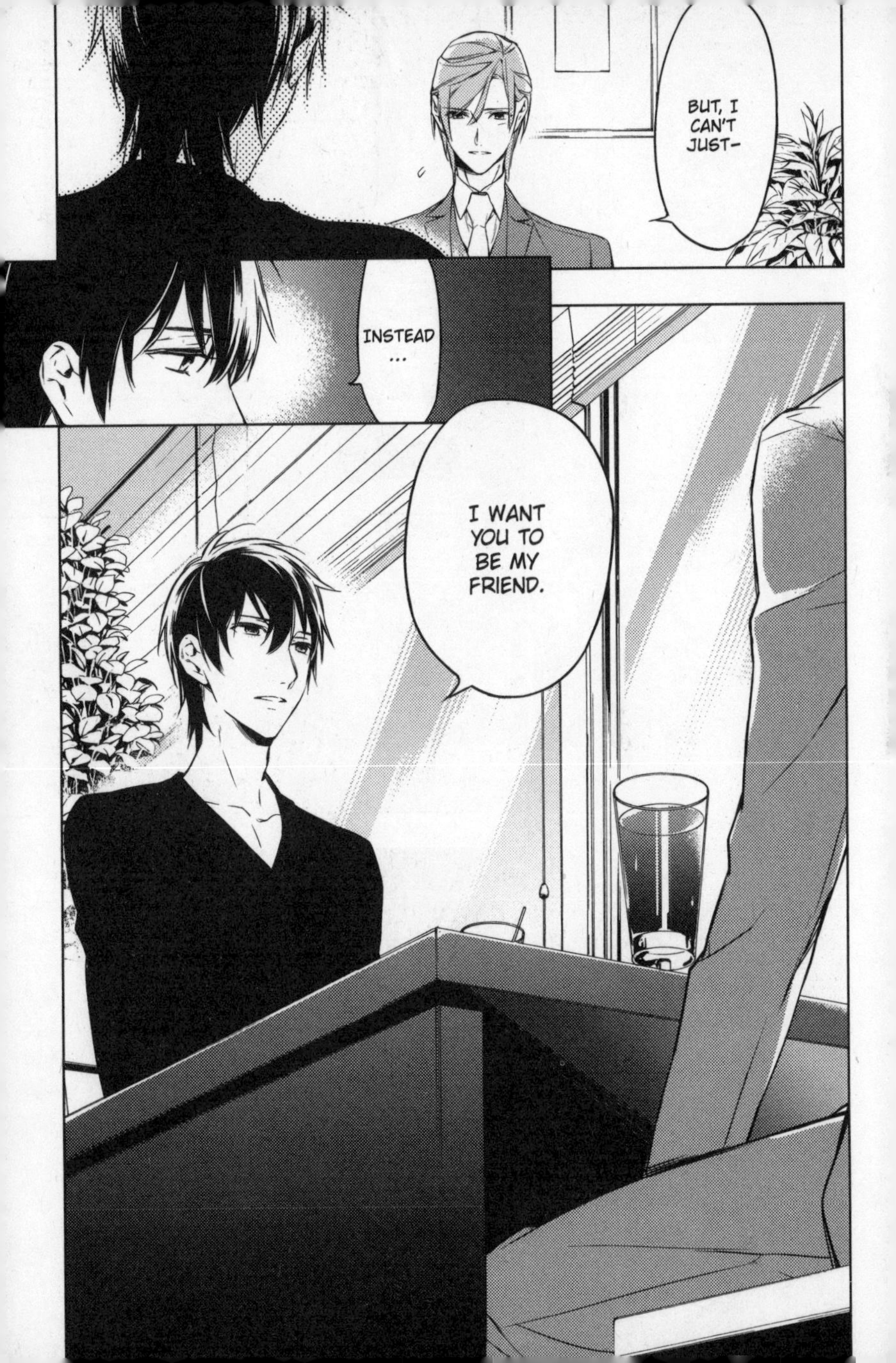
BUT, I CAN'T JUST-
INSTEAD ...
I WANT YOU TO BE MY FRIEND.

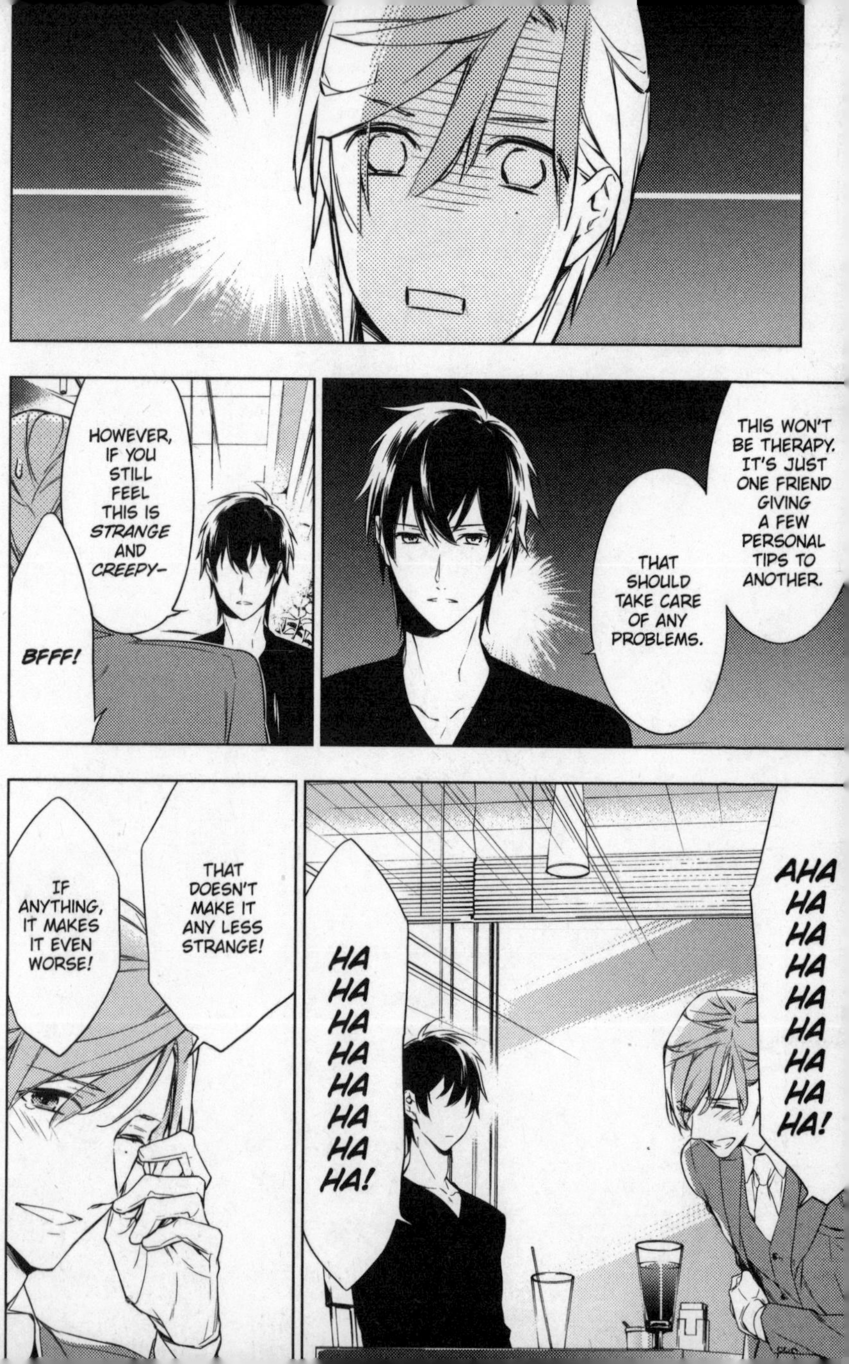
THIS WON'T BE THERAPY. IT'S JUST ONE FRIEND GIVING A FEW PERSONAL TIPS TO ANOTHER.
THAT SHOULD TAKE CARE OF ANY PROBLEMS.
HOWEVER, IF YOU STILL FEEL THIS IS *STRANGE* AND *CREEPY*-
BFFF!
AHA HA HA HA HA HA HA HA HA!
HA HA HA HA HA HA HA HA!
THAT DOESN'T MAKE IT ANY LESS STRANGE!
IF ANYTHING, IT MAKES IT EVEN WORSE!

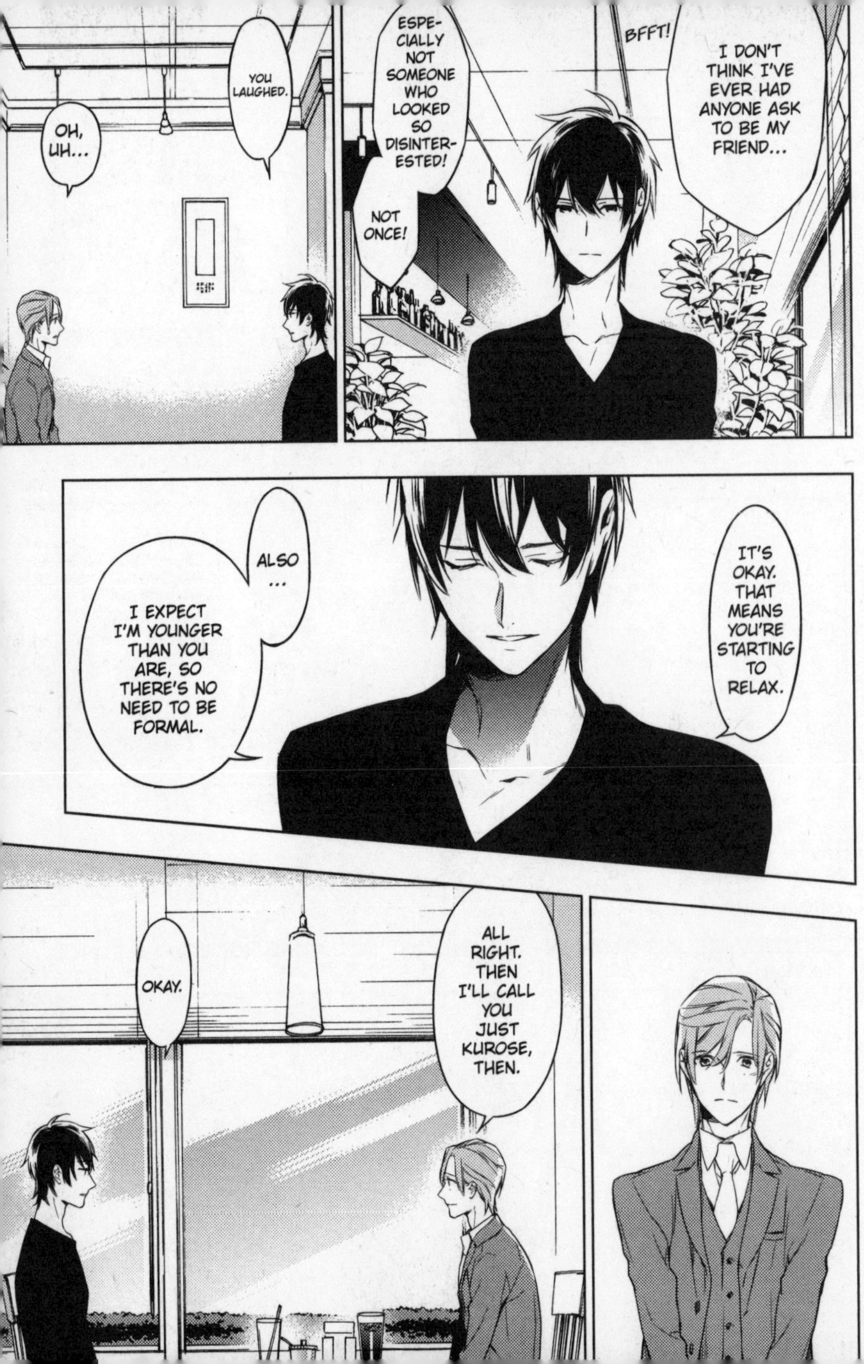
I DON'T THINK I'VE EVER HAD ANYONE ASK TO BE MY FRIEND...
BFFT!
ESPECIALLY NOT SOMEONE WHO LOOKED SO DISINTERESTED!
NOT ONCE!
YOU LAUGHED.
OH, UH...
IT'S OKAY. THAT MEANS YOU'RE STARTING TO RELAX.
ALSO...
I EXPECT I'M YOUNGER THAN YOU ARE, SO THERE'S NO NEED TO BE FORMAL.
ALL RIGHT. THEN I'LL CALL YOU JUST KUROSE, THEN.
OKAY.

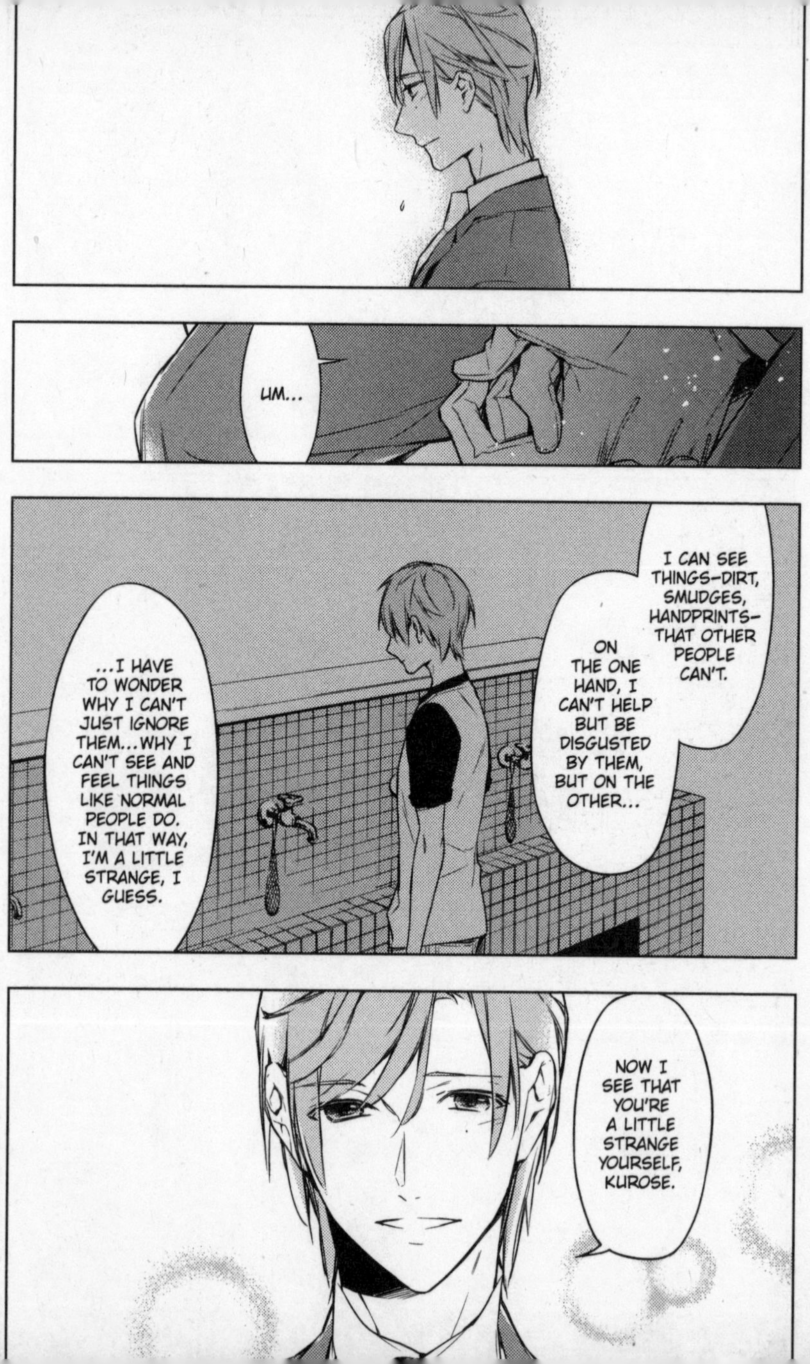
UM...
I CAN SEE THINGS—DIRT, SMUDGES, HANDPRINTS—THAT OTHER PEOPLE CAN'T.
ON THE ONE HAND, I CAN'T HELP BUT BE DISGUSTED BY THEM, BUT ON THE OTHER...
...I HAVE TO WONDER WHY I CAN'T JUST IGNORE THEM...WHY I CAN'T SEE AND FEEL THINGS LIKE NORMAL PEOPLE DO. IN THAT WAY, I'M A LITTLE STRANGE, I GUESS.
NOW I SEE THAT YOU'RE A LITTLE STRANGE YOURSELF, KUROSE.

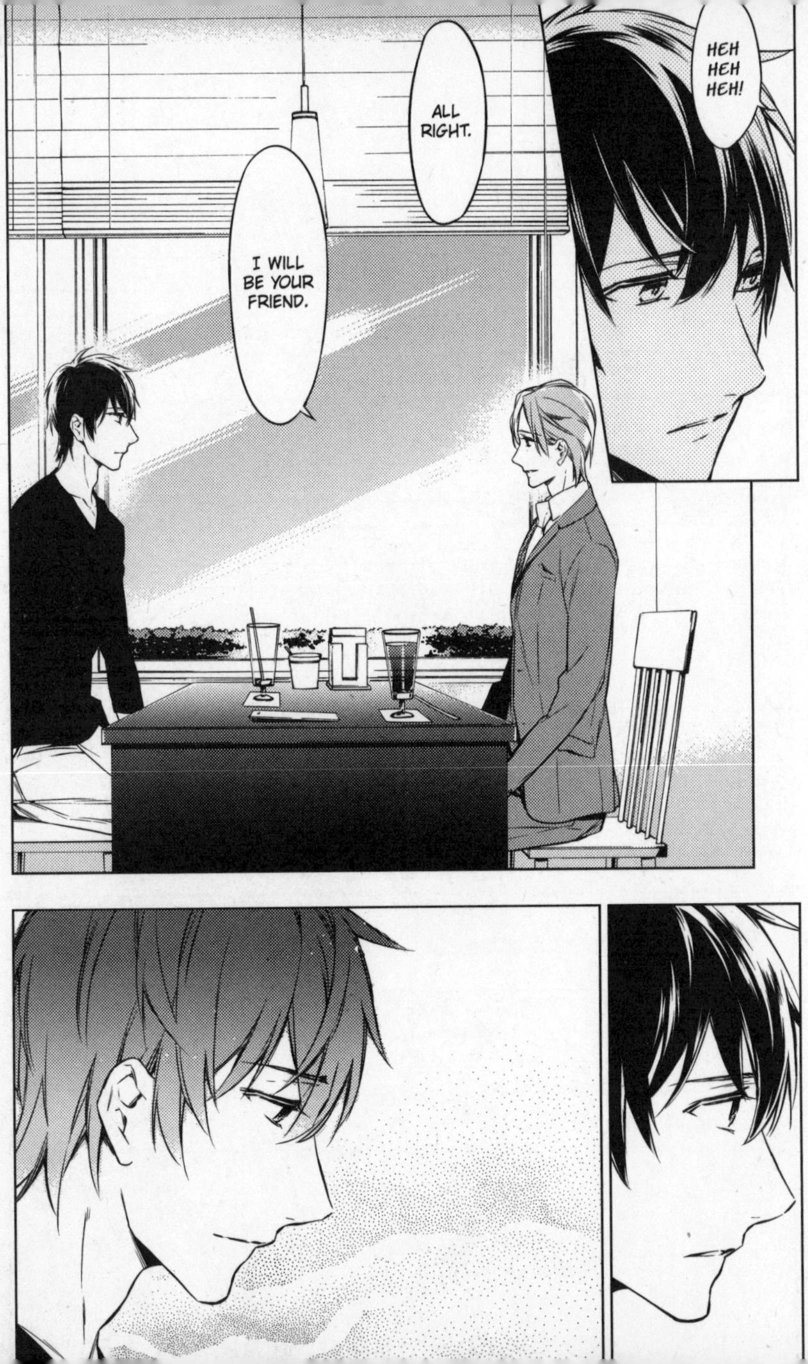
HEH HEH HEH!
ALL RIGHT.
I WILL BE YOUR FRIEND.

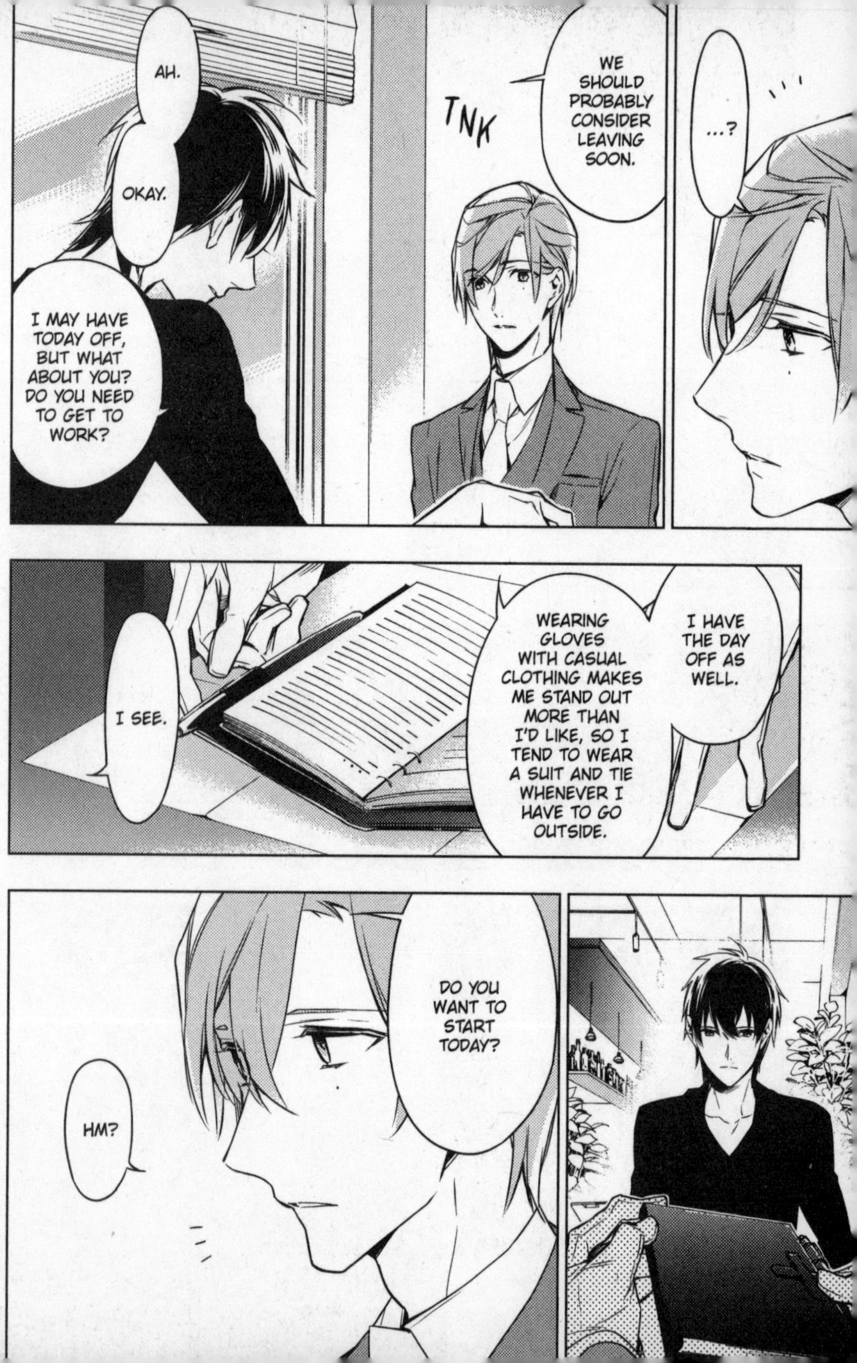
...?
WE SHOULD PROBABLY CONSIDER LEAVING SOON.
TNK
AH.
OKAY.
I MAY HAVE TODAY OFF, BUT WHAT ABOUT YOU? DO YOU NEED TO GET TO WORK?
I HAVE THE DAY OFF AS WELL.
WEARING GLOVES WITH CASUAL CLOTHING MAKES ME STAND OUT MORE THAN I'D LIKE, SO I TEND TO WEAR A SUIT AND TIE WHENEVER I HAVE TO GO OUTSIDE.
I SEE.
DO YOU WANT TO START TODAY?
HM?

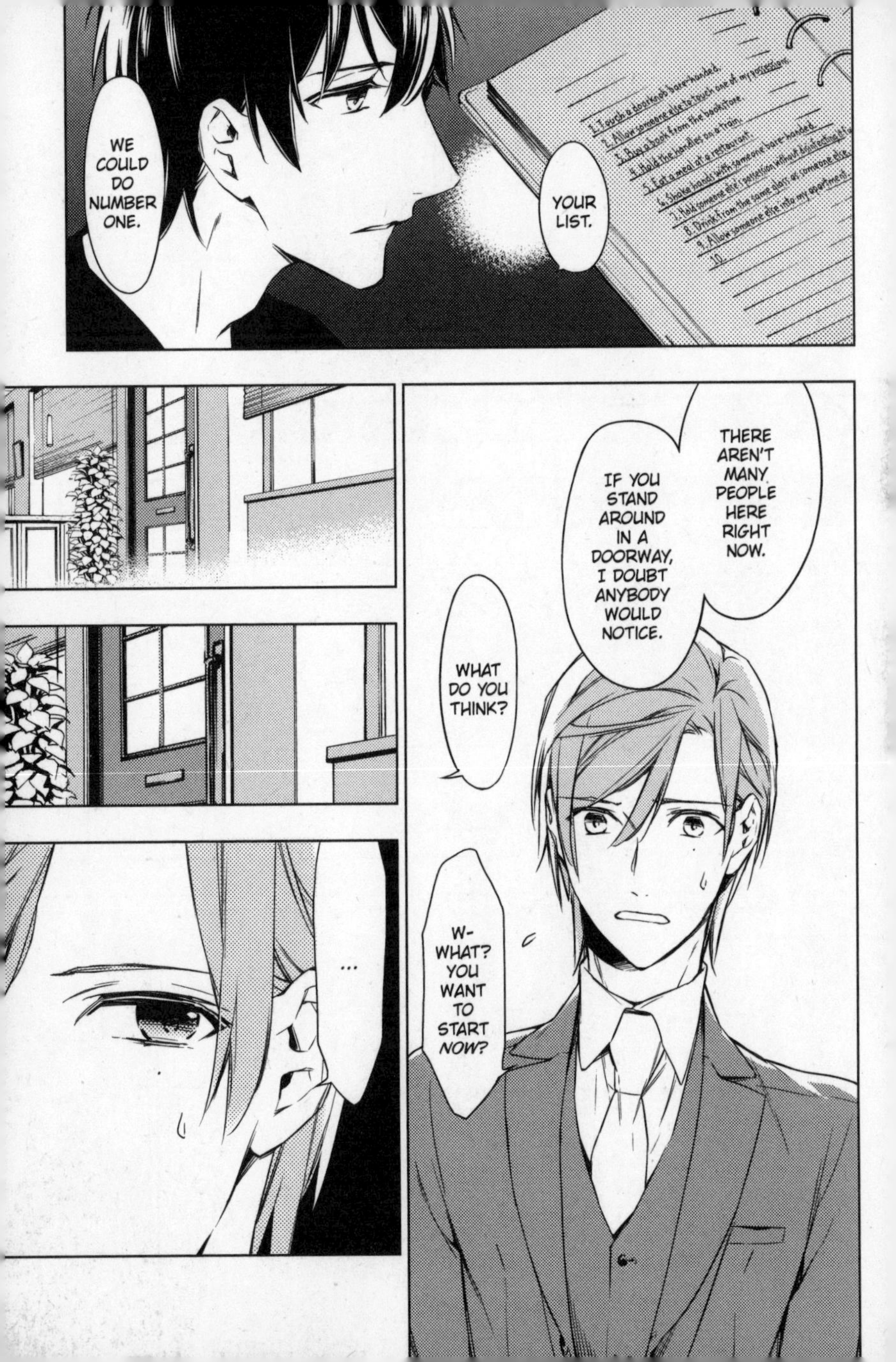
1. Touch a doorknob bare-handed.
2. Allow someone else to touch one of my possessions.
3. Buy a book from the bookstore.
4. Hold the handles on a train.
5. Eat a meal at a restaurant.
6. Shake hands with someone bare-handed.
7. Hold someone else's possession without disinfecting it
8. Drink from the same glass as someone else.
9. Allow someone else into my apartment.
10.
YOUR LIST.
WE COULD DO NUMBER ONE.
THERE AREN'T MANY PEOPLE HERE RIGHT NOW.
IF YOU STAND AROUND IN A DOORWAY, I DOUBT ANYBODY WOULD NOTICE.
WHAT DO YOU THINK?
W- WHAT? YOU WANT TO START *NOW*?
...

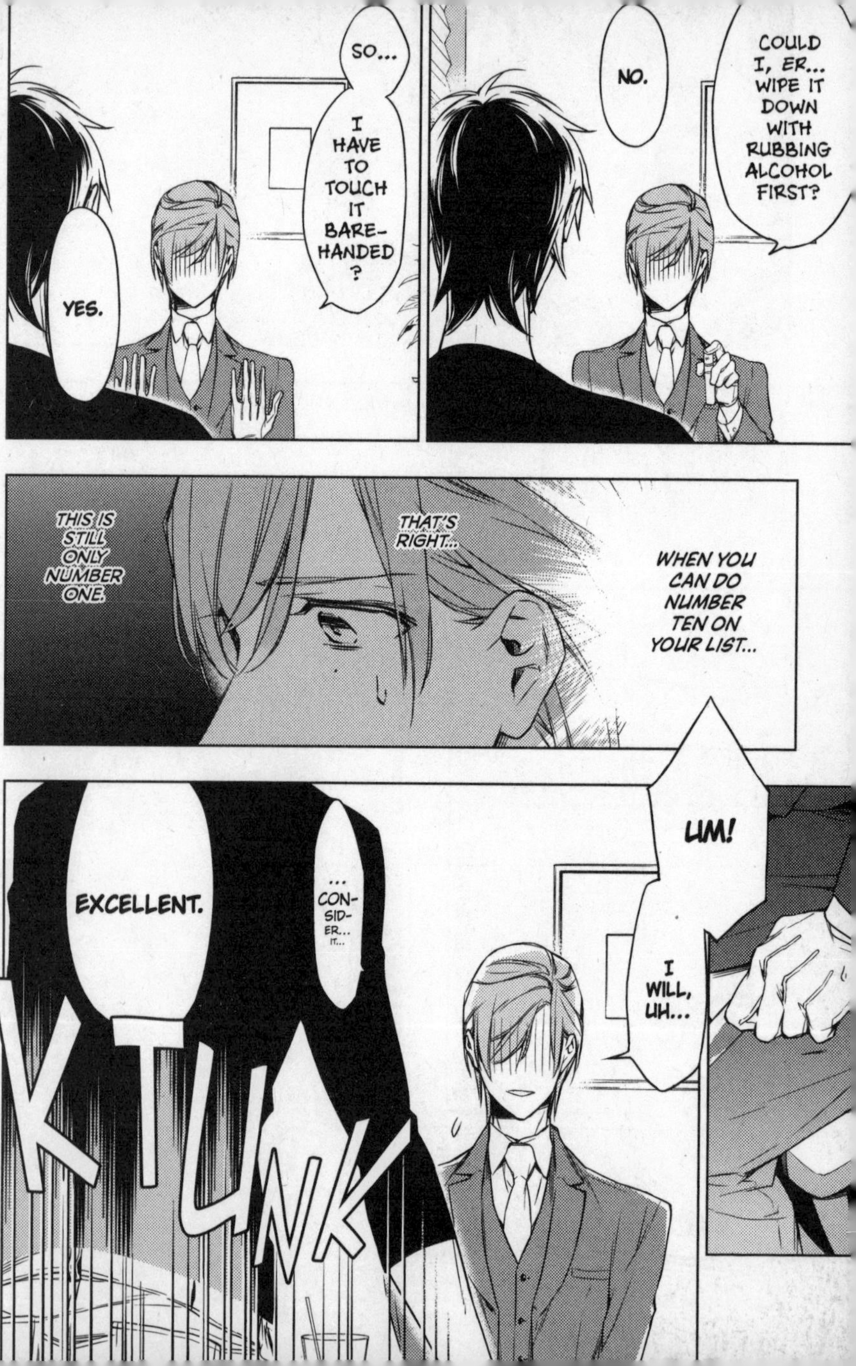
COULD I, ER... WIPE IT DOWN WITH RUBBING ALCOHOL FIRST?
NO.
SO... I HAVE TO TOUCH IT BARE-HANDED?
YES.
WHEN YOU CAN DO NUMBER TEN ON YOUR LIST...
THAT'S RIGHT...
THIS IS STILL ONLY NUMBER ONE.
UM!
I WILL, UH...
... CONSID-ER... IT...
EXCELLENT.
KTUNK

WSH

HUH ?!

I'LL TAKE AS LONG AS I CAN TO PAY THE CASHIER.

PLEASE USE THAT TIME TO WALK OUT THE DOOR.

WAIT!

I'M STILL CONSIDERING...

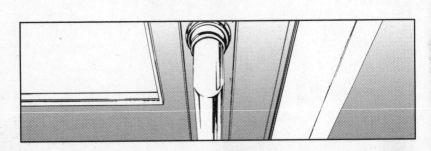

THAT WILL BE 1,365 YEN, SIR.

I THINK I HAVE CHANGE... UMM...

Total 13
Paid
Change

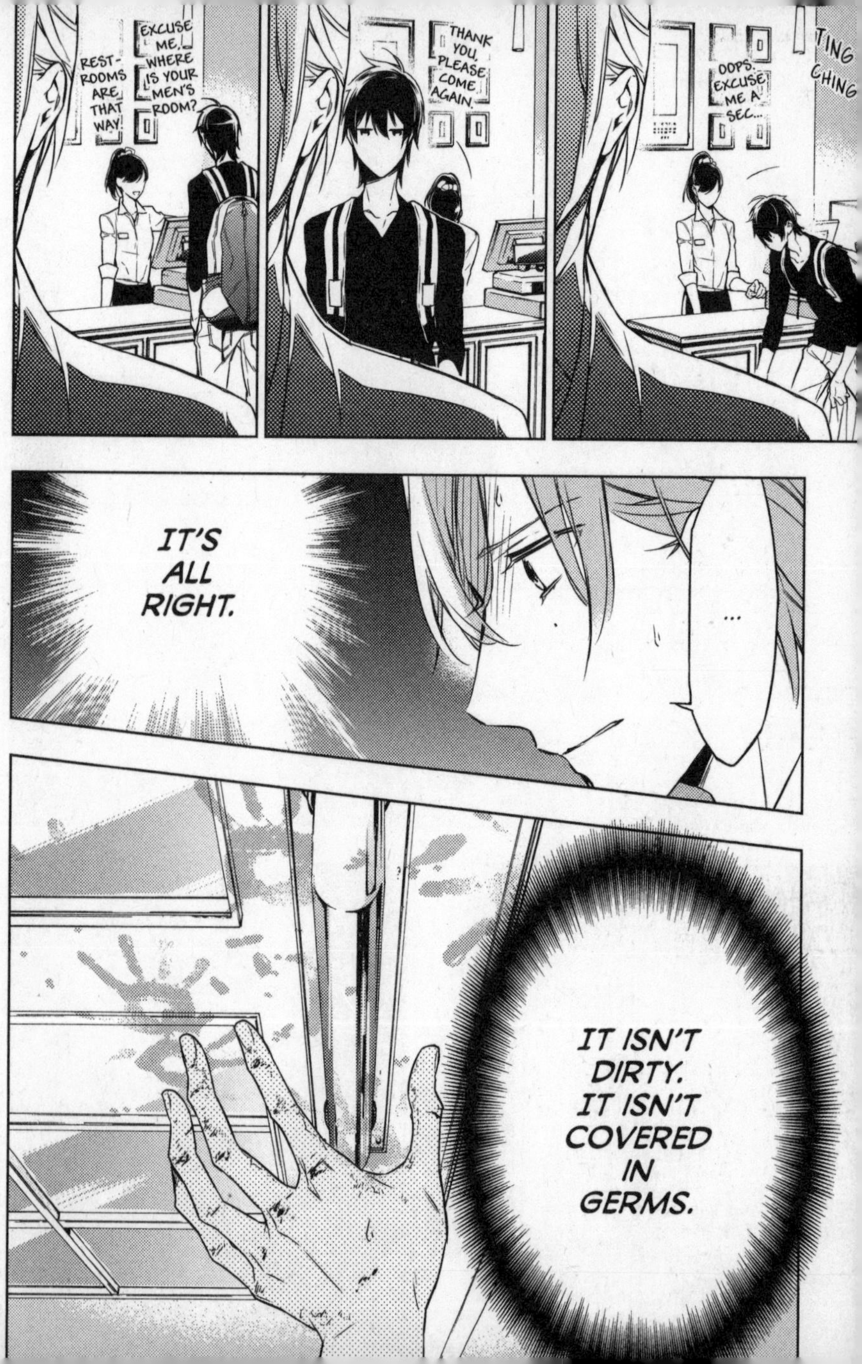
TING CHING
OOPS. EXCUSE ME A SEC...
THANK YOU, PLEASE COME AGAIN.
EXCUSE ME, WHERE IS YOUR MEN'S ROOM?
REST-ROOMS ARE THAT WAY.
...
IT'S ALL RIGHT.
IT ISN'T DIRTY. IT ISN'T COVERED IN GERMS.

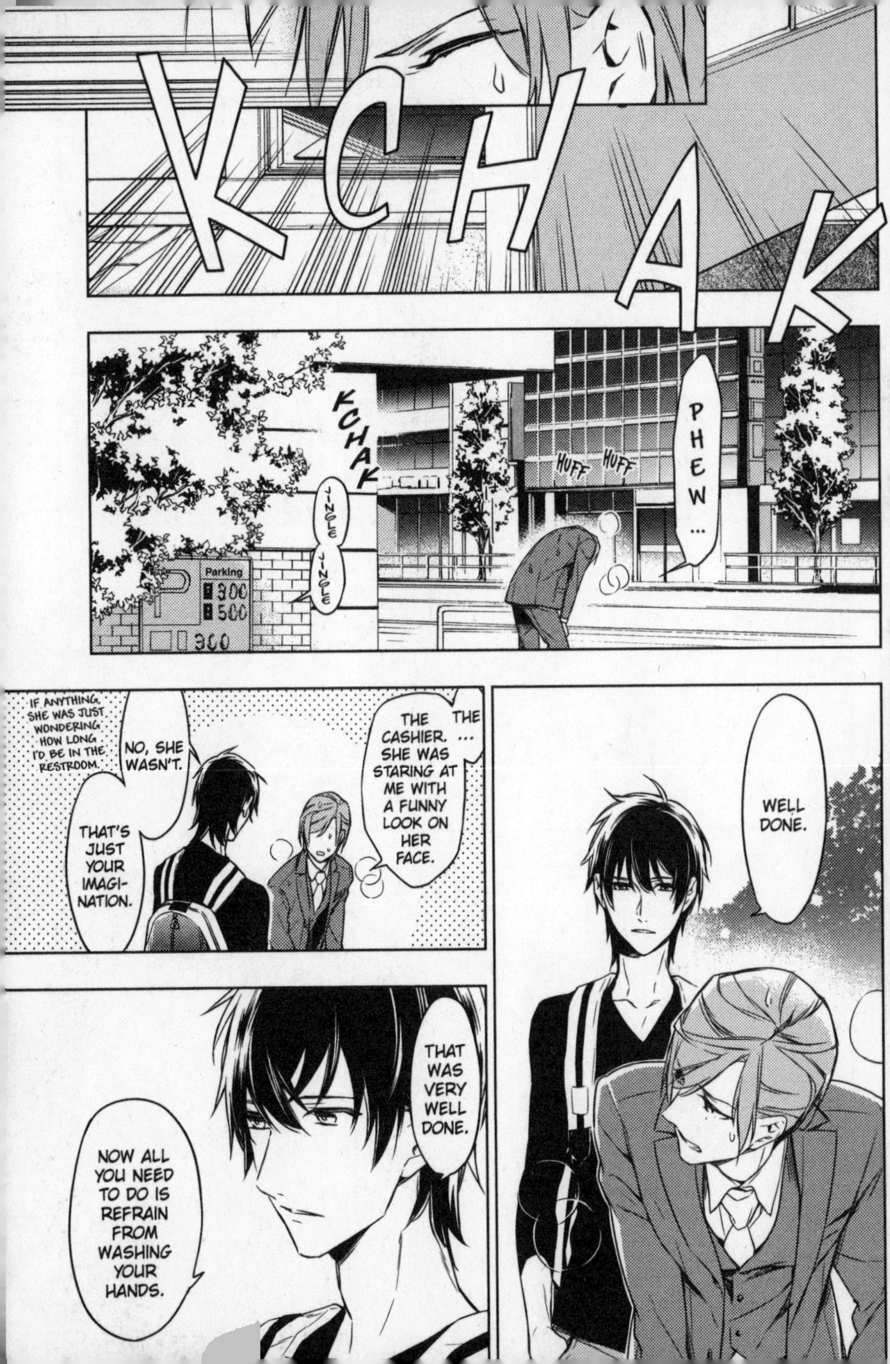
KCHAK
PHEW...
HUFF
HUFF
KCHAK
JINGLE
JINGLE
Parking
300
500
300
WELL DONE.
THE...
THE CASHIER. SHE WAS STARING AT ME WITH A FUNNY LOOK ON HER FACE.
NO, SHE WASN'T.
THAT'S JUST YOUR IMAGINATION.
IF ANYTHING, SHE WAS JUST WONDERING HOW LONG I'D BE IN THE RESTROOM.
THAT WAS VERY WELL DONE.
NOW ALL YOU NEED TO DO IS REFRAIN FROM WASHING YOUR HANDS.

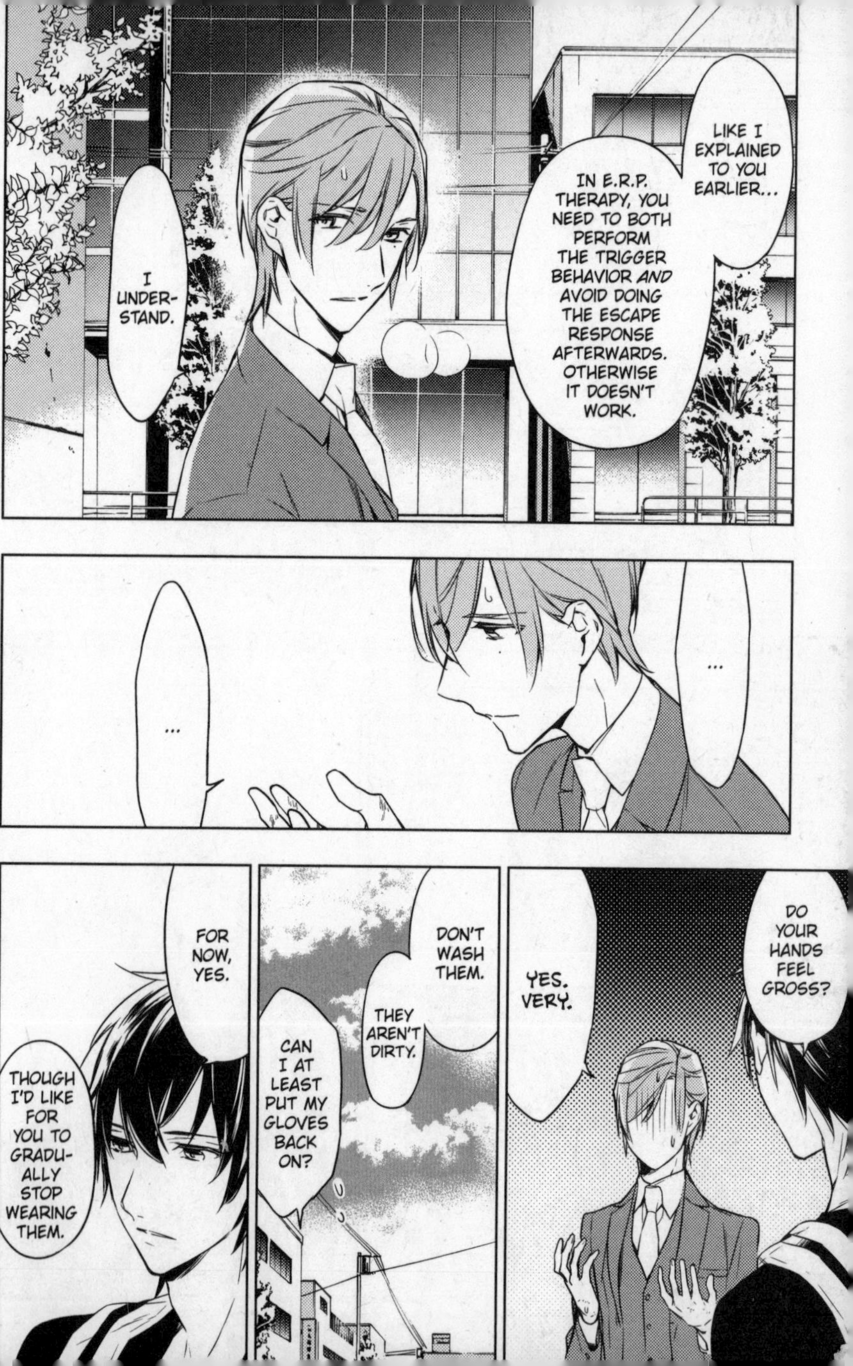
LIKE I EXPLAINED TO YOU EARLIER...
IN E.R.P. THERAPY, YOU NEED TO BOTH PERFORM THE TRIGGER BEHAVIOR *AND* AVOID DOING THE ESCAPE RESPONSE AFTERWARDS. OTHERWISE IT DOESN'T WORK.
I UNDER-STAND.
...
...
DO YOUR HANDS FEEL GROSS?
YES. VERY.
DON'T WASH THEM.
THEY AREN'T DIRTY.
CAN I AT LEAST PUT MY GLOVES BACK ON?
FOR NOW, YES.
THOUGH I'D LIKE FOR YOU TO GRADU-ALLY STOP WEARING THEM.

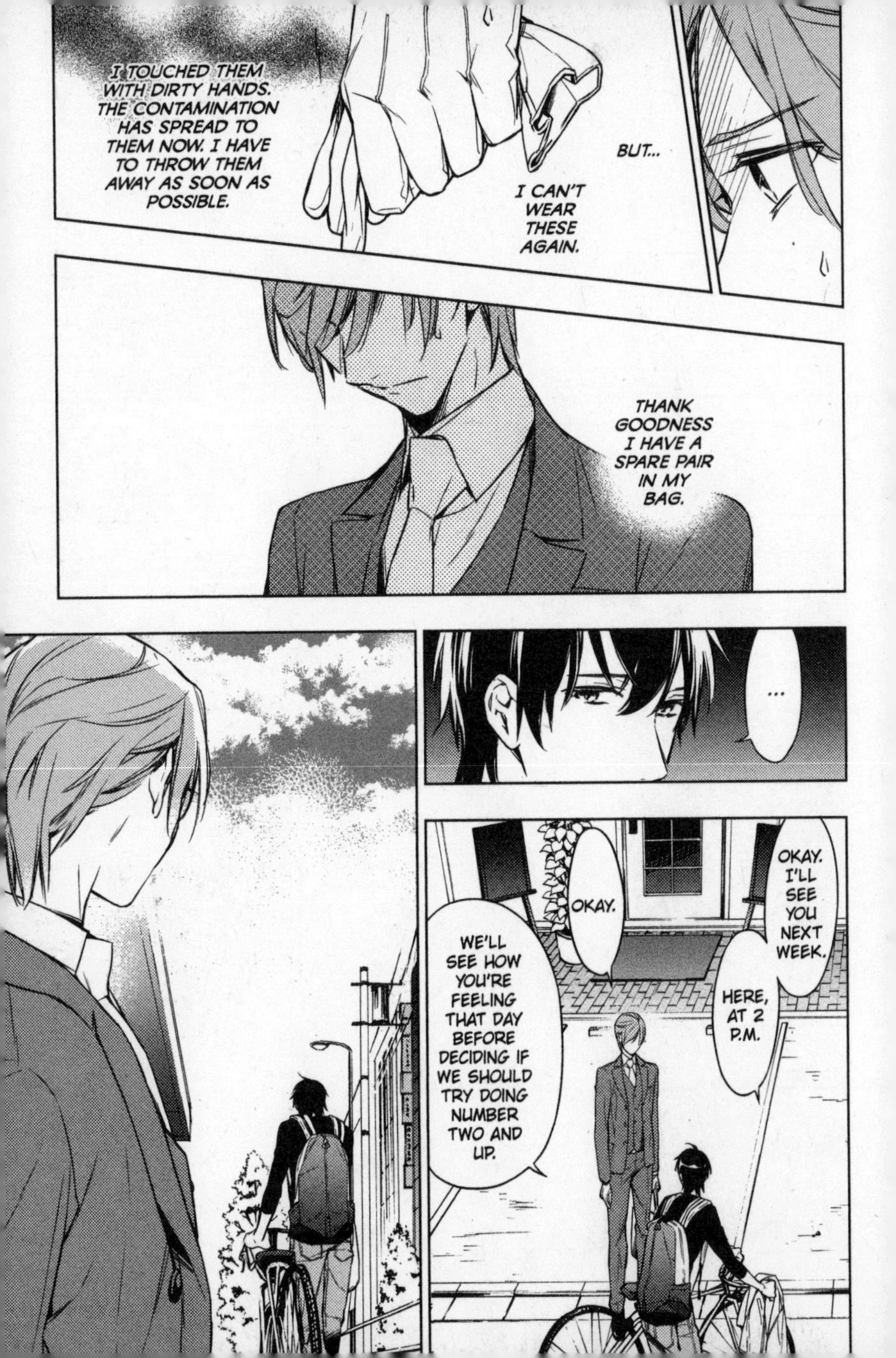
I TOUCHED THEM WITH DIRTY HANDS. THE CONTAMINATION HAS SPREAD TO THEM NOW. I HAVE TO THROW THEM AWAY AS SOON AS POSSIBLE.
BUT...
I CAN'T WEAR THESE AGAIN.
THANK GOODNESS I HAVE A SPARE PAIR IN MY BAG.
...
OKAY. I'LL SEE YOU NEXT WEEK.
HERE, AT 2 P.M.
OKAY.
WE'LL SEE HOW YOU'RE FEELING THAT DAY BEFORE DECIDING IF WE SHOULD TRY DOING NUMBER TWO AND UP.

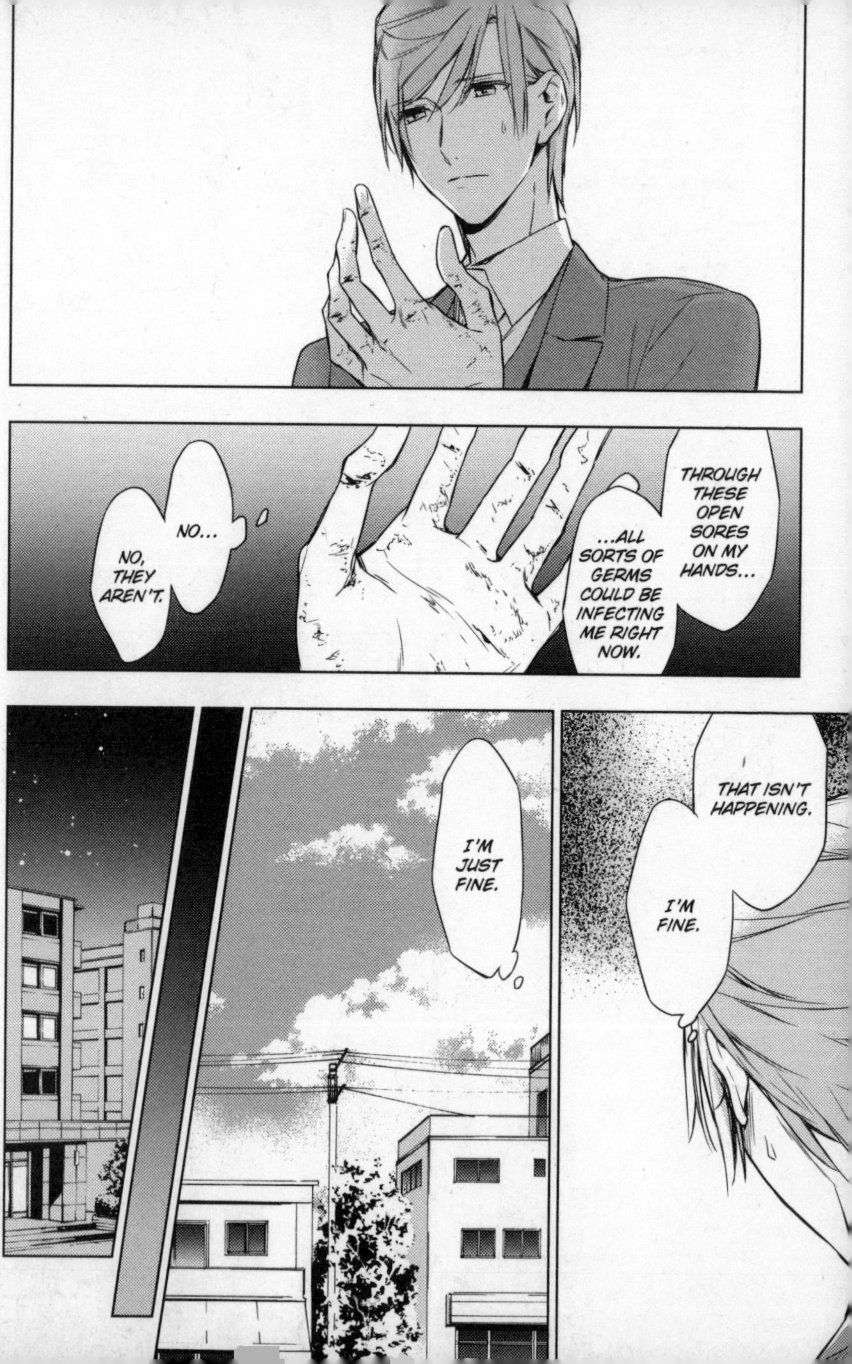
THROUGH THESE OPEN SORES ON MY HANDS...
...ALL SORTS OF GERMS COULD BE INFECTING ME RIGHT NOW.
NO...
NO, THEY AREN'T.
THAT ISN'T HAPPENING.
I'M FINE.
I'M JUST FINE.

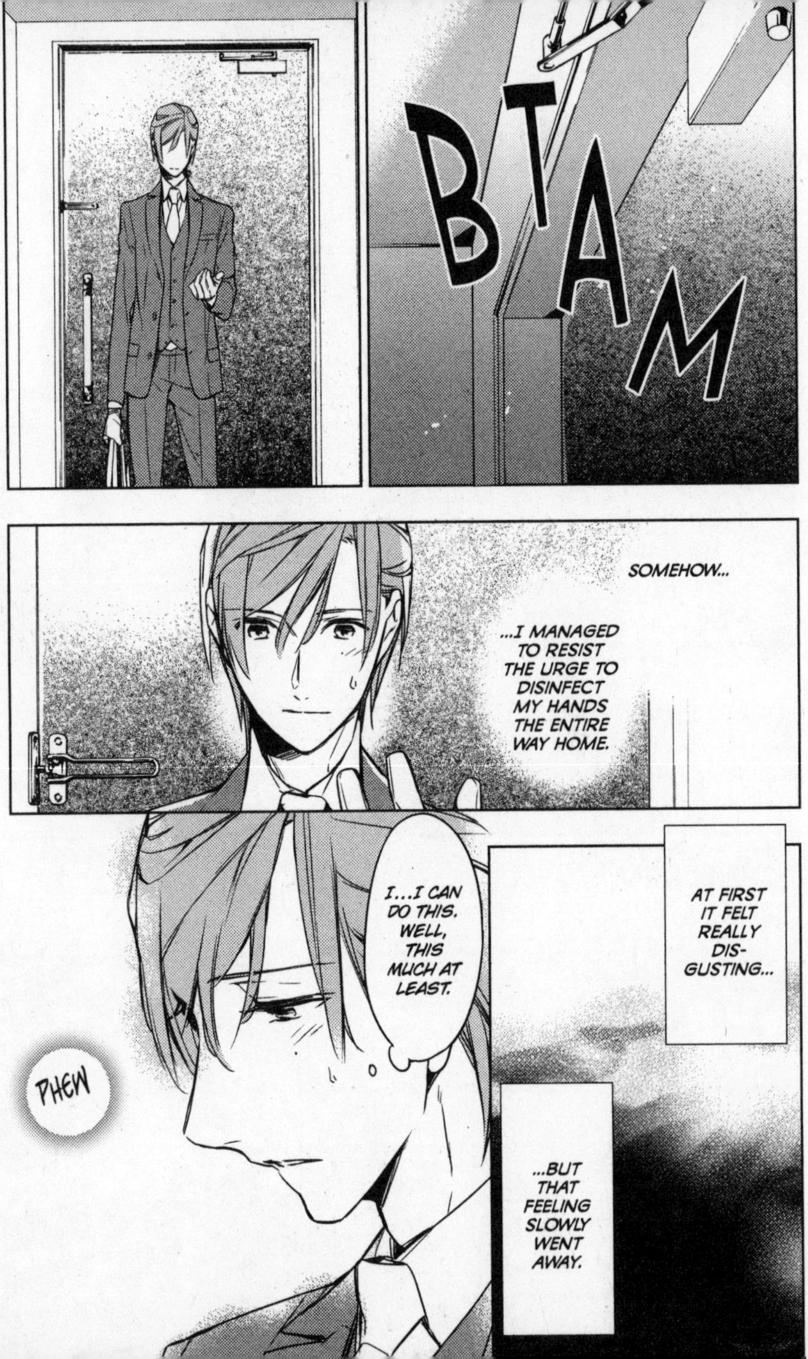
BTAM
SOMEHOW...
...I MANAGED TO RESIST THE URGE TO DISINFECT MY HANDS THE ENTIRE WAY HOME.
AT FIRST IT FELT REALLY DIS-GUSTING...
I...I CAN DO THIS. WELL, THIS MUCH AT LEAST.
...BUT THAT FEELING SLOWLY WENT AWAY.
PHEW

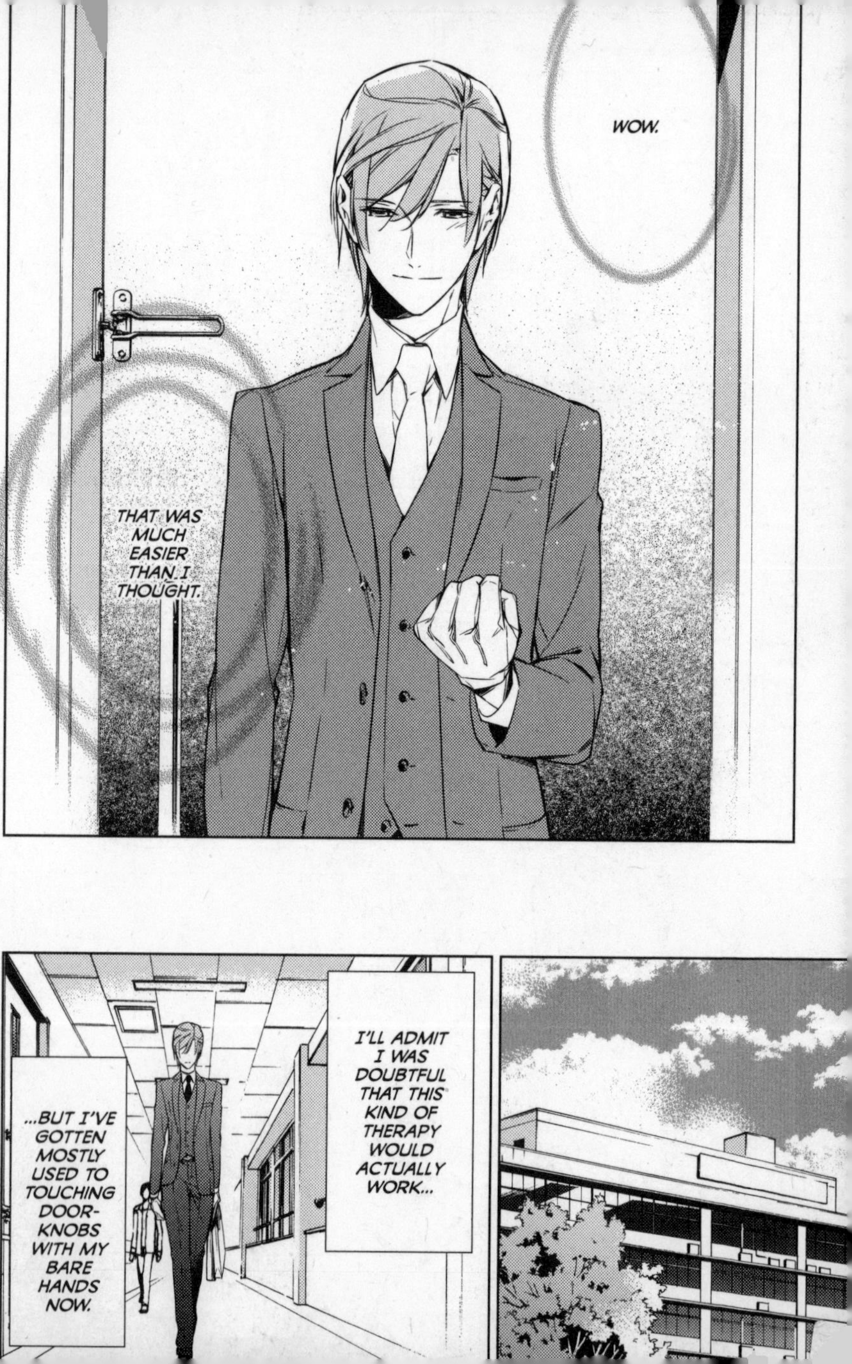
WOW.
THAT WAS MUCH EASIER THAN I THOUGHT.
I'LL ADMIT I WAS DOUBTFUL THAT THIS KIND OF THERAPY WOULD ACTUALLY WORK...
...BUT I'VE GOTTEN MOSTLY USED TO TOUCHING DOOR-KNOBS WITH MY BARE HANDS NOW.

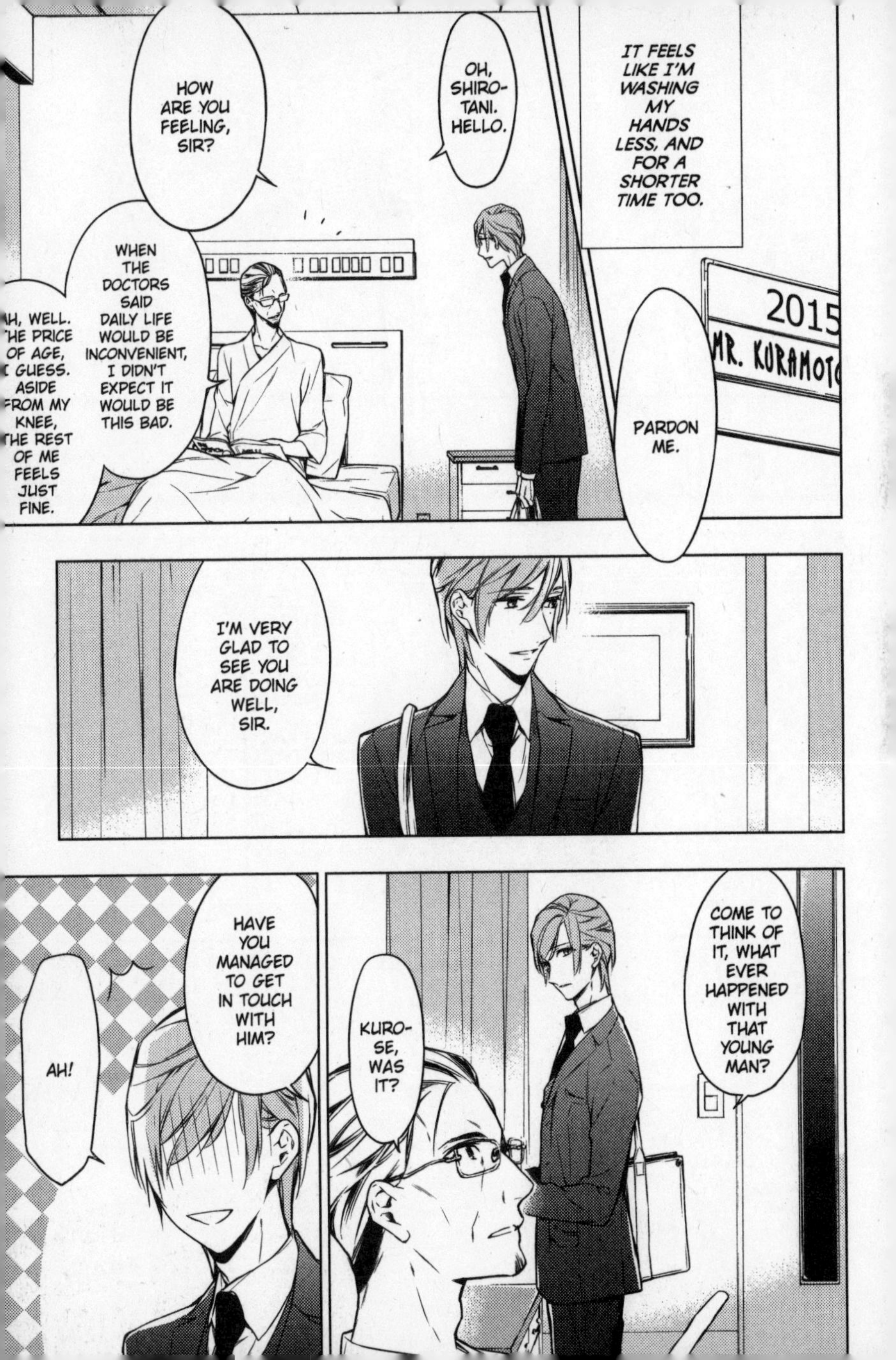
IT FEELS LIKE I'M WASHING MY HANDS LESS, AND FOR A SHORTER TIME TOO.
2015
MR. KURAMOTO
PARDON ME.
OH, SHIRO-TANI. HELLO.
HOW ARE YOU FEELING, SIR?
WHEN THE DOCTORS SAID DAILY LIFE WOULD BE INCONVENIENT, I DIDN'T EXPECT IT WOULD BE THIS BAD.
AH, WELL. THE PRICE OF AGE, I GUESS. ASIDE FROM MY KNEE, THE REST OF ME FEELS JUST FINE.
I'M VERY GLAD TO SEE YOU ARE DOING WELL, SIR.
COME TO THINK OF IT, WHAT EVER HAPPENED WITH THAT YOUNG MAN?
KURO-SE, WAS IT?
HAVE YOU MANAGED TO GET IN TOUCH WITH HIM?
AH!

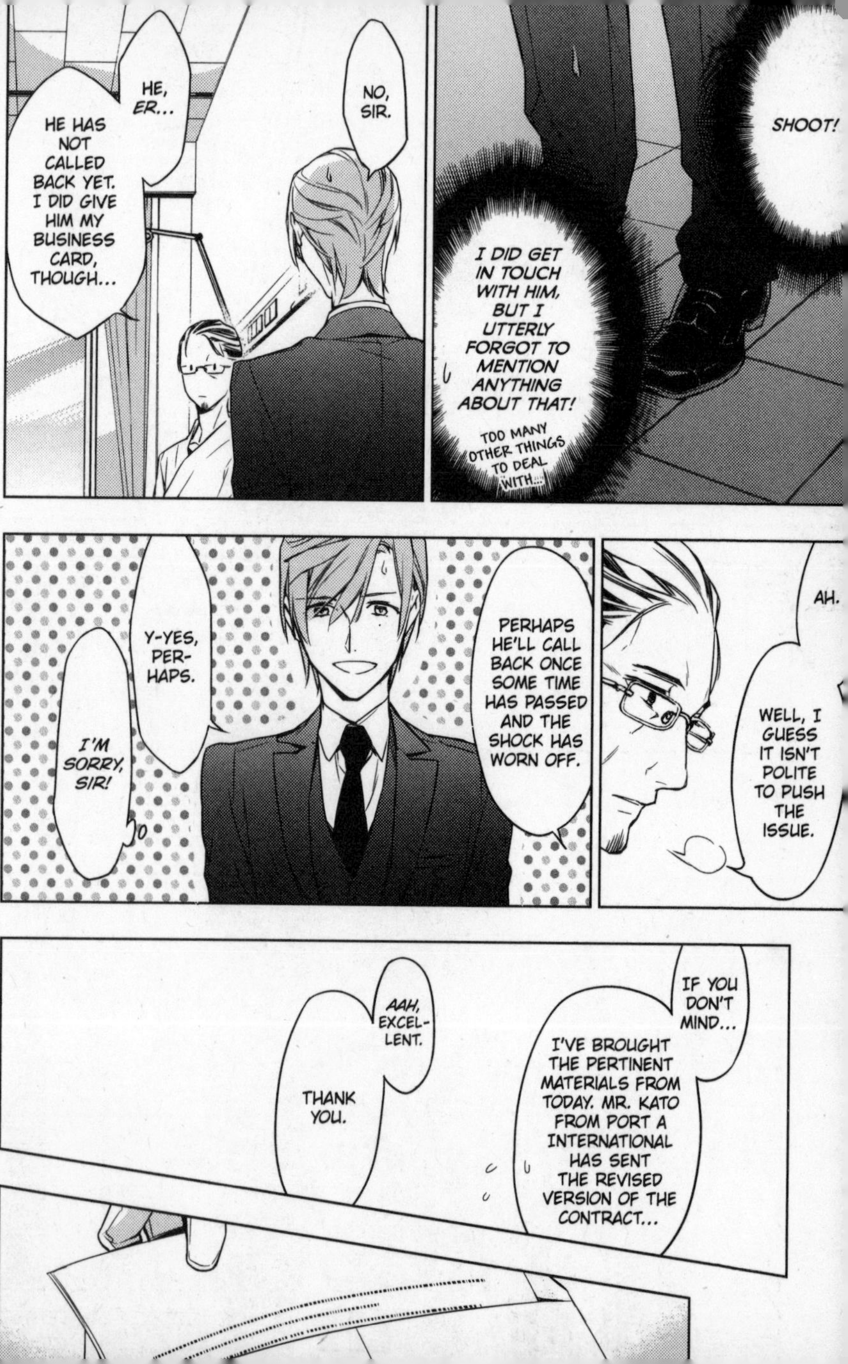
SHOOT!
I DID GET IN TOUCH WITH HIM, BUT I UTTERLY FORGOT TO MENTION ANYTHING ABOUT THAT!
TOO MANY OTHER THINGS TO DEAL WITH...
NO, SIR.
HE, ER...
HE HAS NOT CALLED BACK YET. I DID GIVE HIM MY BUSINESS CARD, THOUGH...
AH.
WELL, I GUESS IT ISN'T POLITE TO PUSH THE ISSUE.
PERHAPS HE'LL CALL BACK ONCE SOME TIME HAS PASSED AND THE SHOCK HAS WORN OFF.
Y-YES, PER-HAPS.
I'M SORRY, SIR!
IF YOU DON'T MIND...
I'VE BROUGHT THE PERTINENT MATERIALS FROM TODAY. MR. KATO FROM PORT A INTERNATIONAL HAS SENT THE REVISED VERSION OF THE CONTRACT...
AAH, EXCEL-LENT.
THANK YOU.

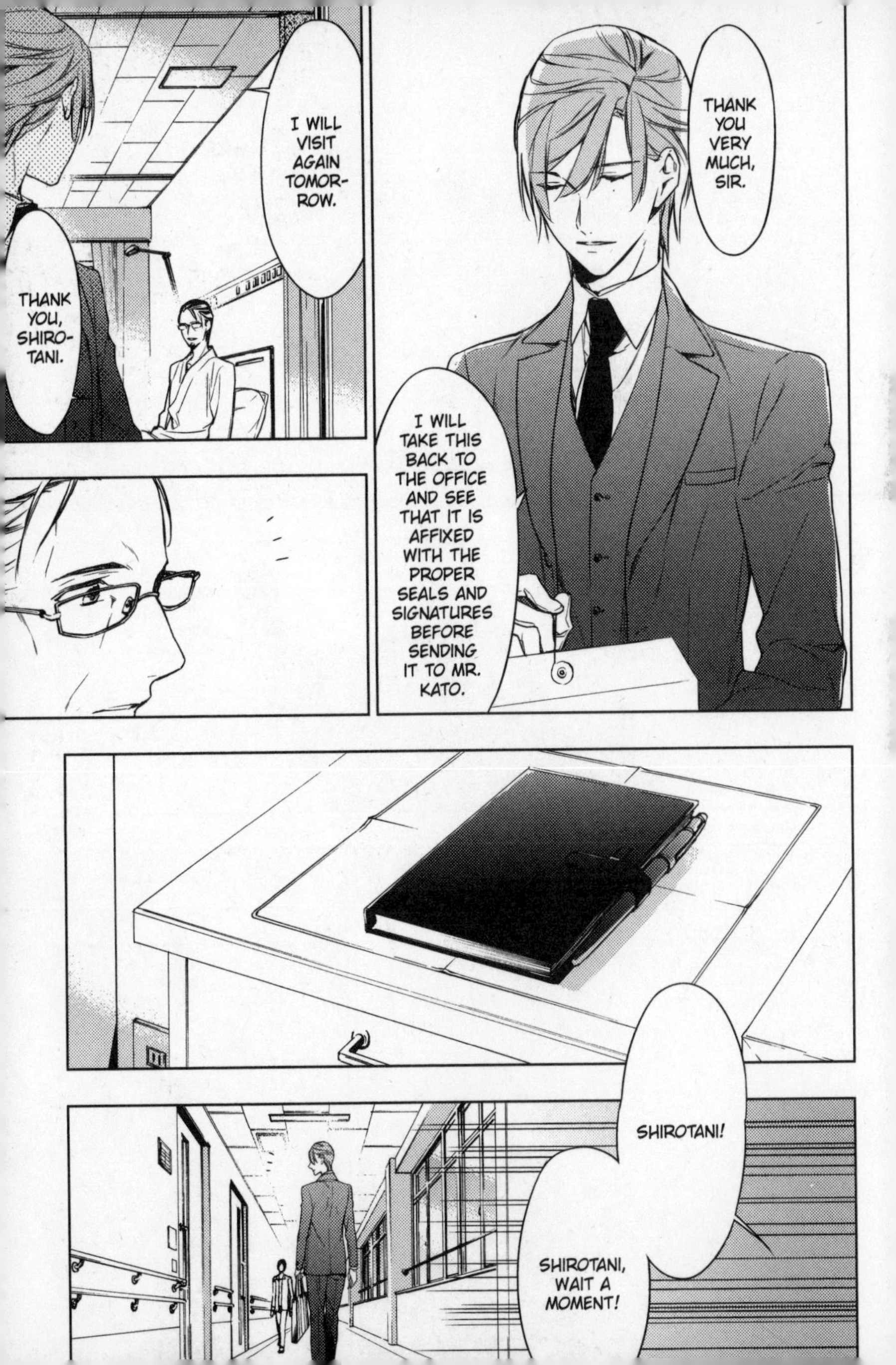
THANK YOU VERY MUCH, SIR.
I WILL TAKE THIS BACK TO THE OFFICE AND SEE THAT IT IS AFFIXED WITH THE PROPER SEALS AND SIGNATURES BEFORE SENDING IT TO MR. KATO.
I WILL VISIT AGAIN TOMOR-ROW.
THANK YOU, SHIRO-TANI.
SHIROTANI!
SHIROTANI, WAIT A MOMENT!

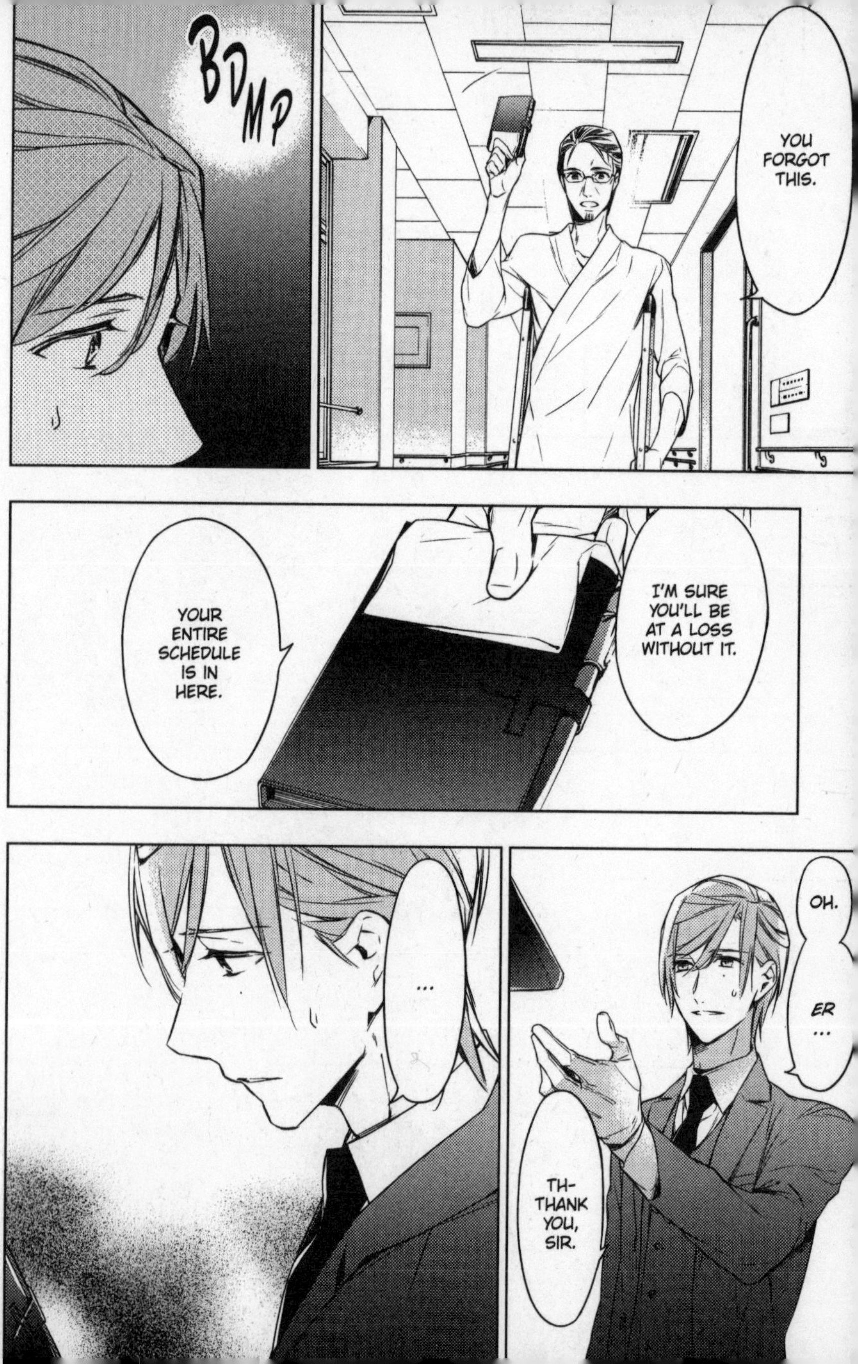
YOU FORGOT THIS.
BDMP
I'M SURE YOU'LL BE AT A LOSS WITHOUT IT.
YOUR ENTIRE SCHEDULE IS IN HERE.
OH.
ER ...
TH- THANK YOU, SIR.
...

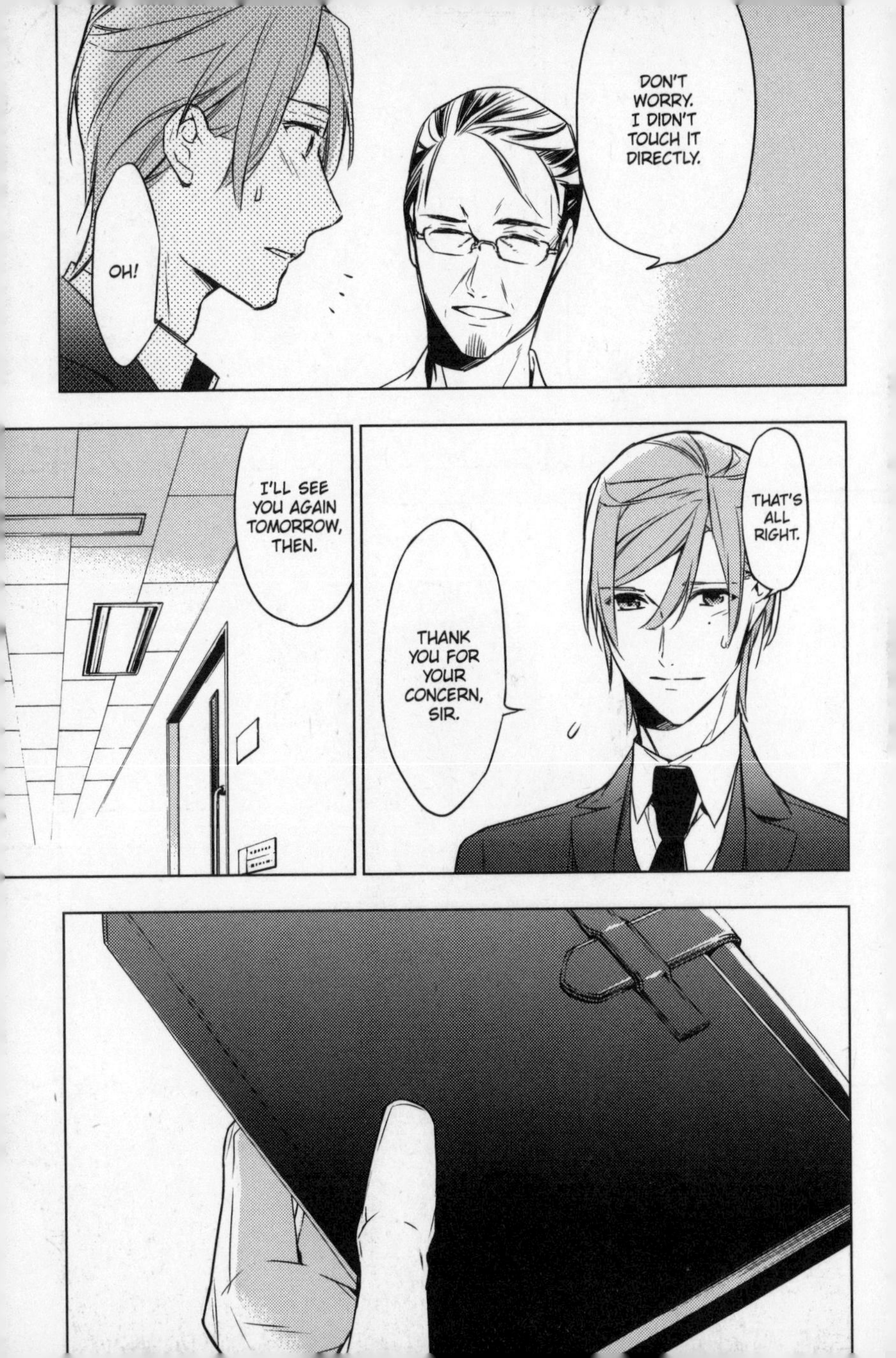
DON'T WORRY. I DIDN'T TOUCH IT DIRECTLY.
OH!
THAT'S ALL RIGHT.
THANK YOU FOR YOUR CONCERN, SIR.
I'LL SEE YOU AGAIN TOMORROW, THEN.

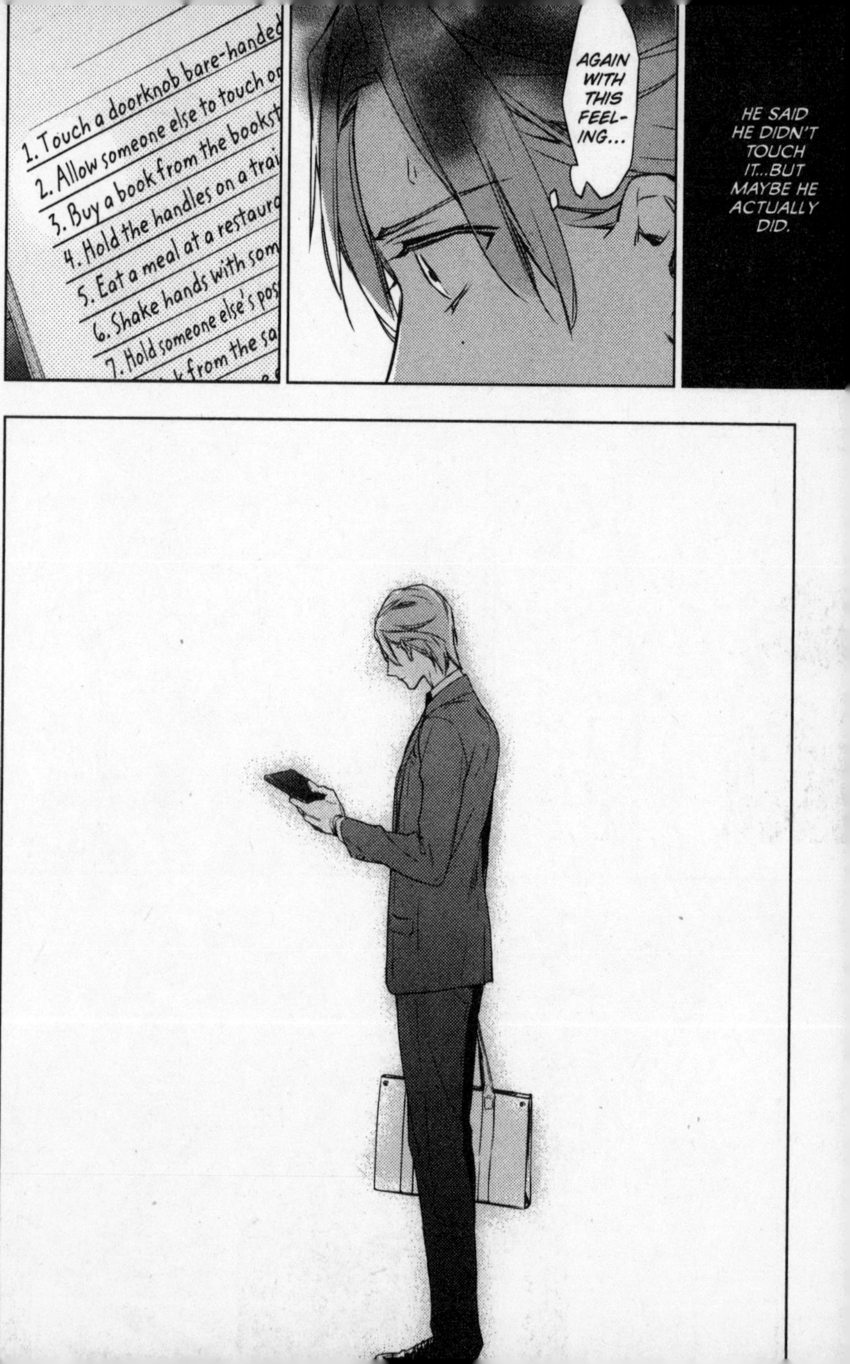
HE SAID HE DIDN'T TOUCH IT...BUT MAYBE HE ACTUALLY DID.
AGAIN WITH THIS FEEL-ING...
1. Touch a doorknob bare-handed
2. Allow someone else to touch o
3. Buy a book from the bookst
4. Hold the handles on a trai
5. Eat a meal at a restaura
6. Shake hands with som
7. Hold someone else's pos
k from the sa

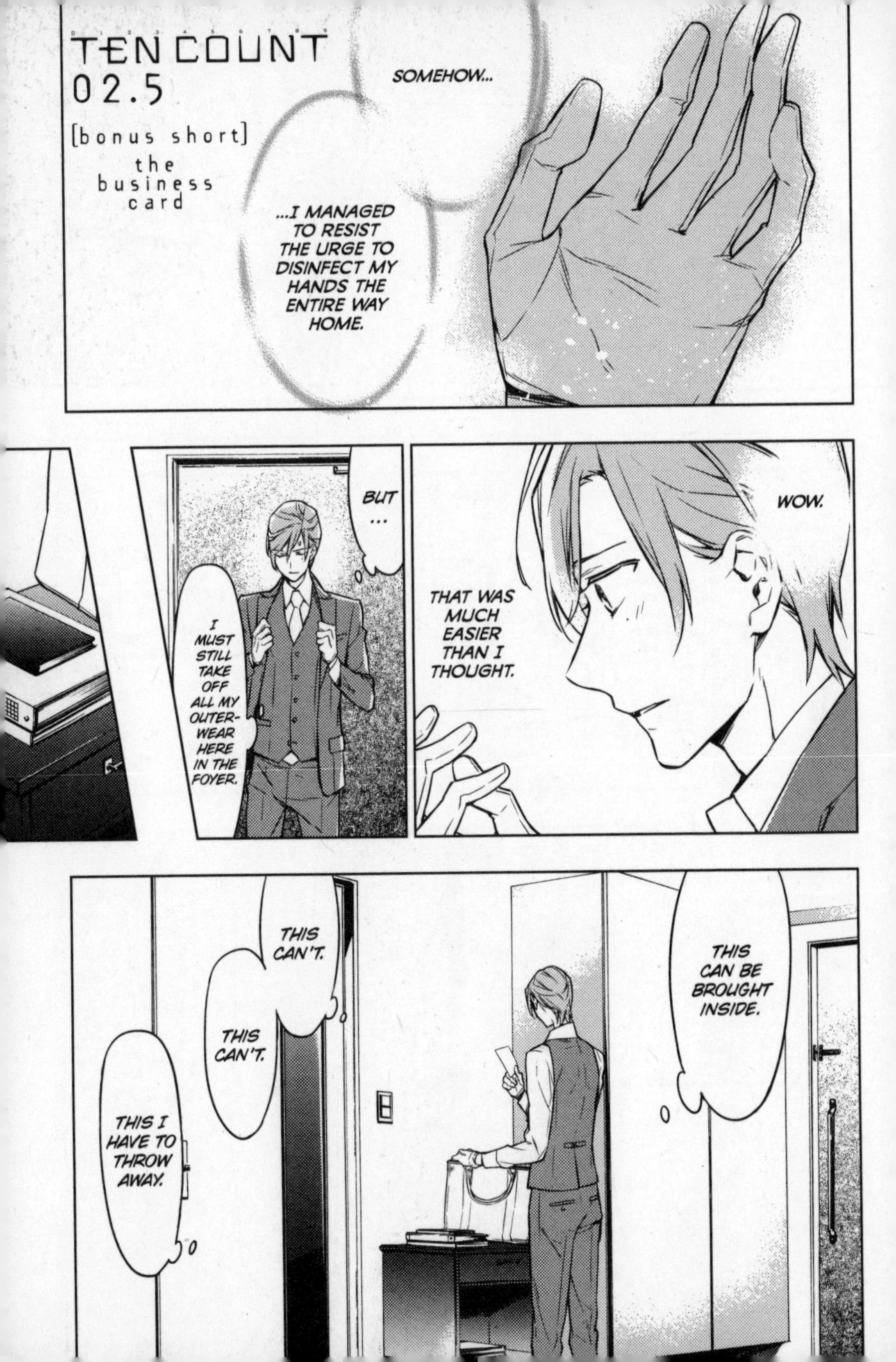
TEN COUNT
02.5
[bonus short]
the business card
SOMEHOW...
...I MANAGED TO RESIST THE URGE TO DISINFECT MY HANDS THE ENTIRE WAY HOME.
WOW.
THAT WAS MUCH EASIER THAN I THOUGHT.
BUT ...
I MUST STILL TAKE OFF ALL MY OUTER-WEAR HERE IN THE FOYER.
THIS CAN BE BROUGHT INSIDE.
THIS CAN'T.
THIS CAN'T.
THIS I HAVE TO THROW AWAY.

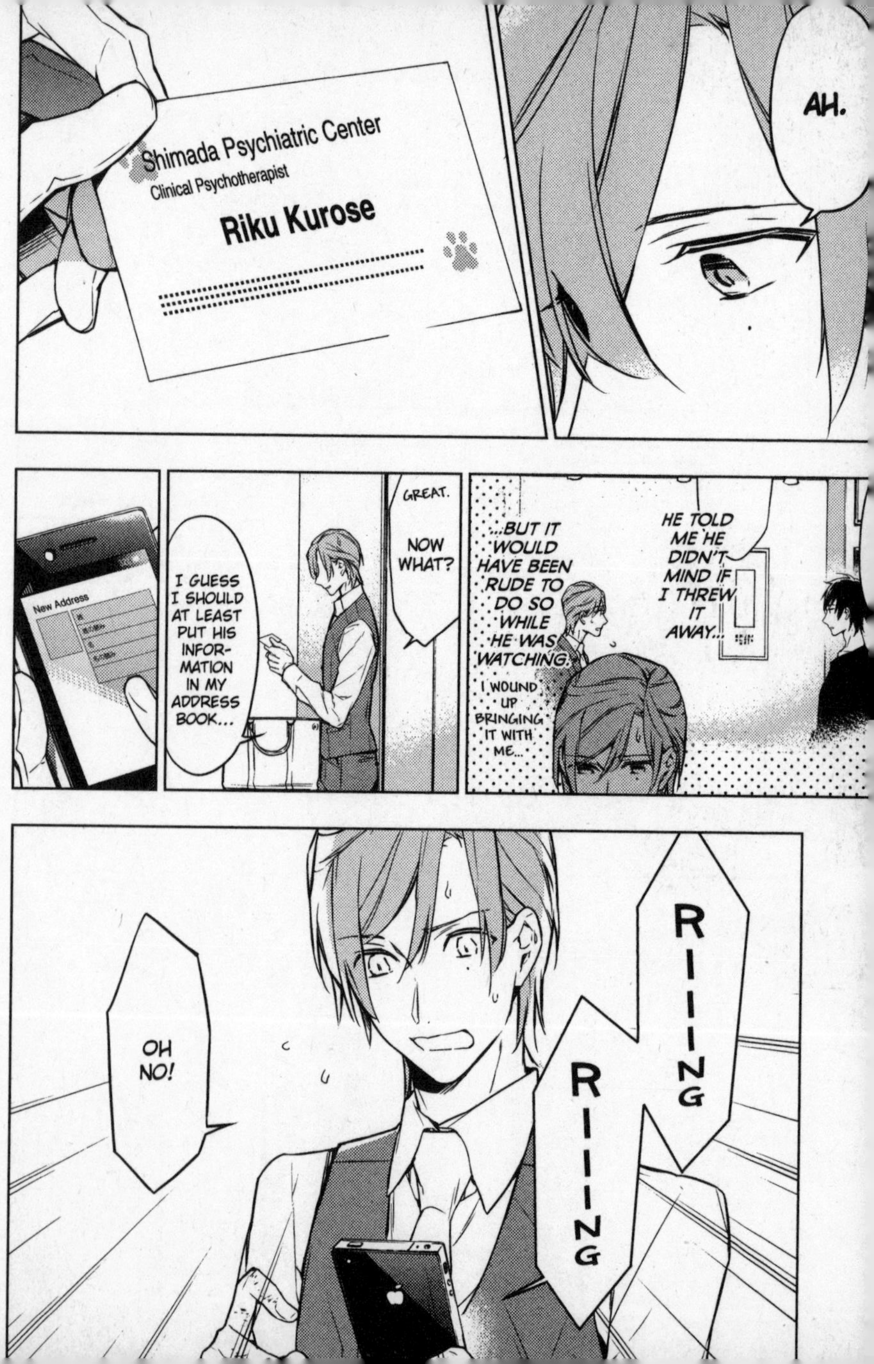
AH.
Shimada Psychiatric Center
Clinical Psychotherapist
Riku Kurose
HE TOLD ME HE DIDN'T MIND IF I THREW IT AWAY...
...BUT IT WOULD HAVE BEEN RUDE TO DO SO WHILE HE WAS WATCHING.
I WOUND UP BRINGING IT WITH ME...
GREAT.
NOW WHAT?
I GUESS I SHOULD AT LEAST PUT HIS INFORMATION IN MY ADDRESS BOOK...
New Address
RIIING
RIIING
OH NO!

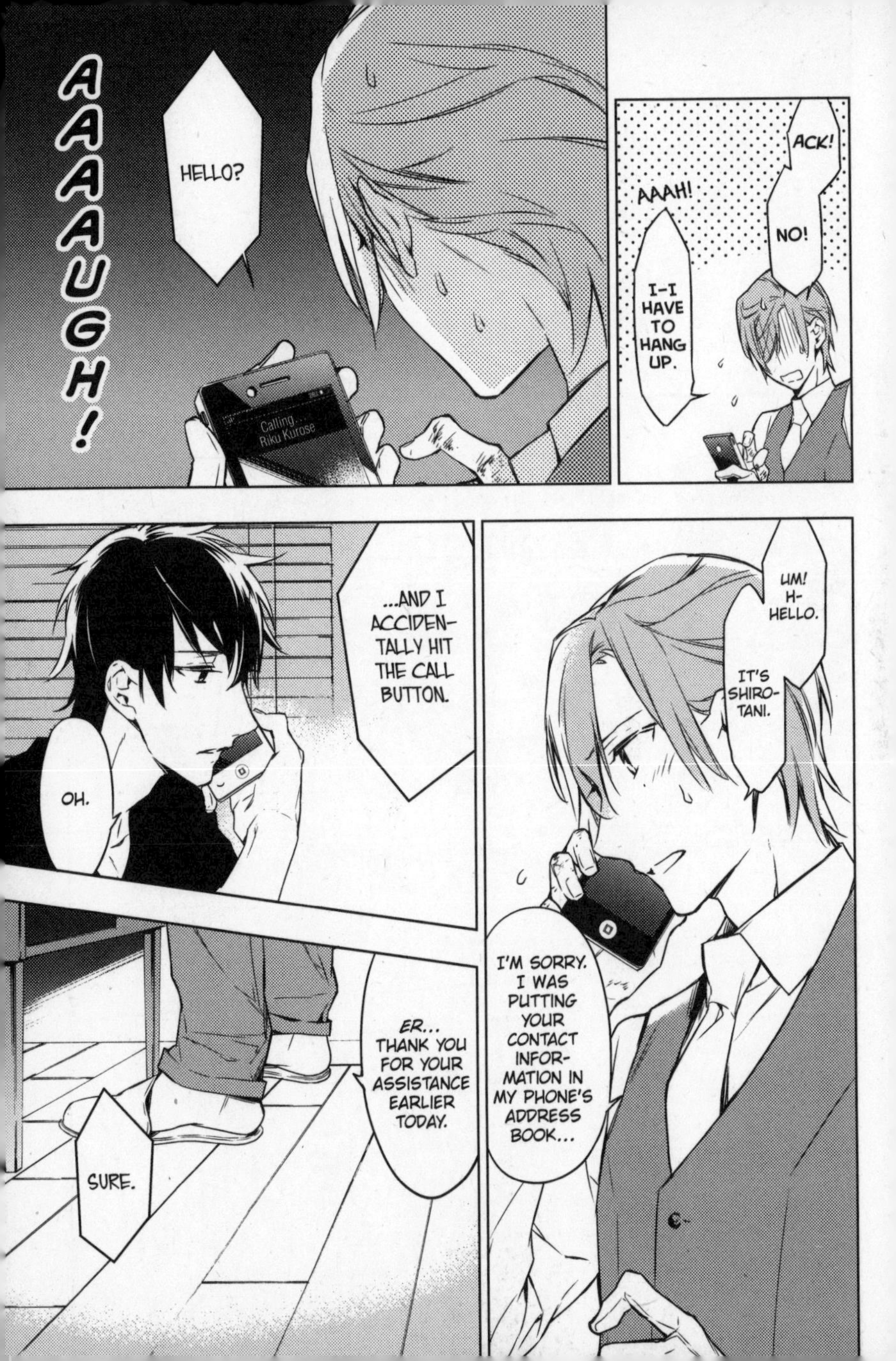
ACK! NO!
AAAH! I-I HAVE TO HANG UP.
HELLO?
AAAAAUGH!
Calling... Riku Kurose
UM! H-HELLO.
IT'S SHIRO-TANI.
I'M SORRY. I WAS PUTTING YOUR CONTACT INFOR-MATION IN MY PHONE'S ADDRESS BOOK...
...AND I ACCIDEN-TALLY HIT THE CALL BUTTON.
OH.
ER... THANK YOU FOR YOUR ASSISTANCE EARLIER TODAY.
SURE.

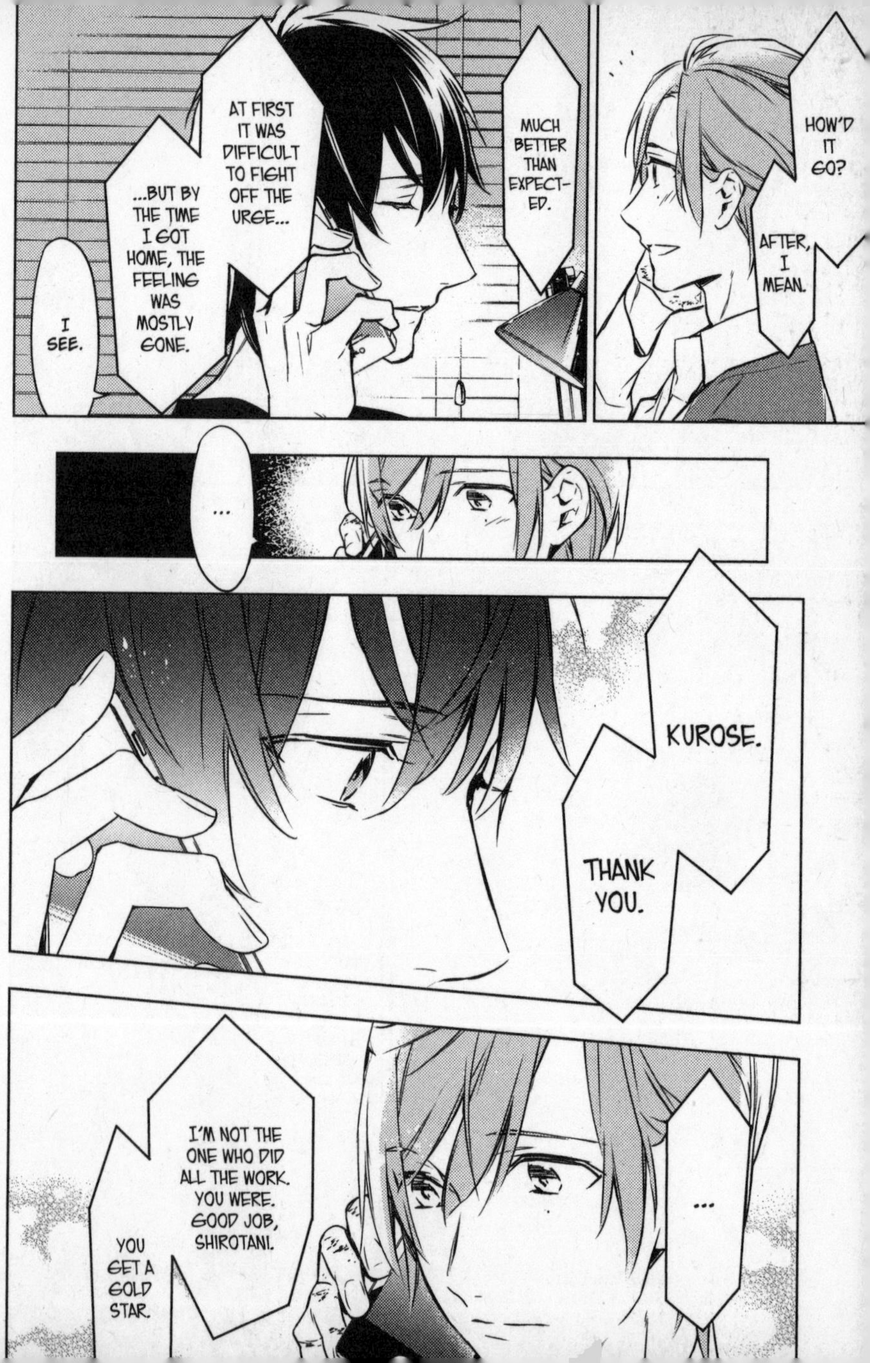
HOW'D IT GO?
AFTER, I MEAN.
MUCH BETTER THAN EXPECT-ED.
AT FIRST IT WAS DIFFICULT TO FIGHT OFF THE URGE...
...BUT BY THE TIME I GOT HOME, THE FEELING WAS MOSTLY GONE.
I SEE.
...
KUROSE.
THANK YOU.
...
I'M NOT THE ONE WHO DID ALL THE WORK. YOU WERE. GOOD JOB, SHIROTANI.
YOU GET A GOLD STAR.

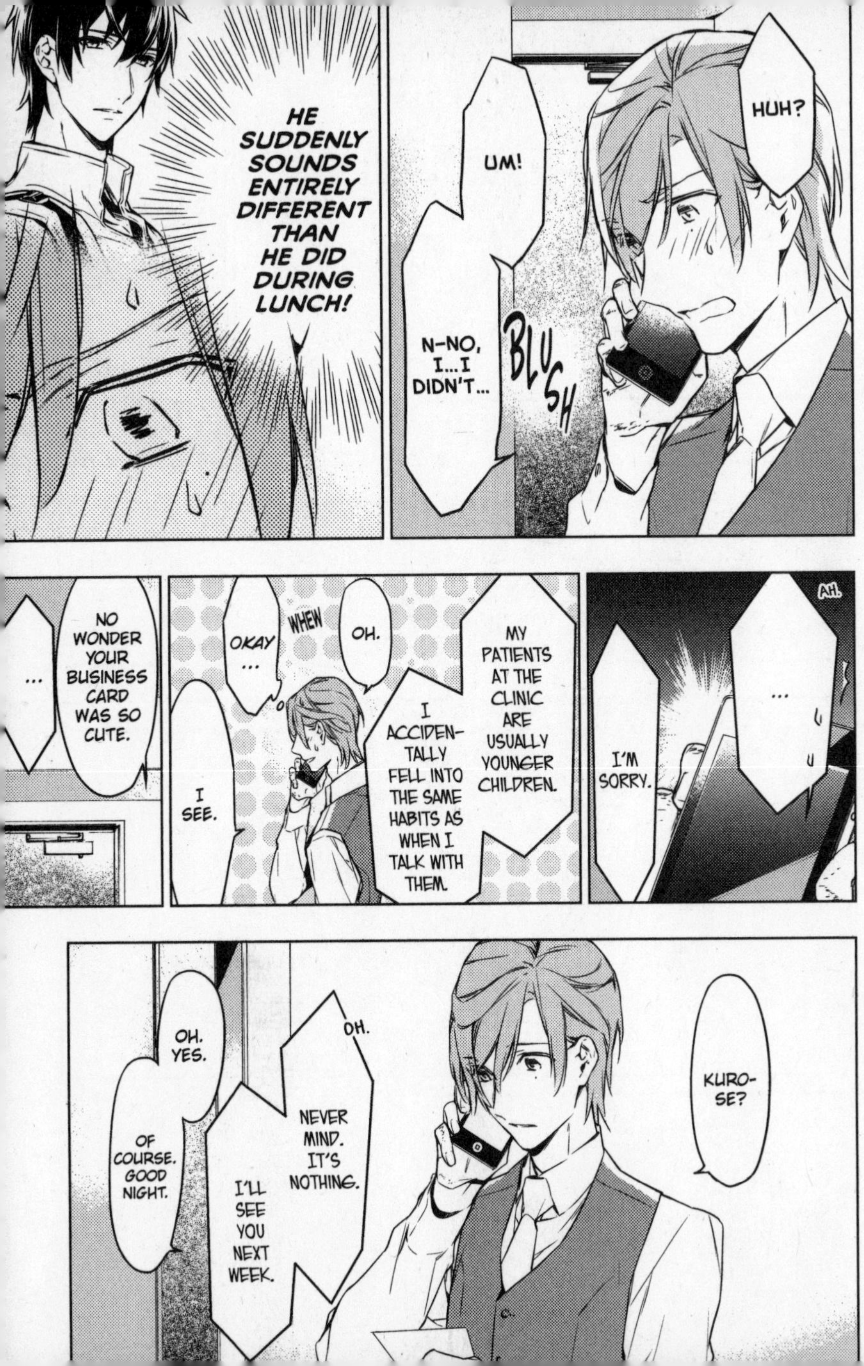
HUH?
UM!
BLUSH
N-NO, I...I DIDN'T...
HE SUDDENLY SOUNDS ENTIRELY DIFFERENT THAN HE DID DURING LUNCH!
AH.
...
I'M SORRY.
MY PATIENTS AT THE CLINIC ARE USUALLY YOUNGER CHILDREN.
I ACCIDEN-TALLY FELL INTO THE SAME HABITS AS WHEN I TALK WITH THEM.
OH.
WHEW
OKAY...
I SEE.
NO WONDER YOUR BUSINESS CARD WAS SO CUTE.
...
KURO-SE?
OH.
NEVER MIND. IT'S NOTHING.
I'LL SEE YOU NEXT WEEK.
OH. YES.
OF COURSE. GOOD NIGHT.

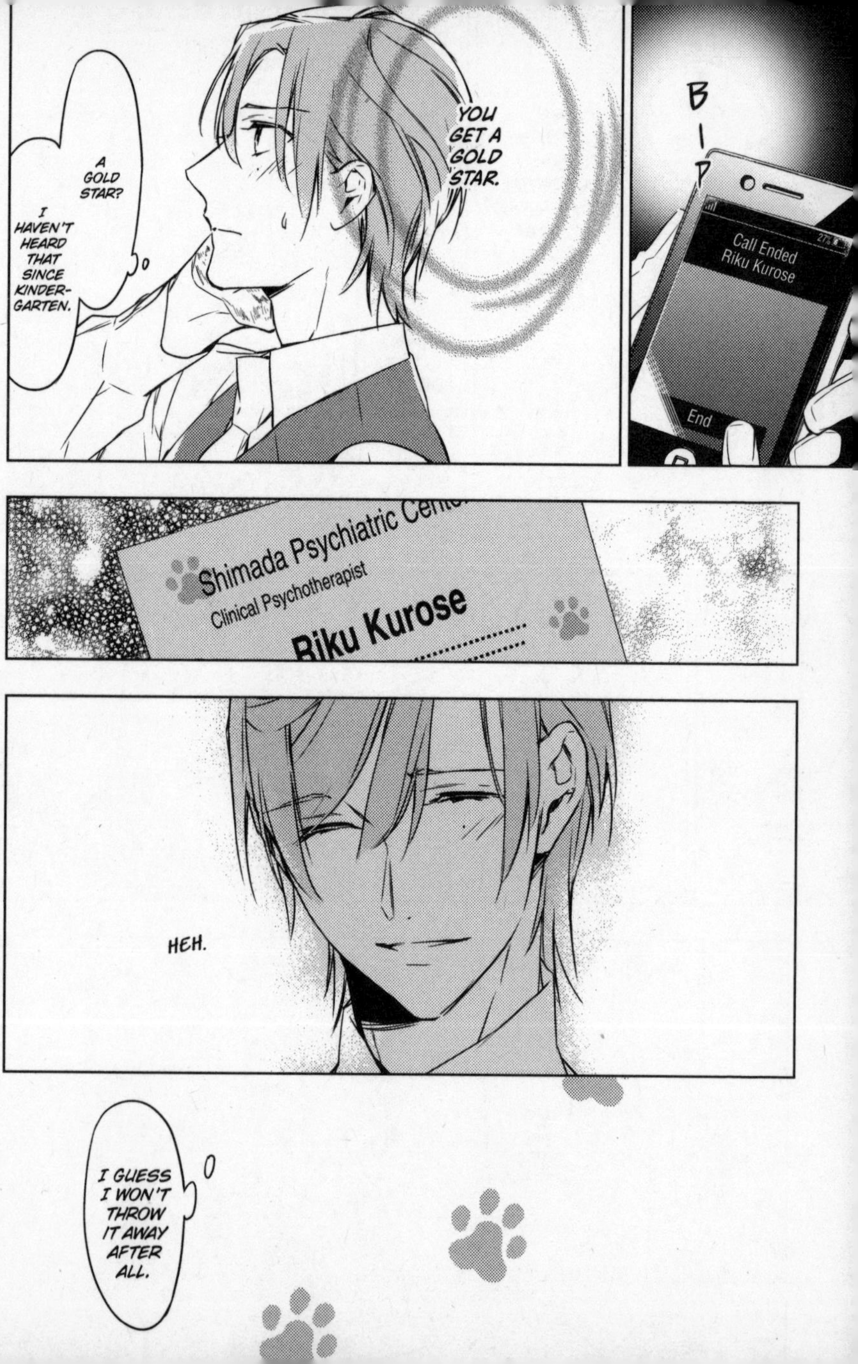

BIP
27%
Call Ended
Riku Kurose
End
YOU GET A GOLD STAR.
A GOLD STAR? I HAVEN'T HEARD THAT SINCE KINDERGARTEN.
Shimada Psychiatric Cent
Clinical Psychotherapist
Riku Kurose
HEH.
I GUESS I WON'T THROW IT AWAY AFTER ALL.

ten count by rihito takarai

ten count by rihito takarai

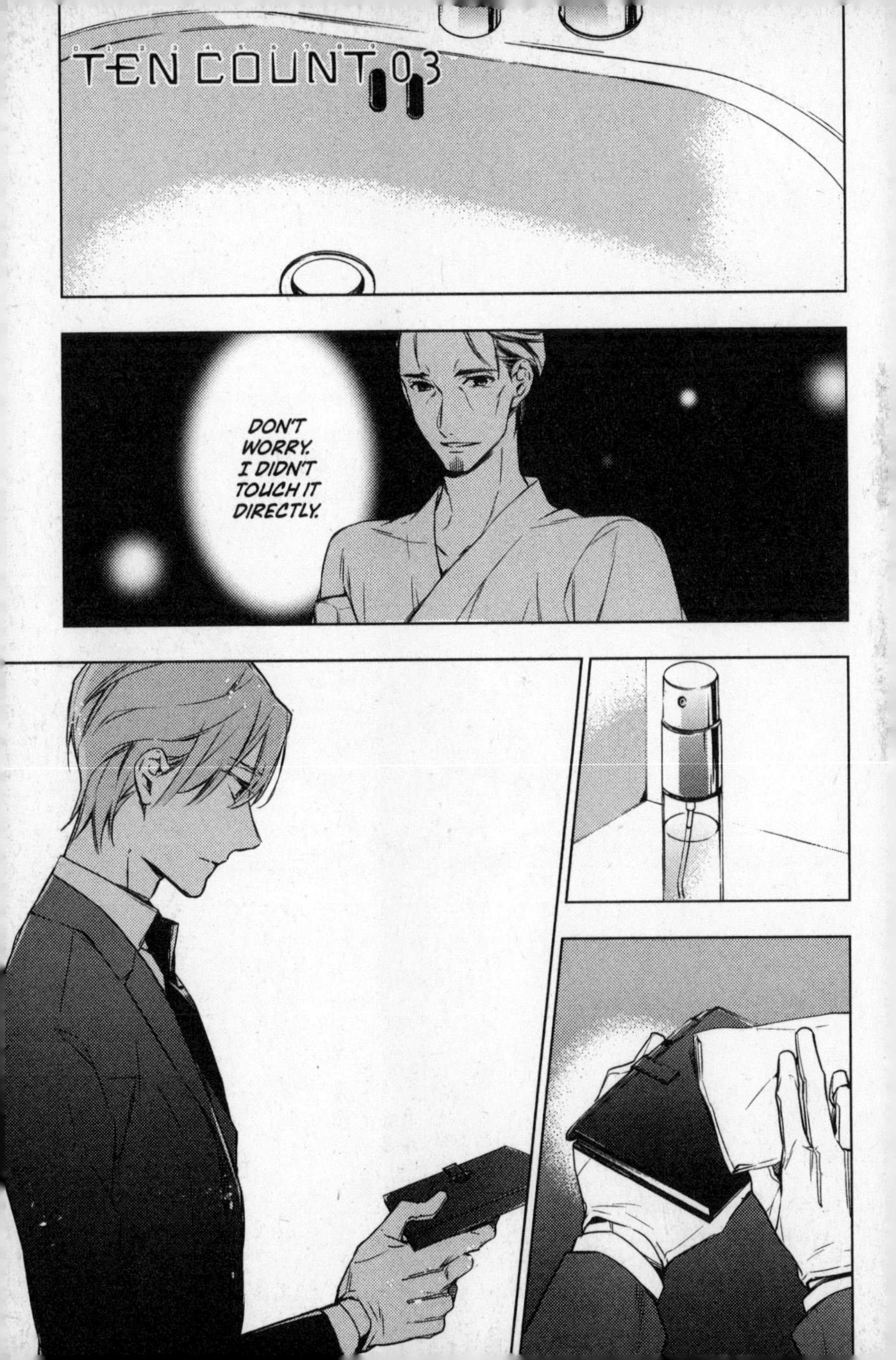
TEN COUNT 03
DON'T WORRY. I DIDN'T TOUCH IT DIRECTLY.

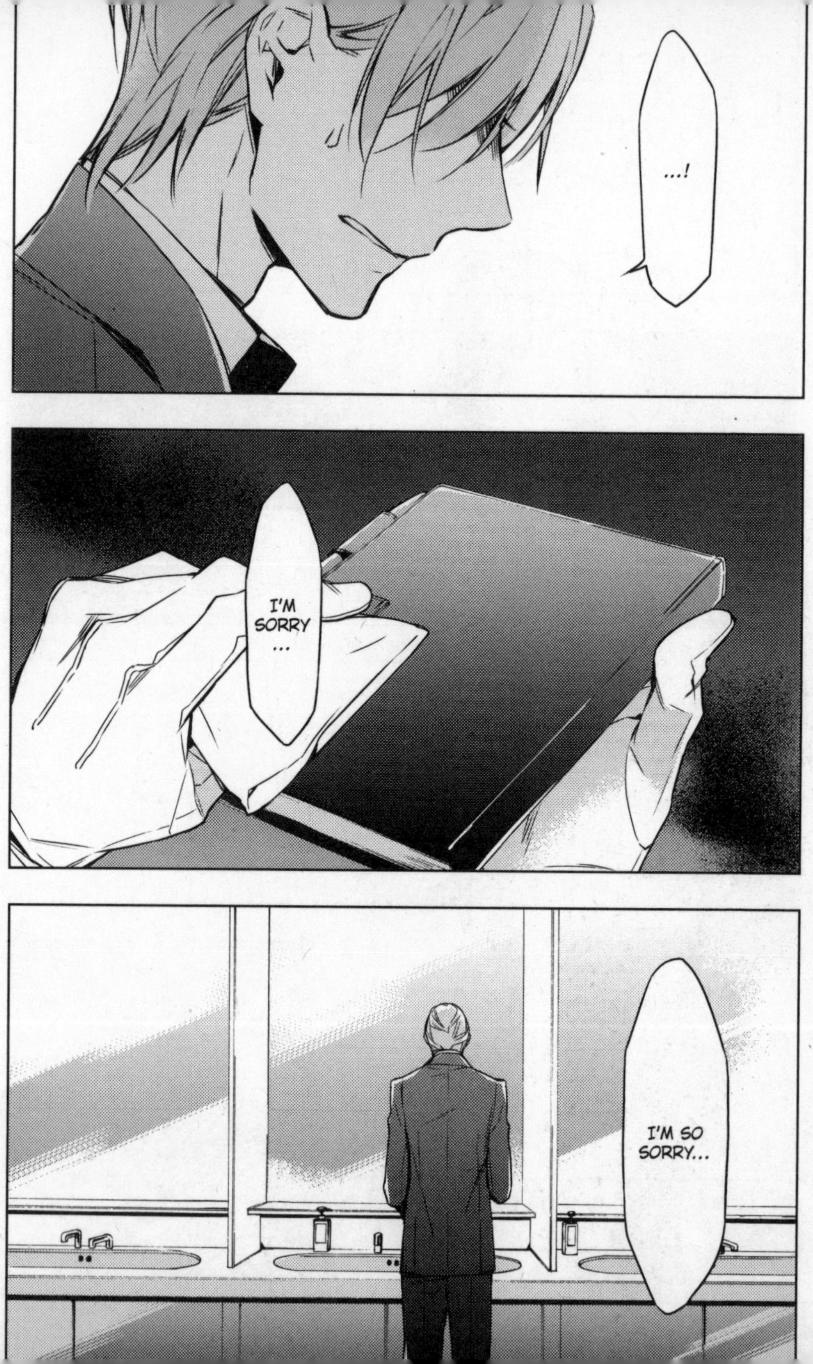
...!
I'M SORRY ...
I'M SO SORRY...

TEN COUNT 03

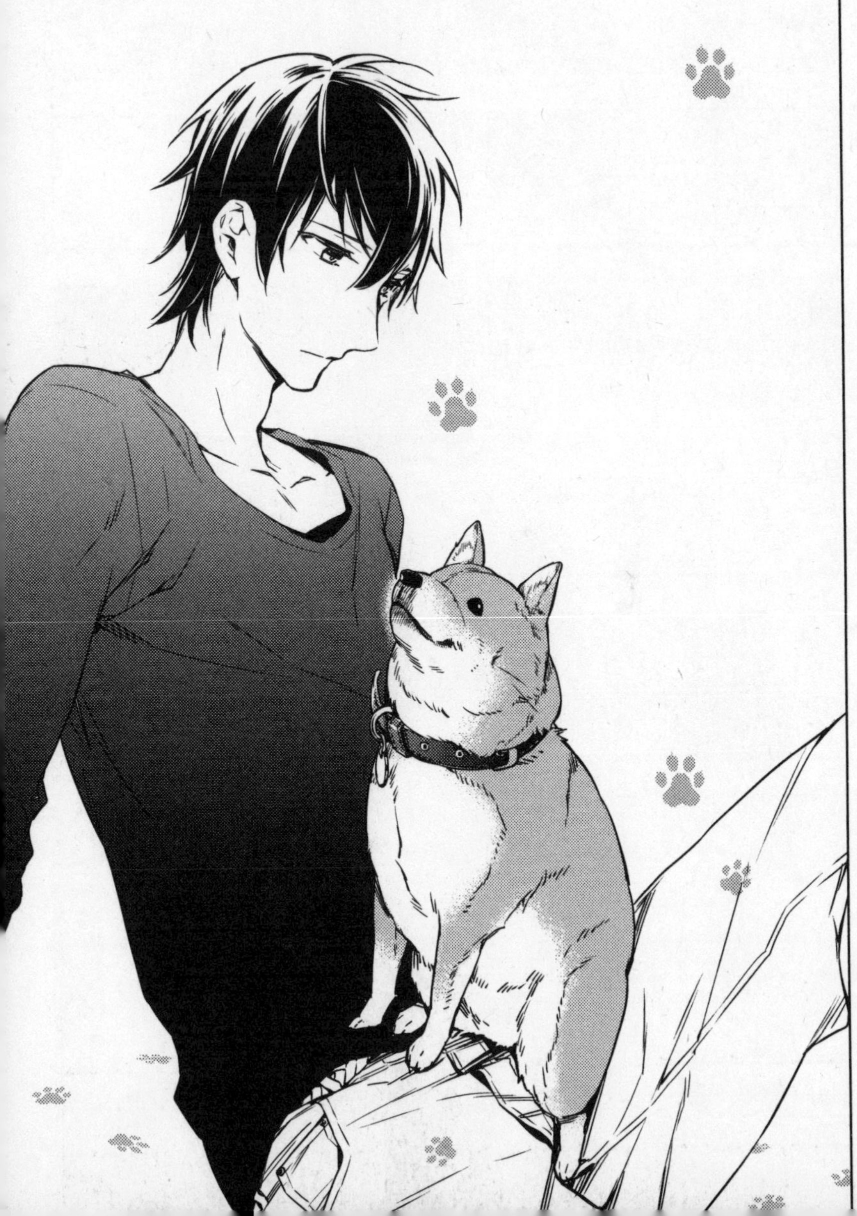

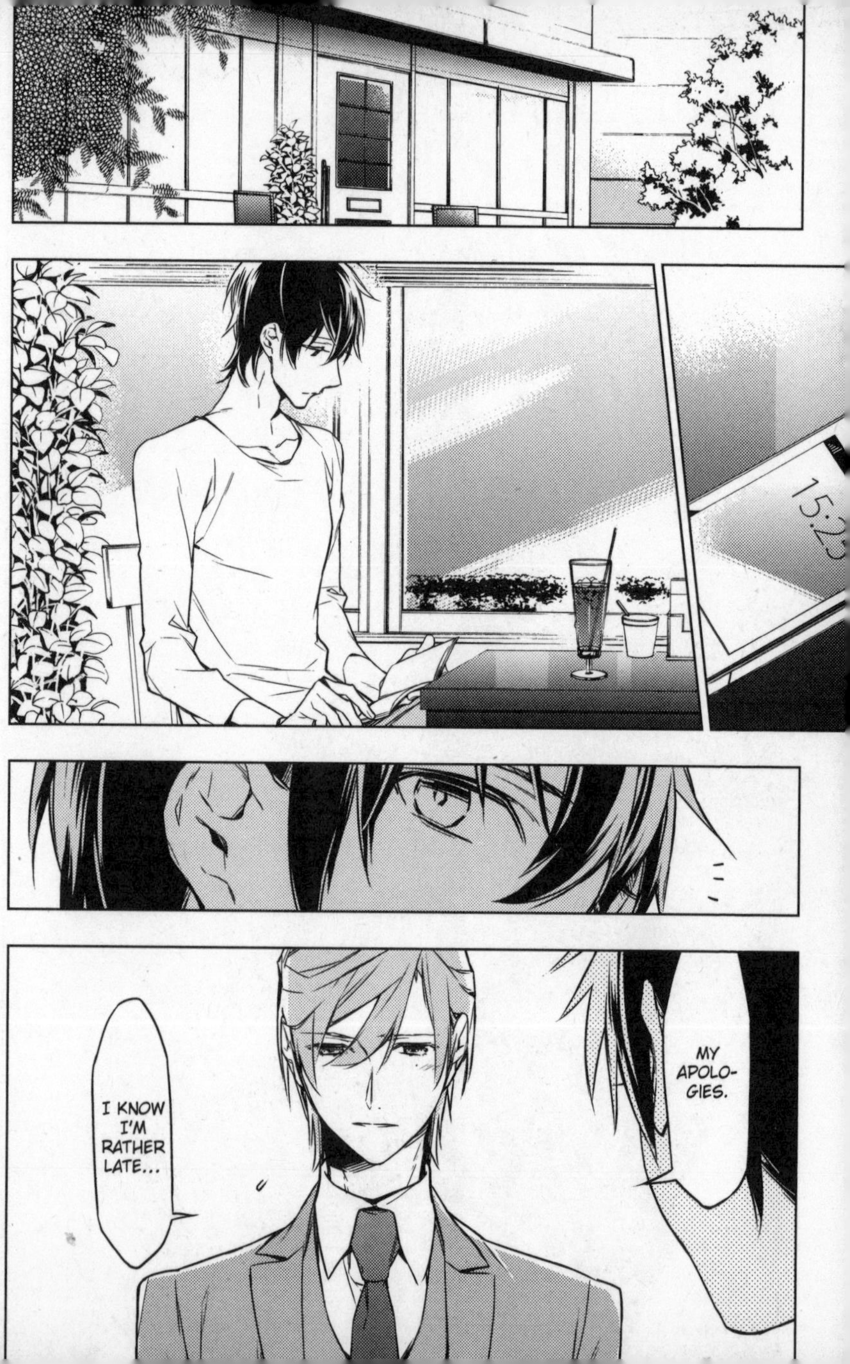
MY APOLO-
GIES.
I KNOW I'M RATHER LATE...

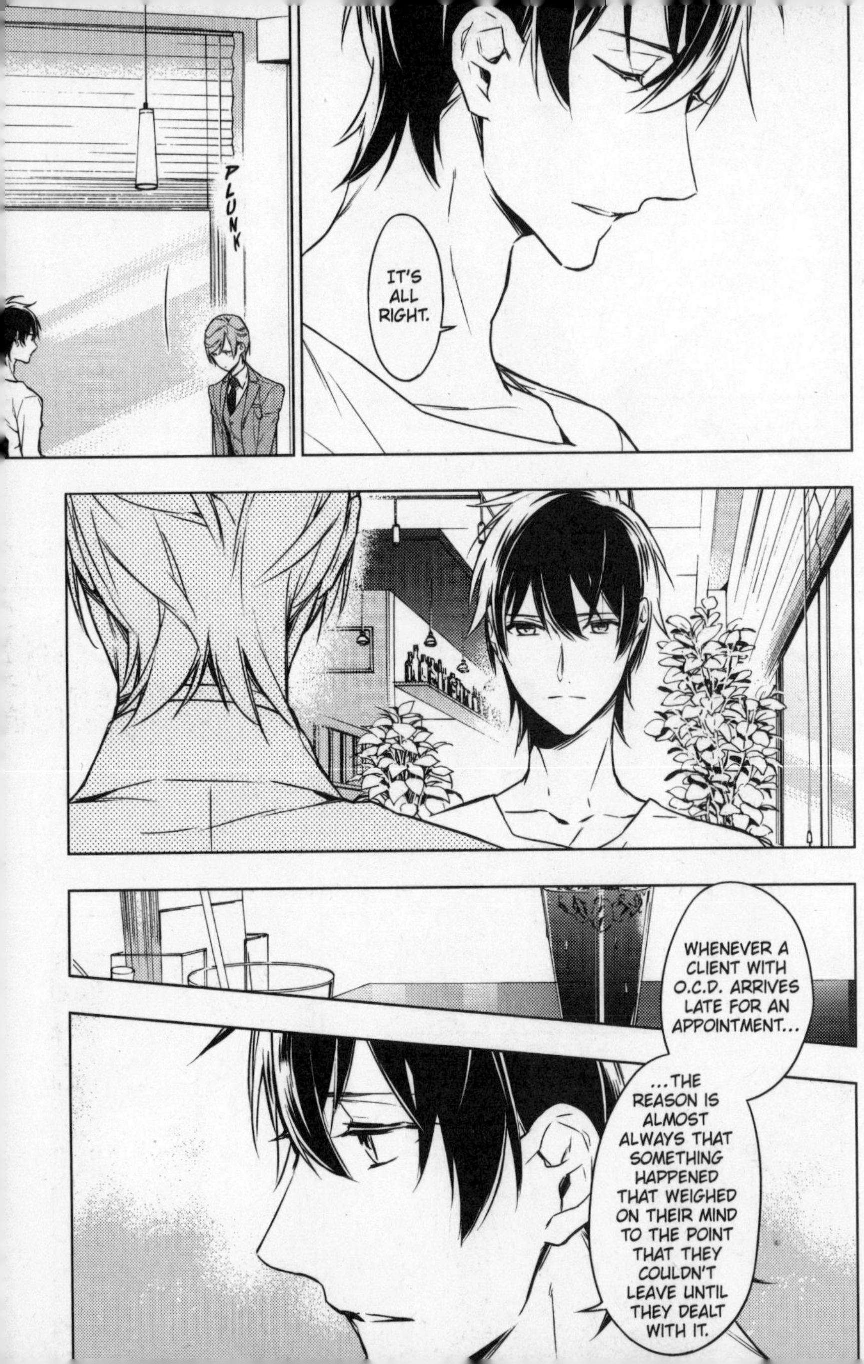
IT'S ALL RIGHT.
PLUNK
WHENEVER A CLIENT WITH O.C.D. ARRIVES LATE FOR AN APPOINTMENT...
...THE REASON IS ALMOST ALWAYS THAT SOMETHING HAPPENED THAT WEIGHED ON THEIR MIND TO THE POINT THAT THEY COULDN'T LEAVE UNTIL THEY DEALT WITH IT.

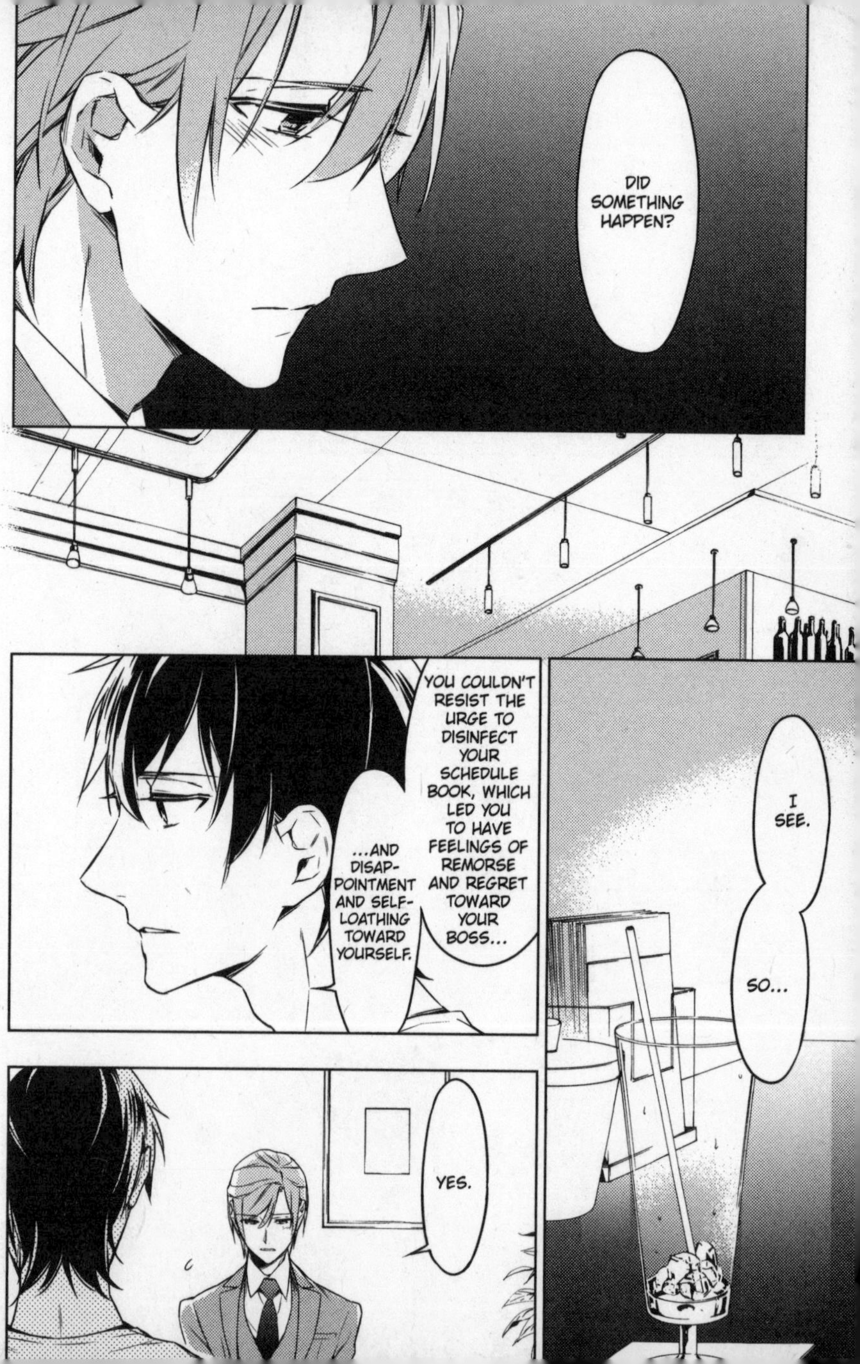
DID SOMETHING HAPPEN?
I SEE.
SO...
YOU COULDN'T RESIST THE URGE TO DISINFECT YOUR SCHEDULE BOOK, WHICH LED YOU TO HAVE FEELINGS OF REMORSE AND REGRET TOWARD YOUR BOSS...
...AND DISAP-POINTMENT AND SELF-LOATHING TOWARD YOURSELF.
YES.

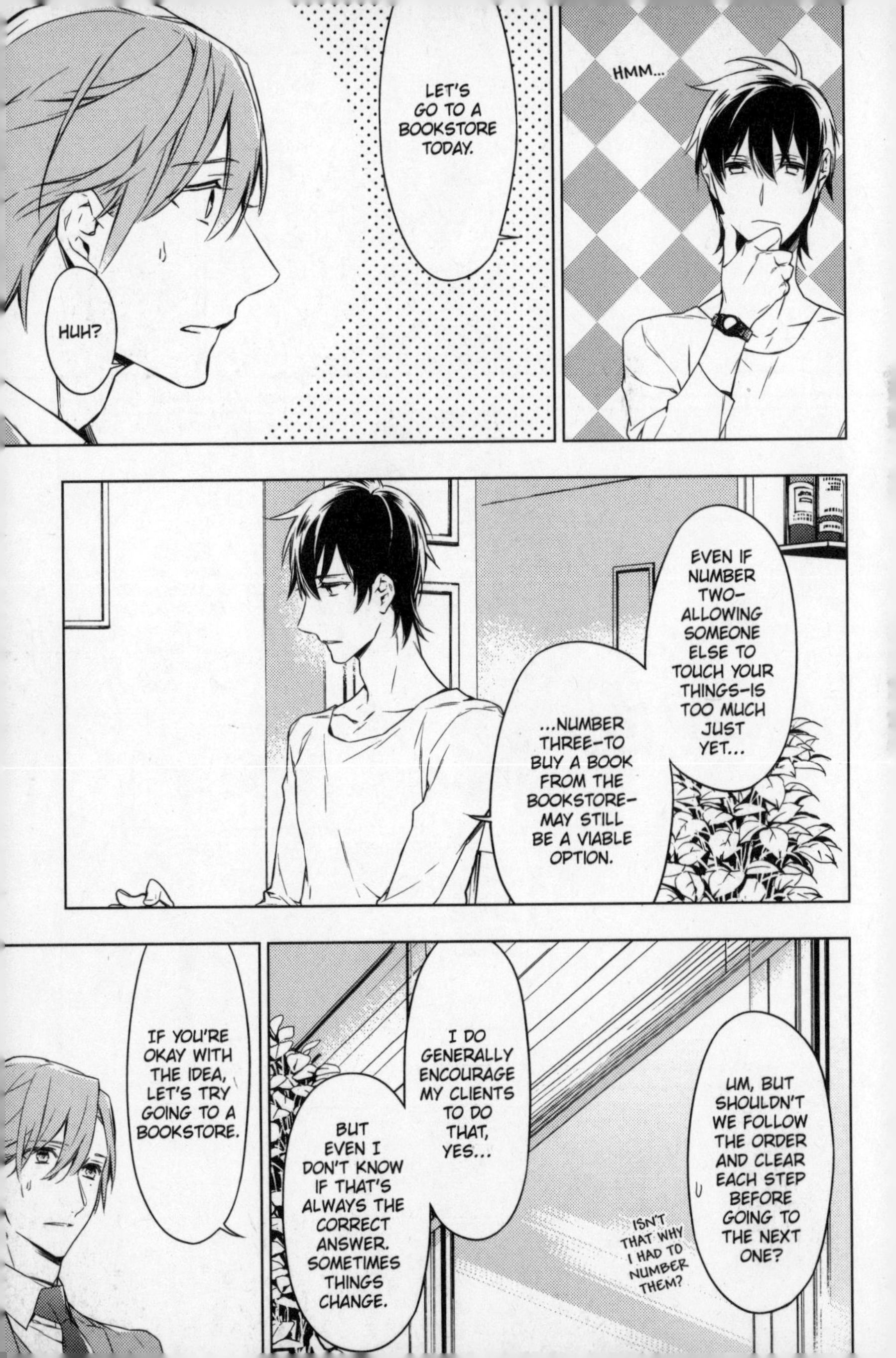
HMM...
LET'S GO TO A BOOKSTORE TODAY.
HUH?
EVEN IF NUMBER TWO—ALLOWING SOMEONE ELSE TO TOUCH YOUR THINGS—IS TOO MUCH JUST YET...
...NUMBER THREE—TO BUY A BOOK FROM THE BOOKSTORE—MAY STILL BE A VIABLE OPTION.
UM, BUT SHOULDN'T WE FOLLOW THE ORDER AND CLEAR EACH STEP BEFORE GOING TO THE NEXT ONE?
ISN'T THAT WHY I HAD TO NUMBER THEM?
I DO GENERALLY ENCOURAGE MY CLIENTS TO DO THAT, YES...
BUT EVEN I DON'T KNOW IF THAT'S ALWAYS THE CORRECT ANSWER. SOMETIMES THINGS CHANGE.
IF YOU'RE OKAY WITH THE IDEA, LET'S TRY GOING TO A BOOKSTORE.

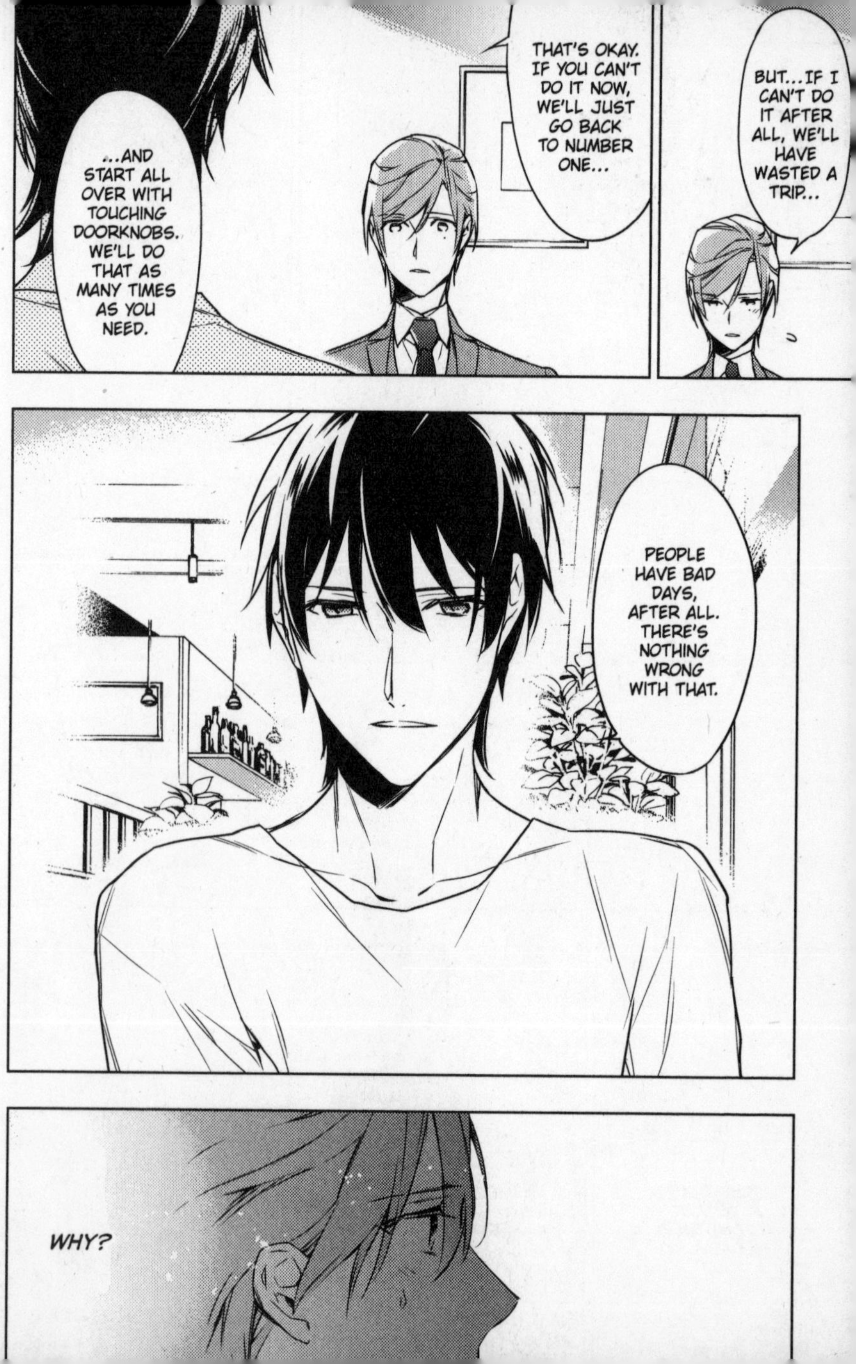
BUT...IF I CAN'T DO IT AFTER ALL, WE'LL HAVE WASTED A TRIP...
THAT'S OKAY. IF YOU CAN'T DO IT NOW, WE'LL JUST GO BACK TO NUMBER ONE...
...AND START ALL OVER WITH TOUCHING DOORKNOBS. WE'LL DO THAT AS MANY TIMES AS YOU NEED.
PEOPLE HAVE BAD DAYS, AFTER ALL. THERE'S NOTHING WRONG WITH THAT.
WHY?

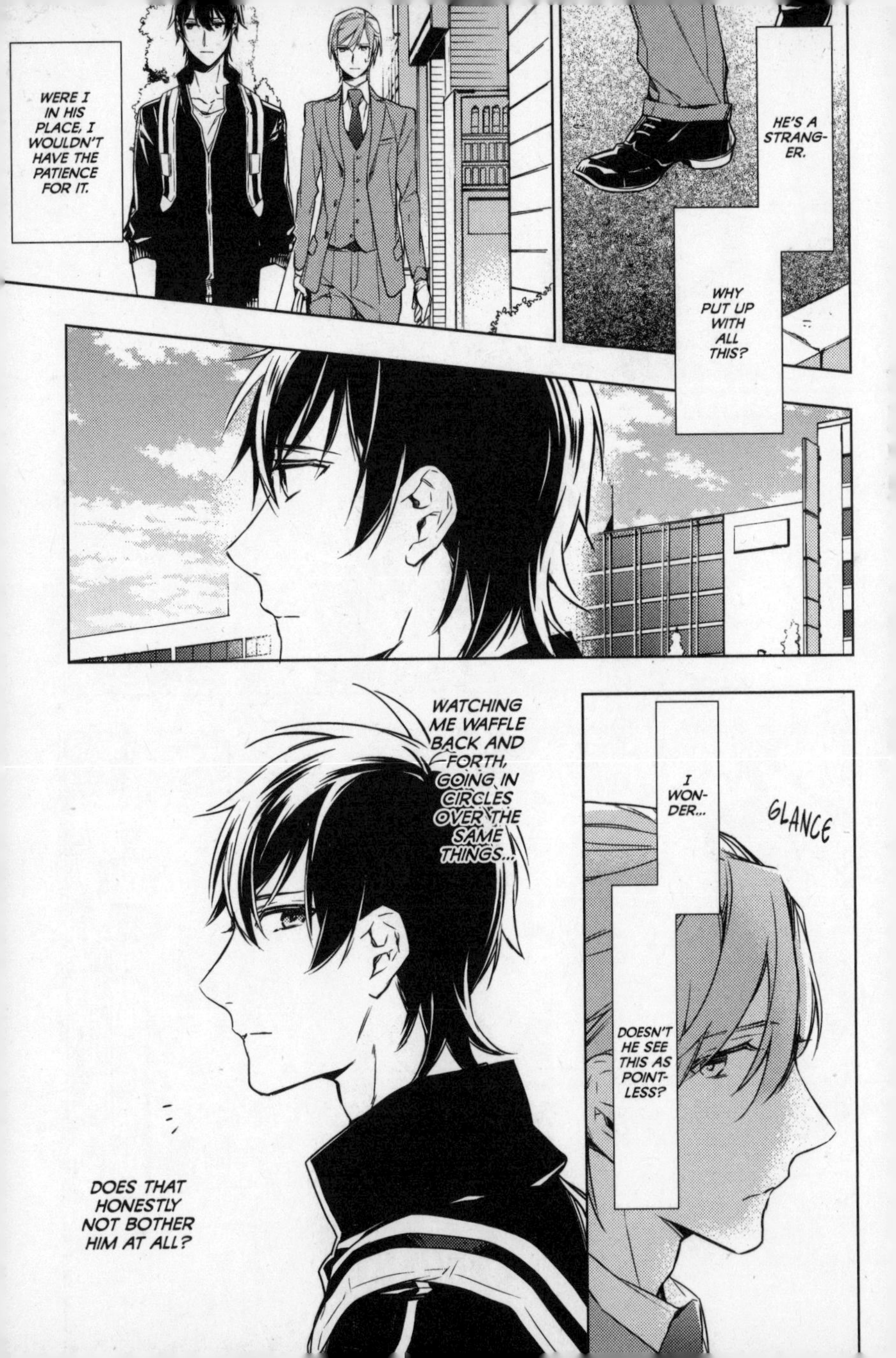
HE'S A STRANGER.
WHY PUT UP WITH ALL THIS?
WERE I IN HIS PLACE, I WOULDN'T HAVE THE PATIENCE FOR IT.
I WONDER...
GLANCE
DOESN'T HE SEE THIS AS POINTLESS?
WATCHING ME WAFFLE BACK AND FORTH, GOING IN CIRCLES OVER THE SAME THINGS...
DOES THAT HONESTLY NOT BOTHER HIM AT ALL?

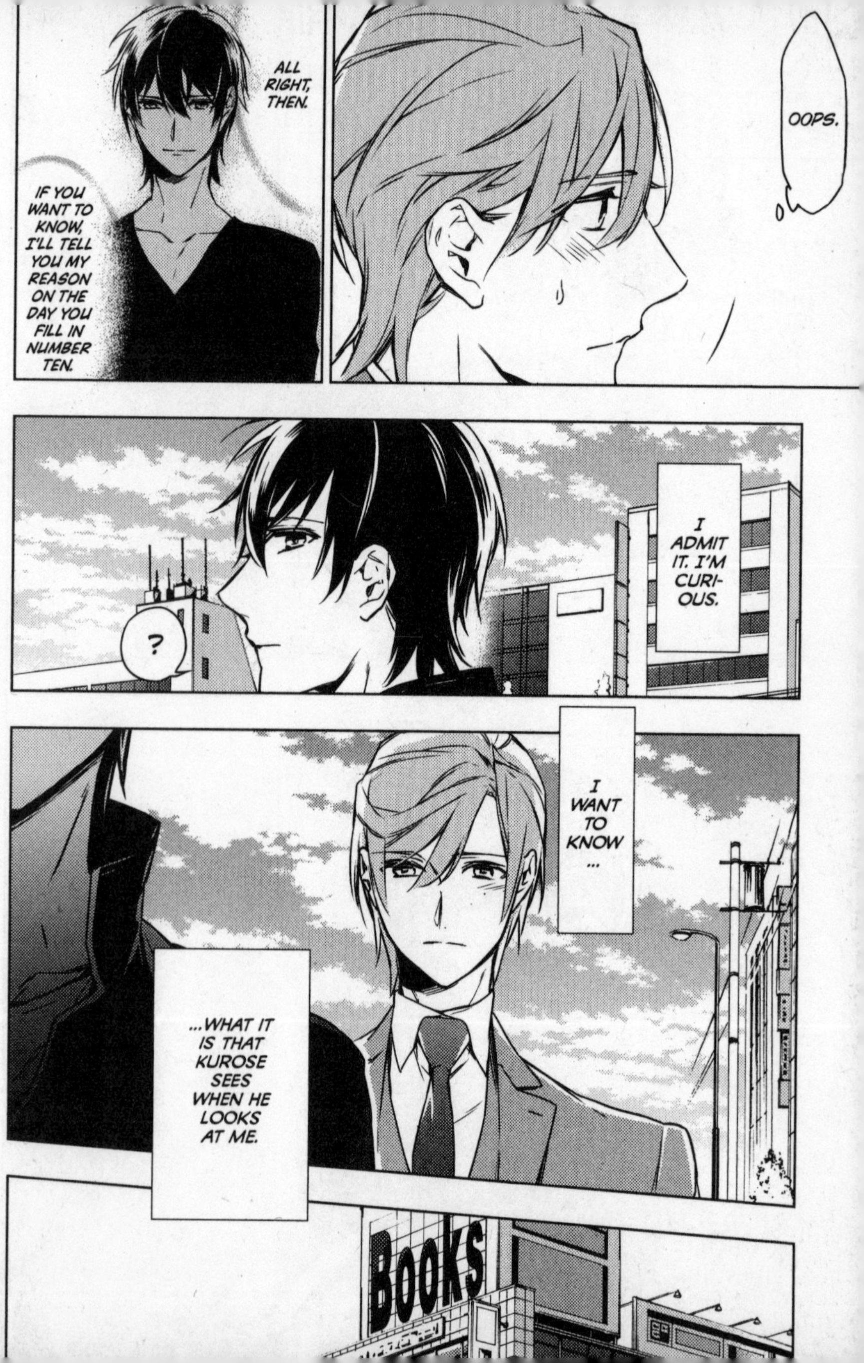
OOPS.
ALL RIGHT, THEN.
IF YOU WANT TO KNOW, I'LL TELL YOU MY REASON ON THE DAY YOU FILL IN NUMBER TEN.
I ADMIT IT. I'M CURIOUS.
?
I WANT TO KNOW...
...WHAT IT IS THAT KUROSE SEES WHEN HE LOOKS AT ME.
BOOKS

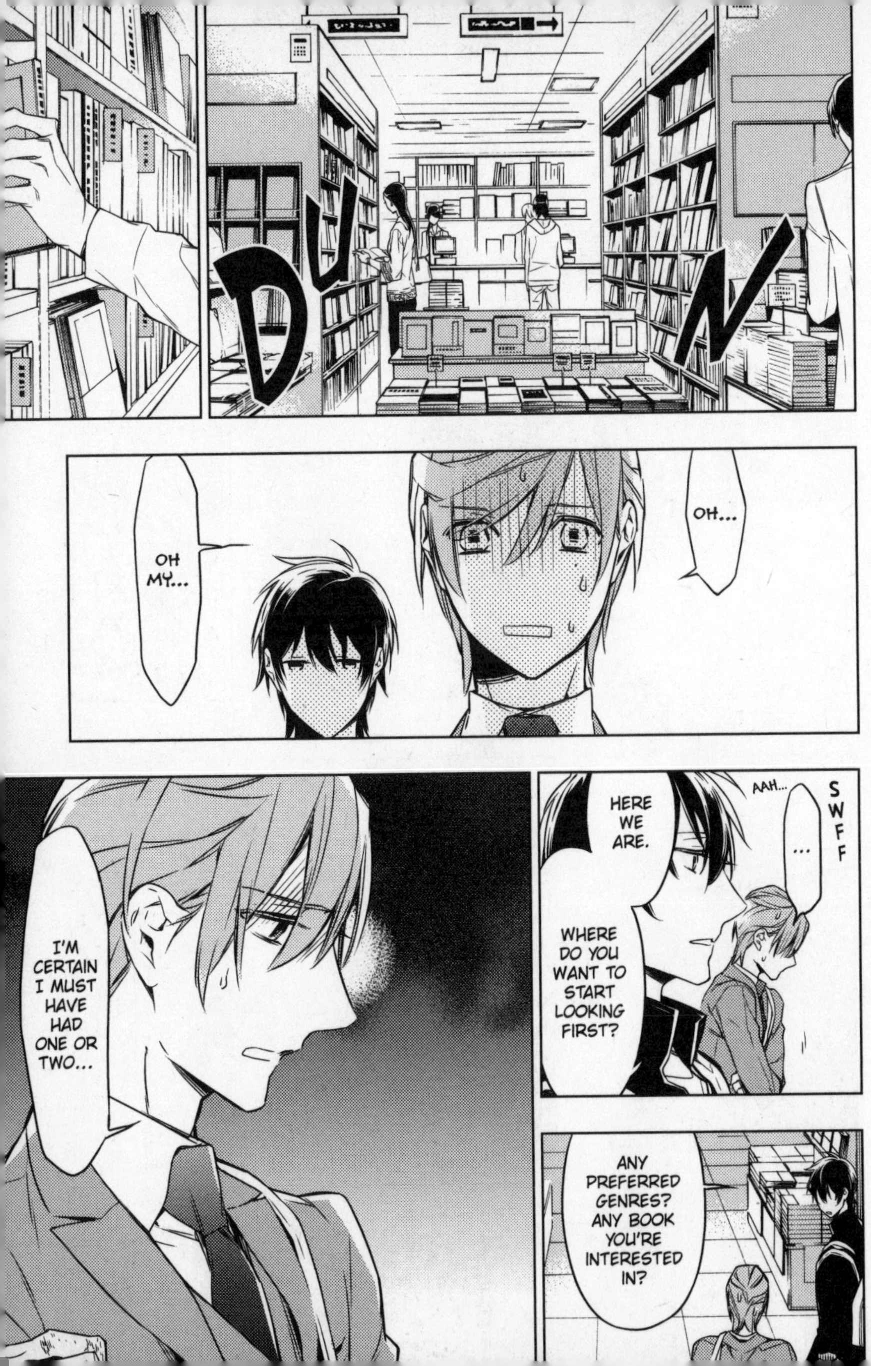
DUN
OH...
OH MY...
SWFF
AAH...
...
HERE WE ARE.
WHERE DO YOU WANT TO START LOOKING FIRST?
ANY PREFERRED GENRES? ANY BOOK YOU'RE INTERESTED IN?
I'M CERTAIN I MUST HAVE HAD ONE OR TWO...

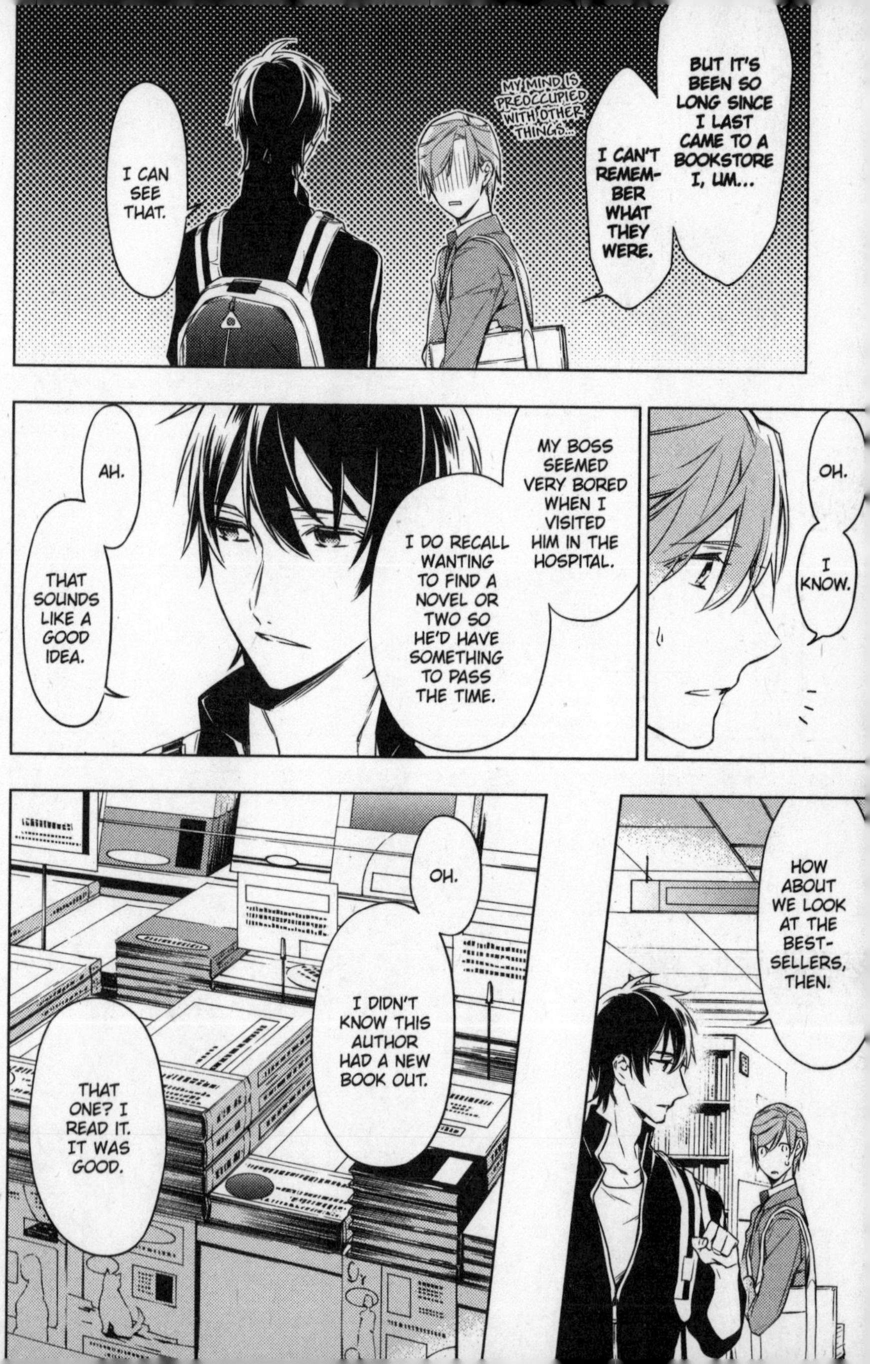
BUT IT'S BEEN SO LONG SINCE I LAST CAME TO A BOOKSTORE I, UM...
I CAN'T REMEMBER WHAT THEY WERE.
MY MIND IS PREOCCUPIED WITH OTHER THINGS...
I CAN SEE THAT.
OH.
I KNOW.
MY BOSS SEEMED VERY BORED WHEN I VISITED HIM IN THE HOSPITAL.
I DO RECALL WANTING TO FIND A NOVEL OR TWO SO HE'D HAVE SOMETHING TO PASS THE TIME.
AH.
THAT SOUNDS LIKE A GOOD IDEA.
HOW ABOUT WE LOOK AT THE BEST-SELLERS, THEN.
OH.
I DIDN'T KNOW THIS AUTHOR HAD A NEW BOOK OUT.
THAT ONE? I READ IT. IT WAS GOOD.

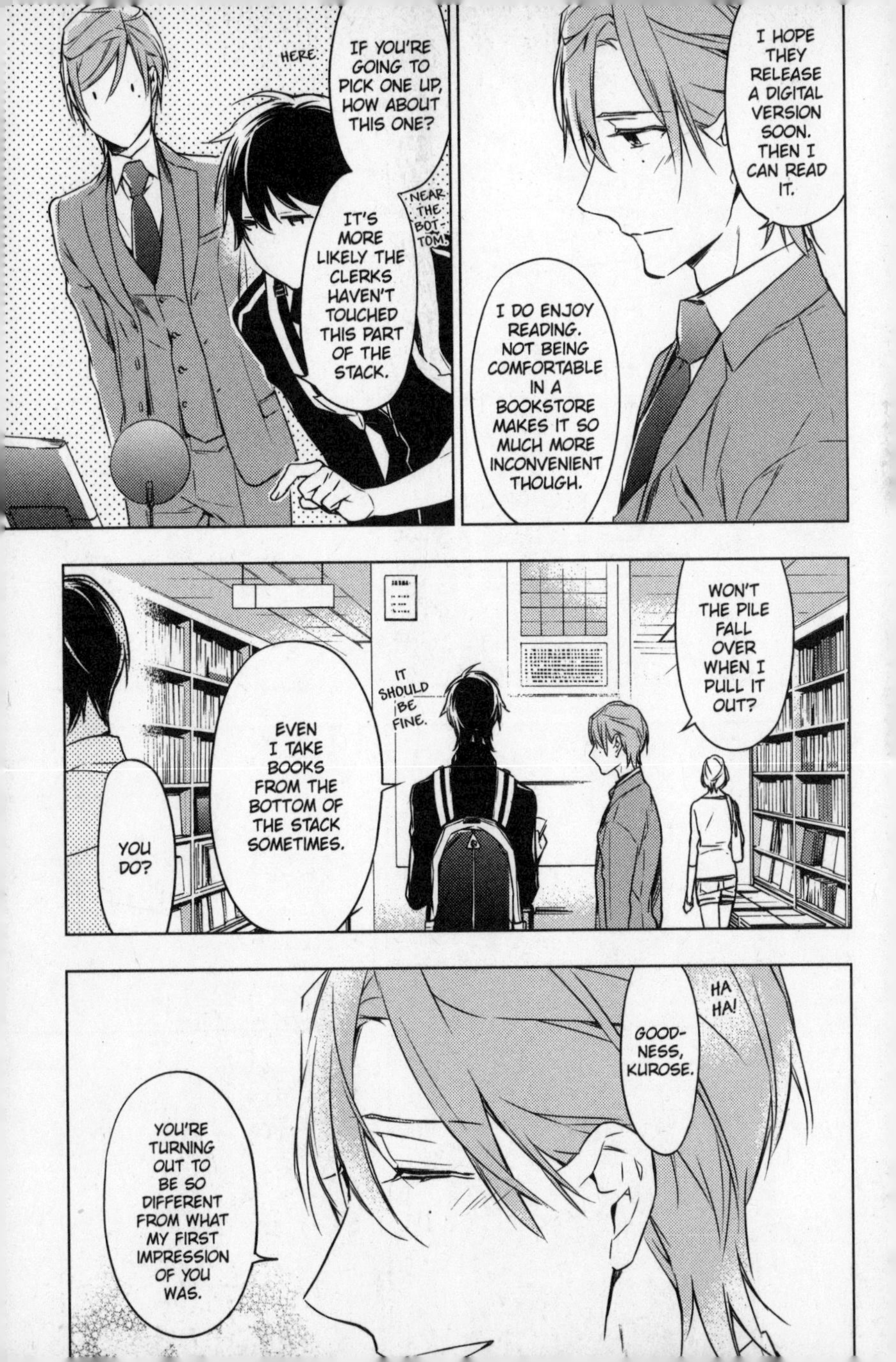
I HOPE THEY RELEASE A DIGITAL VERSION SOON. THEN I CAN READ IT.
I DO ENJOY READING. NOT BEING COMFORTABLE IN A BOOKSTORE MAKES IT SO MUCH MORE INCONVENIENT THOUGH.
IF YOU'RE GOING TO PICK ONE UP, HOW ABOUT THIS ONE?
HERE.
NEAR THE BOT-TOM.
IT'S MORE LIKELY THE CLERKS HAVEN'T TOUCHED THIS PART OF THE STACK.
WON'T THE PILE FALL OVER WHEN I PULL IT OUT?
IT SHOULD BE FINE.
EVEN I TAKE BOOKS FROM THE BOTTOM OF THE STACK SOMETIMES.
YOU DO?
HA HA!
GOOD-NESS, KUROSE.
YOU'RE TURNING OUT TO BE SO DIFFERENT FROM WHAT MY FIRST IMPRESSION OF YOU WAS.

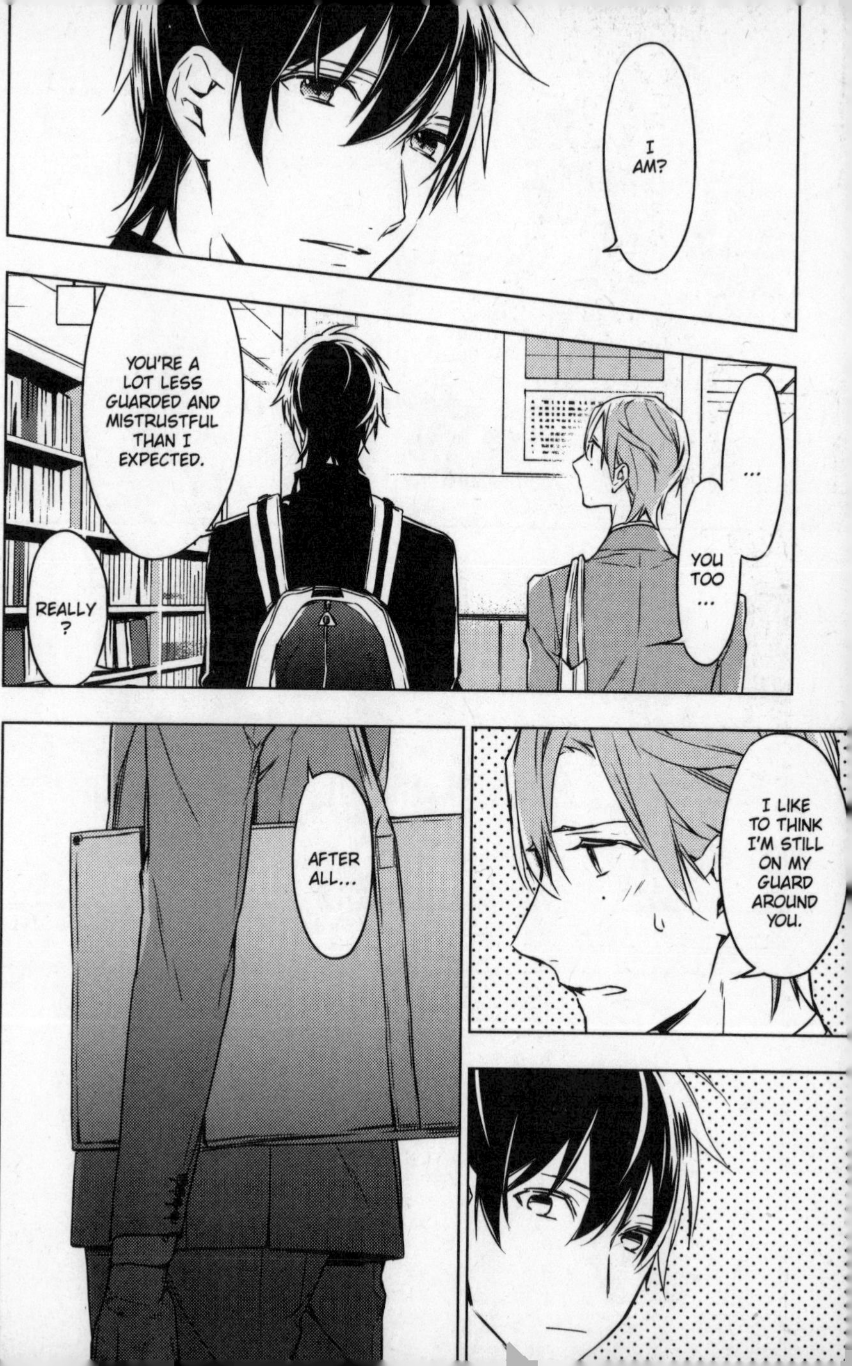

I AM?
...
YOU TOO ...
YOU'RE A LOT LESS GUARDED AND MISTRUSTFUL THAN I EXPECTED.
REALLY ?
I LIKE TO THINK I'M STILL ON MY GUARD AROUND YOU.
AFTER ALL...

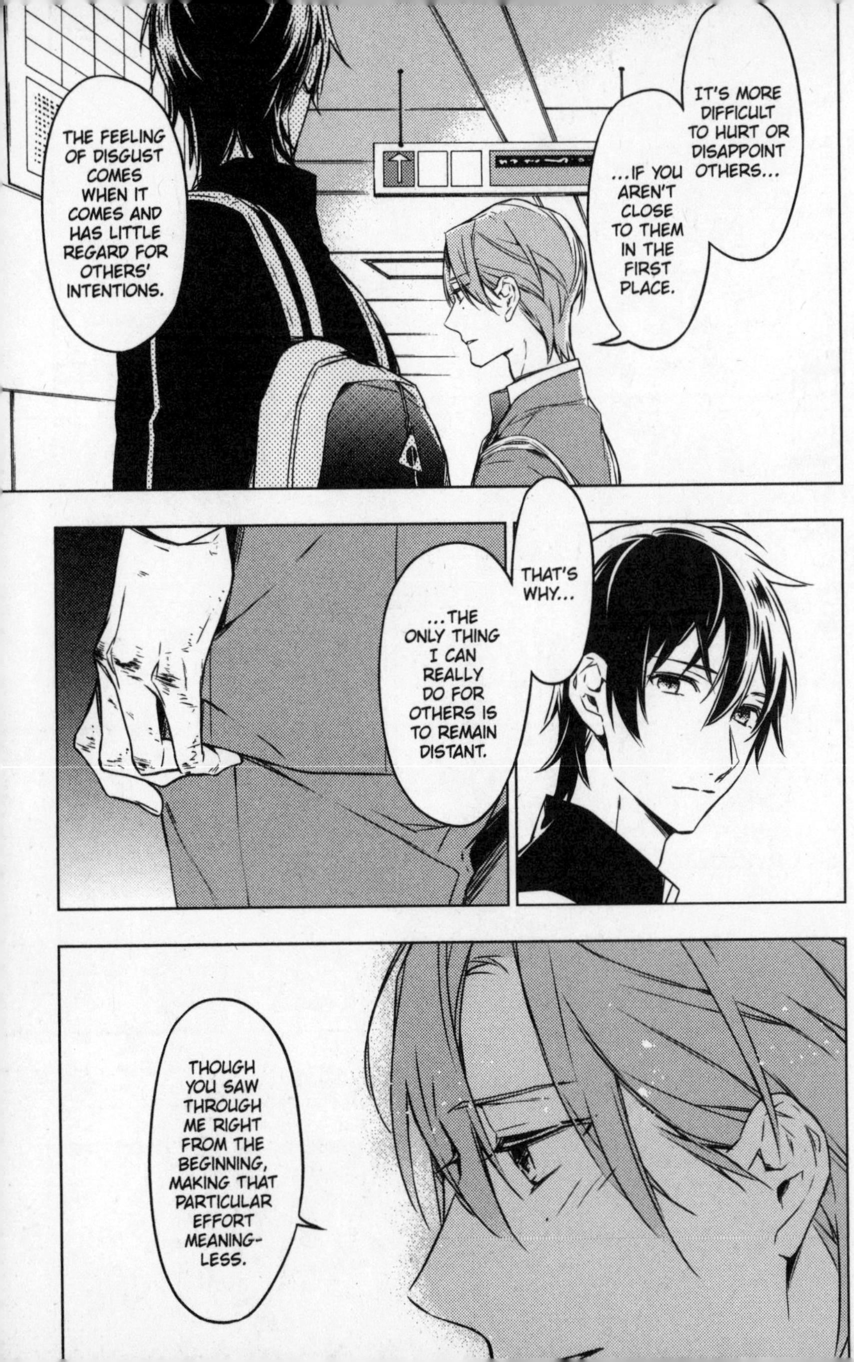
IT'S MORE DIFFICULT TO HURT OR DISAPPOINT OTHERS...
...IF YOU AREN'T CLOSE TO THEM IN THE FIRST PLACE.
THE FEELING OF DISGUST COMES WHEN IT COMES AND HAS LITTLE REGARD FOR OTHERS' INTENTIONS.
THAT'S WHY...
...THE ONLY THING I CAN REALLY DO FOR OTHERS IS TO REMAIN DISTANT.
THOUGH YOU SAW THROUGH ME RIGHT FROM THE BEGINNING, MAKING THAT PARTICULAR EFFORT MEANING-LESS.

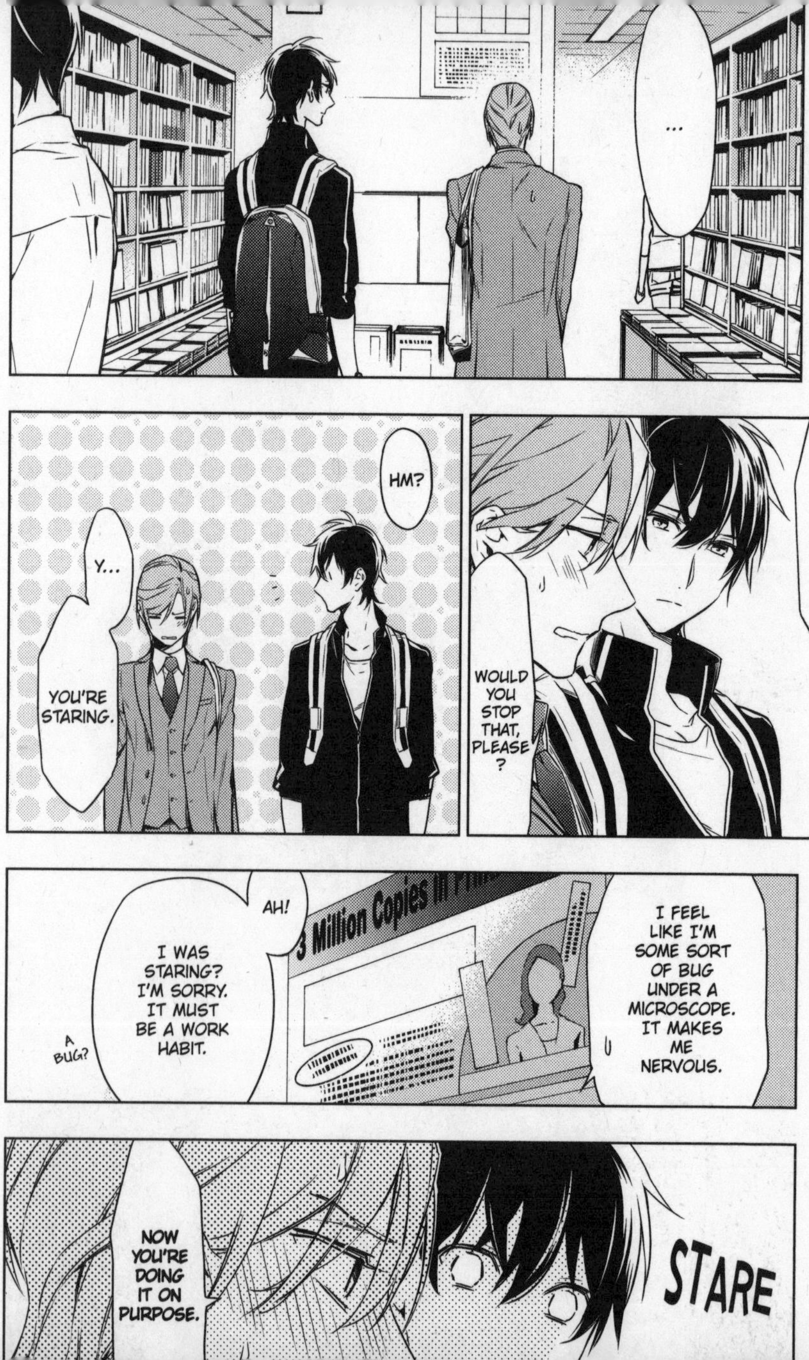
...
...
WOULD YOU STOP THAT, PLEASE?
HM?
Y... YOU'RE STARING.
I FEEL LIKE I'M SOME SORT OF BUG UNDER A MICROSCOPE. IT MAKES ME NERVOUS.
3 Million Copies In
AH! I WAS STARING? I'M SORRY. IT MUST BE A WORK HABIT.
A BUG?
STARE
NOW YOU'RE DOING IT ON PURPOSE.

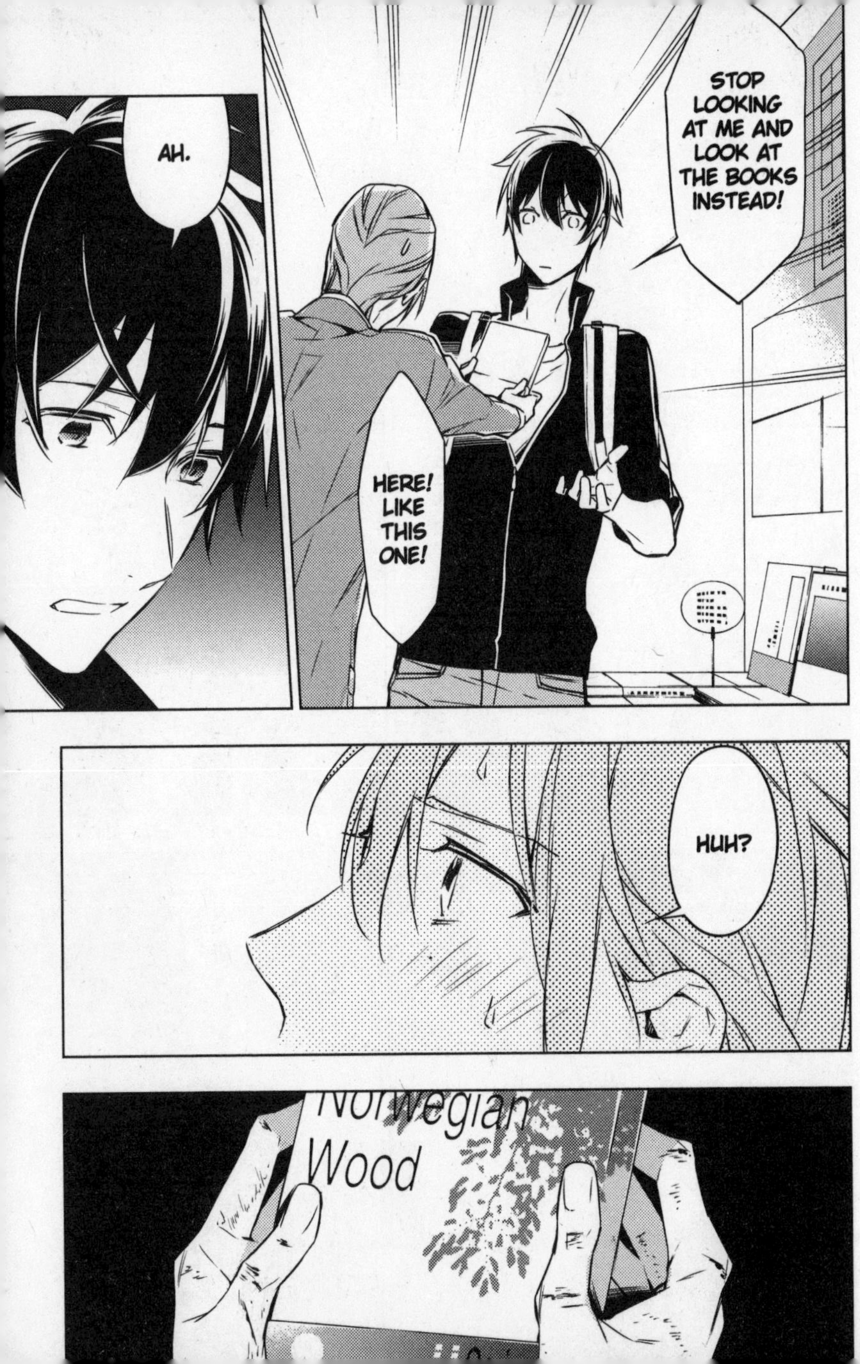
STOP LOOKING AT ME AND LOOK AT THE BOOKS INSTEAD!
HERE! LIKE THIS ONE!
AH.
HUH?
Norwegian Wood

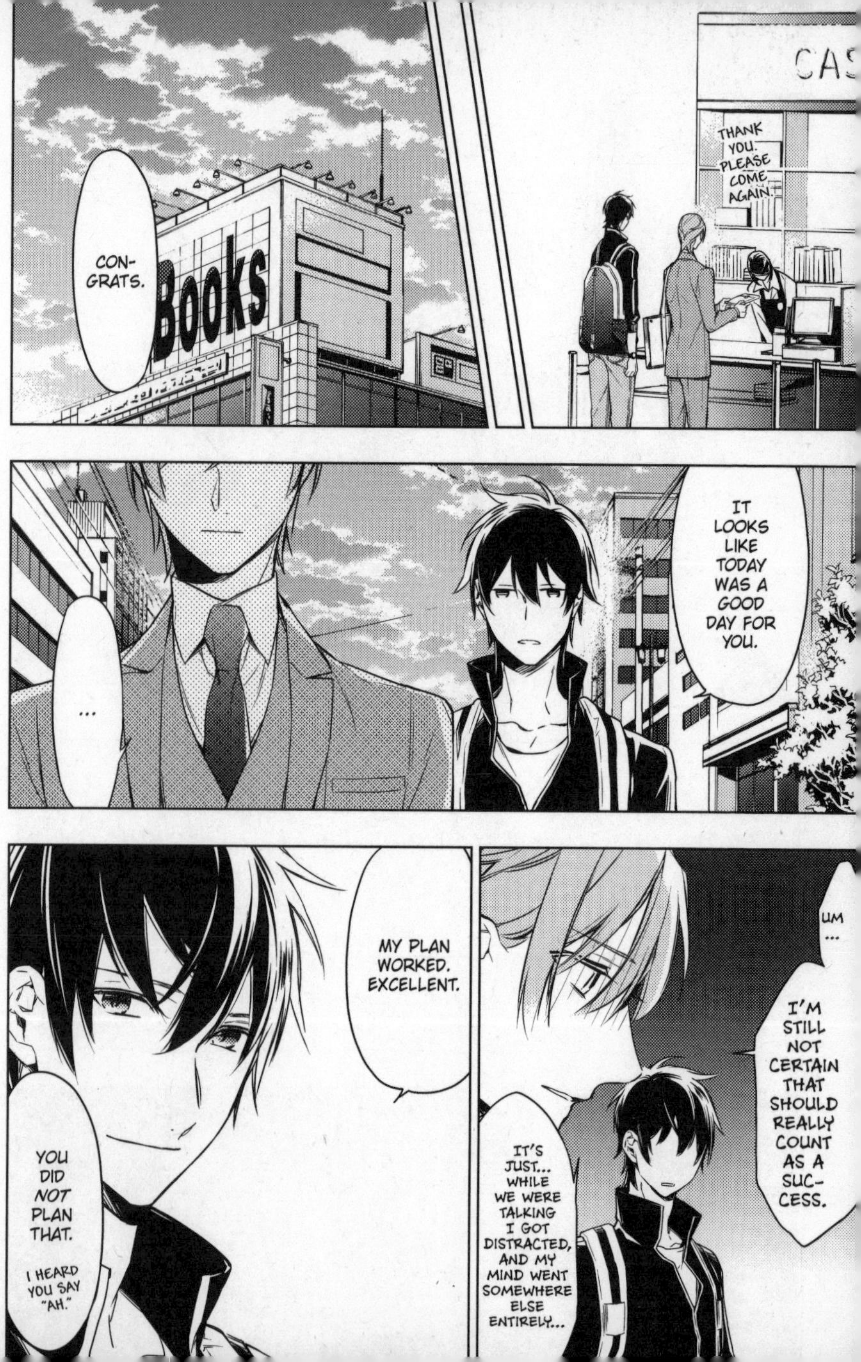
THANK YOU. PLEASE COME AGAIN.
CON-GRATS.
IT LOOKS LIKE TODAY WAS A GOOD DAY FOR YOU.
...
UM...
I'M STILL NOT CERTAIN THAT SHOULD REALLY COUNT AS A SUC-CESS.
IT'S JUST... WHILE WE WERE TALKING I GOT DISTRACTED, AND MY MIND WENT SOMEWHERE ELSE ENTIRELY...
MY PLAN WORKED. EXCELLENT.
YOU DID *NOT* PLAN THAT.
I HEARD YOU SAY "AH."

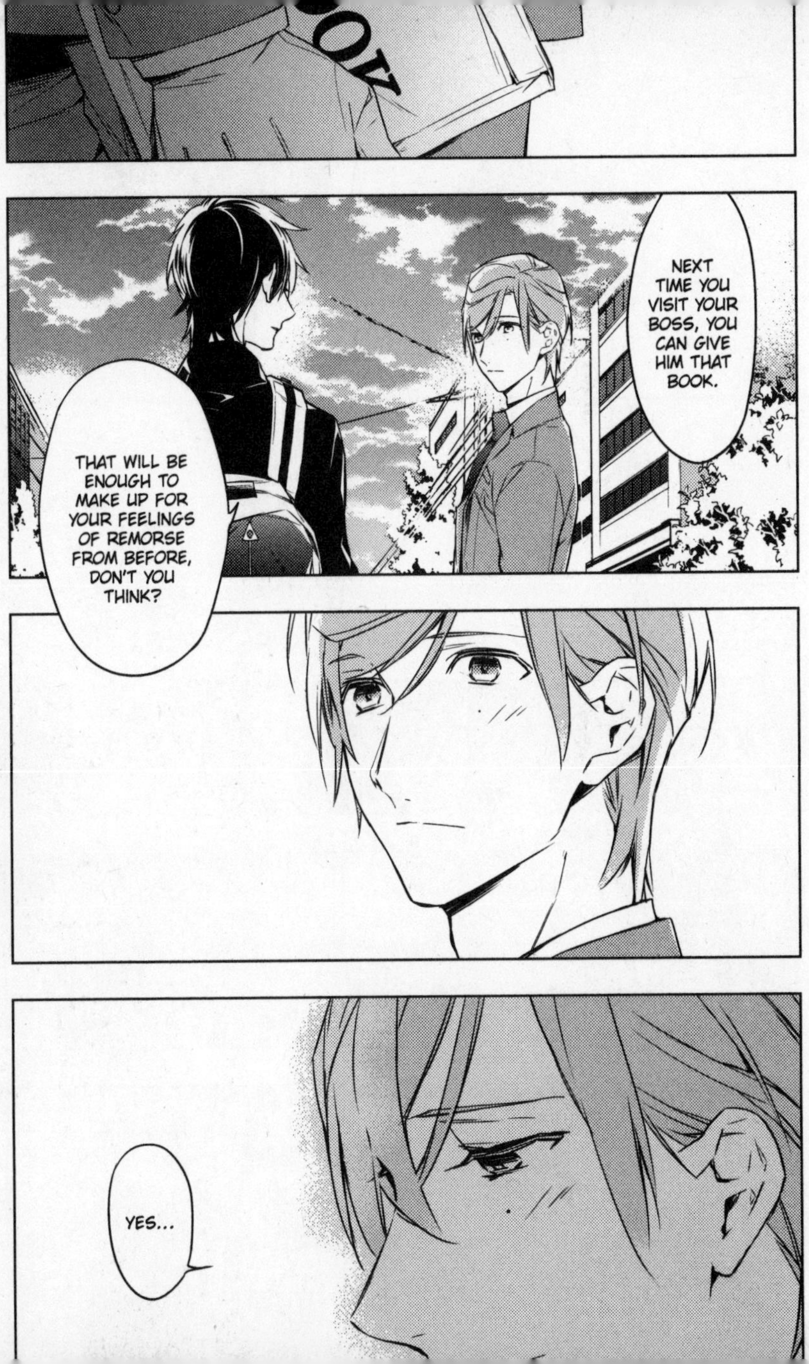
NEXT TIME YOU VISIT YOUR BOSS, YOU CAN GIVE HIM THAT BOOK.
THAT WILL BE ENOUGH TO MAKE UP FOR YOUR FEELINGS OF REMORSE FROM BEFORE, DON'T YOU THINK?
YES...

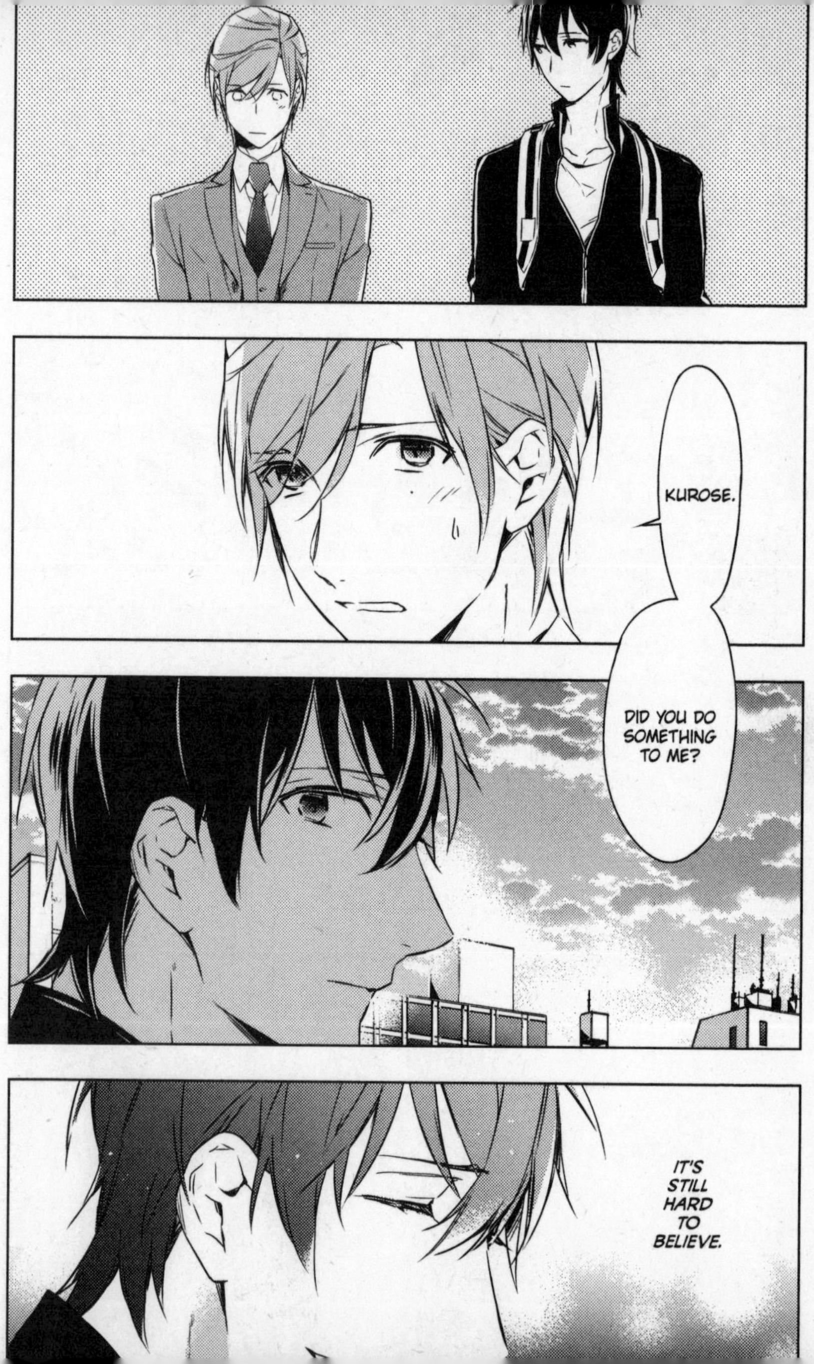
KUROSE.
DID YOU DO SOMETHING TO ME?
IT'S STILL HARD TO BELIEVE.

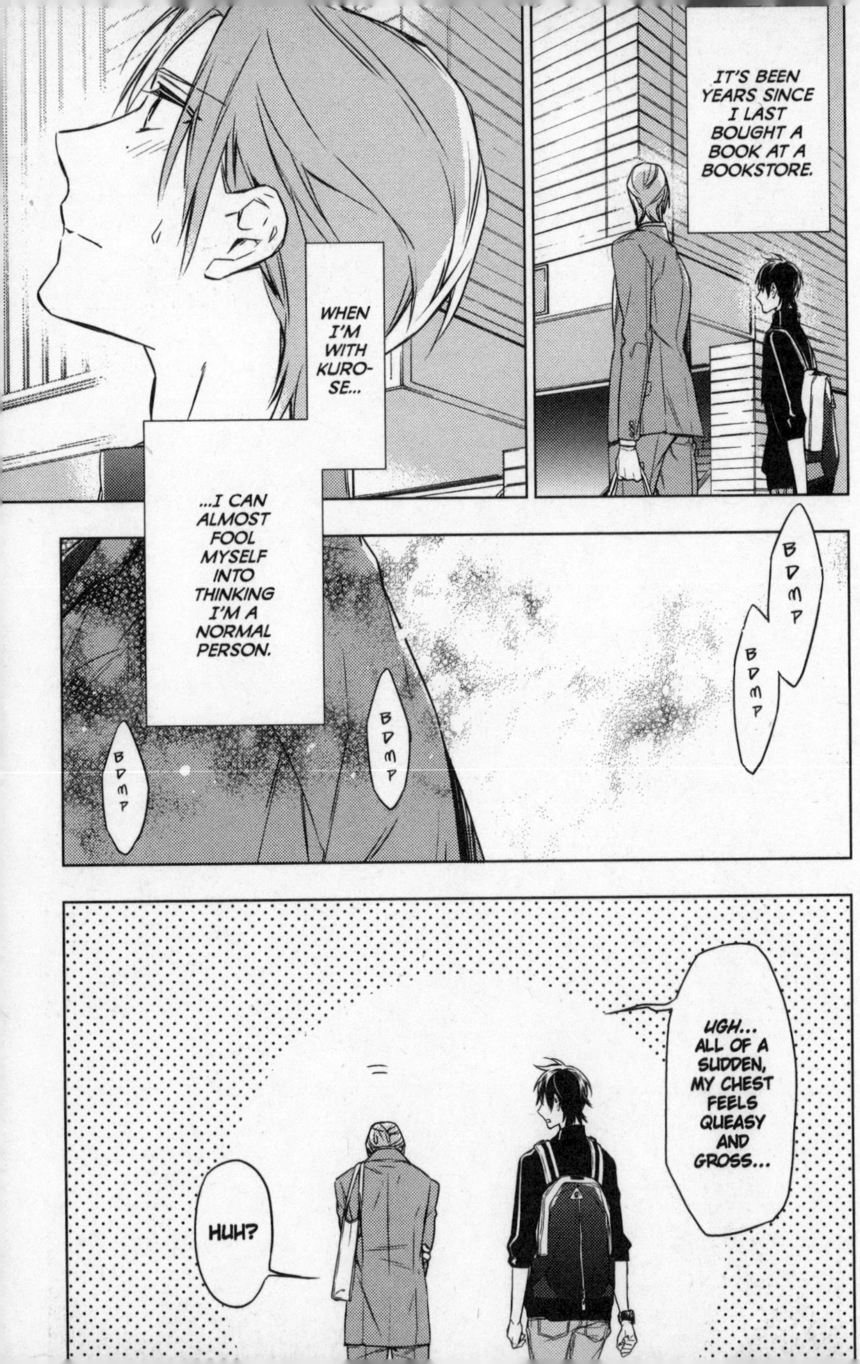
IT'S BEEN YEARS SINCE I LAST BOUGHT A BOOK AT A BOOKSTORE.
WHEN I'M WITH KURO-SE...
...I CAN ALMOST FOOL MYSELF INTO THINKING I'M A NORMAL PERSON.
BDMP
BDMP
BDMP
BDMP
UGH... ALL OF A SUDDEN, MY CHEST FEELS QUEASY AND GROSS...
HUH?

ten count by rihito takarai

TEN COUNT 04

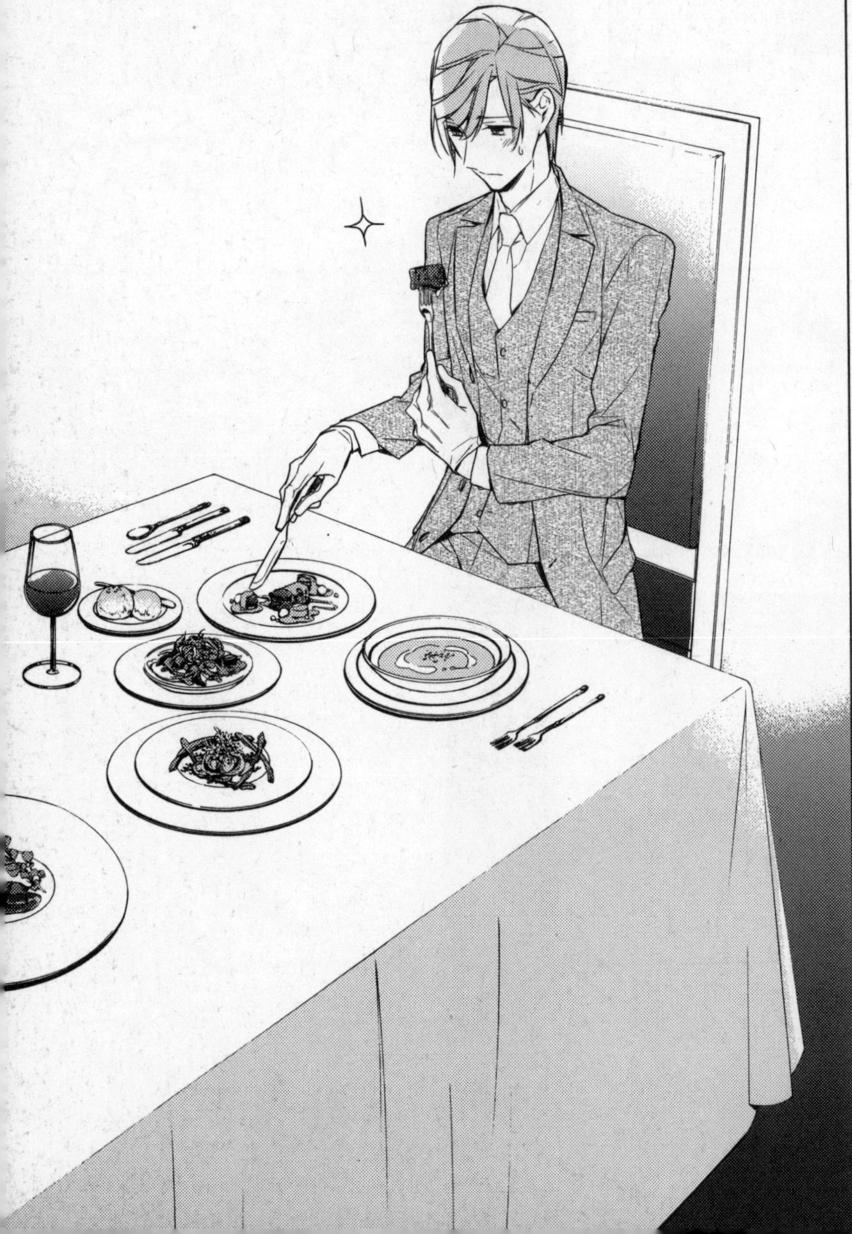

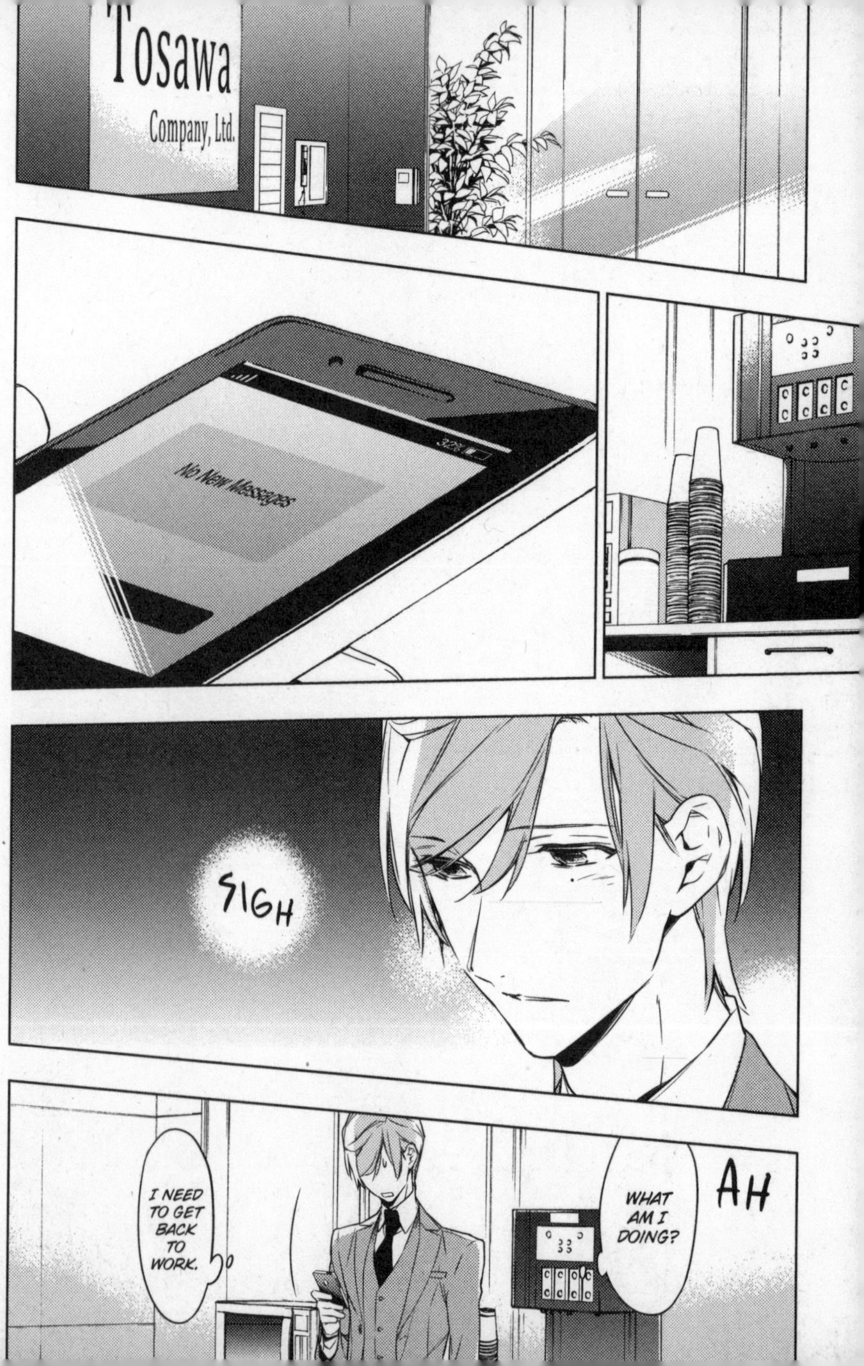
Tosawa
Company, Ltd.
No New Messages
SIGH
AH
WHAT AM I DOING?
I NEED TO GET BACK TO WORK.

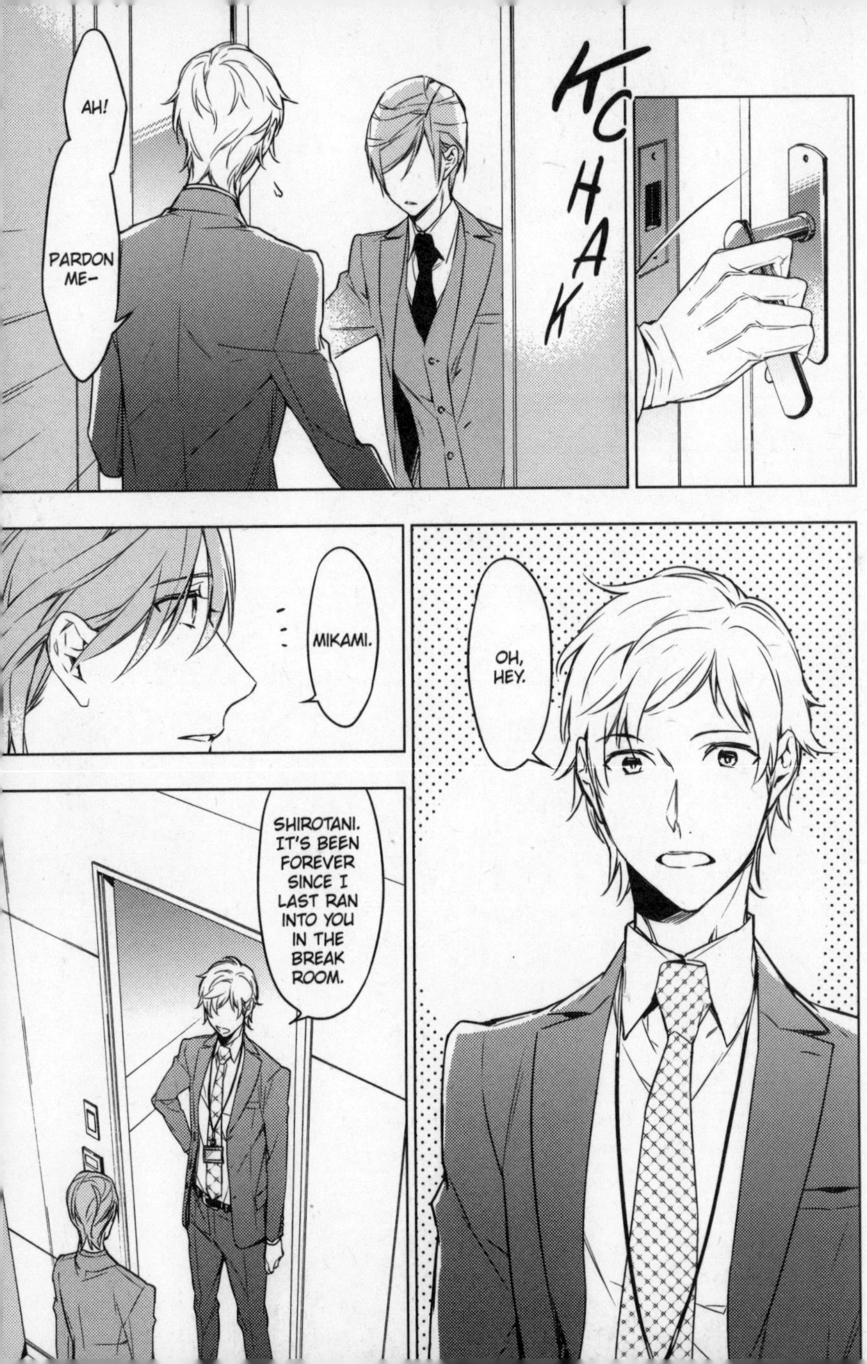
KCHAK
AH!
PARDON ME-
OH, HEY.
...
MIKAMI.
SHIROTANI. IT'S BEEN FOREVER SINCE I LAST RAN INTO YOU IN THE BREAK ROOM.

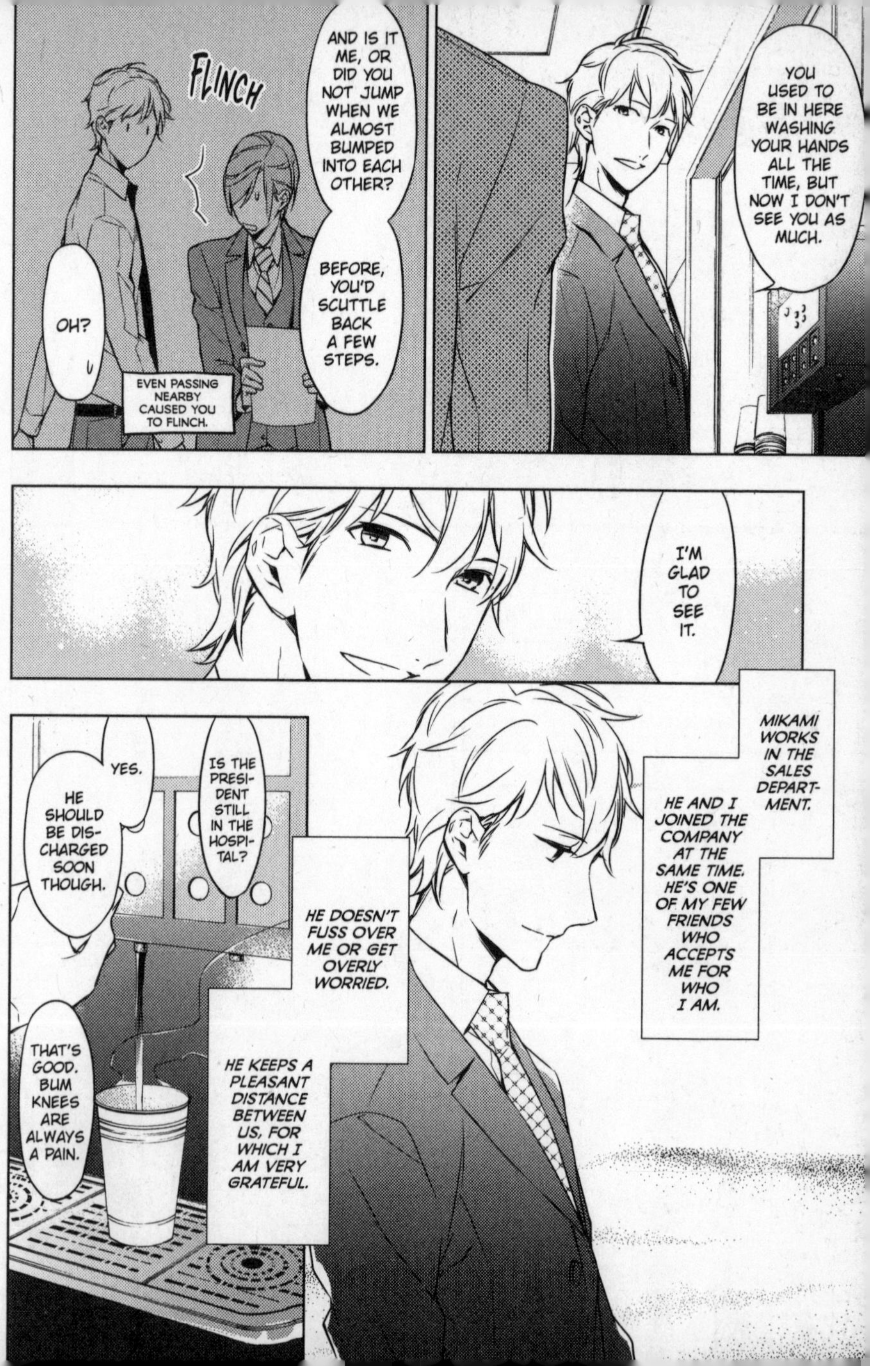

YOU USED TO BE IN HERE WASHING YOUR HANDS ALL THE TIME, BUT NOW I DON'T SEE YOU AS MUCH.
AND IS IT ME, OR DID YOU NOT JUMP WHEN WE ALMOST BUMPED INTO EACH OTHER?
FLINCH
BEFORE, YOU'D SCUTTLE BACK A FEW STEPS.
OH?
EVEN PASSING NEARBY CAUSED YOU TO FLINCH.
I'M GLAD TO SEE IT.
MIKAMI WORKS IN THE SALES DEPARTMENT.
HE AND I JOINED THE COMPANY AT THE SAME TIME. HE'S ONE OF MY FEW FRIENDS WHO ACCEPTS ME FOR WHO I AM.
HE DOESN'T FUSS OVER ME OR GET OVERLY WORRIED.
HE KEEPS A PLEASANT DISTANCE BETWEEN US, FOR WHICH I AM VERY GRATEFUL.
IS THE PRESI-DENT STILL IN THE HOSPI-TAL?
YES.
HE SHOULD BE DIS-CHARGED SOON THOUGH.
THAT'S GOOD. BUM KNEES ARE ALWAYS A PAIN.

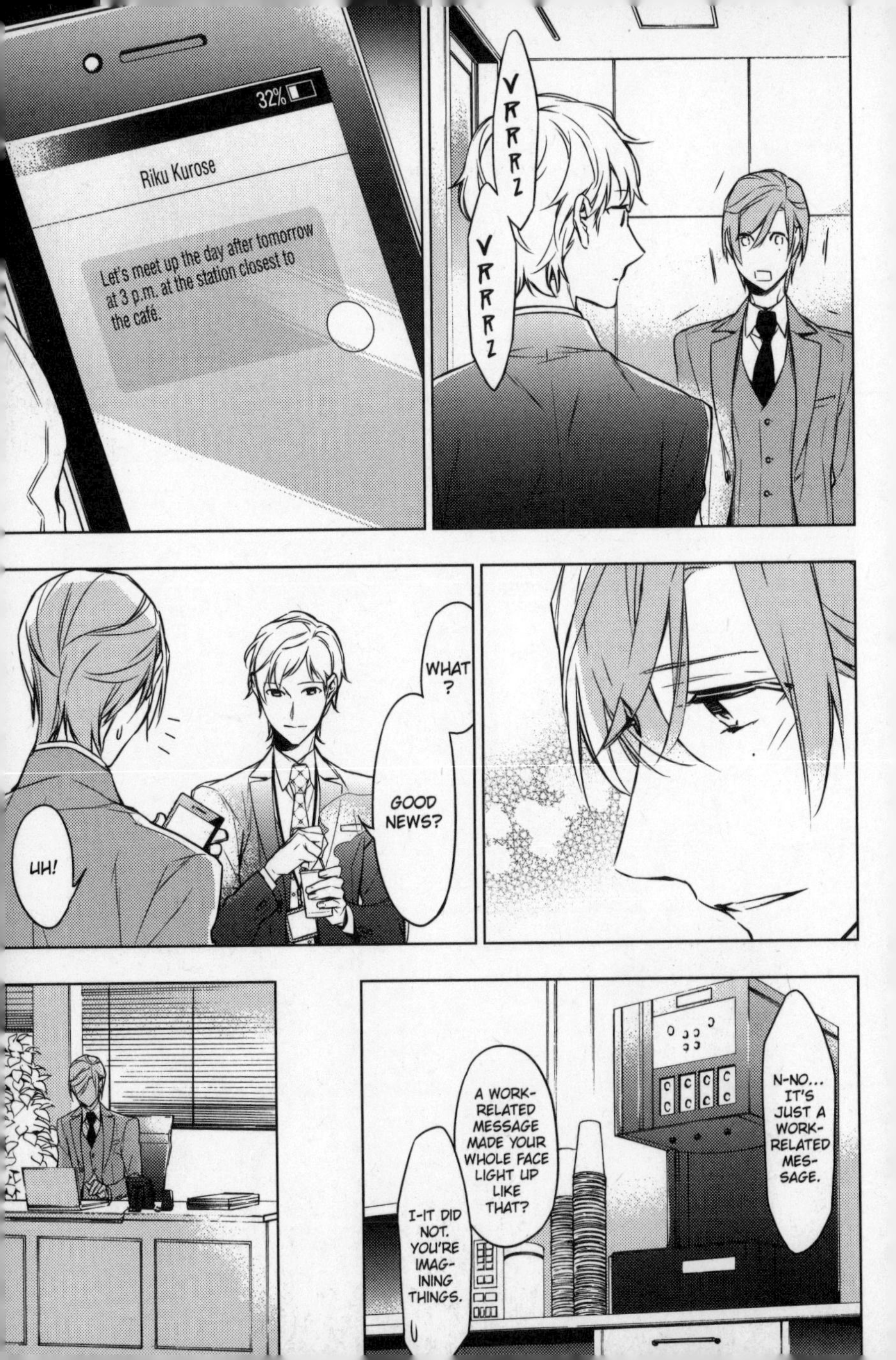
VRRRZ
VRRRZ
32%
Riku Kurose
Let's meet up the day after tomorrow at 3 p.m. at the station closest to the café.
WHAT?
GOOD NEWS?
UH!
N-NO... IT'S JUST A WORK-RELATED MESSAGE.
A WORK-RELATED MESSAGE MADE YOUR WHOLE FACE LIGHT UP LIKE THAT?
I-IT DID NOT. YOU'RE IMAGINING THINGS.

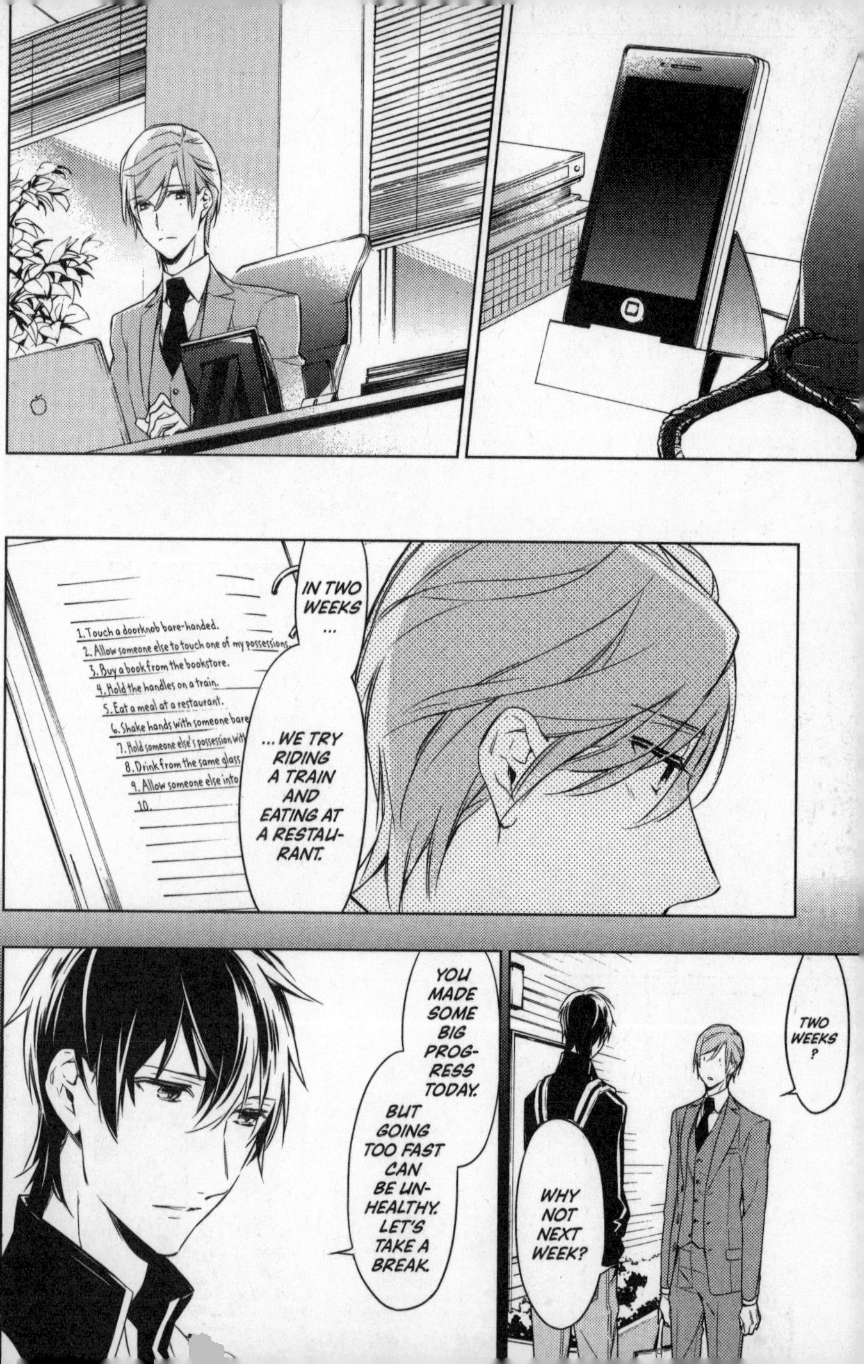
IN TWO WEEKS ...
... WE TRY RIDING A TRAIN AND EATING AT A RESTAU-RANT.
1. Touch a doorknob bare-handed.
2. Allow someone else to touch one of my possessions
3. Buy a book from the bookstore.
4. Hold the handles on a train.
5. Eat a meal at a restaurant.
6. Shake hands with someone bare
7. Hold someone else's possession with
8. Drink from the same glass
9. Allow someone else into
10.
TWO WEEKS ?
WHY NOT NEXT WEEK?
YOU MADE SOME BIG PROG-RESS TODAY.
BUT GOING TOO FAST CAN BE UN-HEALTHY. LET'S TAKE A BREAK.

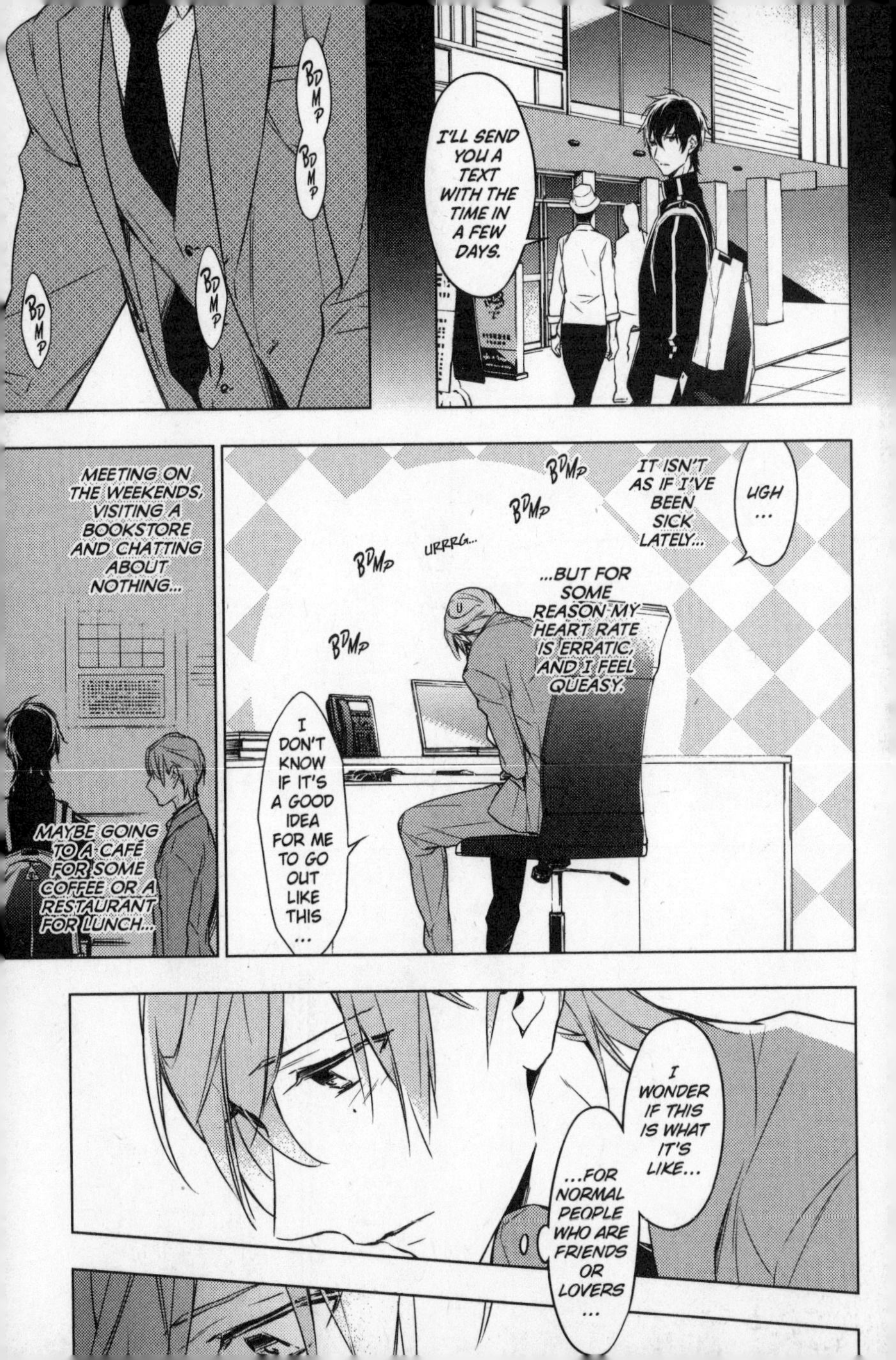
I'LL SEND YOU A TEXT WITH THE TIME IN A FEW DAYS.
BDMP
BDMP
BDMP
BDMP
UGH...
IT ISN'T AS IF I'VE BEEN SICK LATELY...
BDMP
...BUT FOR SOME REASON MY HEART RATE IS ERRATIC, AND I FEEL QUEASY.
BDMP
URRRG...
BDMP
BDMP
I DON'T KNOW IF IT'S A GOOD IDEA FOR ME TO GO OUT LIKE THIS...
MEETING ON THE WEEKENDS, VISITING A BOOKSTORE AND CHATTING ABOUT NOTHING...
MAYBE GOING TO A CAFÉ FOR SOME COFFEE OR A RESTAURANT FOR LUNCH...
I WONDER IF THIS IS WHAT IT'S LIKE...
...FOR NORMAL PEOPLE WHO ARE FRIENDS OR LOVERS...

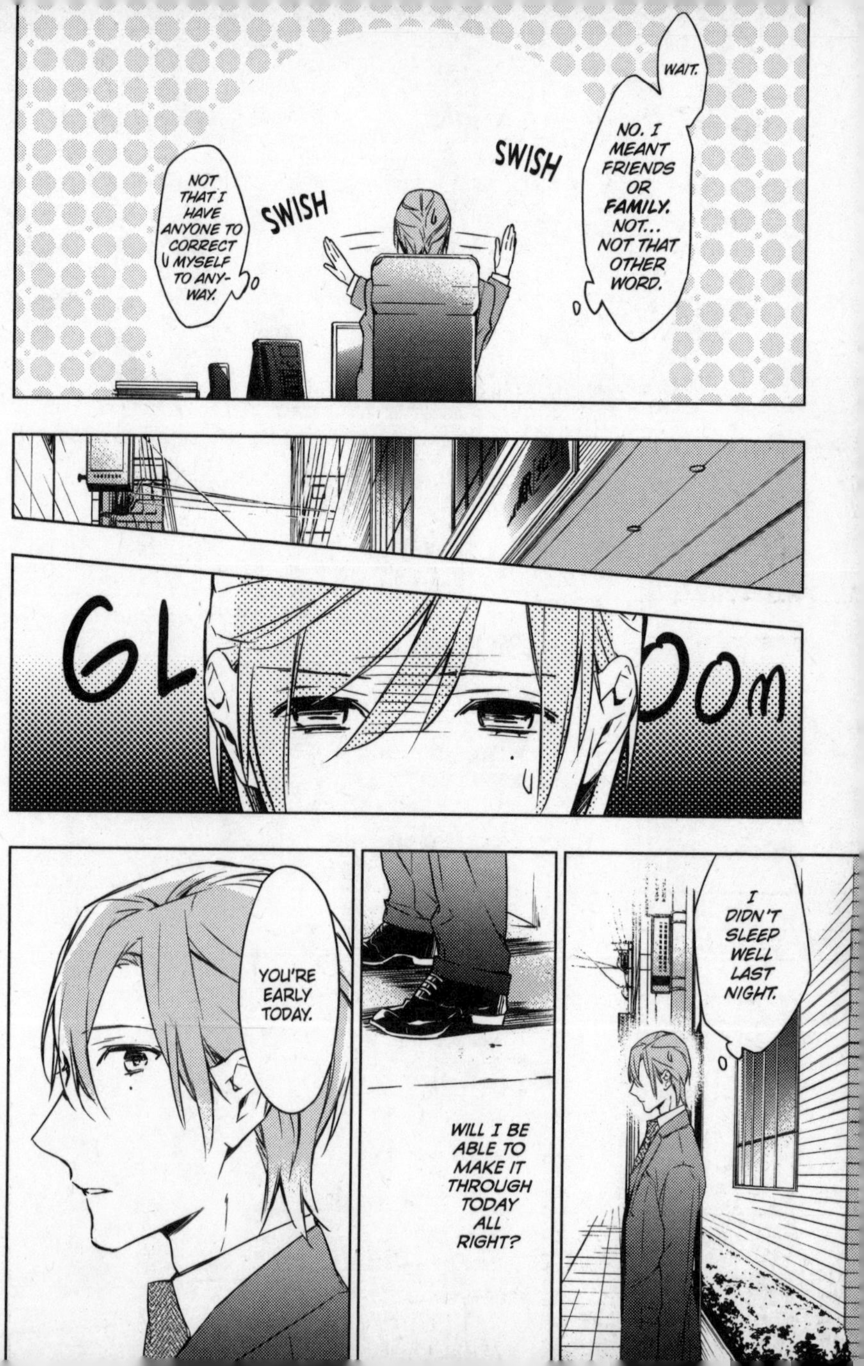
WAIT.
NO. I MEANT FRIENDS OR FAMILY. NOT... NOT THAT OTHER WORD.
SWISH
SWISH
NOT THAT I HAVE ANYONE TO CORRECT MYSELF TO ANY-WAY.
GL OOM
I DIDN'T SLEEP WELL LAST NIGHT.
WILL I BE ABLE TO MAKE IT THROUGH TODAY ALL RIGHT?
YOU'RE EARLY TODAY.

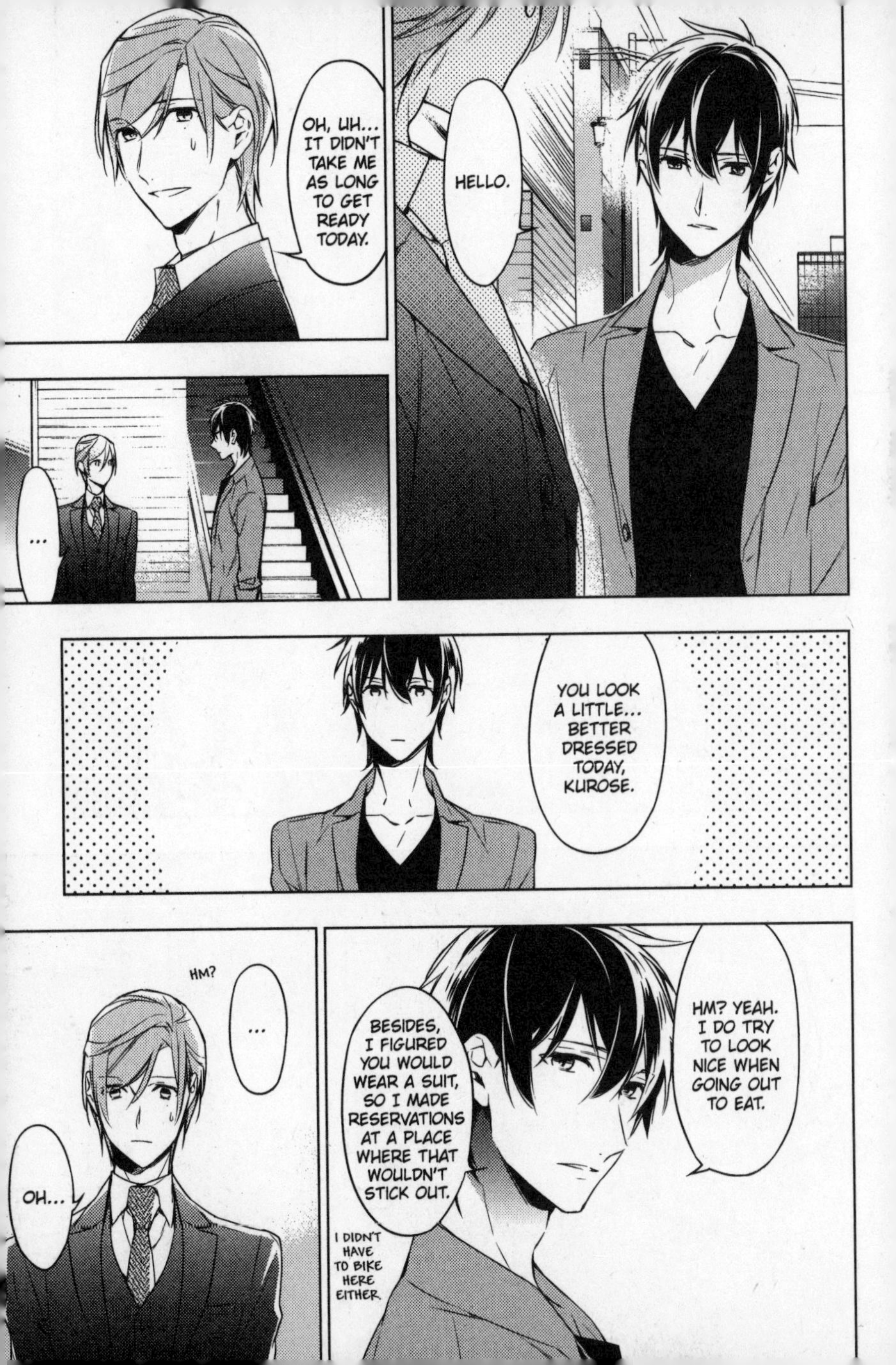
HELLO.
OH, UH... IT DIDN'T TAKE ME AS LONG TO GET READY TODAY.
...
YOU LOOK A LITTLE... BETTER DRESSED TODAY, KUROSE.
HM? YEAH. I DO TRY TO LOOK NICE WHEN GOING OUT TO EAT.
BESIDES, I FIGURED YOU WOULD WEAR A SUIT, SO I MADE RESERVATIONS AT A PLACE WHERE THAT WOULDN'T STICK OUT.
I DIDN'T HAVE TO BIKE HERE EITHER.
HM?
...
OH...

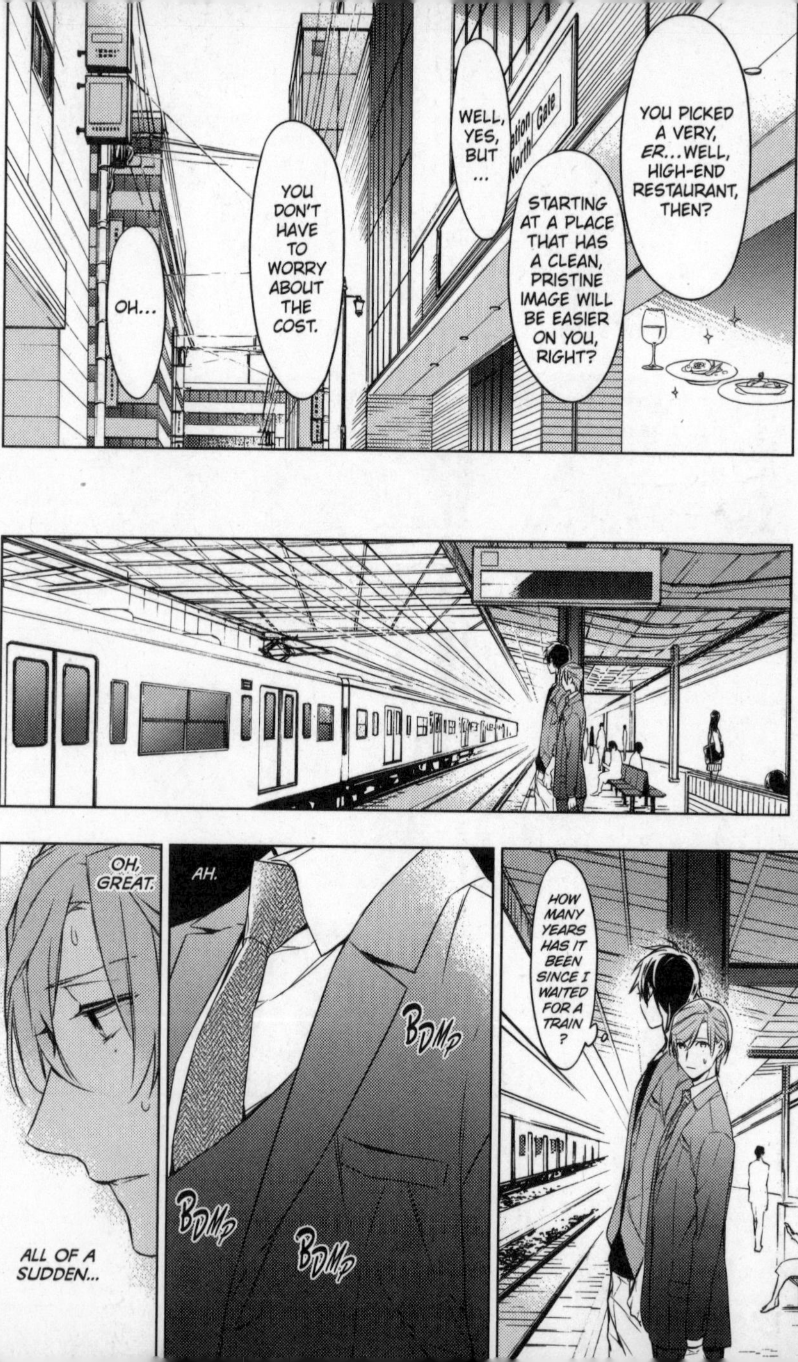
YOU PICKED A VERY, ER...WELL, HIGH-END RESTAURANT, THEN?
STARTING AT A PLACE THAT HAS A CLEAN, PRISTINE IMAGE WILL BE EASIER ON YOU, RIGHT?
WELL, YES, BUT ...
YOU DON'T HAVE TO WORRY ABOUT THE COST.
OH...
HOW MANY YEARS HAS IT BEEN SINCE I WAITED FOR A TRAIN?
AH.
BDMP
BDMP
BDMP
OH, GREAT.
ALL OF A SUDDEN...

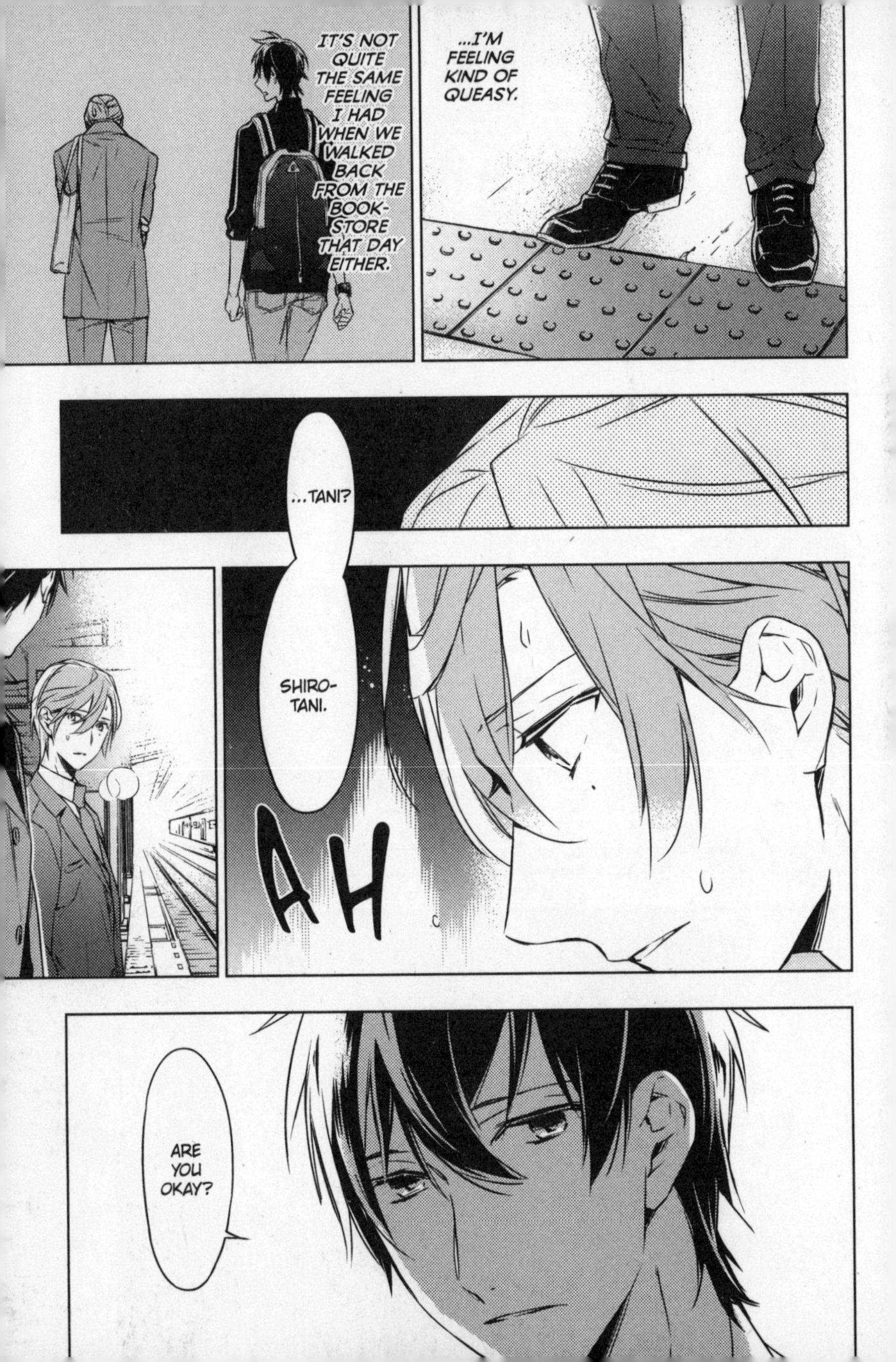
...I'M FEELING KIND OF QUEASY.
IT'S NOT QUITE THE SAME FEELING I HAD WHEN WE WALKED BACK FROM THE BOOK-STORE THAT DAY EITHER.
...TANI?
SHIRO-TANI.
AH
ARE YOU OKAY?

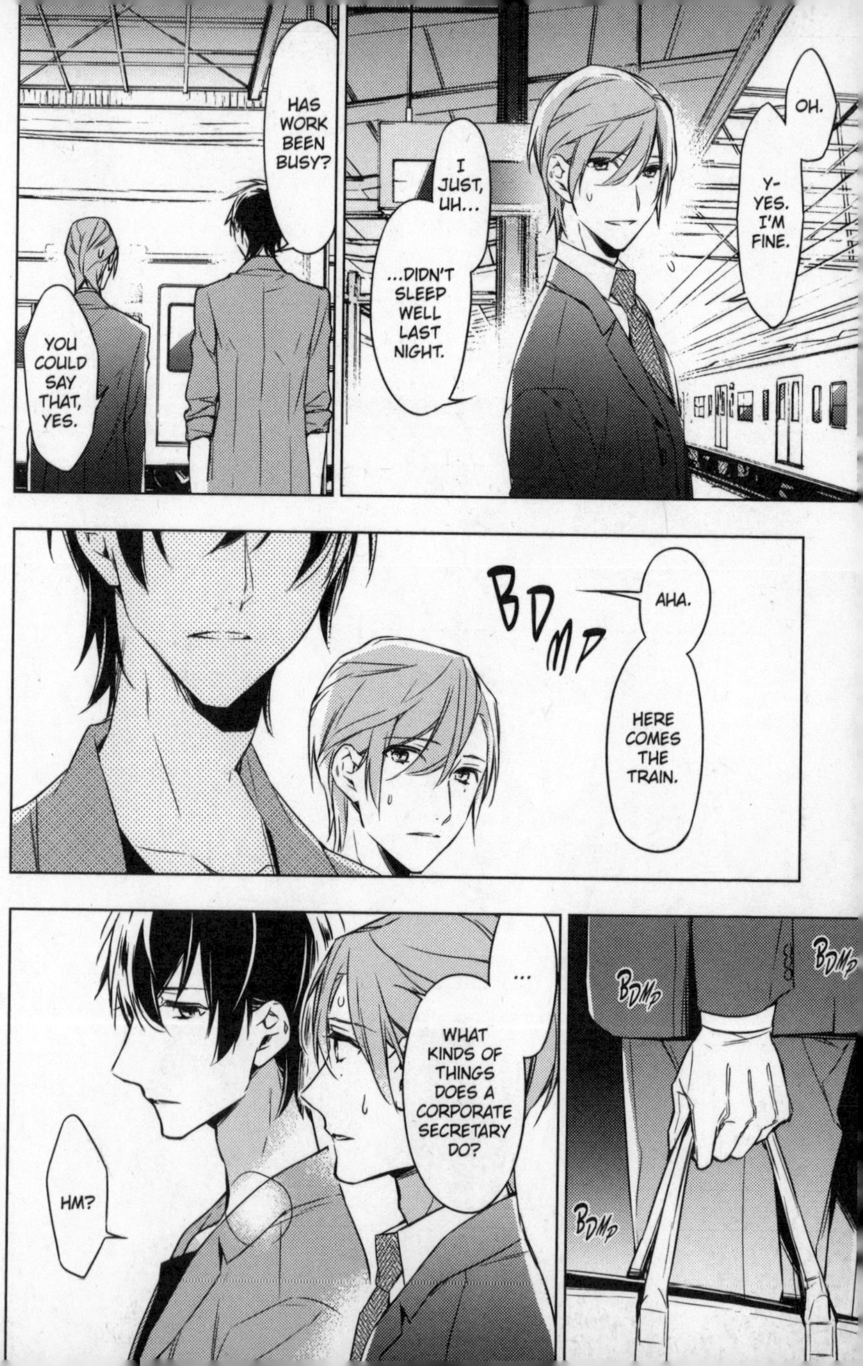
OH.
Y- YES. I'M FINE.
I JUST, UH...
...DIDN'T SLEEP WELL LAST NIGHT.
HAS WORK BEEN BUSY?
YOU COULD SAY THAT, YES.
BDMP
AHA.
HERE COMES THE TRAIN.
BDMP
BDMP
BDMP
...
WHAT KINDS OF THINGS DOES A CORPORATE SECRETARY DO?
HM?

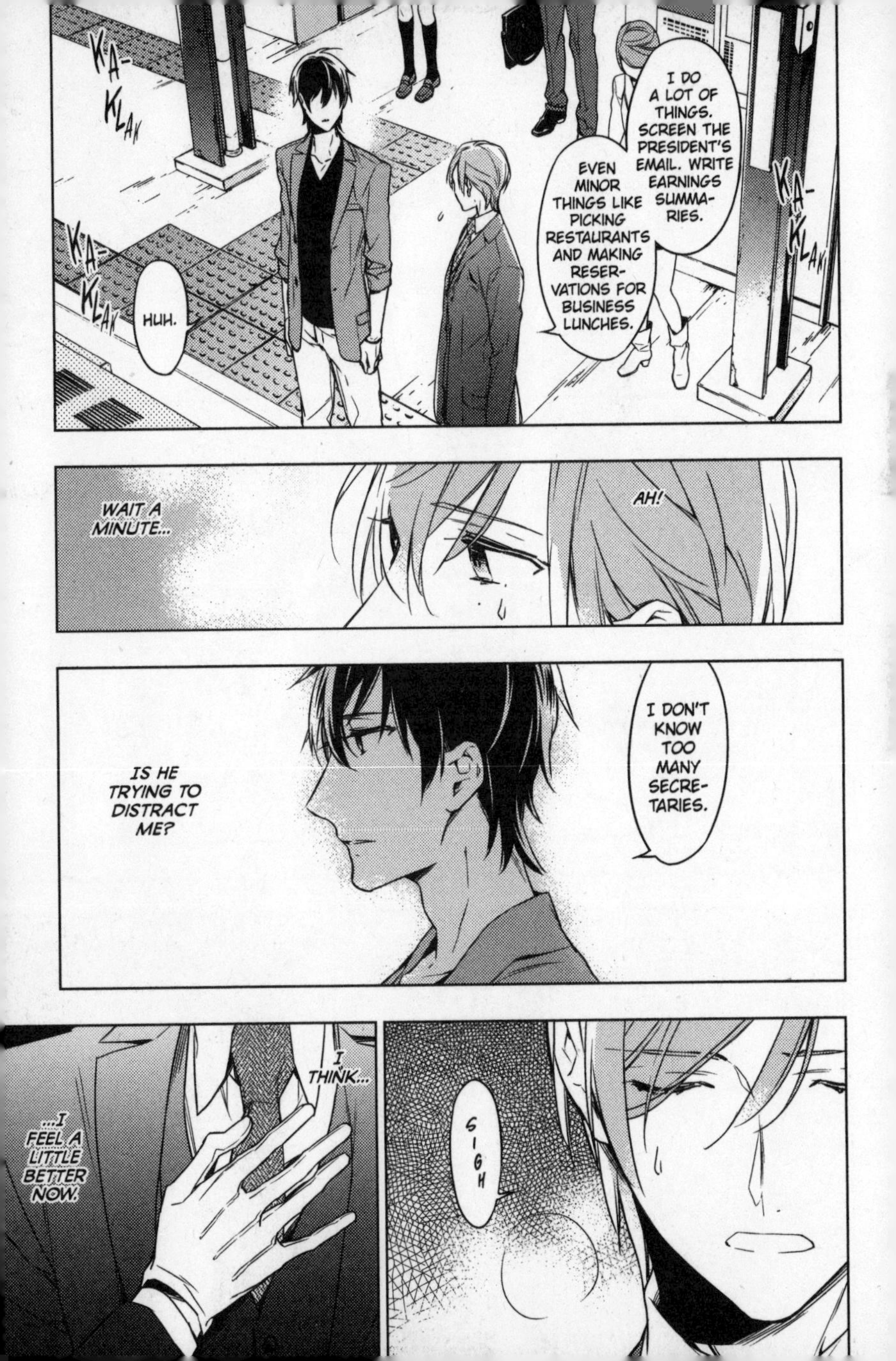
KA-KLAK
I DO A LOT OF THINGS. SCREEN THE PRESIDENT'S EMAIL. WRITE EARNINGS SUMMA-RIES.
EVEN MINOR THINGS LIKE PICKING RESTAURANTS AND MAKING RESER-VATIONS FOR BUSINESS LUNCHES.
KA-KLAK
KA-KLAK
HUH.
AH!
WAIT A MINUTE...
I DON'T KNOW TOO MANY SECRE-TARIES.
IS HE TRYING TO DISTRACT ME?
SIGH
I THINK...
...I FEEL A LITTLE BETTER NOW.

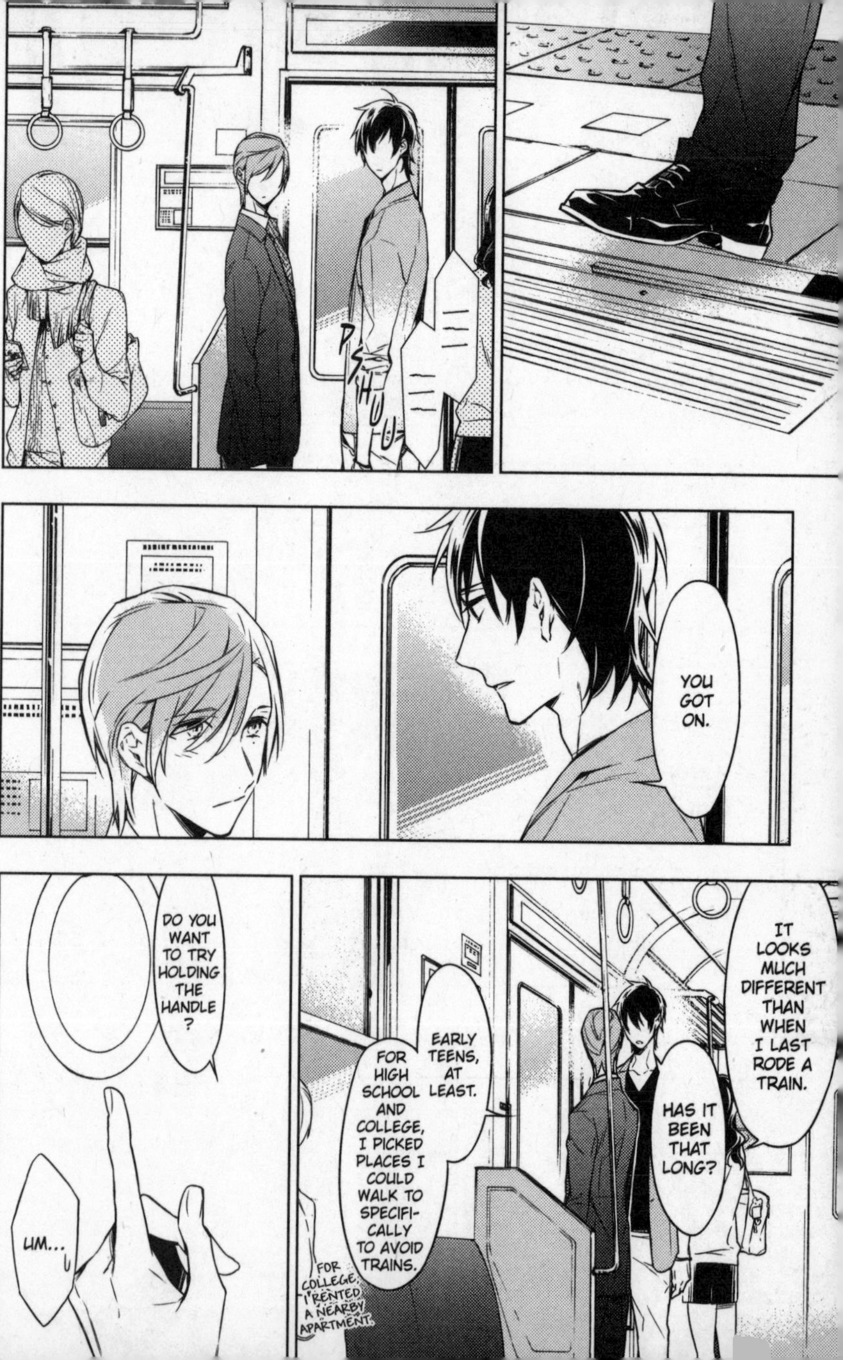
PSHUU
YOU GOT ON.
IT LOOKS MUCH DIFFERENT THAN WHEN I LAST RODE A TRAIN.
HAS IT BEEN THAT LONG?
EARLY TEENS, AT LEAST.
FOR HIGH SCHOOL AND COLLEGE, I PICKED PLACES I COULD WALK TO SPECIFICALLY TO AVOID TRAINS.
FOR COLLEGE, I RENTED A NEARBY APARTMENT.
DO YOU WANT TO TRY HOLDING THE HANDLE?
UM...

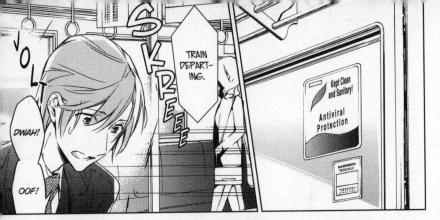

Kept Clean and Sanitary!
Antiviral Protection
TRAIN DEPART-ING.
SKREEE
VOLT
DWAH!
OOF!
BDMP
BDMP
BDMP
SEE?
YOU MIGHT FALL.
KA-KLAK
KA-KLAK
KA-KLAK

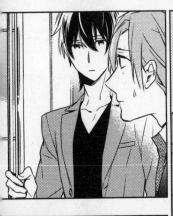

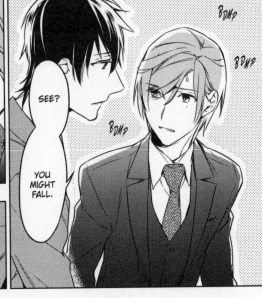

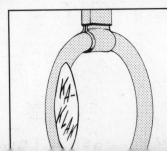

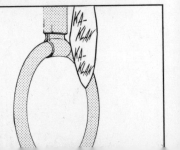

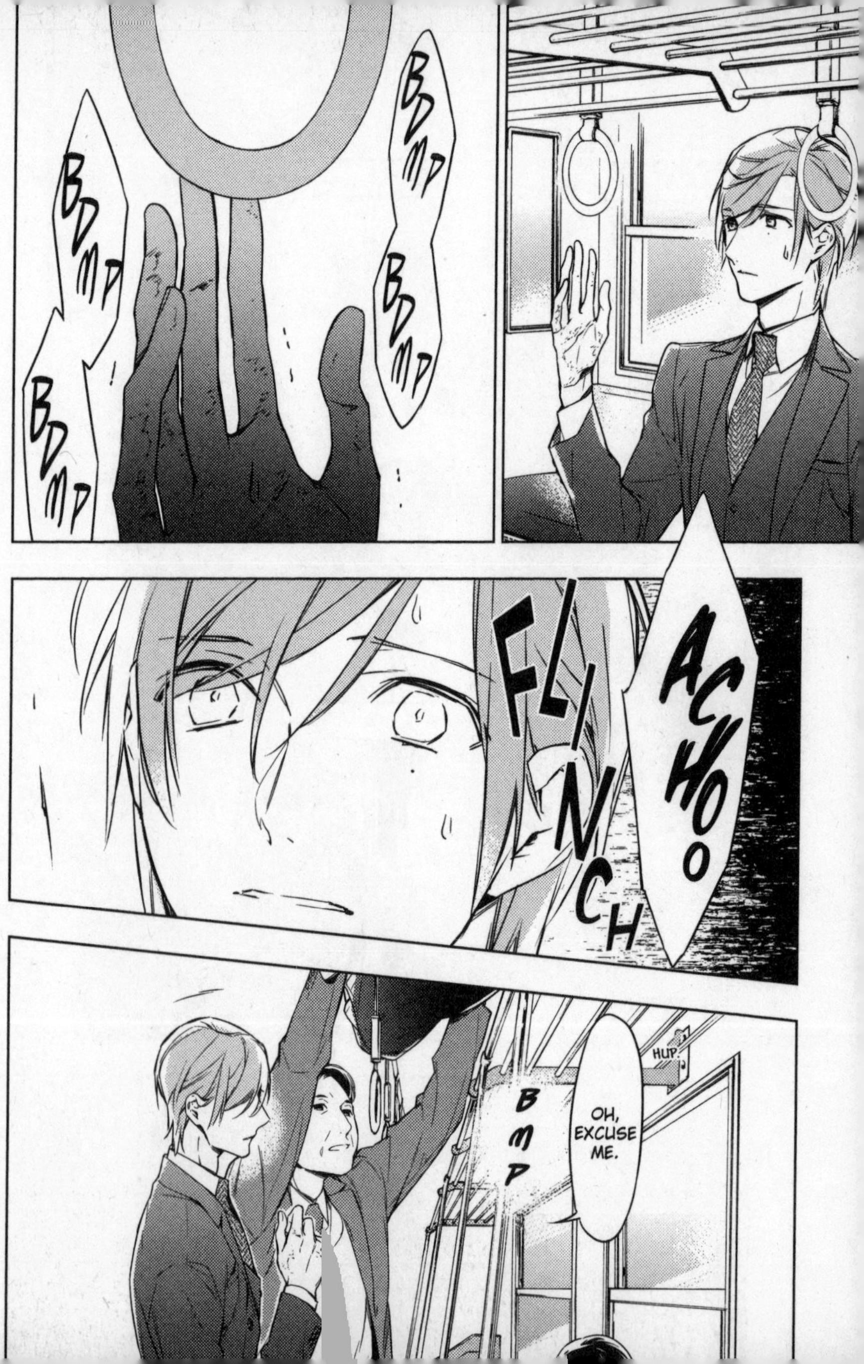
BDMP
BDMP
BDMP
BDMP
ACHOO
FLINCH
HUP.
OH, EXCUSE ME.
BMP

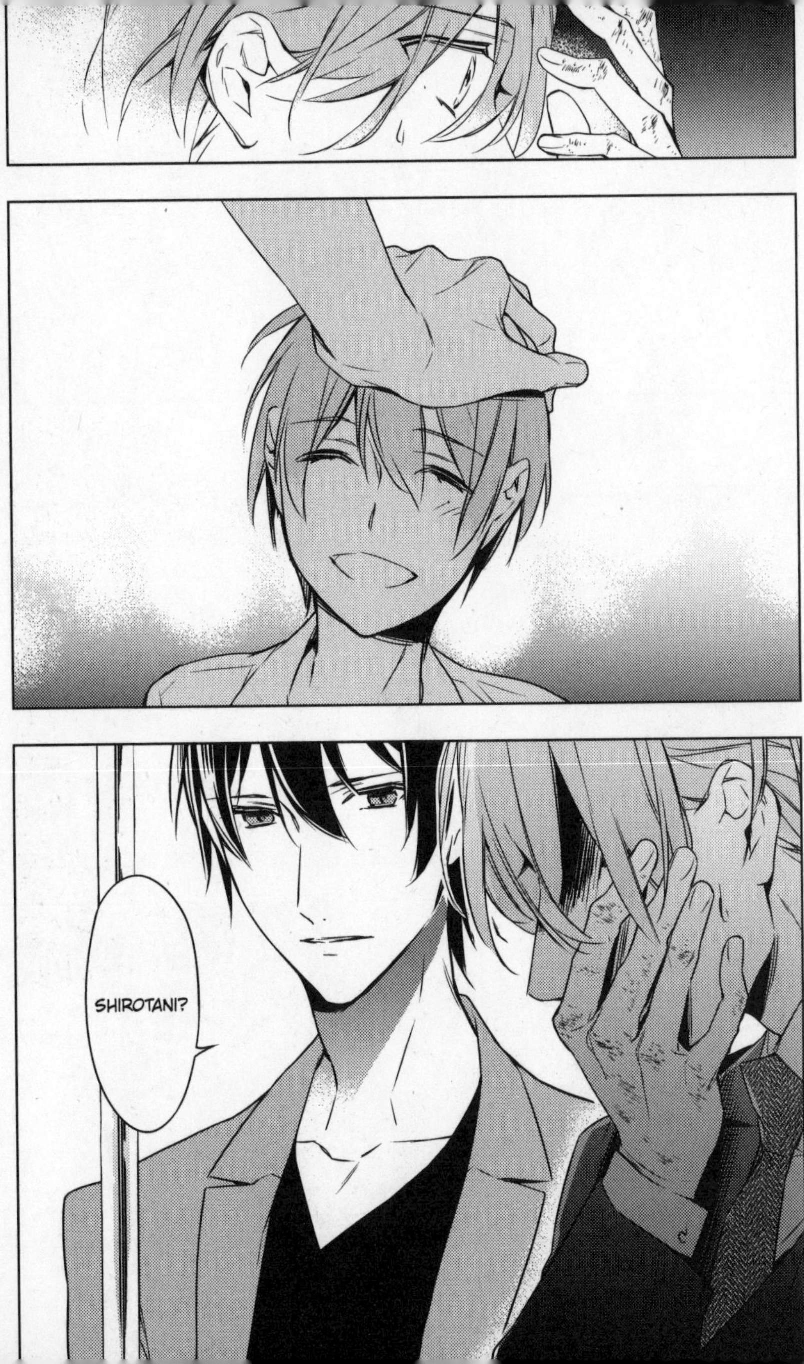
SHIROTANI?

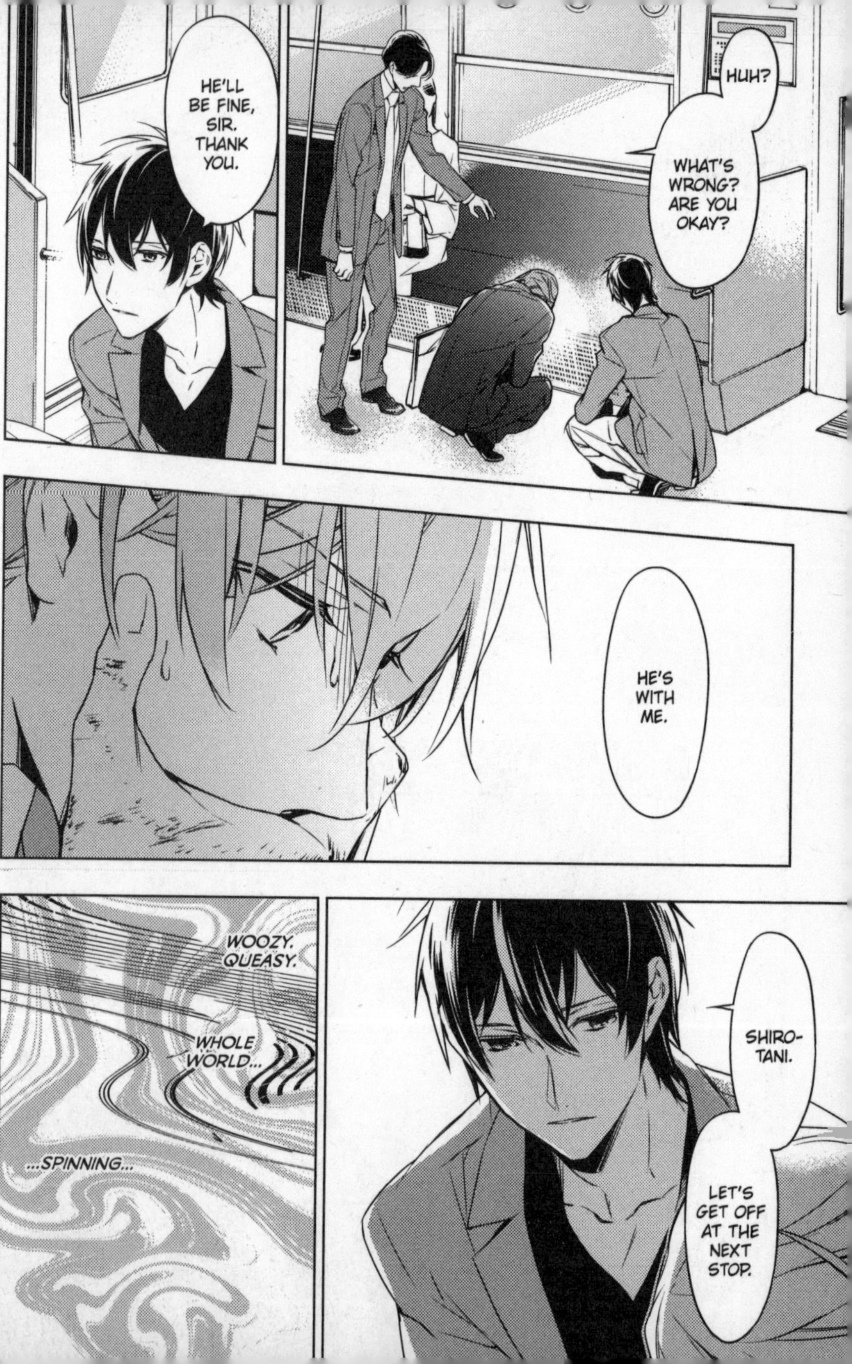
HUH?
WHAT'S WRONG? ARE YOU OKAY?
HE'LL BE FINE, SIR. THANK YOU.
HE'S WITH ME.
SHIRO-TANI.
LET'S GET OFF AT THE NEXT STOP.
WOOZY. QUEASY.
WHOLE WORLD...
...SPINNING...

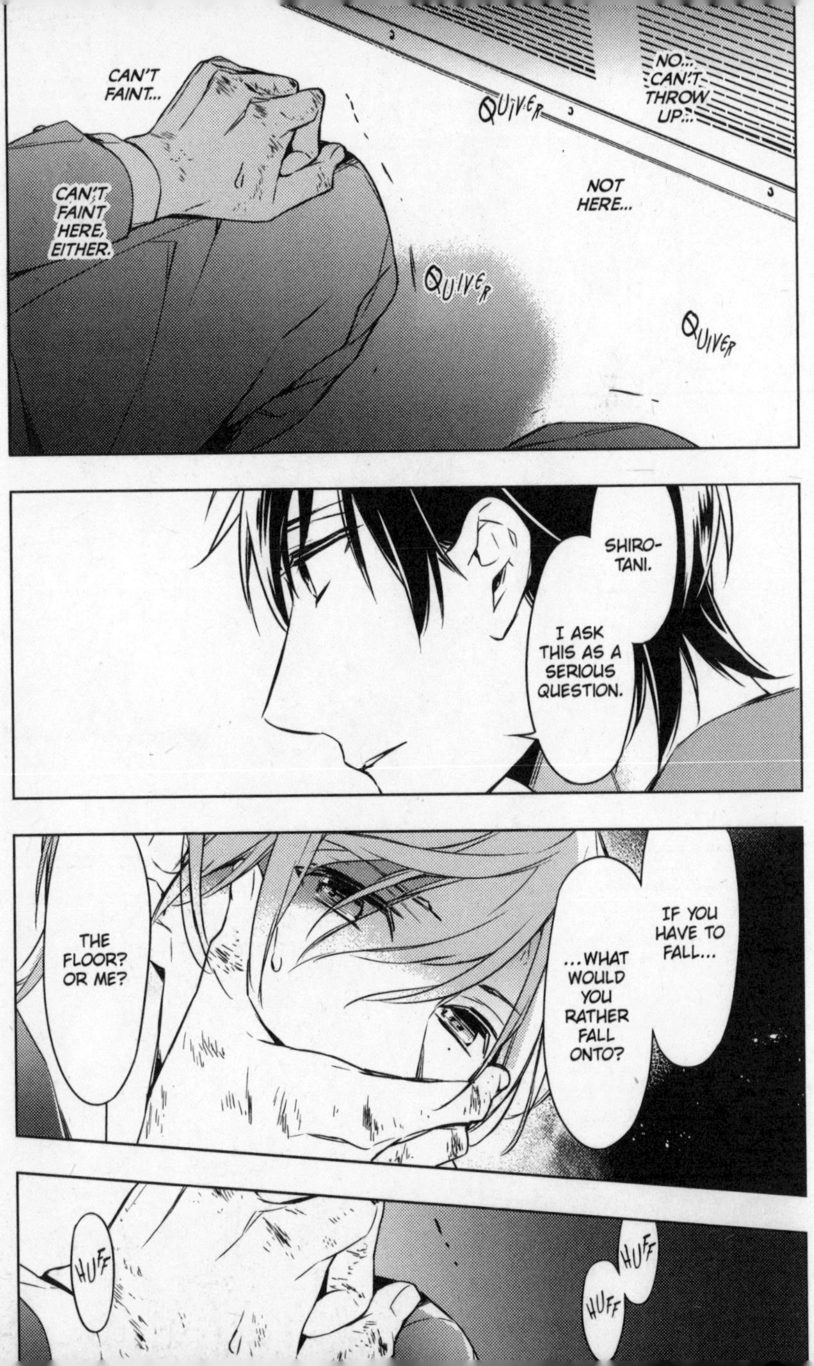
NO... CAN'T THROW UP...
QUIVER
NOT HERE...
QUIVER
QUIVER
CAN'T FAINT...
CAN'T FAINT HERE, EITHER.
SHIRO-TANI.
I ASK THIS AS A SERIOUS QUESTION.
IF YOU HAVE TO FALL...
...WHAT WOULD YOU RATHER FALL ONTO?
THE FLOOR? OR ME?
HUFF
HUFF
HUFF

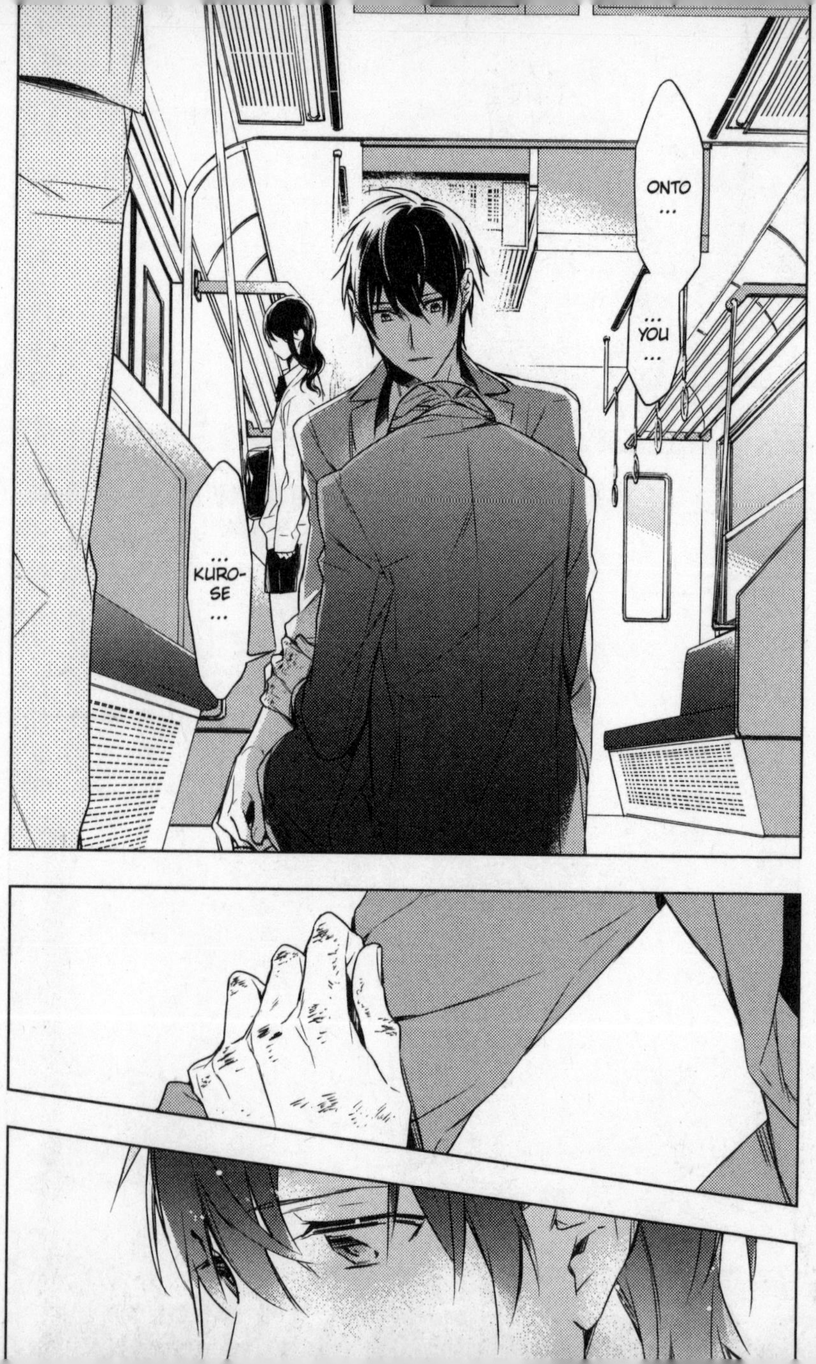
ONTO ...
... YOU ...
... KURO-SE ...

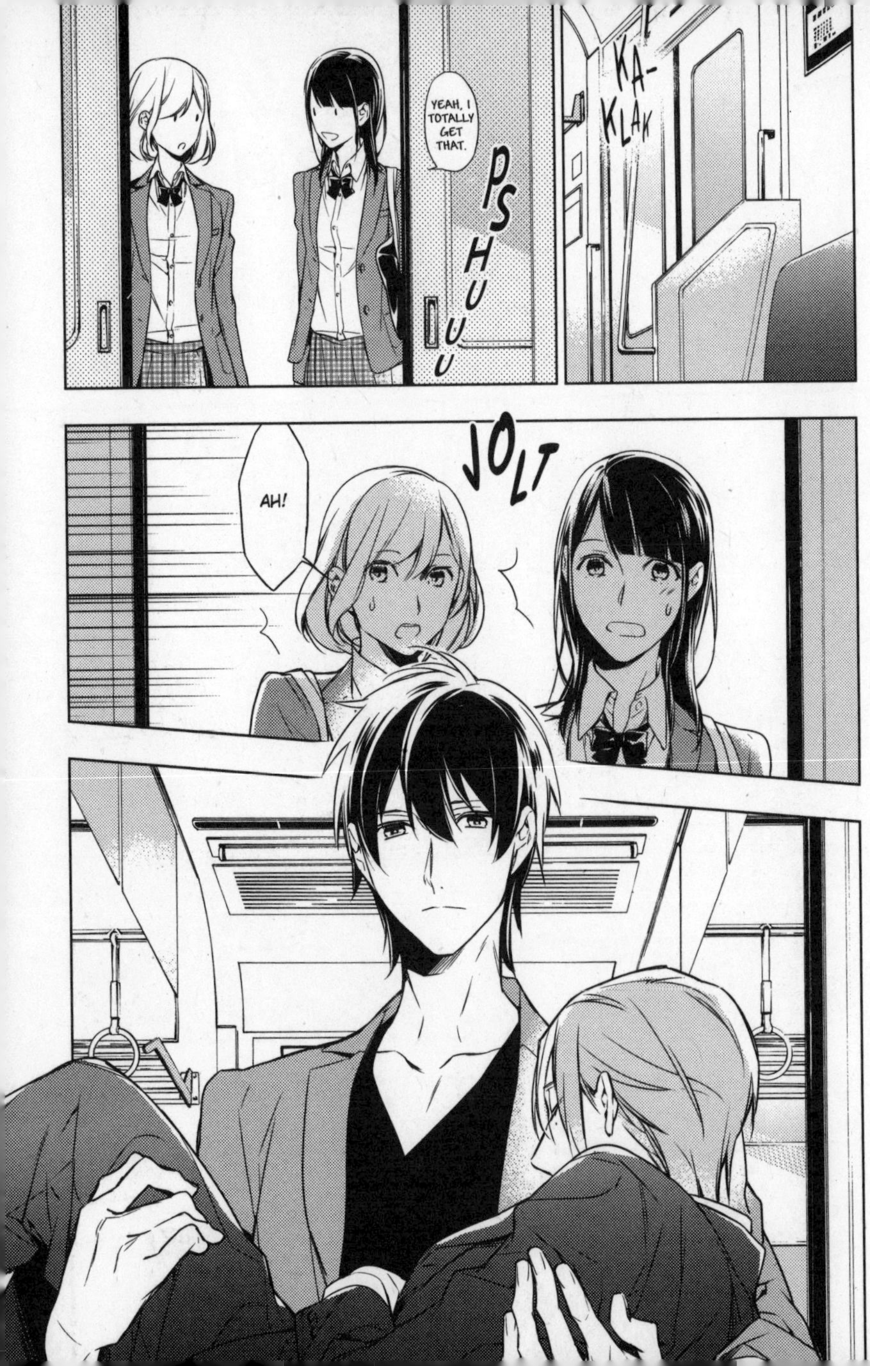
KA-KLAK
YEAH, I TOTALLY GET THAT.
PSHUUUU
JOLT
AH!

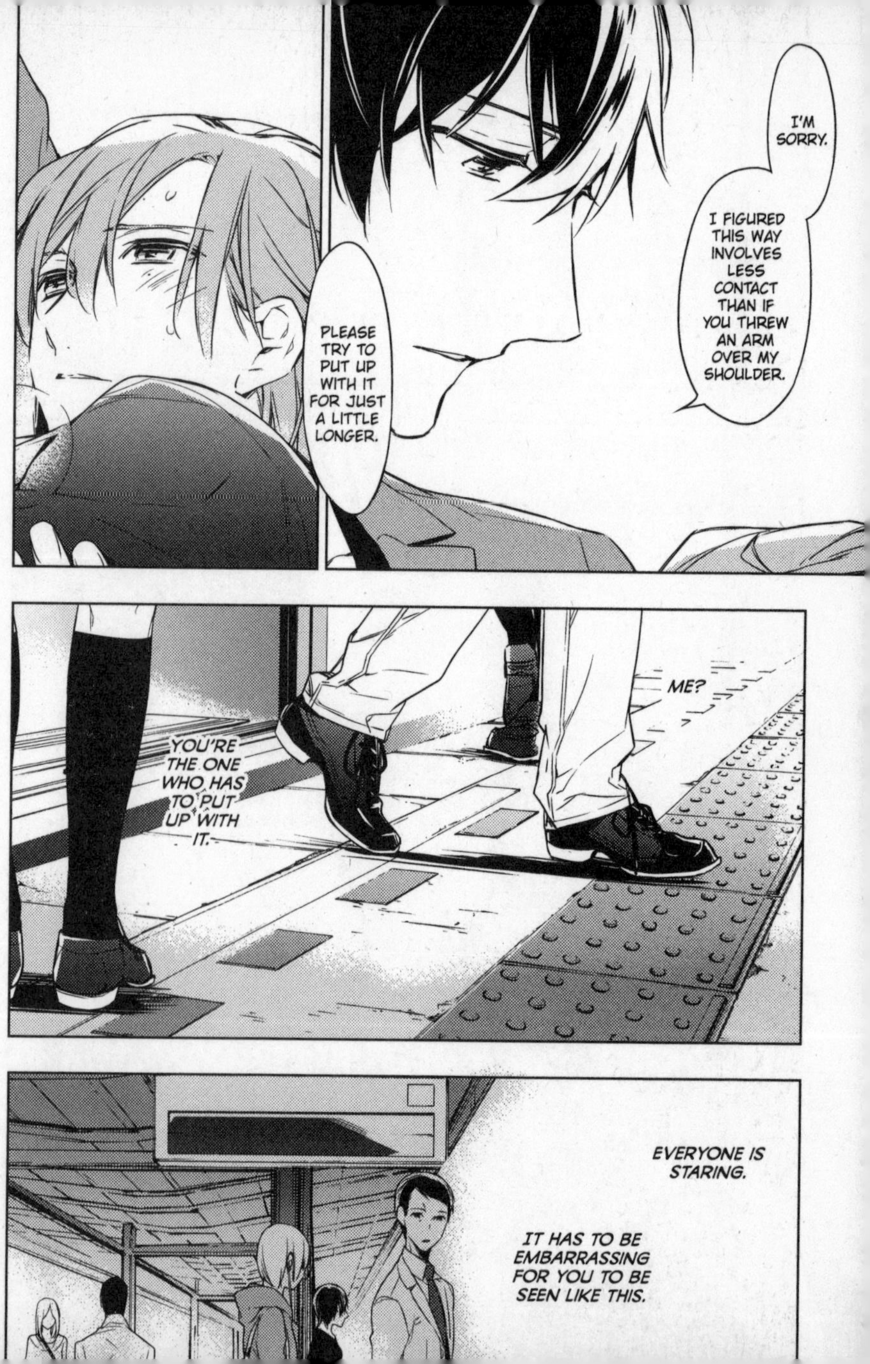
I'M SORRY.
I FIGURED THIS WAY INVOLVES LESS CONTACT THAN IF YOU THREW AN ARM OVER MY SHOULDER.
PLEASE TRY TO PUT UP WITH IT FOR JUST A LITTLE LONGER.
ME?
YOU'RE THE ONE WHO HAS TO PUT UP WITH IT.
EVERYONE IS STARING.
IT HAS TO BE EMBARRASSING FOR YOU TO BE SEEN LIKE THIS.

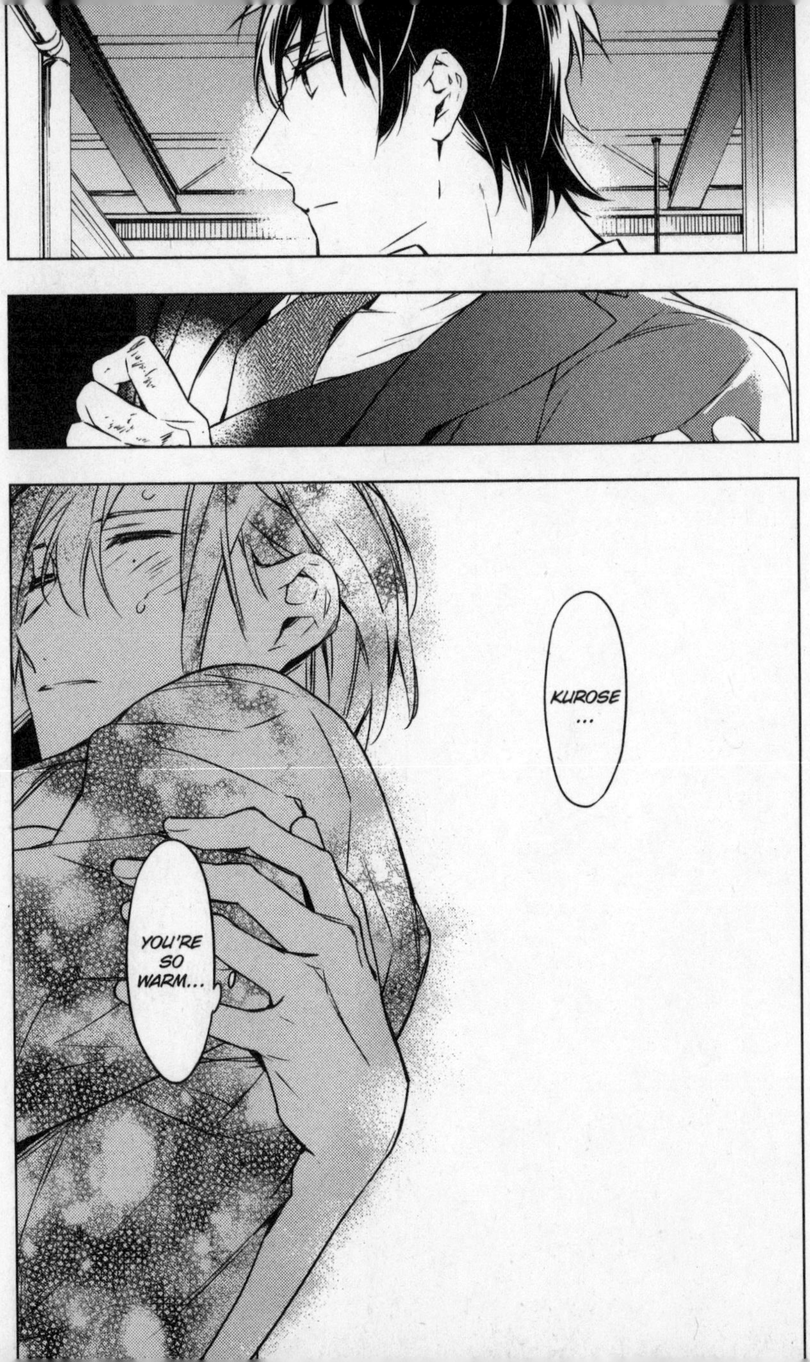
KUROSE ...
YOU'RE SO WARM...

ten count by rihito takarai

TEN COUNT 05

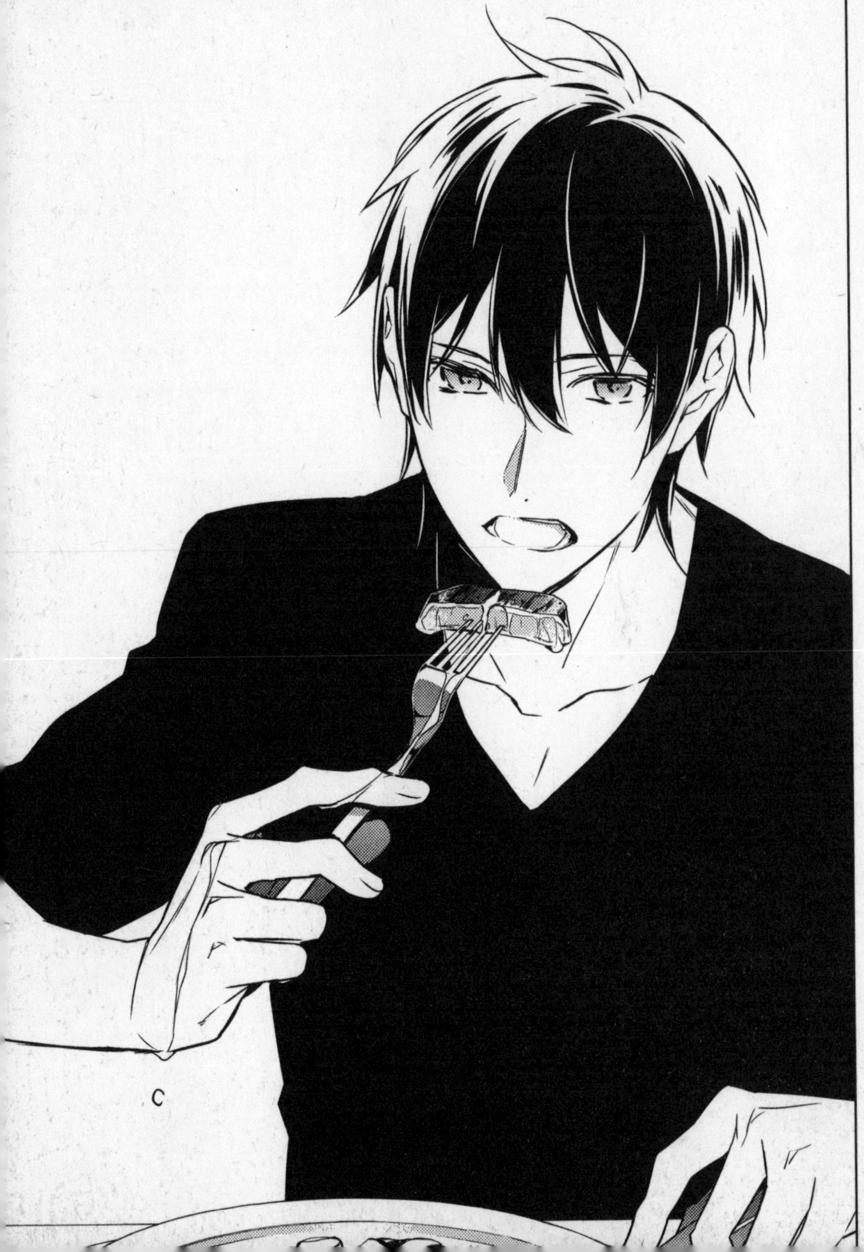

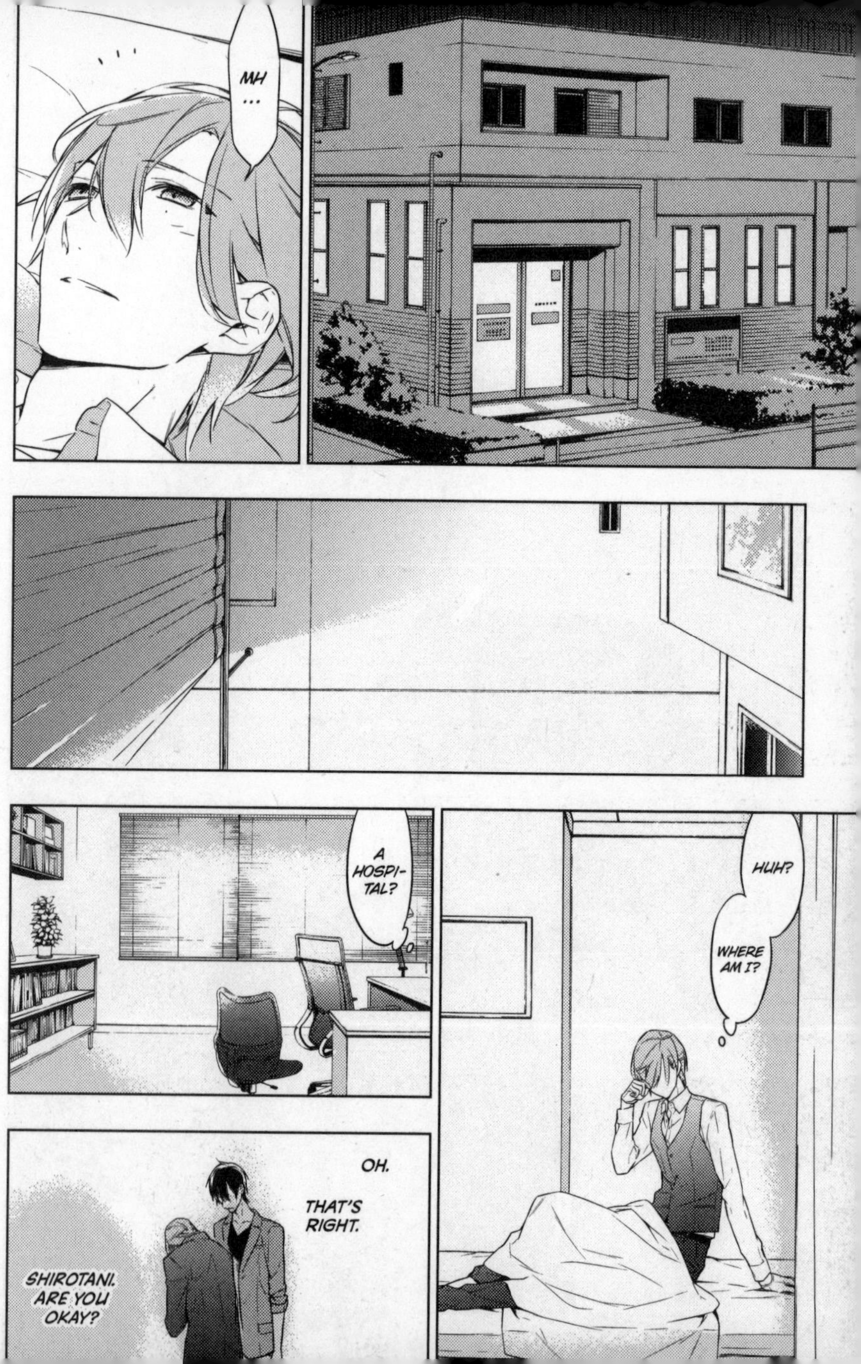
MH ...
HUH?
WHERE AM I?
A HOSPI-TAL?
OH.
THAT'S RIGHT.
SHIROTANI. ARE YOU OKAY?

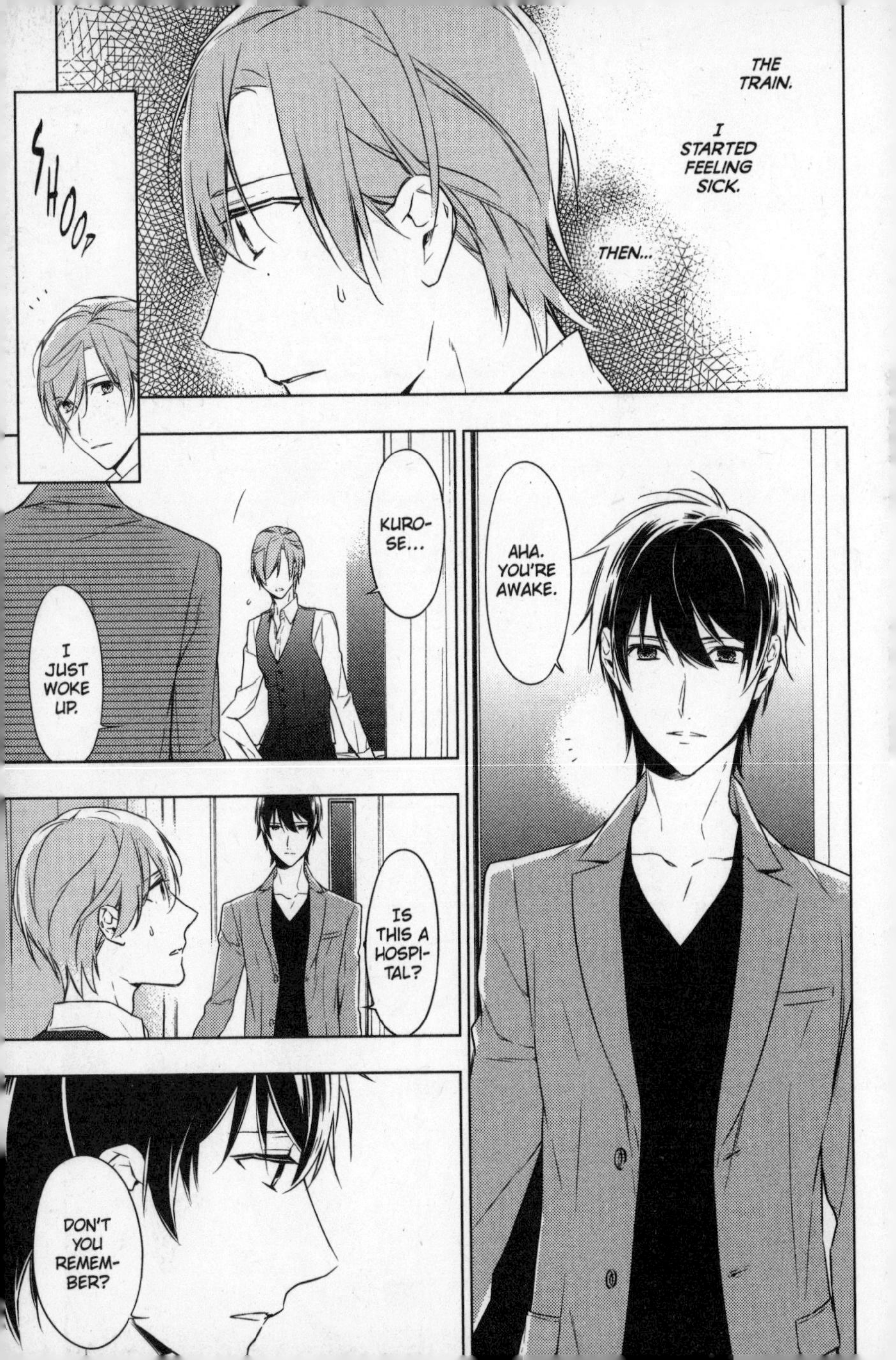
THE TRAIN.
I STARTED FEELING SICK.
THEN...
SHOOP
AHA. YOU'RE AWAKE.
KURO-SE...
I JUST WOKE UP.
IS THIS A HOSPI-TAL?
DON'T YOU REMEM-BER?

THIS IS THE CLINIC WHERE I WORK.

I TOLD THE DIRECTOR WHAT HAPPENED AND ASKED TO BORROW AN EMPTY ROOM.

himada Ps Cent

● Practice
Psychiatry

HOURS	Mo	Tu
10:00~12:00	○	○
15:00~20:00	○	

IT WAS THE CLOSEST PLACE TO THE STATION WHERE WE GOT OFF.

...

I ASKED YOU IF YOU PREFERRED THAT I CALL AN AMBULANCE, BUT YOU KEPT INSISTING YOU WERE OKAY.

I COULDN'T ALLOW YOU TO GO HOME BY YOURSELF IN THAT STATE, SO I HAILED A TAXI AND BROUGHT US HERE.

I'M SORRY.

I'M...

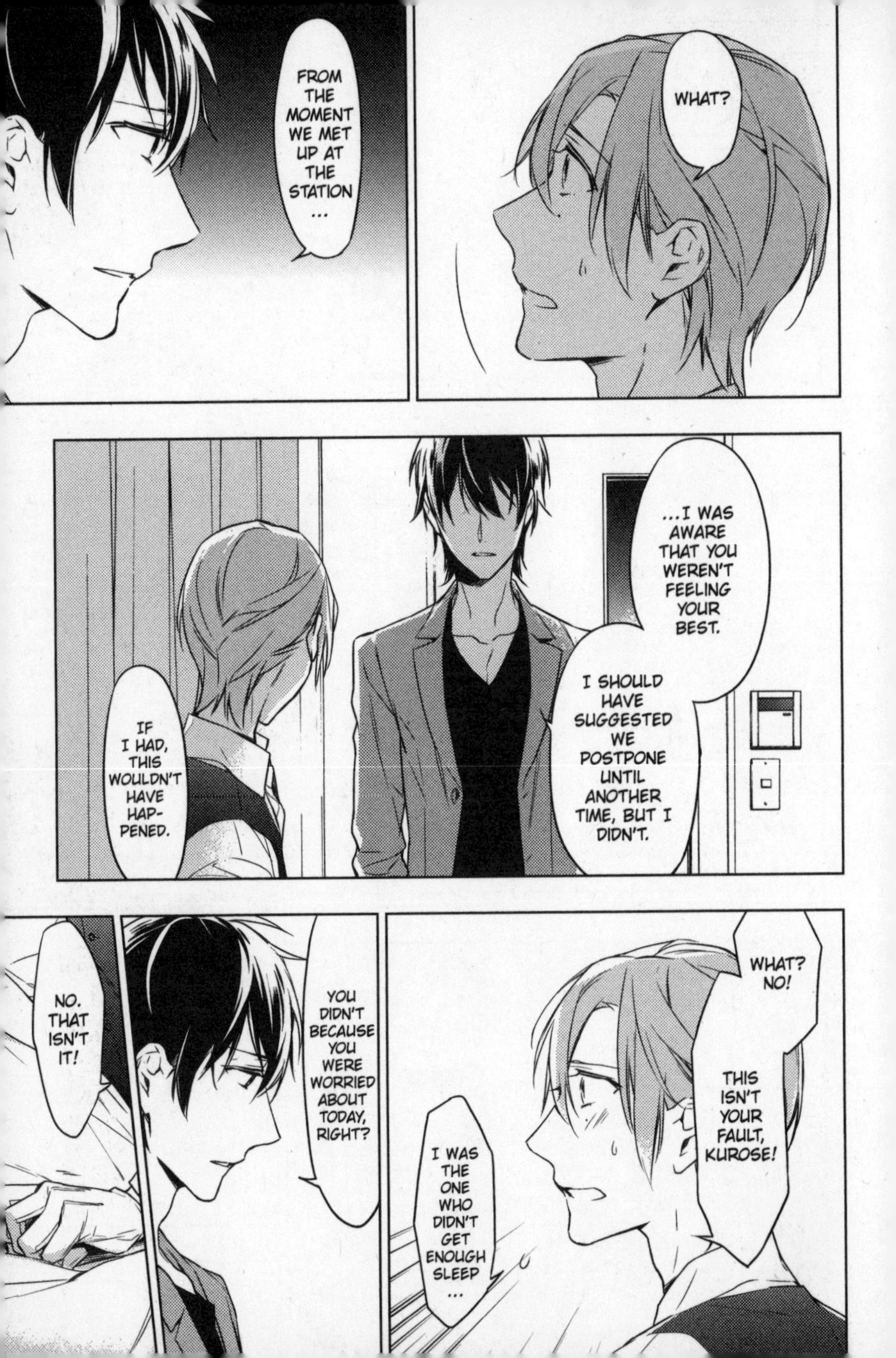
WHAT?
FROM THE MOMENT WE MET UP AT THE STATION ...
...I WAS AWARE THAT YOU WEREN'T FEELING YOUR BEST.
I SHOULD HAVE SUGGESTED WE POSTPONE UNTIL ANOTHER TIME, BUT I DIDN'T.
IF I HAD, THIS WOULDN'T HAVE HAP-PENED.
WHAT? NO!
THIS ISN'T YOUR FAULT, KUROSE!
I WAS THE ONE WHO DIDN'T GET ENOUGH SLEEP ...
YOU DIDN'T BECAUSE YOU WERE WORRIED ABOUT TODAY, RIGHT?
NO. THAT ISN'T IT!

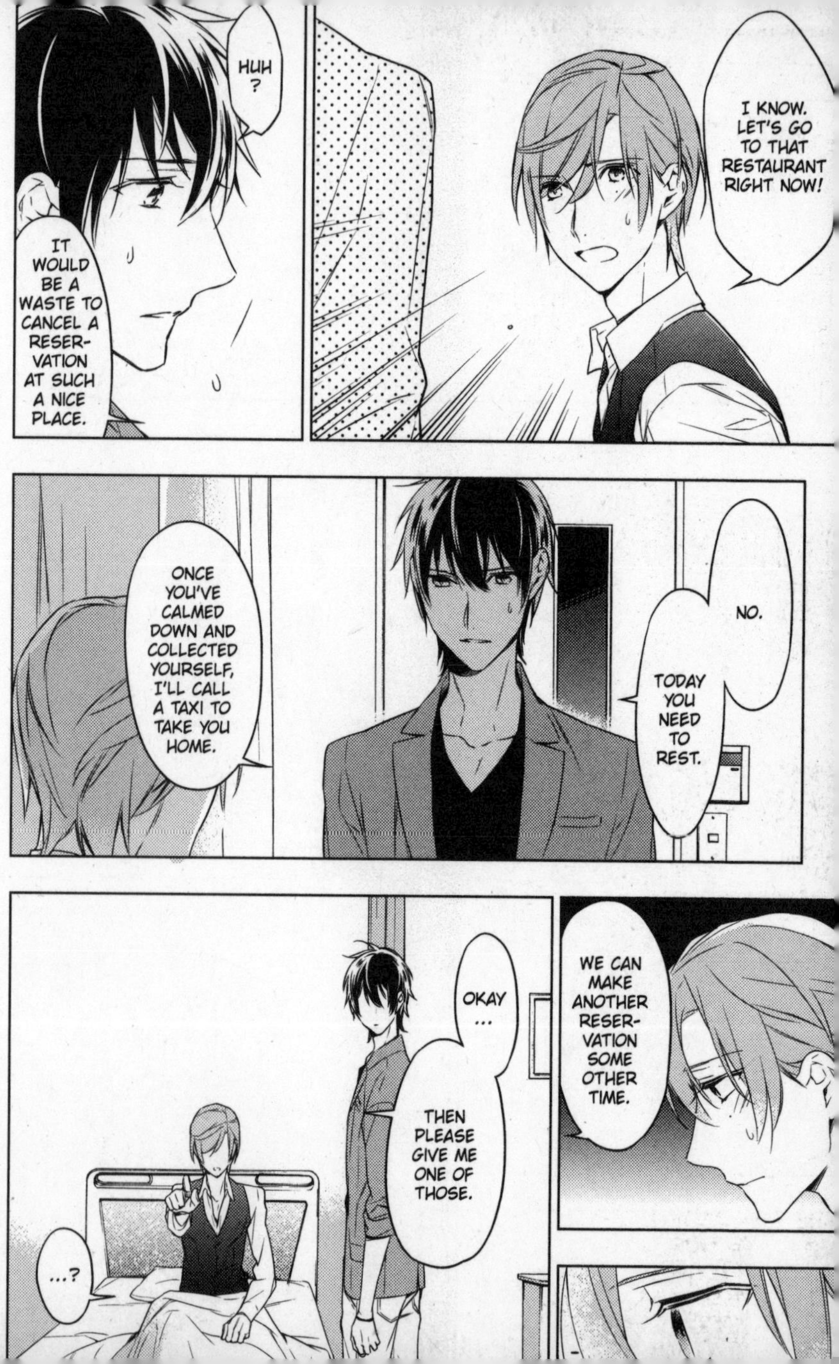
I KNOW. LET'S GO TO THAT RESTAURANT RIGHT NOW!
HUH?
IT WOULD BE A WASTE TO CANCEL A RESERVATION AT SUCH A NICE PLACE.
NO.
TODAY YOU NEED TO REST.
ONCE YOU'VE CALMED DOWN AND COLLECTED YOURSELF, I'LL CALL A TAXI TO TAKE YOU HOME.
WE CAN MAKE ANOTHER RESERVATION SOME OTHER TIME.
OKAY...
THEN PLEASE GIVE ME ONE OF THOSE.
...?

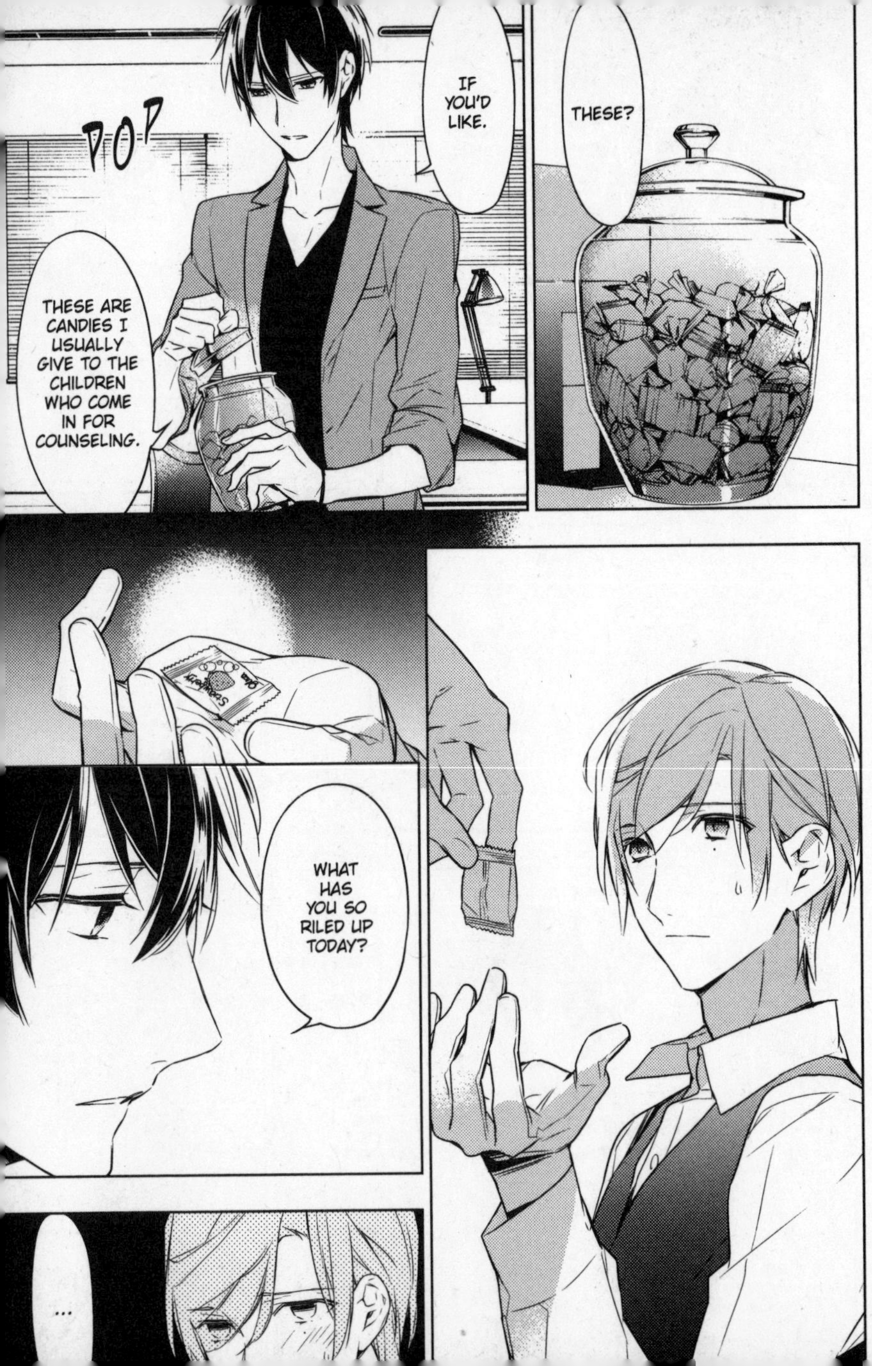
THESE?
IF YOU'D LIKE.
POP
THESE ARE CANDIES I USUALLY GIVE TO THE CHILDREN WHO COME IN FOR COUNSELING.
WHAT HAS YOU SO RILED UP TODAY?
...

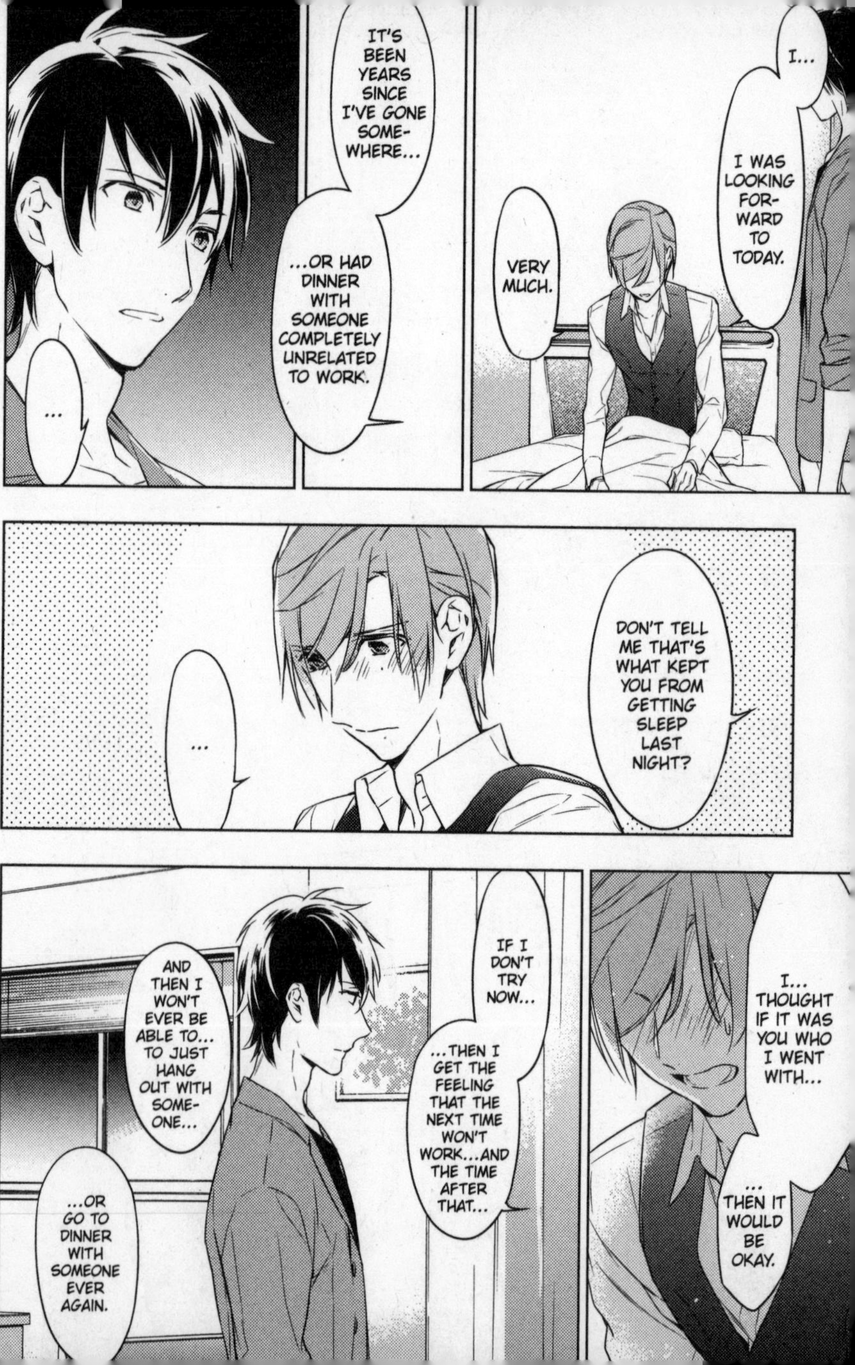
I...
I WAS LOOKING FOR-WARD TO TODAY.
VERY MUCH.
IT'S BEEN YEARS SINCE I'VE GONE SOME-WHERE...
...OR HAD DINNER WITH SOMEONE COMPLETELY UNRELATED TO WORK.
...
DON'T TELL ME THAT'S WHAT KEPT YOU FROM GETTING SLEEP LAST NIGHT?
...
I... THOUGHT IF IT WAS YOU WHO I WENT WITH...
...THEN IT WOULD BE OKAY.
IF I DON'T TRY NOW...
...THEN I GET THE FEELING THAT THE NEXT TIME WON'T WORK...AND THE TIME AFTER THAT...
AND THEN I WON'T EVER BE ABLE TO... TO JUST HANG OUT WITH SOME-ONE...
...OR GO TO DINNER WITH SOMEONE EVER AGAIN.

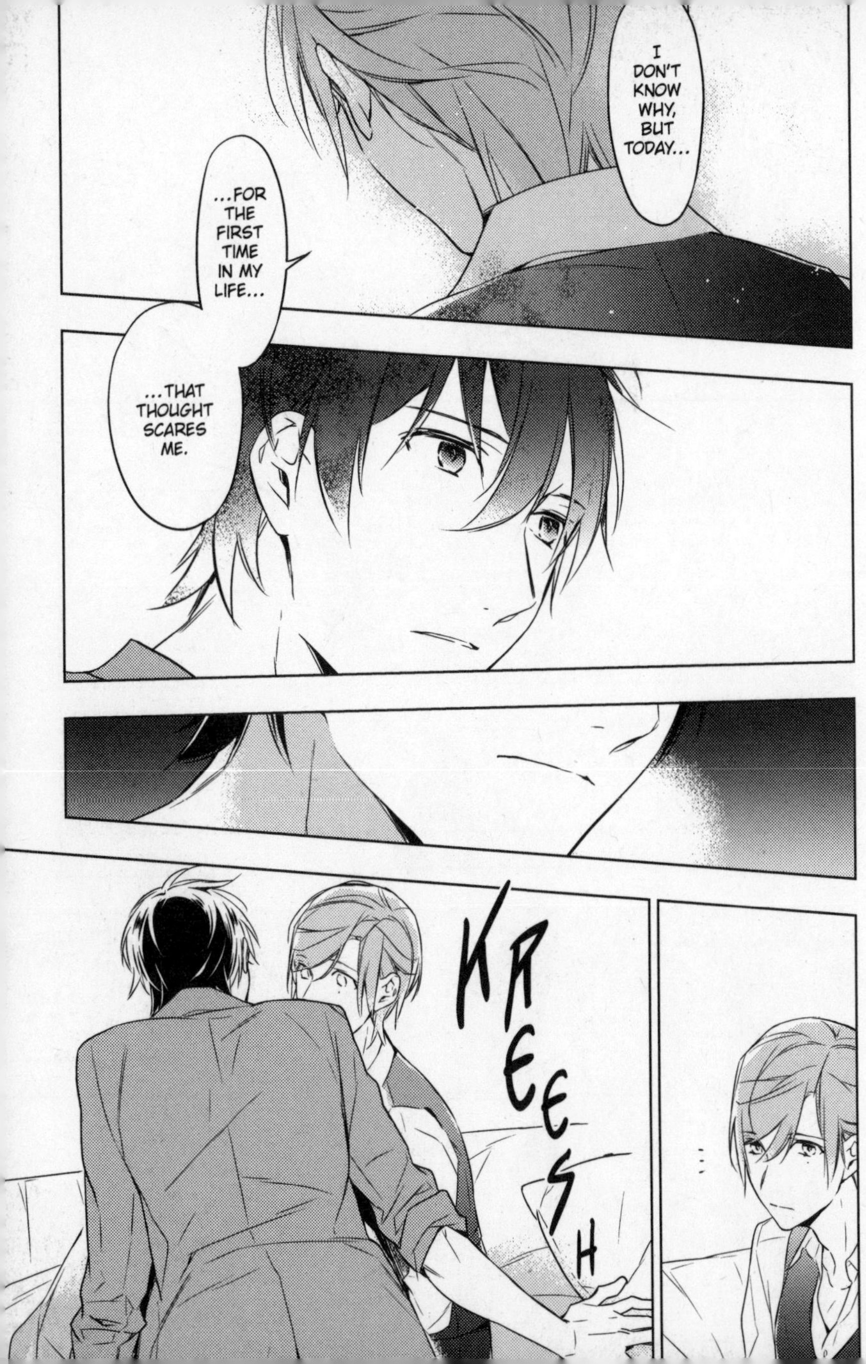
I DON'T KNOW WHY, BUT TODAY...
...FOR THE FIRST TIME IN MY LIFE...
...THAT THOUGHT SCARES ME.
...
KREESH

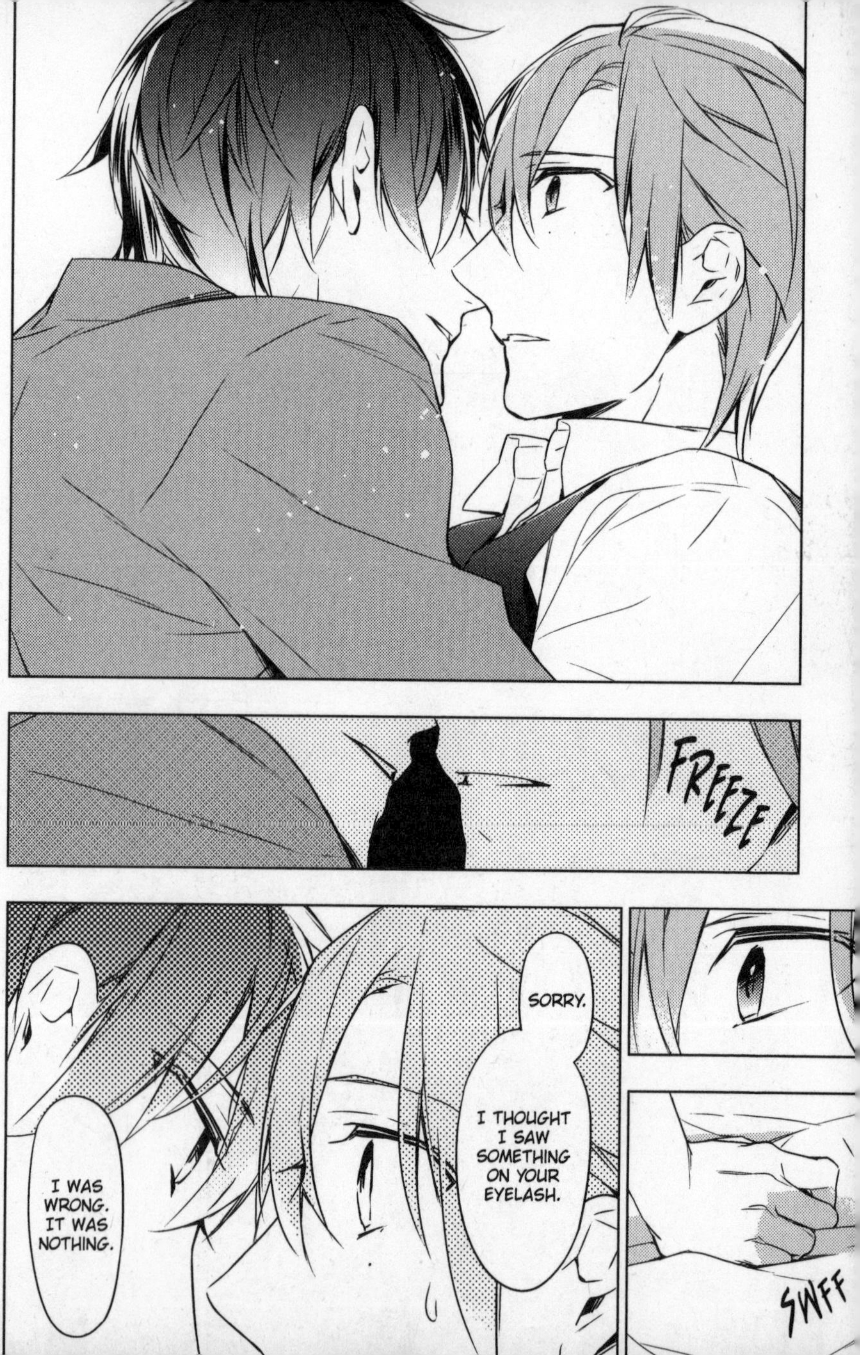
FREEZE
SWFF
SORRY.
I THOUGHT I SAW SOMETHING ON YOUR EYELASH.
I WAS WRONG. IT WAS NOTHING.

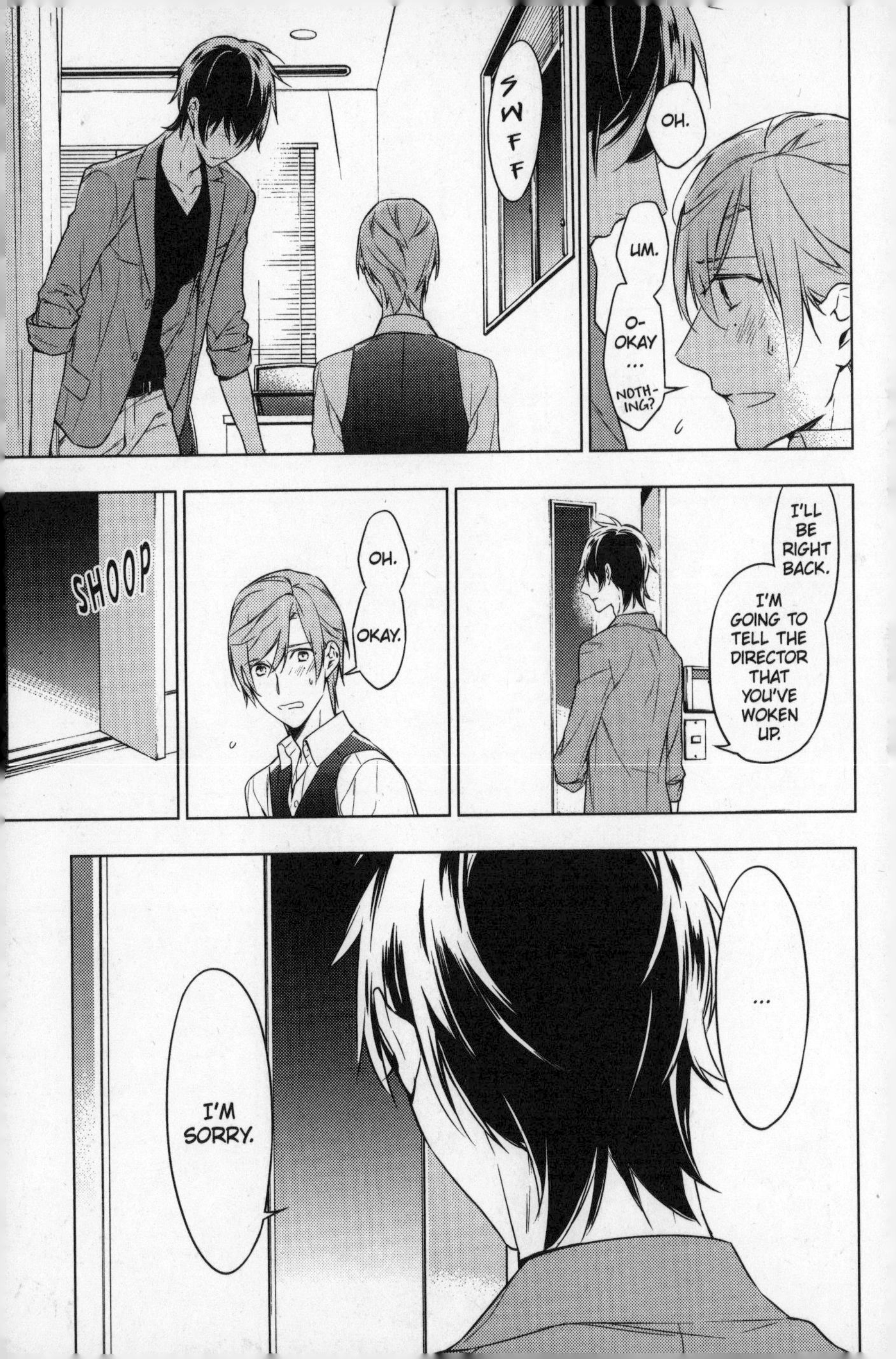
OH.
UM.
O-OKAY... NOTHING?
SWFF
I'LL BE RIGHT BACK.
I'M GOING TO TELL THE DIRECTOR THAT YOU'VE WOKEN UP.
OH.
OKAY.
SHOOP
...
I'M SORRY.

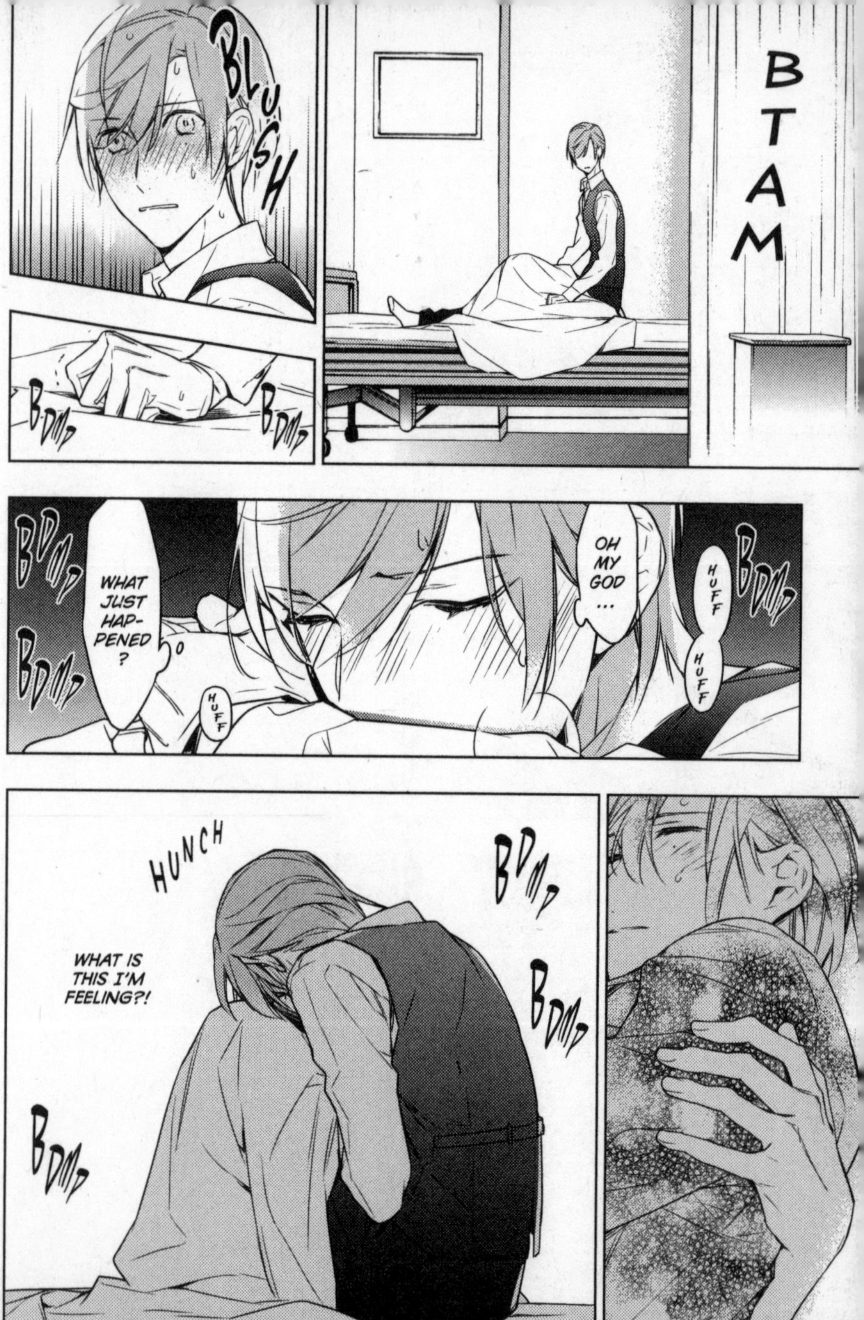
BTAM
BLUSH
BDMP
BDMP
BDMP
HUFF
HUFF
OH MY GOD ...
HUFF
WHAT JUST HAP-PENED?
BDMP
BDMP
BDMP
BDMP
HUNCH
WHAT IS THIS I'M FEELING?!
BDMP

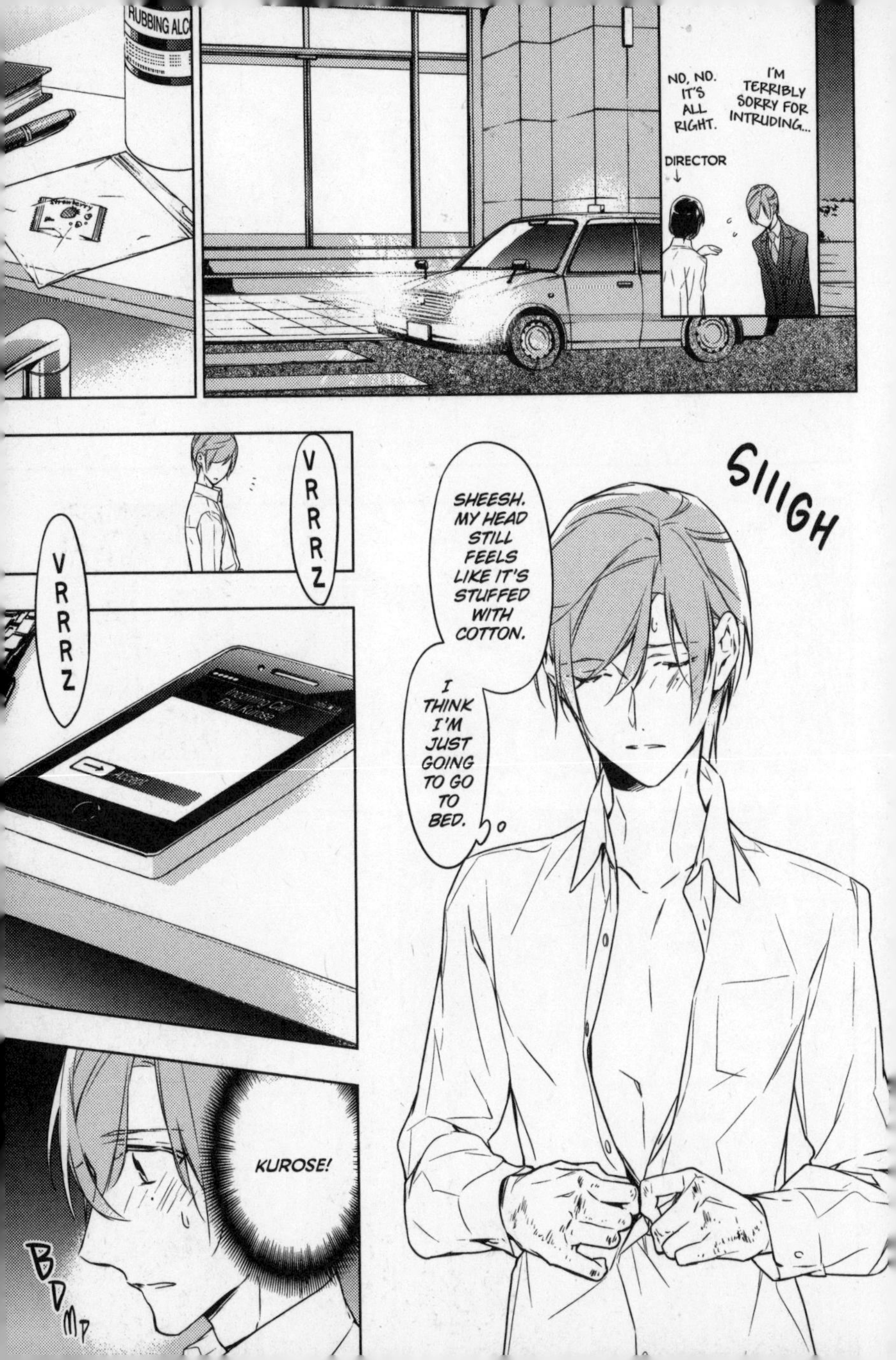
I'M TERRIBLY SORRY FOR INTRUDING...
NO, NO. IT'S ALL RIGHT.
DIRECTOR
RUBBING ALC
SIIIGH
SHEESH. MY HEAD STILL FEELS LIKE IT'S STUFFED WITH COTTON.
I THINK I'M JUST GOING TO GO TO BED.
VRRRZ
VRRRZ
Incoming Call
Riku Kurose
Accept
KUROSE!
BDMP

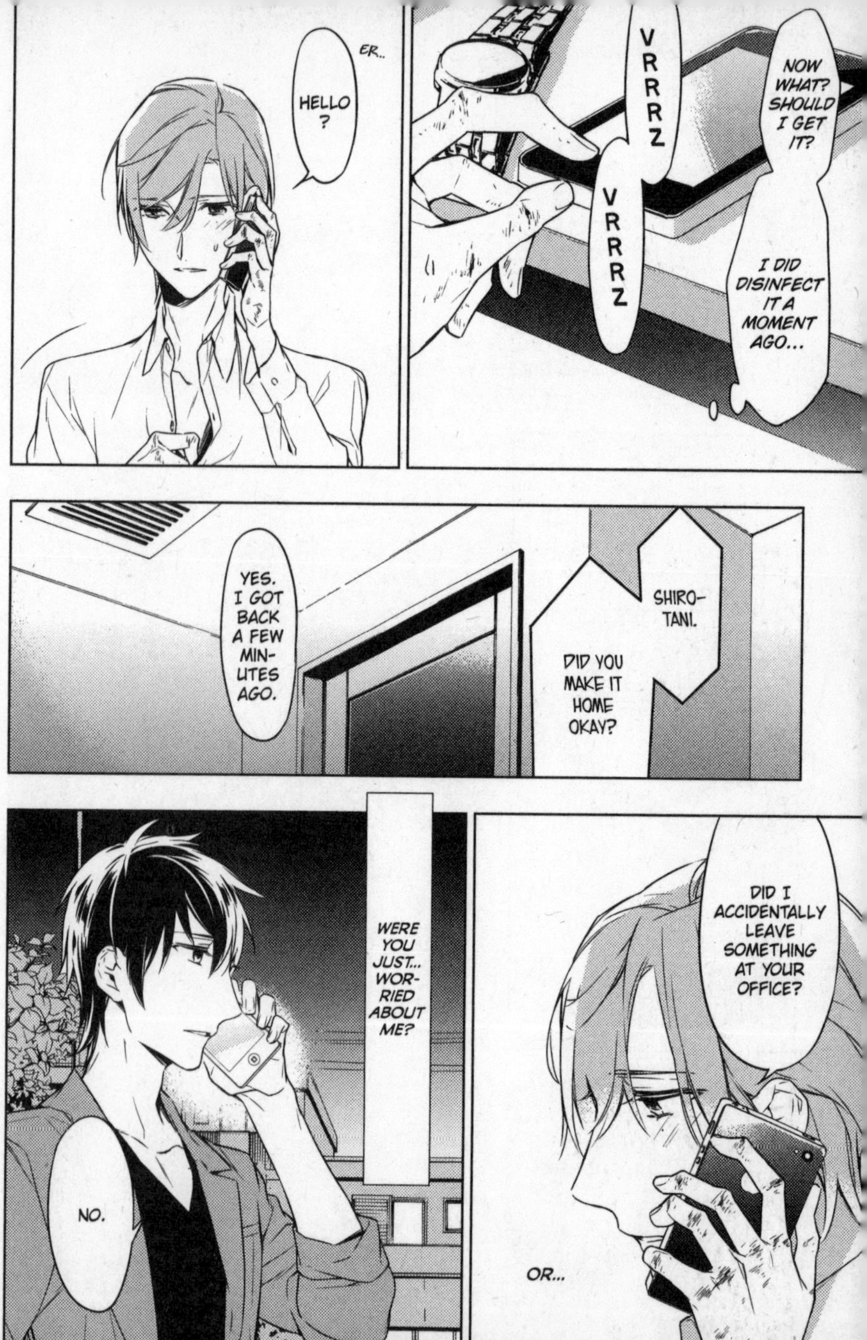
NOW WHAT? SHOULD I GET IT?
VRRRZ
VRRRZ
I DID DISINFECT IT A MOMENT AGO...
ER..
HELLO?
SHIRO-TANI.
DID YOU MAKE IT HOME OKAY?
YES. I GOT BACK A FEW MIN-UTES AGO.
DID I ACCIDENTALLY LEAVE SOMETHING AT YOUR OFFICE?
OR...
WERE YOU JUST... WOR-RIED ABOUT ME?
NO.

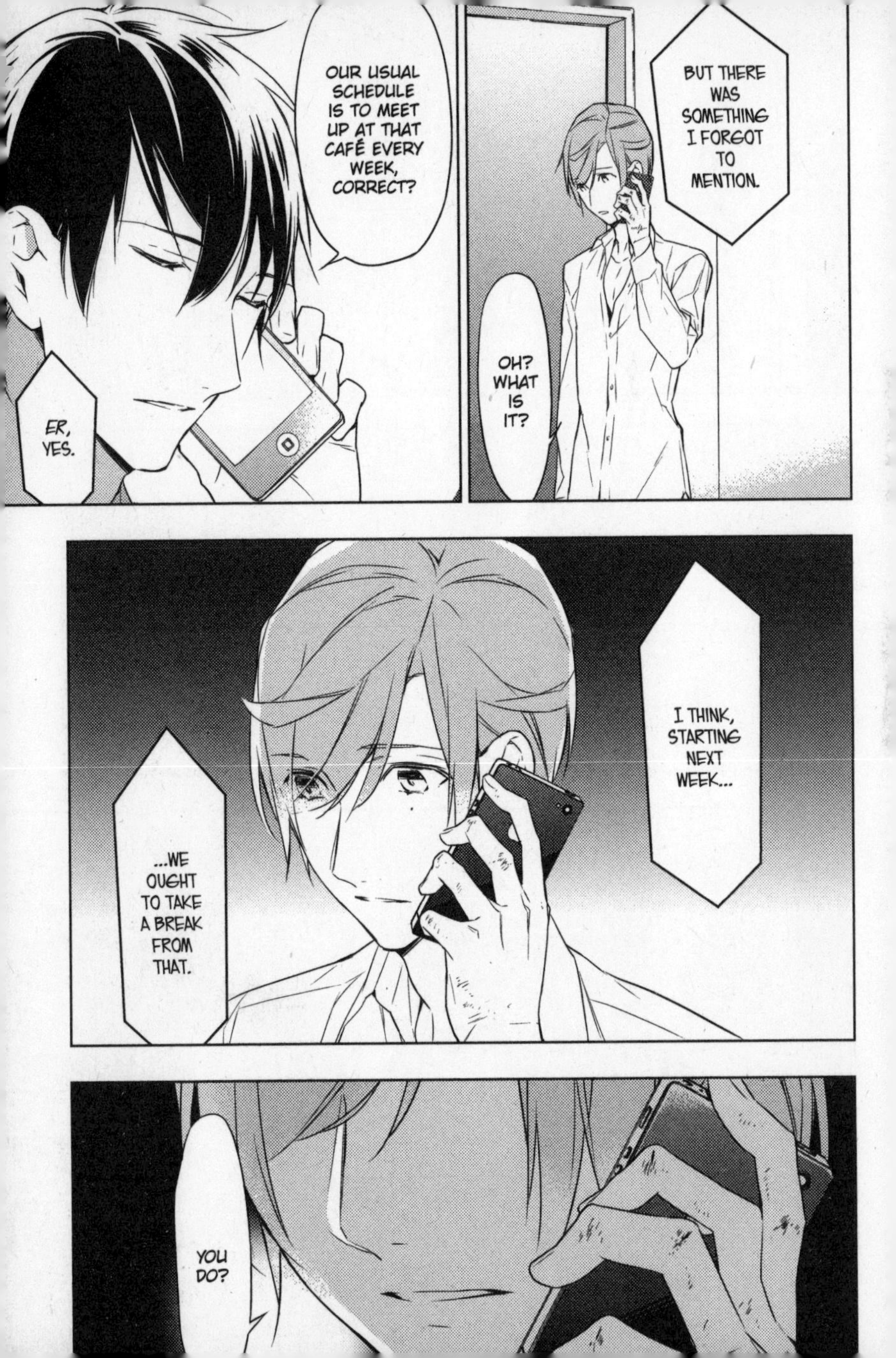
BUT THERE WAS SOMETHING I FORGOT TO MENTION.
OH? WHAT IS IT?
OUR USUAL SCHEDULE IS TO MEET UP AT THAT CAFÉ EVERY WEEK, CORRECT?
ER, YES.
I THINK, STARTING NEXT WEEK...
...WE OUGHT TO TAKE A BREAK FROM THAT.
YOU DO?

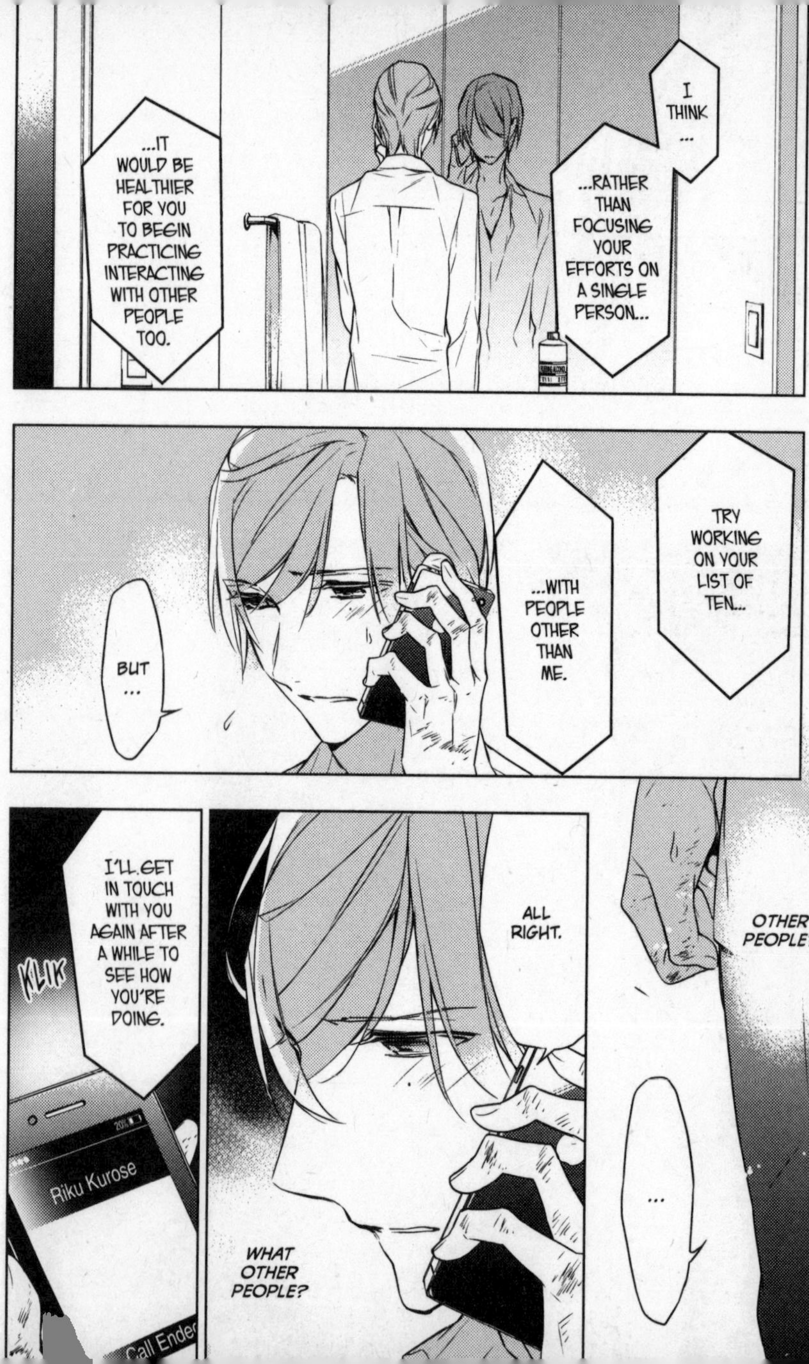
I THINK ...
...RATHER THAN FOCUSING YOUR EFFORTS ON A SINGLE PERSON...
...IT WOULD BE HEALTHIER FOR YOU TO BEGIN PRACTICING INTERACTING WITH OTHER PEOPLE TOO.
TRY WORKING ON YOUR LIST OF TEN...
...WITH PEOPLE OTHER THAN ME.
BUT ...
OTHER PEOPLE?
...
ALL RIGHT.
WHAT OTHER PEOPLE?
I'LL GET IN TOUCH WITH YOU AGAIN AFTER A WHILE TO SEE HOW YOU'RE DOING.
KLIK
Riku Kurose
Call Ende

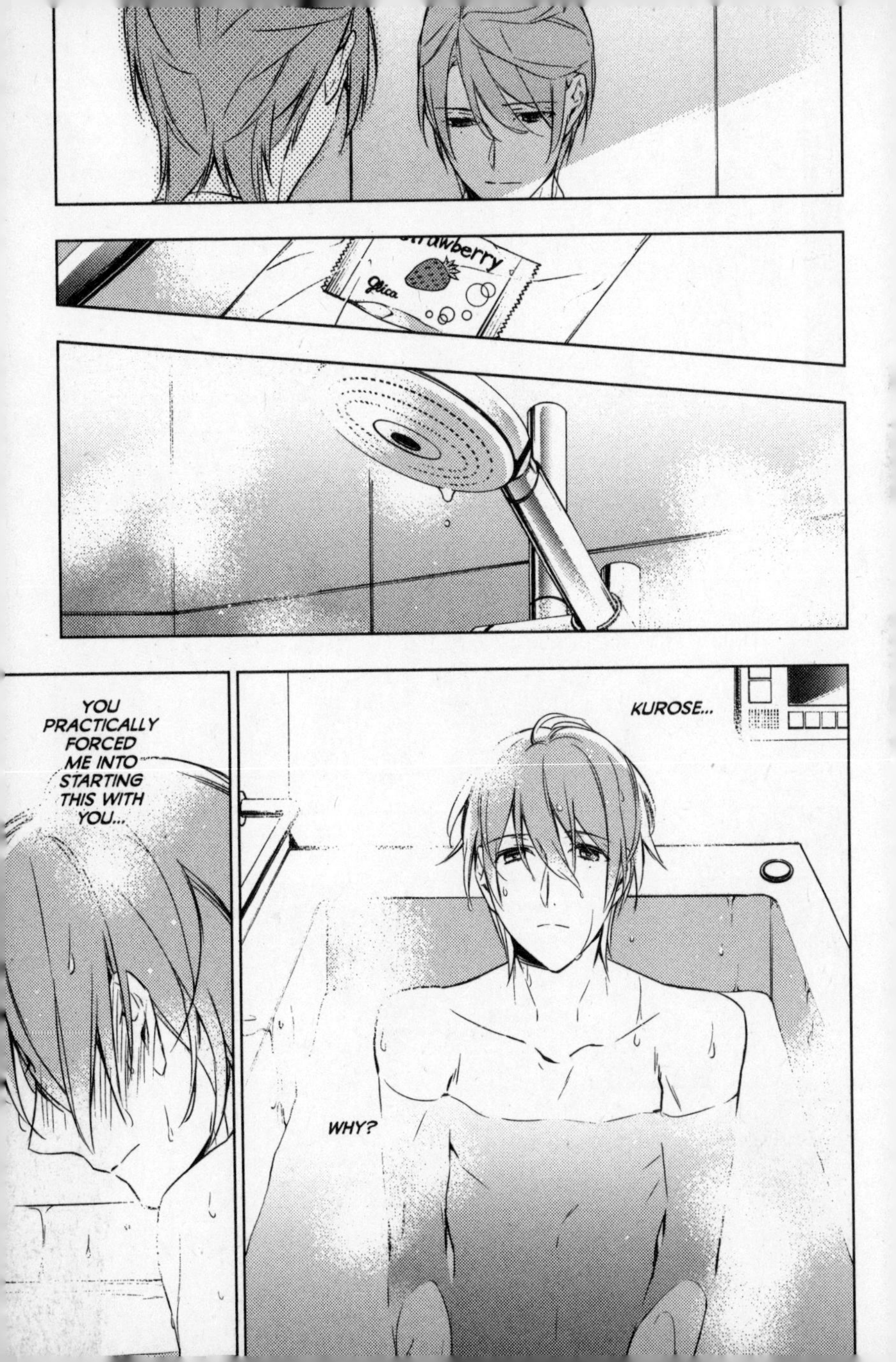
KUROSE...
WHY?
YOU PRACTICALLY FORCED ME INTO STARTING THIS WITH YOU...

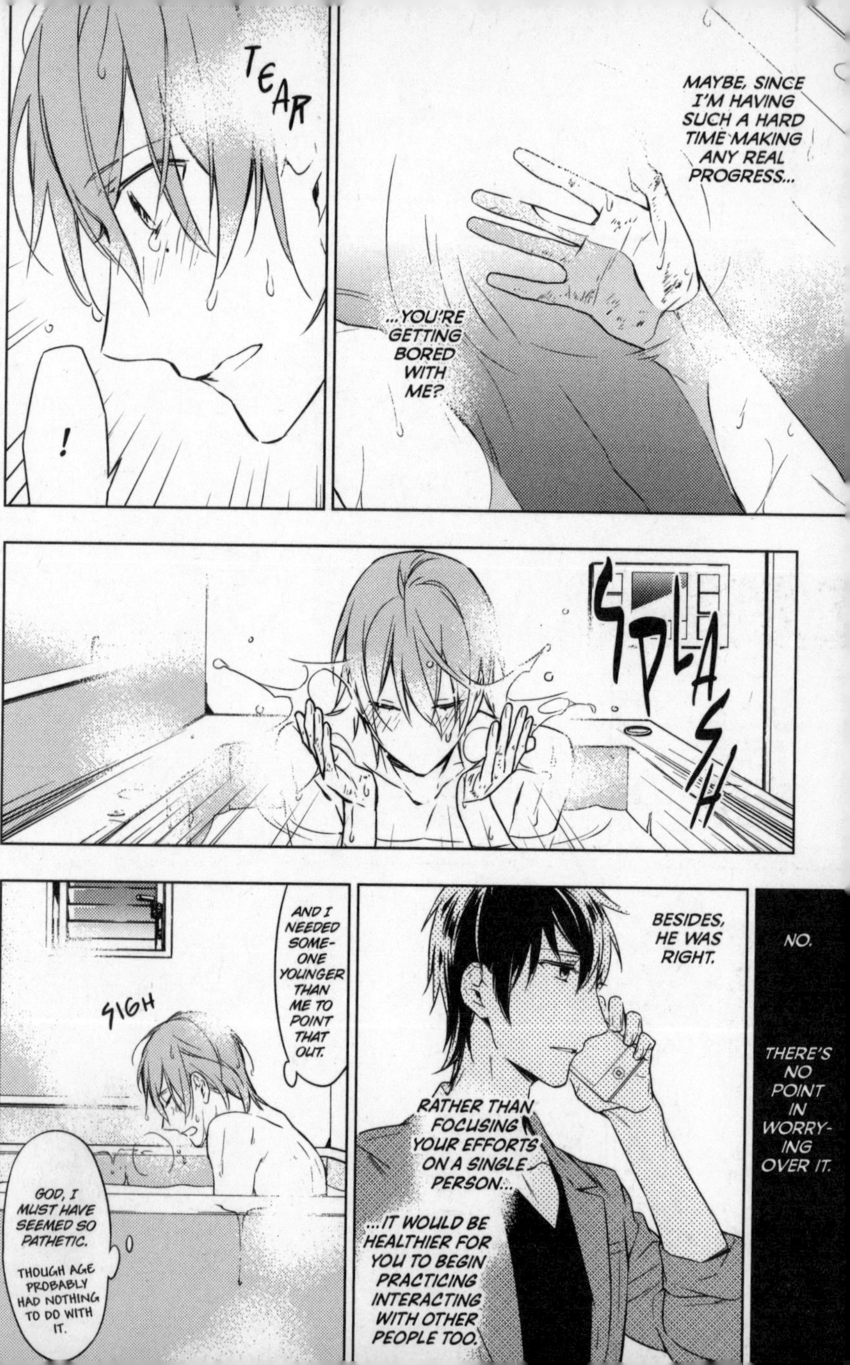
MAYBE, SINCE I'M HAVING SUCH A HARD TIME MAKING ANY REAL PROGRESS...
...YOU'RE GETTING BORED WITH ME?
TEAR
!
SPLASH
NO.
THERE'S NO POINT IN WORRYING OVER IT.
BESIDES, HE WAS RIGHT.
RATHER THAN FOCUSING YOUR EFFORTS ON A SINGLE PERSON...
...IT WOULD BE HEALTHIER FOR YOU TO BEGIN PRACTICING INTERACTING WITH OTHER PEOPLE TOO.
AND I NEEDED SOME-ONE YOUNGER THAN ME TO POINT THAT OUT.
SIGH
GOD, I MUST HAVE SEEMED SO PATHETIC.
THOUGH AGE PROBABLY HAD NOTHING TO DO WITH IT.

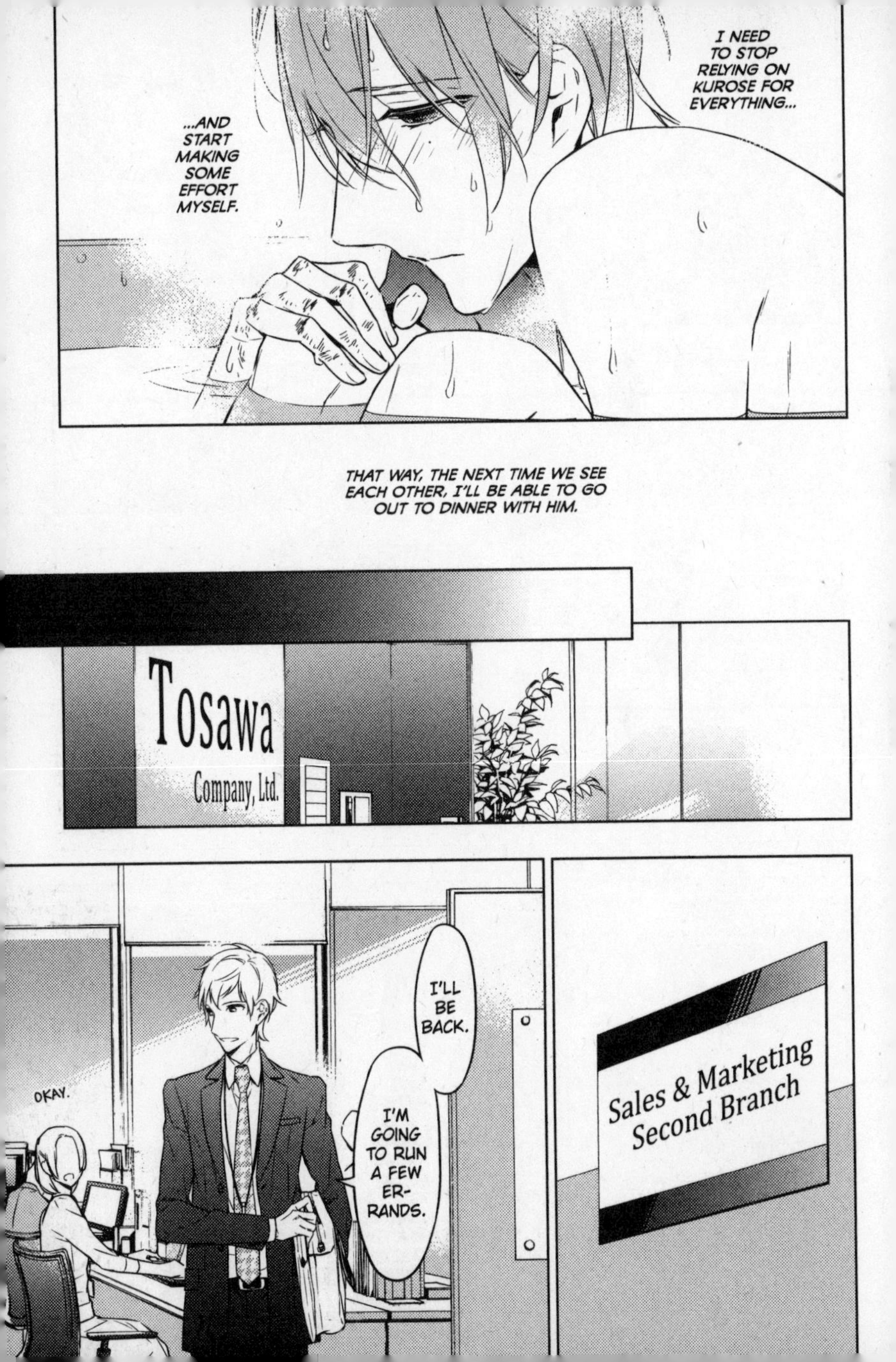
I NEED TO STOP RELYING ON KUROSE FOR EVERYTHING...
...AND START MAKING SOME EFFORT MYSELF.
THAT WAY, THE NEXT TIME WE SEE EACH OTHER, I'LL BE ABLE TO GO OUT TO DINNER WITH HIM.
Tosawa
Company, Ltd.
Sales & Marketing
Second Branch
I'LL BE BACK.
I'M GOING TO RUN A FEW ER-RANDS.
OKAY.

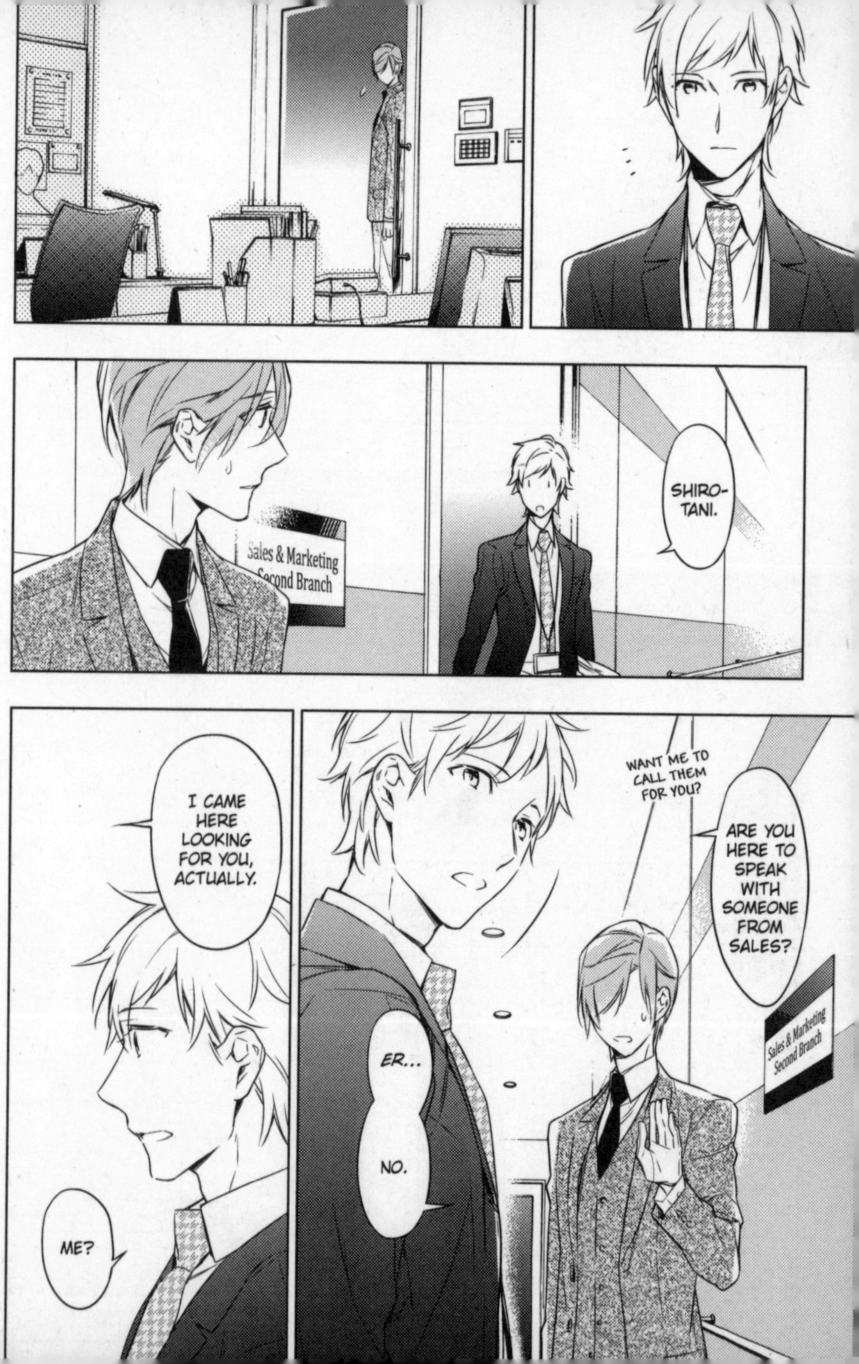
SHIRO-TANI.
Sales & Marketing Second Branch
ARE YOU HERE TO SPEAK WITH SOMEONE FROM SALES?
WANT ME TO CALL THEM FOR YOU?
Sales & Marketing Second Branch
ER...
NO.
I CAME HERE LOOKING FOR YOU, ACTUALLY.
ME?

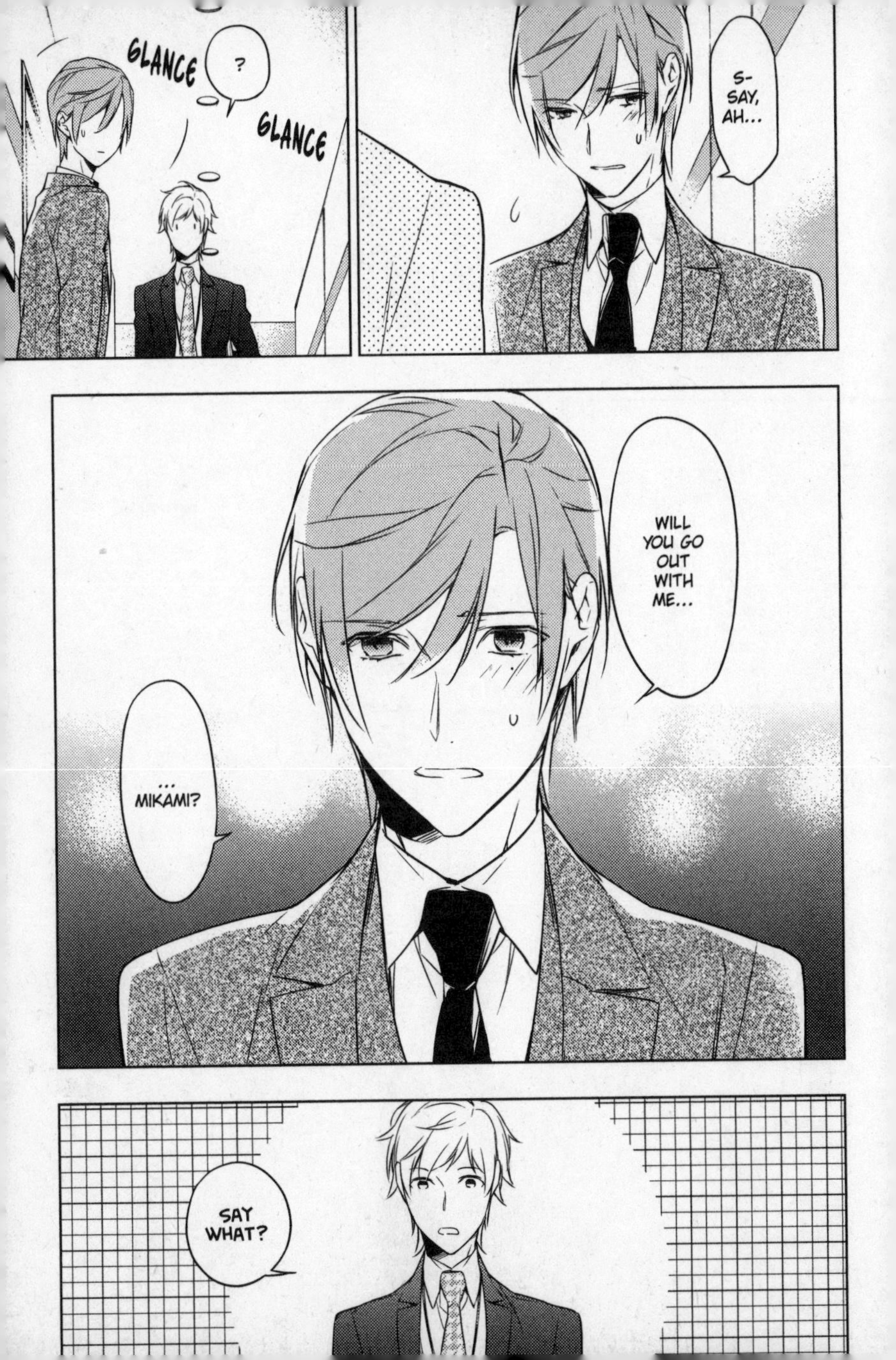
S-SAY, AH...
GLANCE
?
GLANCE
WILL YOU GO OUT WITH ME...
...MIKAMI?
SAY WHAT?

t e n c o u n t b y r i h i t o t a k a r a i

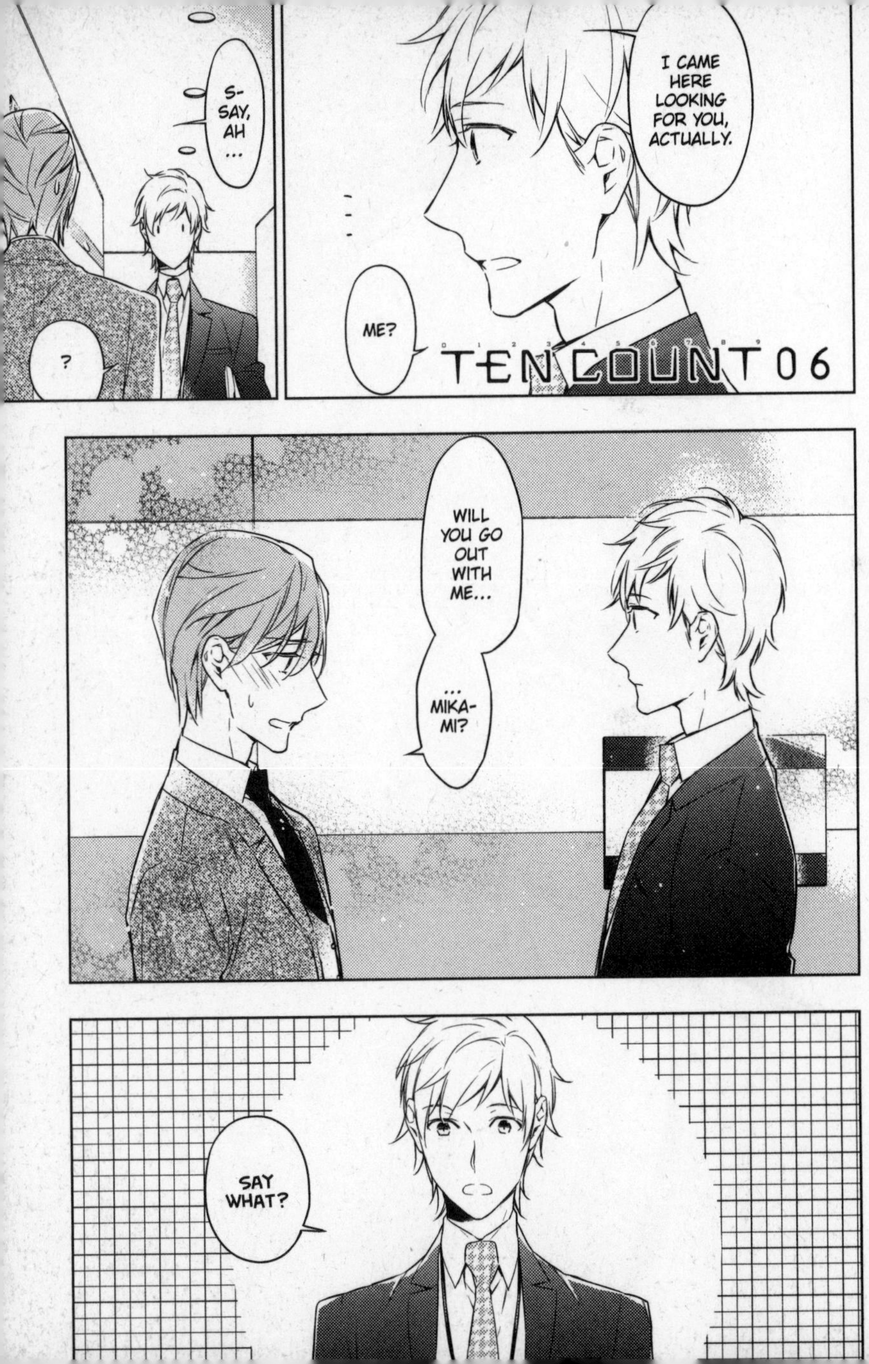
I CAME HERE LOOKING FOR YOU, ACTUALLY.
...
ME?
TEN COUNT 06
S-SAY, AH ...
?
WILL YOU GO OUT WITH ME...
... MIKAMI?
SAY WHAT?

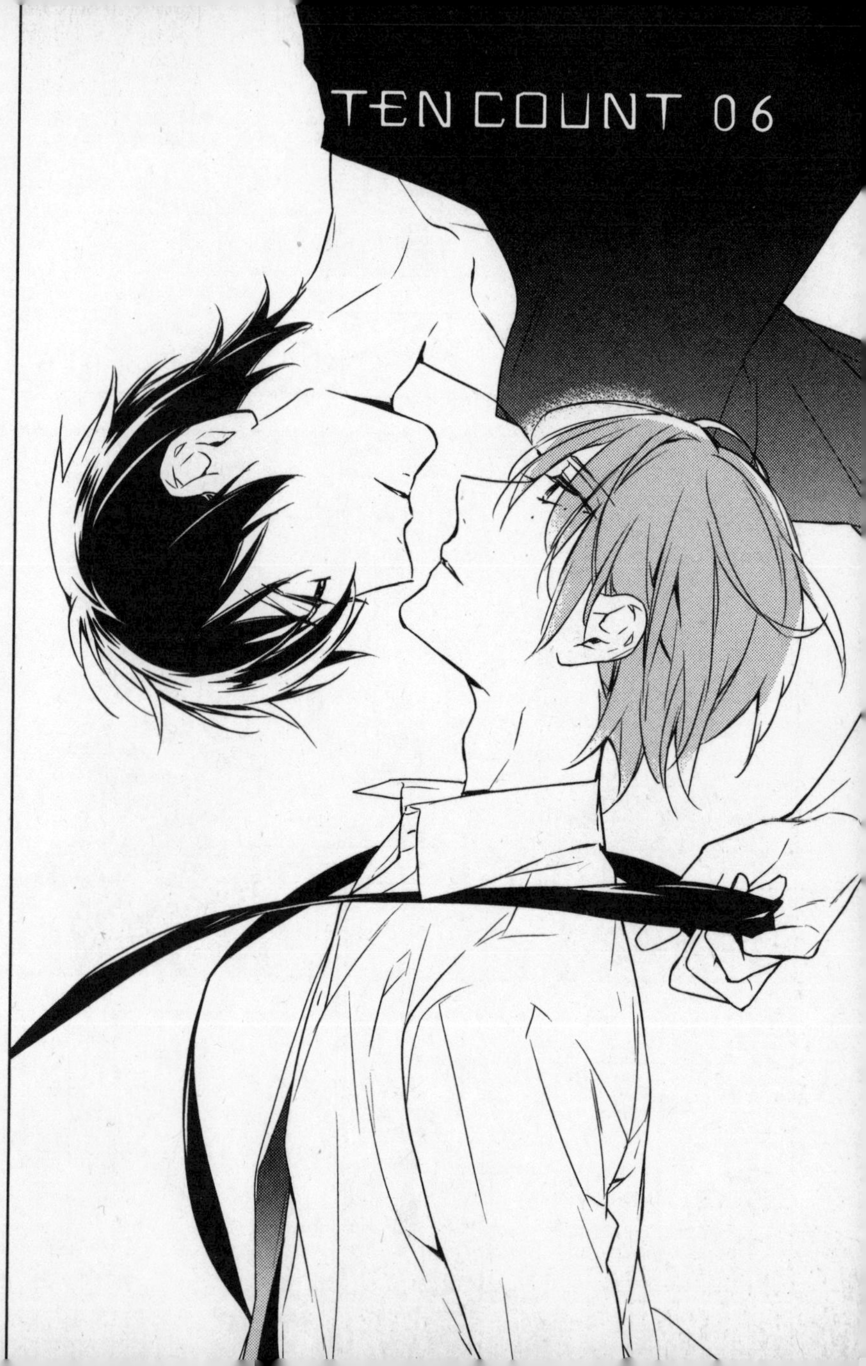
TEN COUNT 06

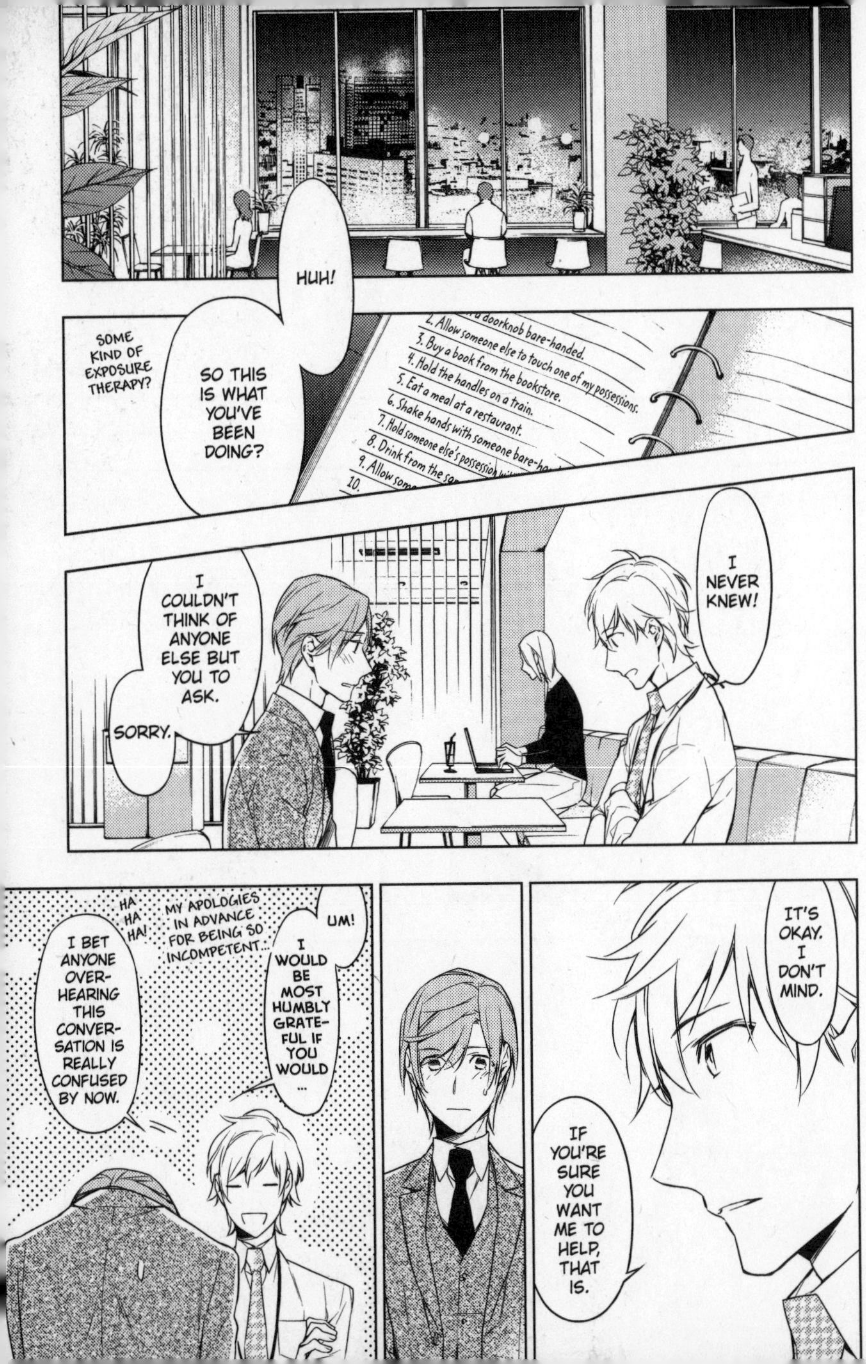
HUH!
a doorknob bare-handed.
2. Allow someone else to touch one of my possessions.
3. Buy a book from the bookstore.
4. Hold the handles on a train.
5. Eat a meal at a restaurant.
6. Shake hands with someone bare-
7. Hold someone else's possession
8. Drink from the
9. Allow
10.
SO THIS IS WHAT YOU'VE BEEN DOING?
SOME KIND OF EXPOSURE THERAPY?
I NEVER KNEW!
I COULDN'T THINK OF ANYONE ELSE BUT YOU TO ASK.
SORRY.
IT'S OKAY. I DON'T MIND.
IF YOU'RE SURE YOU WANT ME TO HELP, THAT IS.
UM!
I WOULD BE MOST HUMBLY GRATEFUL IF YOU WOULD...
MY APOLOGIES IN ADVANCE FOR BEING SO INCOMPETENT...
HA HA HA!
I BET ANYONE OVERHEARING THIS CONVERSATION IS REALLY CONFUSED BY NOW.

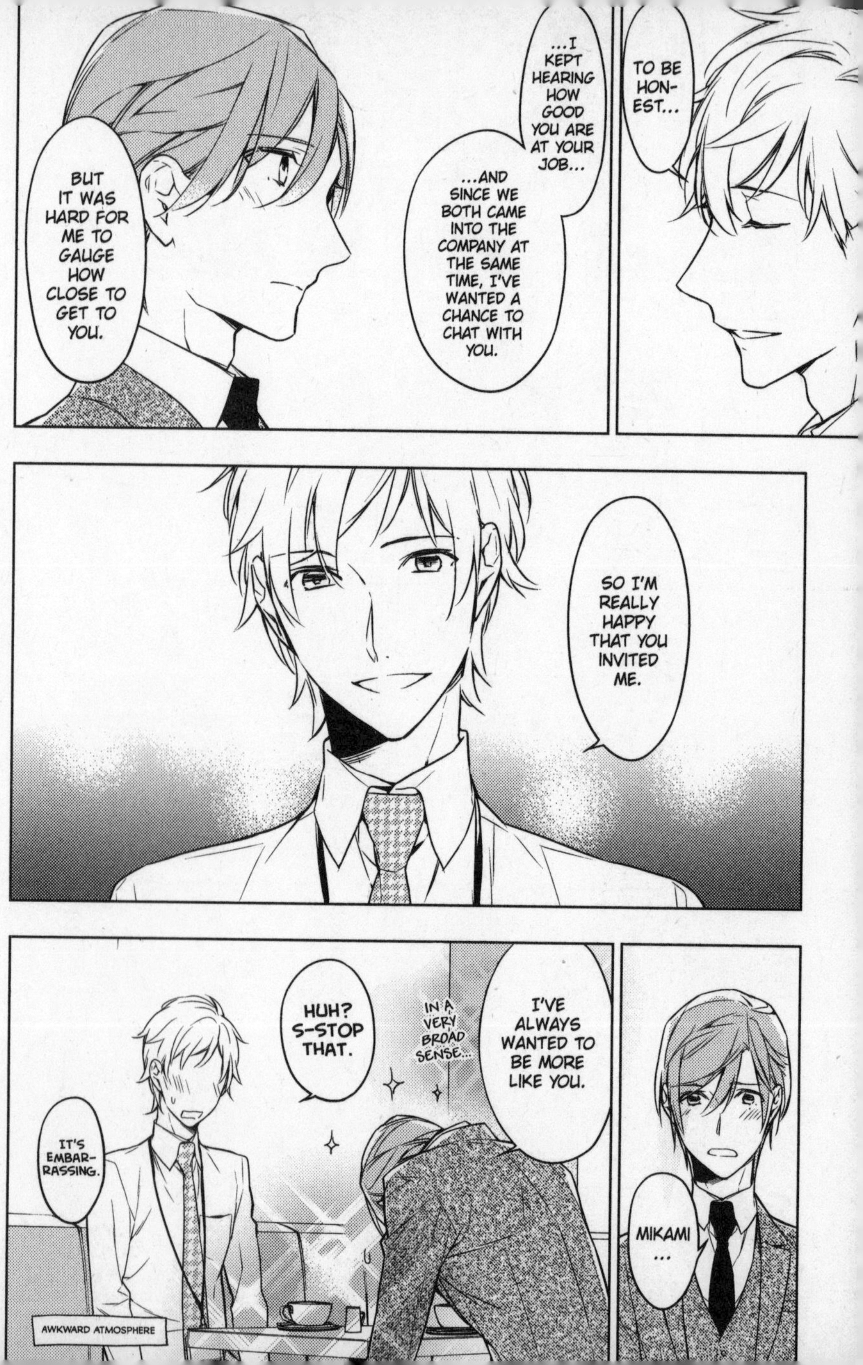
TO BE HON-EST...
...I KEPT HEARING HOW GOOD YOU ARE AT YOUR JOB...
...AND SINCE WE BOTH CAME INTO THE COMPANY AT THE SAME TIME, I'VE WANTED A CHANCE TO CHAT WITH YOU.
BUT IT WAS HARD FOR ME TO GAUGE HOW CLOSE TO GET TO YOU.
SO I'M REALLY HAPPY THAT YOU INVITED ME.
MIKAMI...
I'VE ALWAYS WANTED TO BE MORE LIKE YOU.
IN A VERY BROAD SENSE...
HUH? S-STOP THAT.
IT'S EMBARRASSING.
AWKWARD ATMOSPHERE

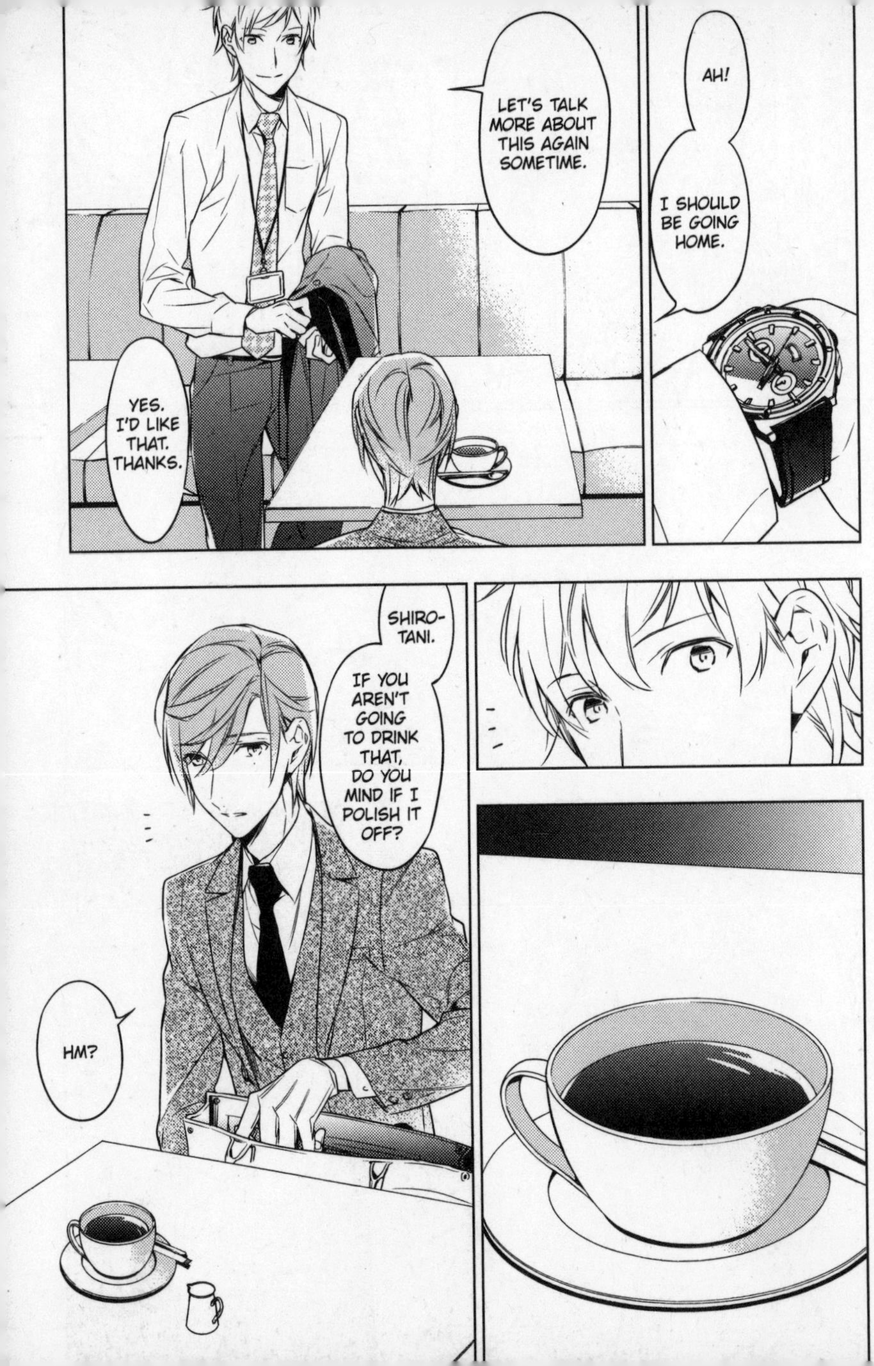
AH!
I SHOULD BE GOING HOME.
LET'S TALK MORE ABOUT THIS AGAIN SOMETIME.
YES. I'D LIKE THAT. THANKS.
SHIRO-TANI.
IF YOU AREN'T GOING TO DRINK THAT, DO YOU MIND IF I POLISH IT OFF?
HM?

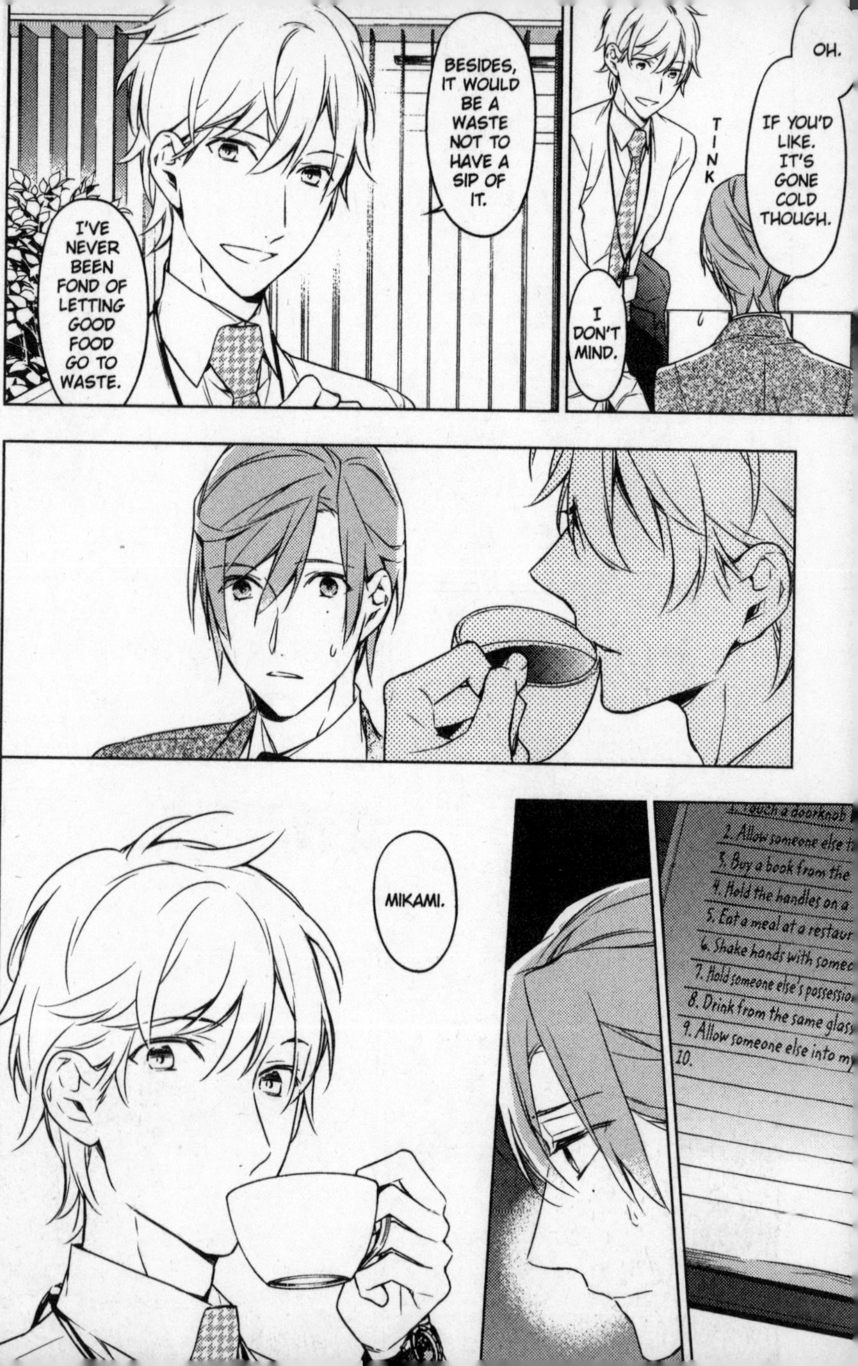
OH.
IF YOU'D LIKE. IT'S GONE COLD THOUGH.
TINK
I DON'T MIND.
I'VE NEVER BEEN FOND OF LETTING GOOD FOOD GO TO WASTE.
BESIDES, IT WOULD BE A WASTE NOT TO HAVE A SIP OF IT.
1. Touch a doorknob
2. Allow someone else t
3. Buy a book from the
4. Hold the handles on a
5. Eat a meal at a restaur
6. Shake hands with somec
7. Hold someone else's possessio
8. Drink from the same glas
9. Allow someone else into m
10.
MIKAMI.

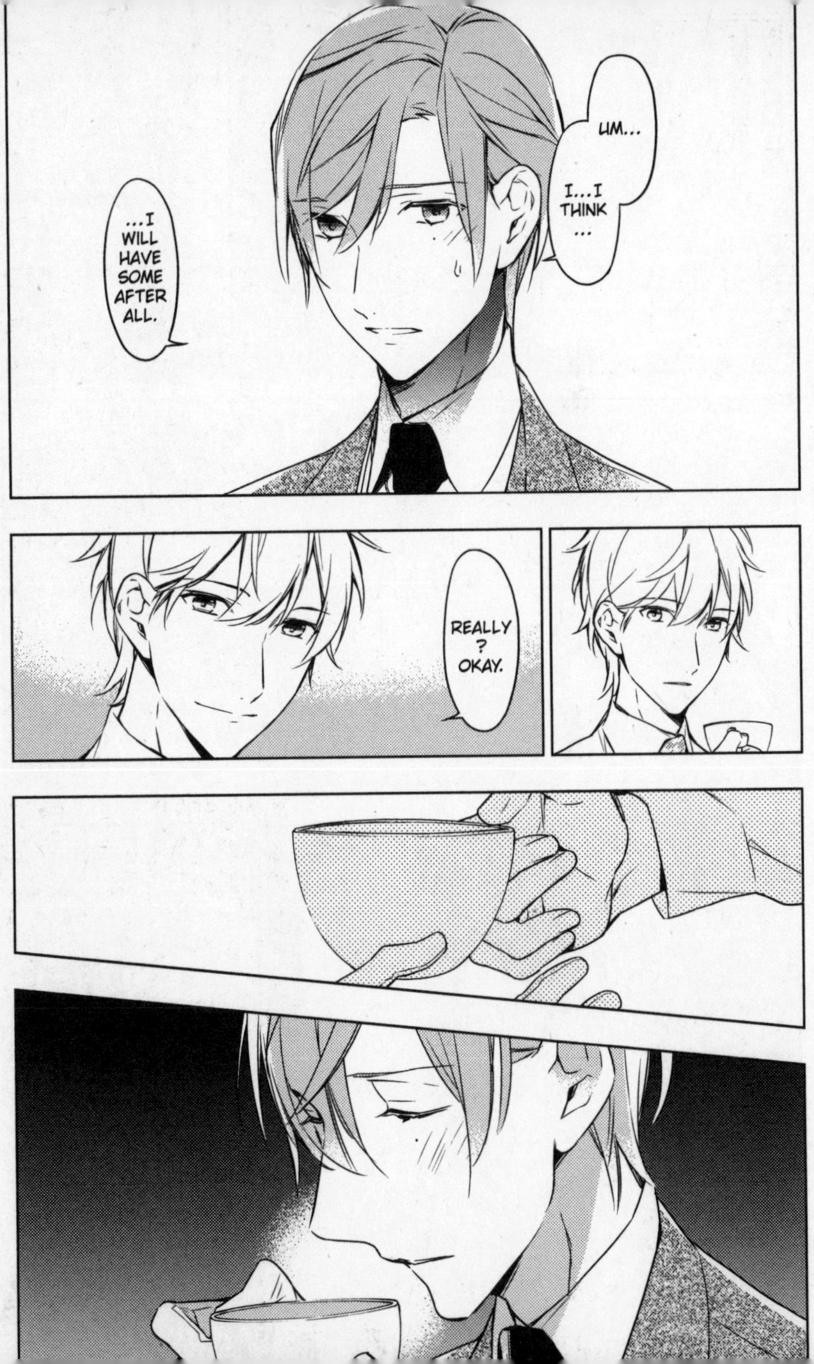
UM... I...I THINK...
...I WILL HAVE SOME AFTER ALL.
REALLY? OKAY.

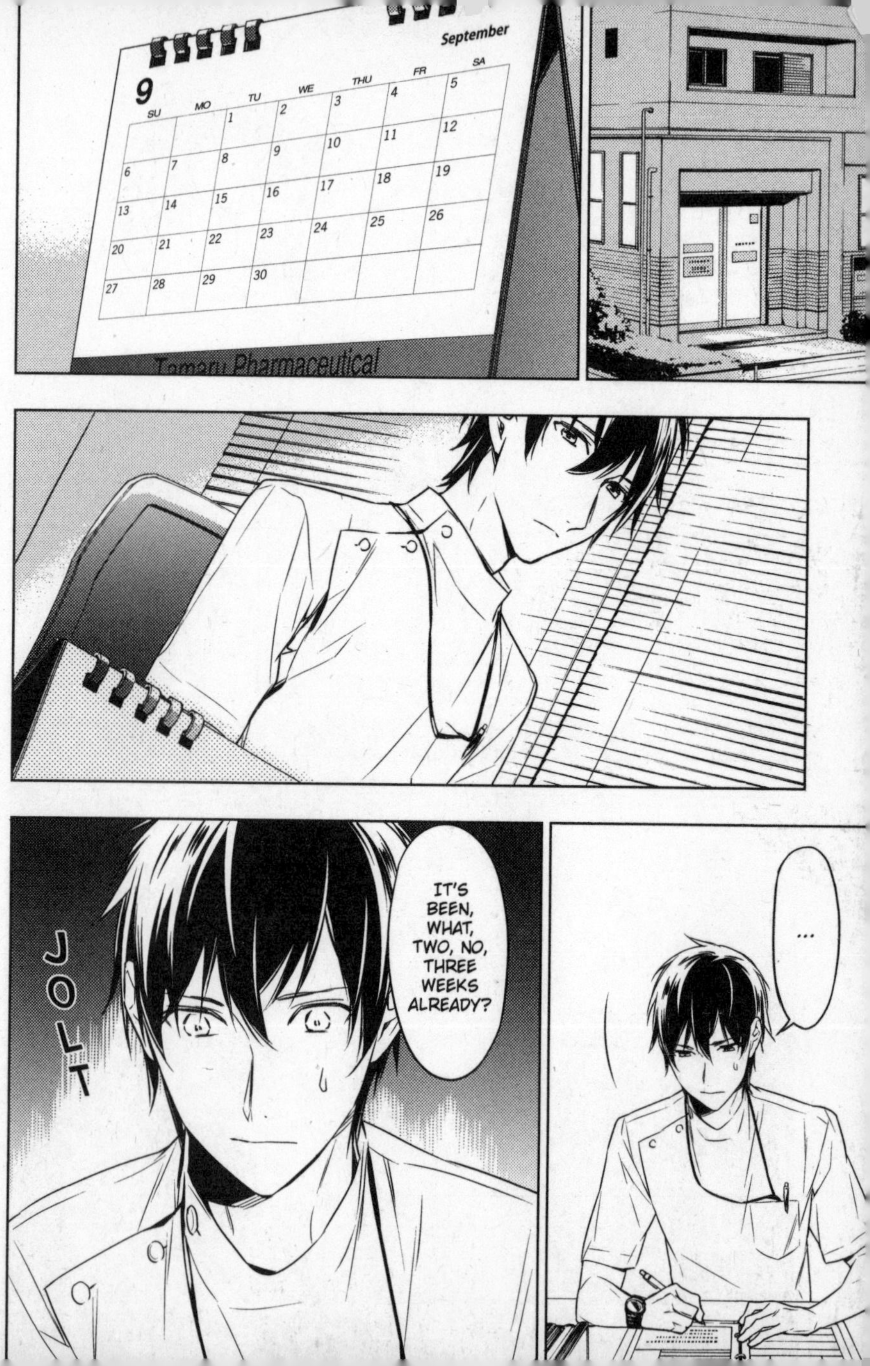
September
Tamaru Pharmaceutical
...
IT'S BEEN, WHAT, TWO, NO, THREE WEEKS ALREADY?
JOLT

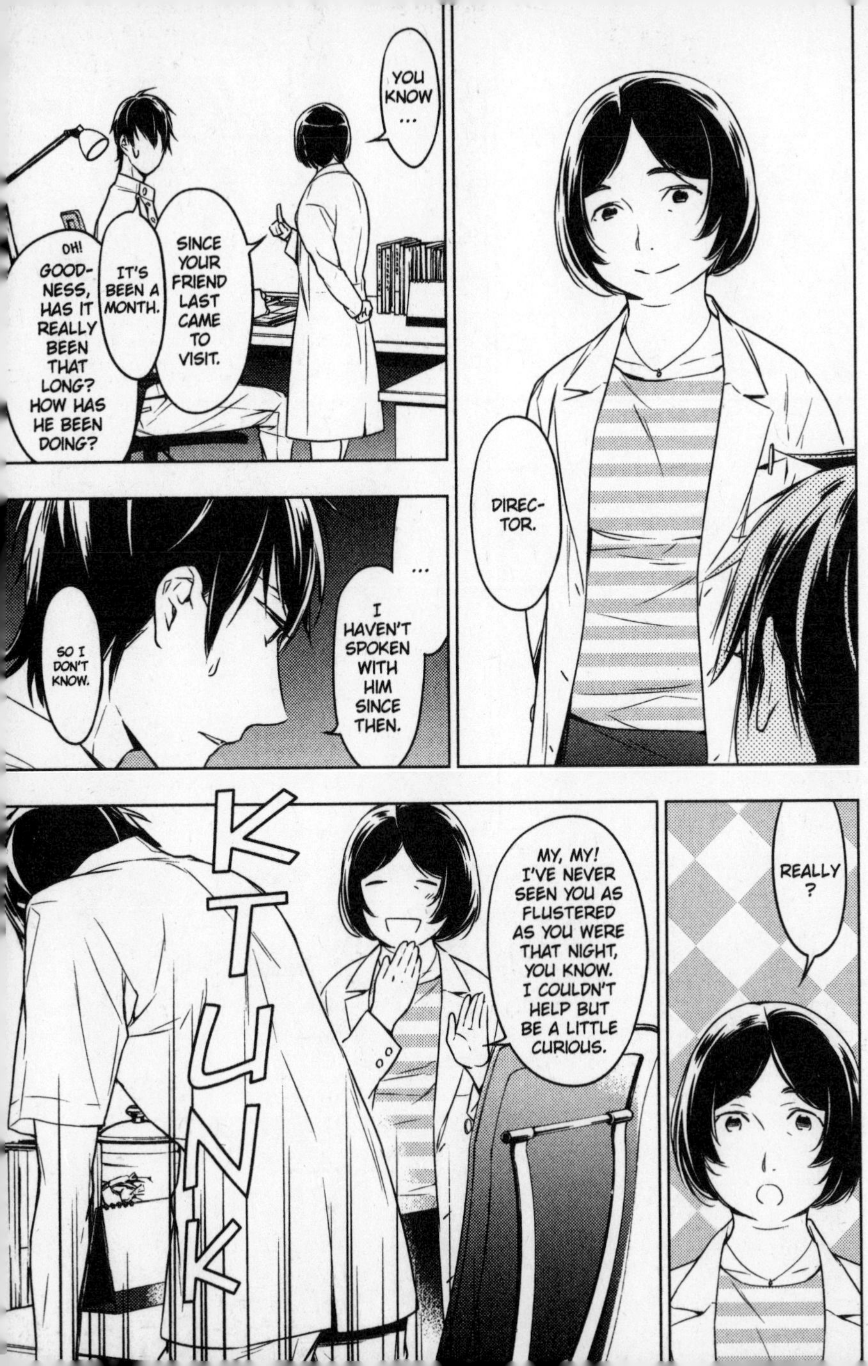
DIRECTOR.
YOU KNOW...
SINCE YOUR FRIEND LAST CAME TO VISIT.
IT'S BEEN A MONTH.
OH! GOODNESS, HAS IT REALLY BEEN THAT LONG? HOW HAS HE BEEN DOING?
...
I HAVEN'T SPOKEN WITH HIM SINCE THEN.
SO I DON'T KNOW.
REALLY?
MY, MY! I'VE NEVER SEEN YOU AS FLUSTERED AS YOU WERE THAT NIGHT, YOU KNOW. I COULDN'T HELP BUT BE A LITTLE CURIOUS.
KTUNK

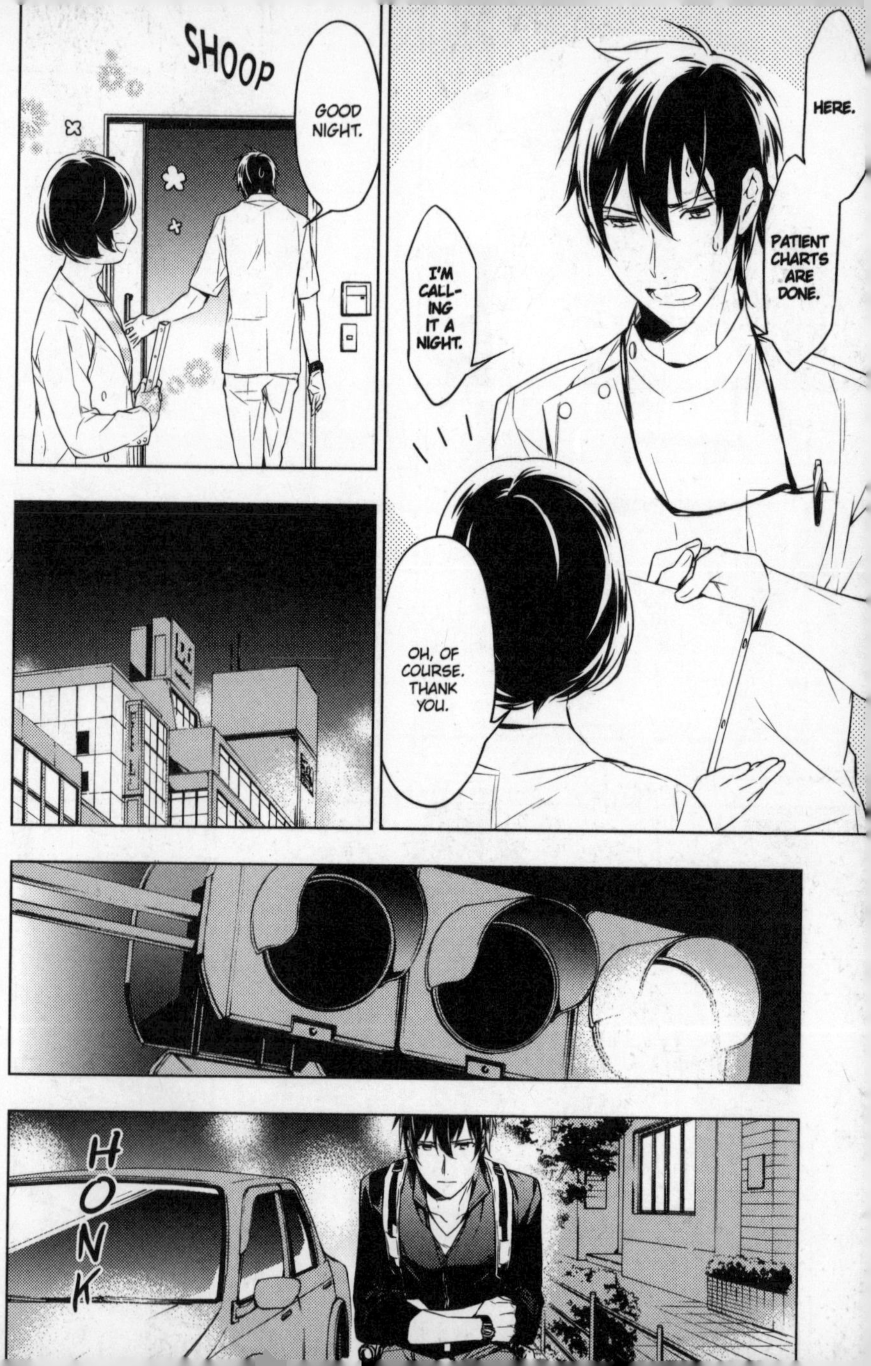
HERE.
PATIENT CHARTS ARE DONE.
I'M CALLING IT A NIGHT.
OH, OF COURSE. THANK YOU.
GOOD NIGHT.
SHOOP
HONK

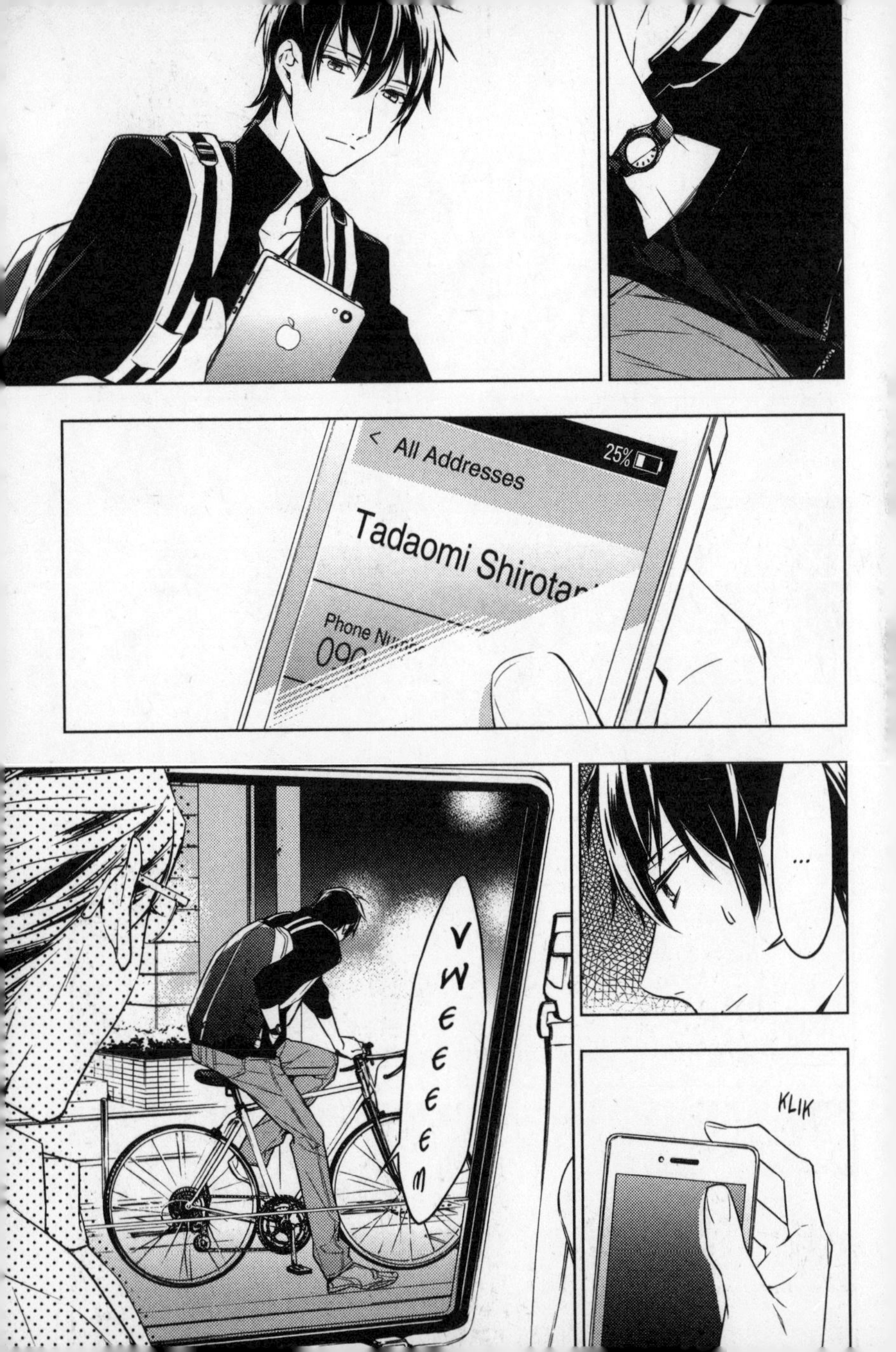
< All Addresses
25%
Tadaomi Shirotan
Phone Nu
090
...
KLIK
VWEEEEEM

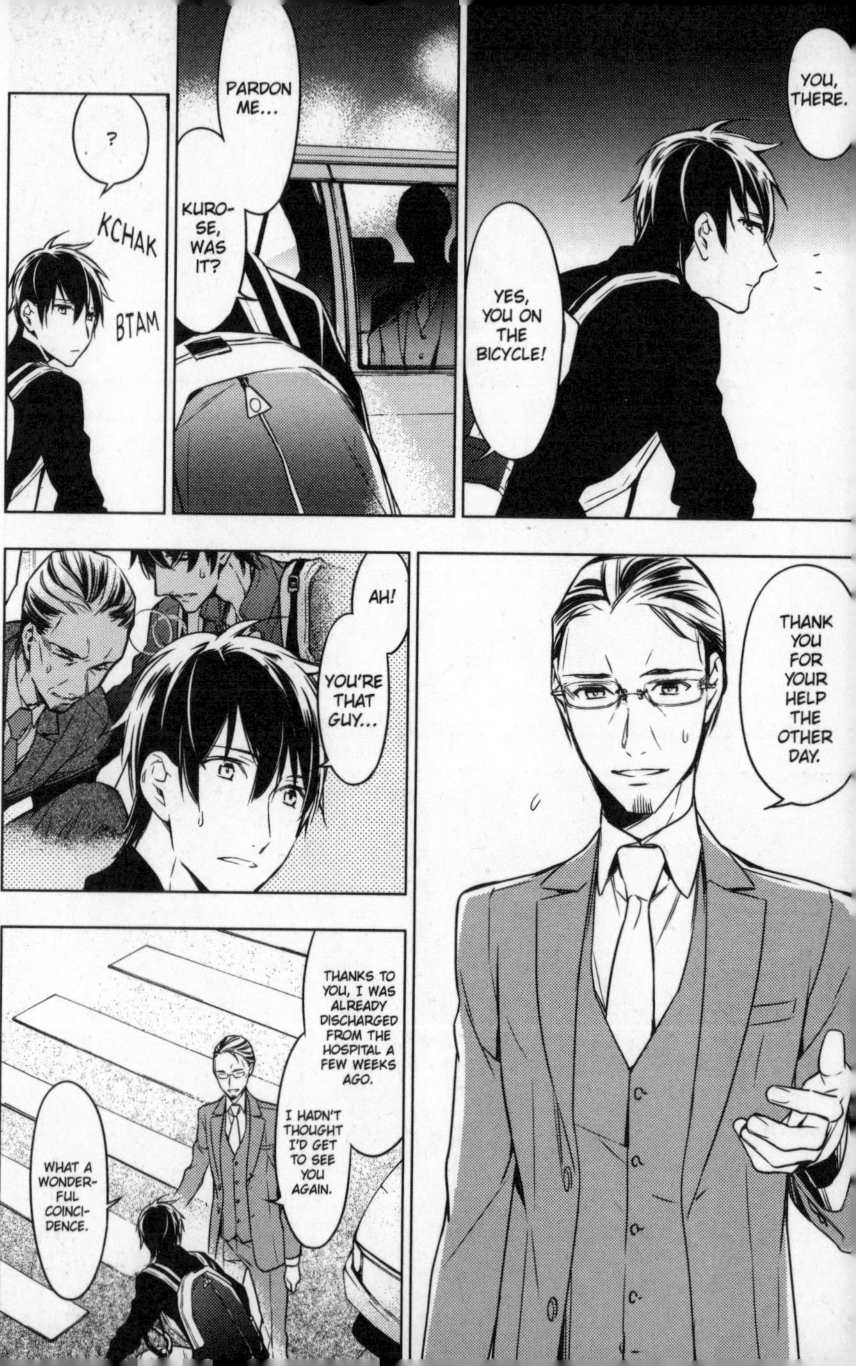
YOU, THERE.
YES, YOU ON THE BICYCLE!
PARDON ME...
KURO-SE, WAS IT?
?
KCHAK
BTAM
THANK YOU FOR YOUR HELP THE OTHER DAY.
AH!
YOU'RE THAT GUY...
THANKS TO YOU, I WAS ALREADY DISCHARGED FROM THE HOSPITAL A FEW WEEKS AGO.
I HADN'T THOUGHT I'D GET TO SEE YOU AGAIN.
WHAT A WONDER-FUL COINCI-DENCE.

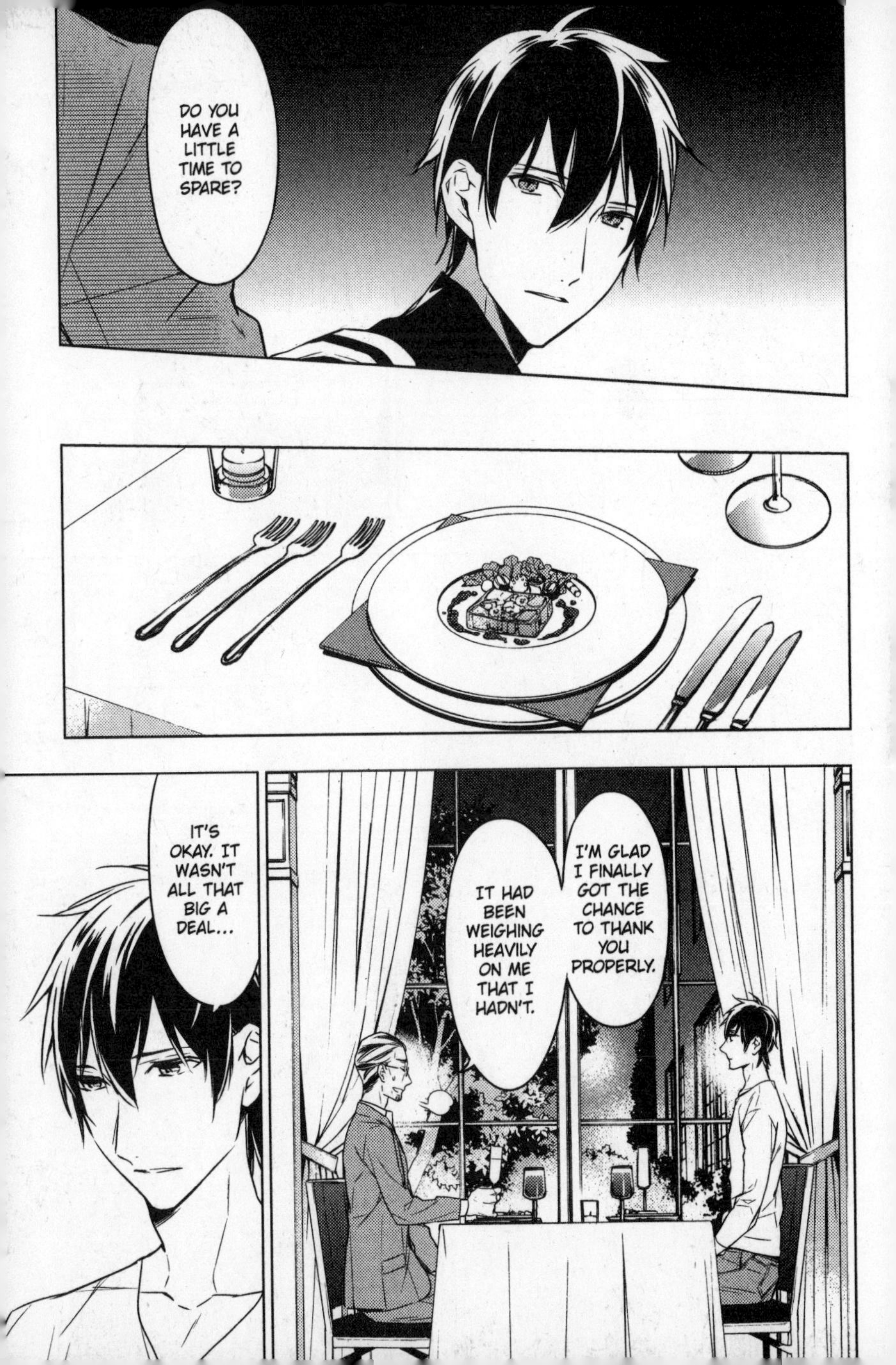
DO YOU HAVE A LITTLE TIME TO SPARE?
I'M GLAD I FINALLY GOT THE CHANCE TO THANK YOU PROPERLY.
IT HAD BEEN WEIGHING HEAVILY ON ME THAT I HADN'T.
IT'S OKAY. IT WASN'T ALL THAT BIG A DEAL...

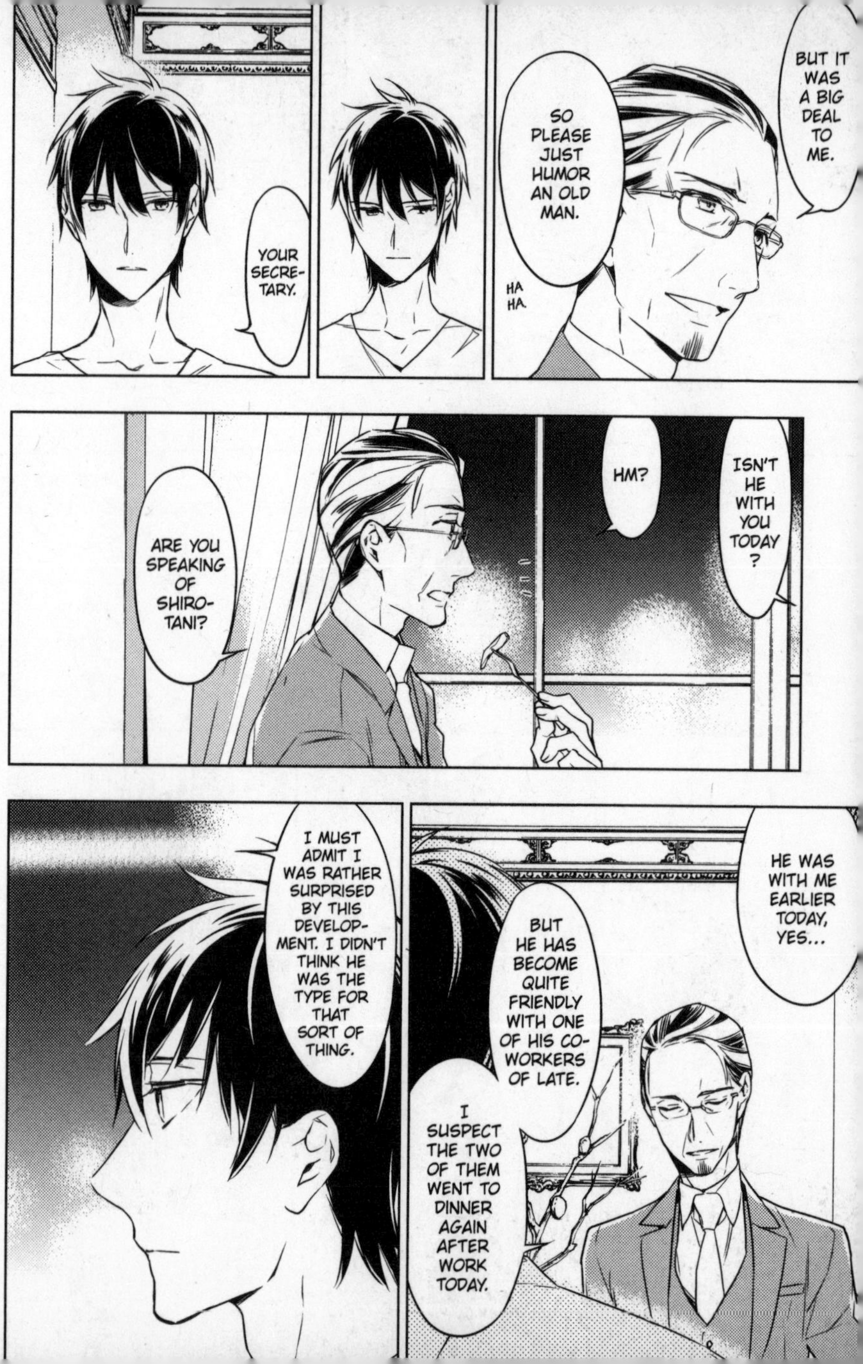
BUT IT WAS A BIG DEAL TO ME.
SO PLEASE JUST HUMOR AN OLD MAN.
HA HA.
YOUR SECRETARY.
ISN'T HE WITH YOU TODAY?
HM?
ARE YOU SPEAKING OF SHIROTANI?
HE WAS WITH ME EARLIER TODAY, YES...
BUT HE HAS BECOME QUITE FRIENDLY WITH ONE OF HIS CO-WORKERS OF LATE.
I SUSPECT THE TWO OF THEM WENT TO DINNER AGAIN AFTER WORK TODAY.
I MUST ADMIT I WAS RATHER SURPRISED BY THIS DEVELOPMENT. I DIDN'T THINK HE WAS THE TYPE FOR THAT SORT OF THING.

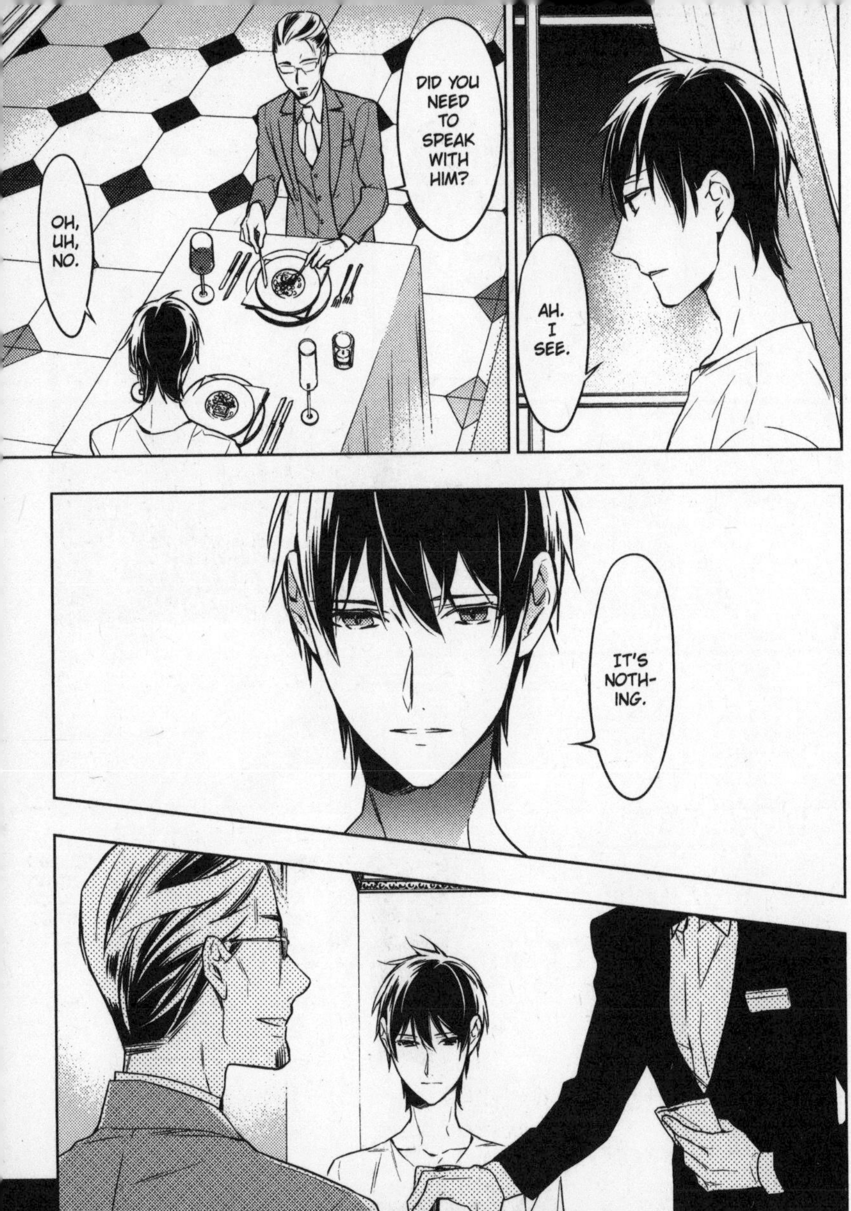
AH. I SEE.
DID YOU NEED TO SPEAK WITH HIM?
OH, UH, NO.
IT'S NOTH-ING.

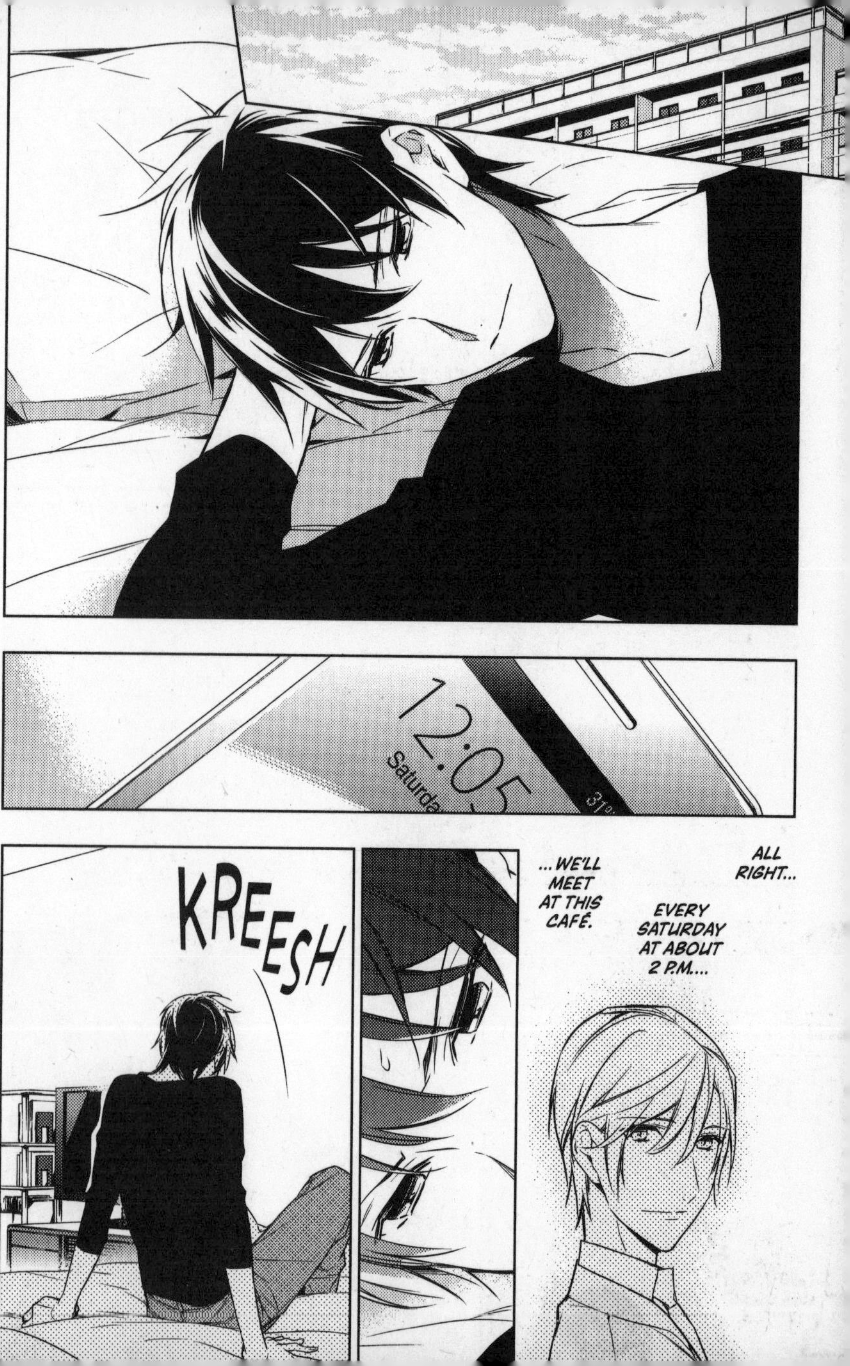
12:05
ALL RIGHT...
EVERY SATURDAY AT ABOUT 2 P.M....
...WE'LL MEET AT THIS CAFÉ.
KREESH

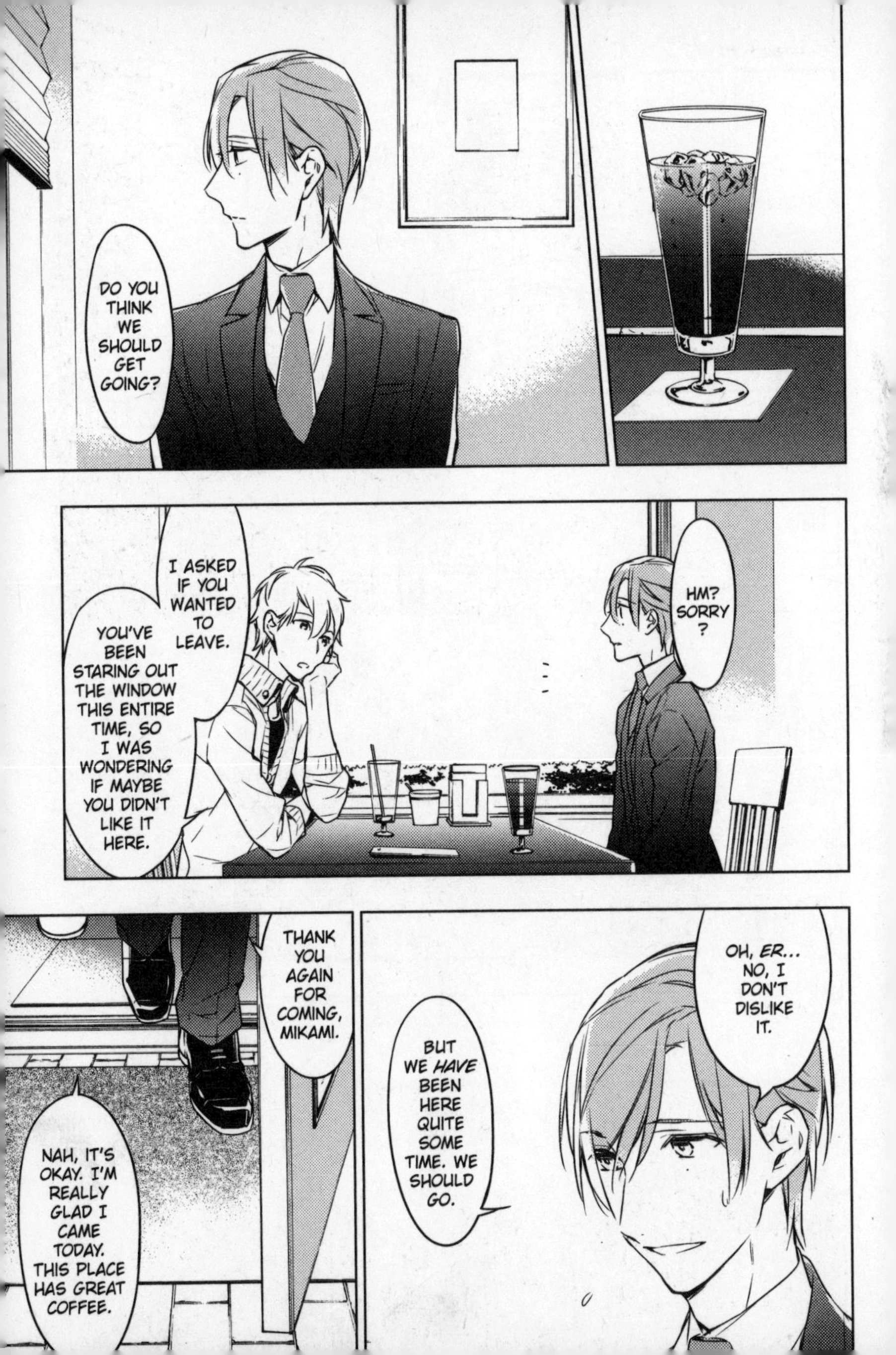

DO YOU THINK WE SHOULD GET GOING?
HM? SORRY?
I ASKED IF YOU WANTED TO LEAVE.
YOU'VE BEEN STARING OUT THE WINDOW THIS ENTIRE TIME, SO I WAS WONDERING IF MAYBE YOU DIDN'T LIKE IT HERE.
OH, *ER*... NO, I DON'T DISLIKE IT.
BUT WE *HAVE* BEEN HERE QUITE SOME TIME. WE SHOULD GO.
THANK YOU AGAIN FOR COMING, MIKAMI.
NAH, IT'S OKAY. I'M REALLY GLAD I CAME TODAY. THIS PLACE HAS GREAT COFFEE.

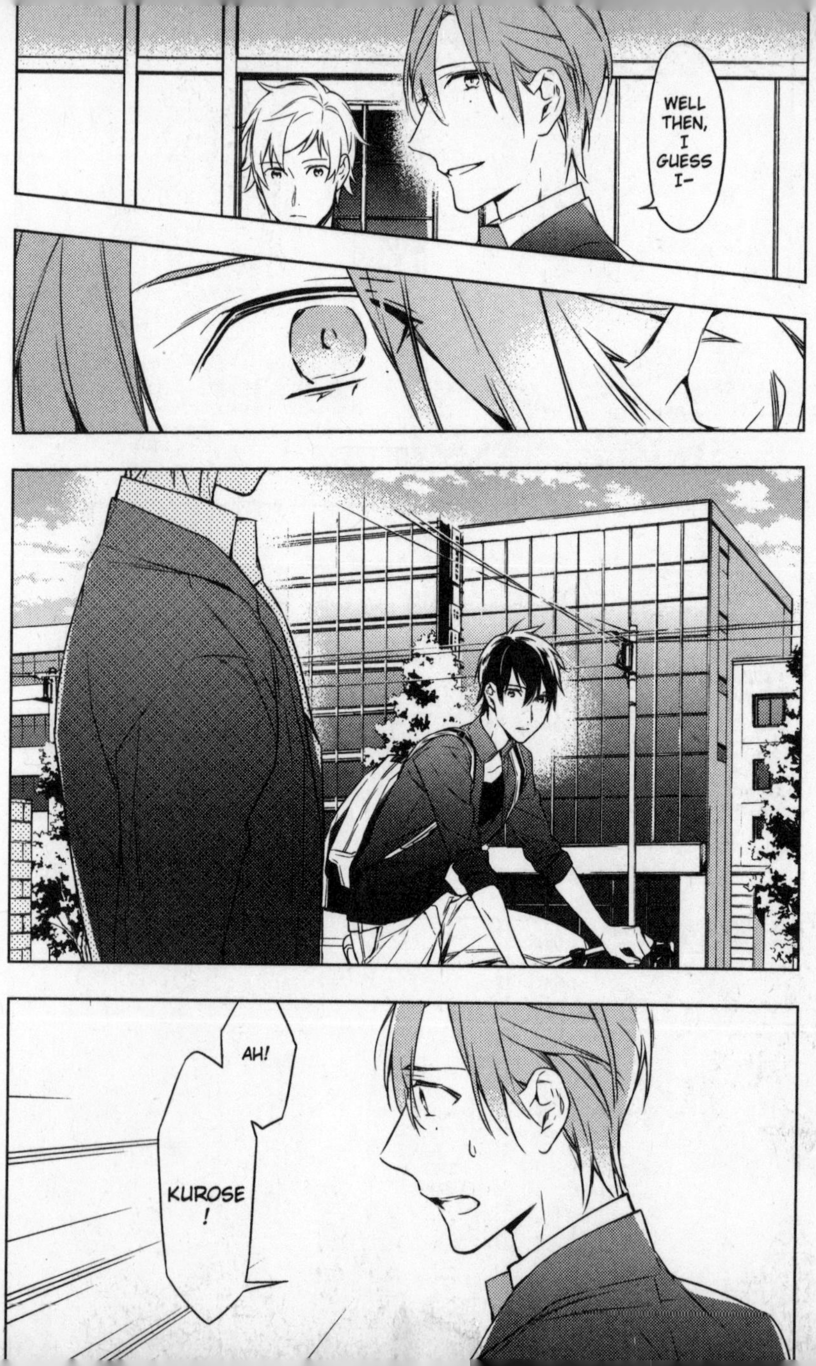
WELL THEN, I GUESS I–
AH!
KUROSE!

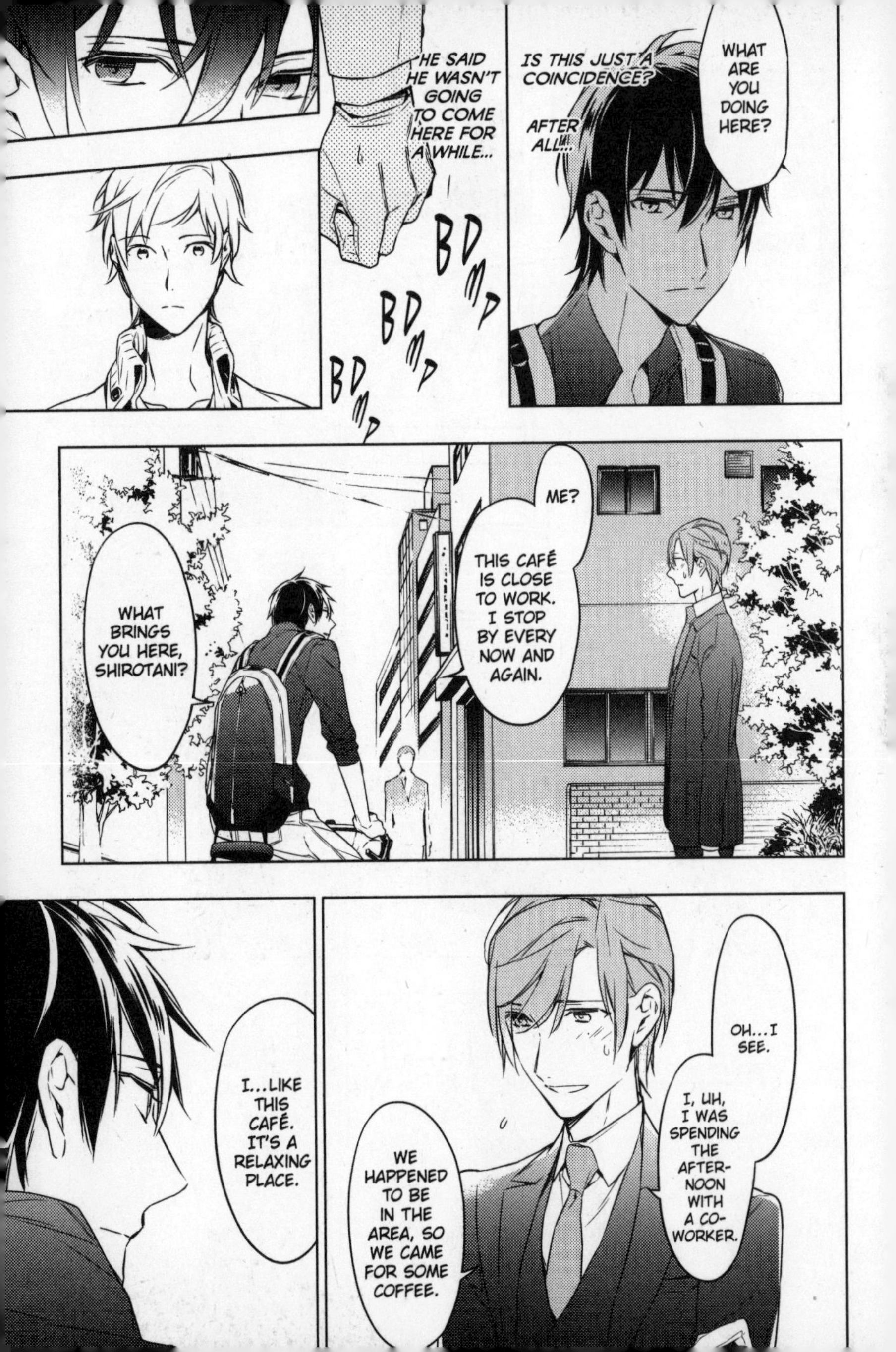
WHAT ARE YOU DOING HERE?
IS THIS JUST A COINCIDENCE?
AFTER ALL...
HE SAID HE WASN'T GOING TO COME HERE FOR A WHILE...
BDMP
BDMP
BDMP
ME?
THIS CAFÉ IS CLOSE TO WORK. I STOP BY EVERY NOW AND AGAIN.
WHAT BRINGS YOU HERE, SHIROTANI?
OH...I SEE.
I, UH, I WAS SPENDING THE AFTERNOON WITH A CO-WORKER.
WE HAPPENED TO BE IN THE AREA, SO WE CAME FOR SOME COFFEE.
I...LIKE THIS CAFÉ. IT'S A RELAXING PLACE.

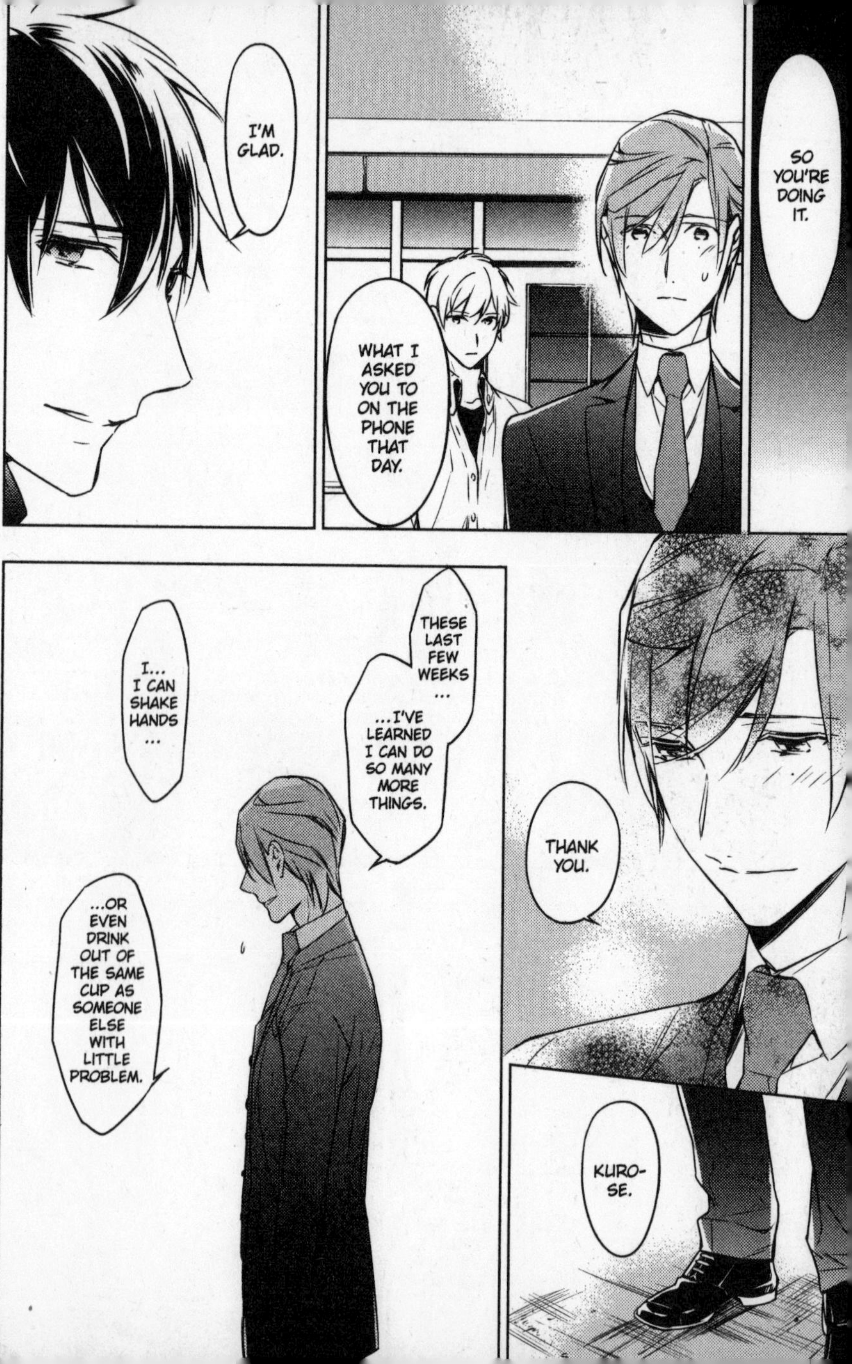
SO YOU'RE DOING IT.
WHAT I ASKED YOU TO ON THE PHONE THAT DAY.
I'M GLAD.
THANK YOU.
KURO-SE.
THESE LAST FEW WEEKS...
...I'VE LEARNED I CAN DO SO MANY MORE THINGS.
I... I CAN SHAKE HANDS...
...OR EVEN DRINK OUT OF THE SAME CUP AS SOMEONE ELSE WITH LITTLE PROBLEM.

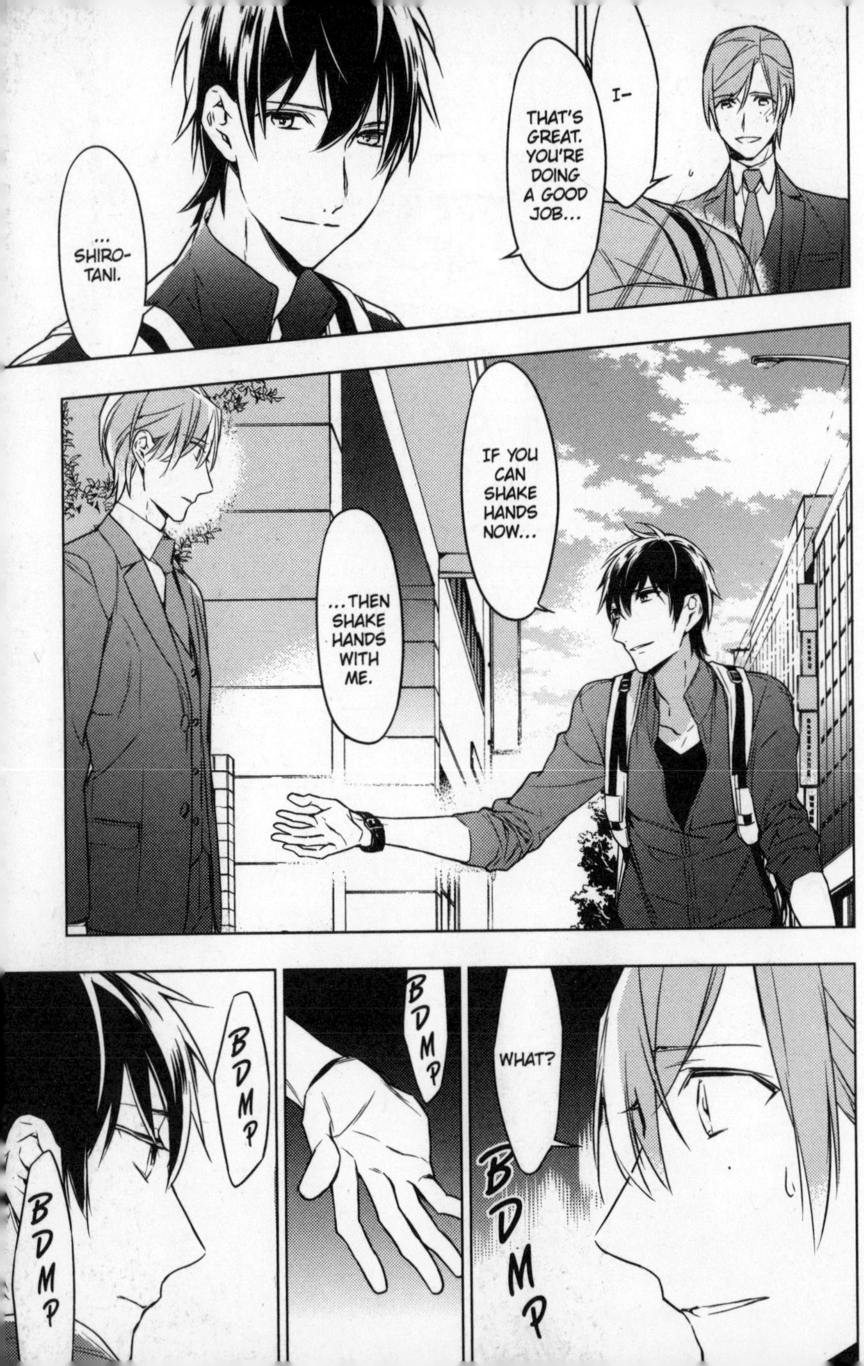
I—
THAT'S GREAT. YOU'RE DOING A GOOD JOB...
... SHIRO-TANI.
IF YOU CAN SHAKE HANDS NOW...
...THEN SHAKE HANDS WITH ME.
WHAT?
BDMP
BDMP
BDMP
BDMP

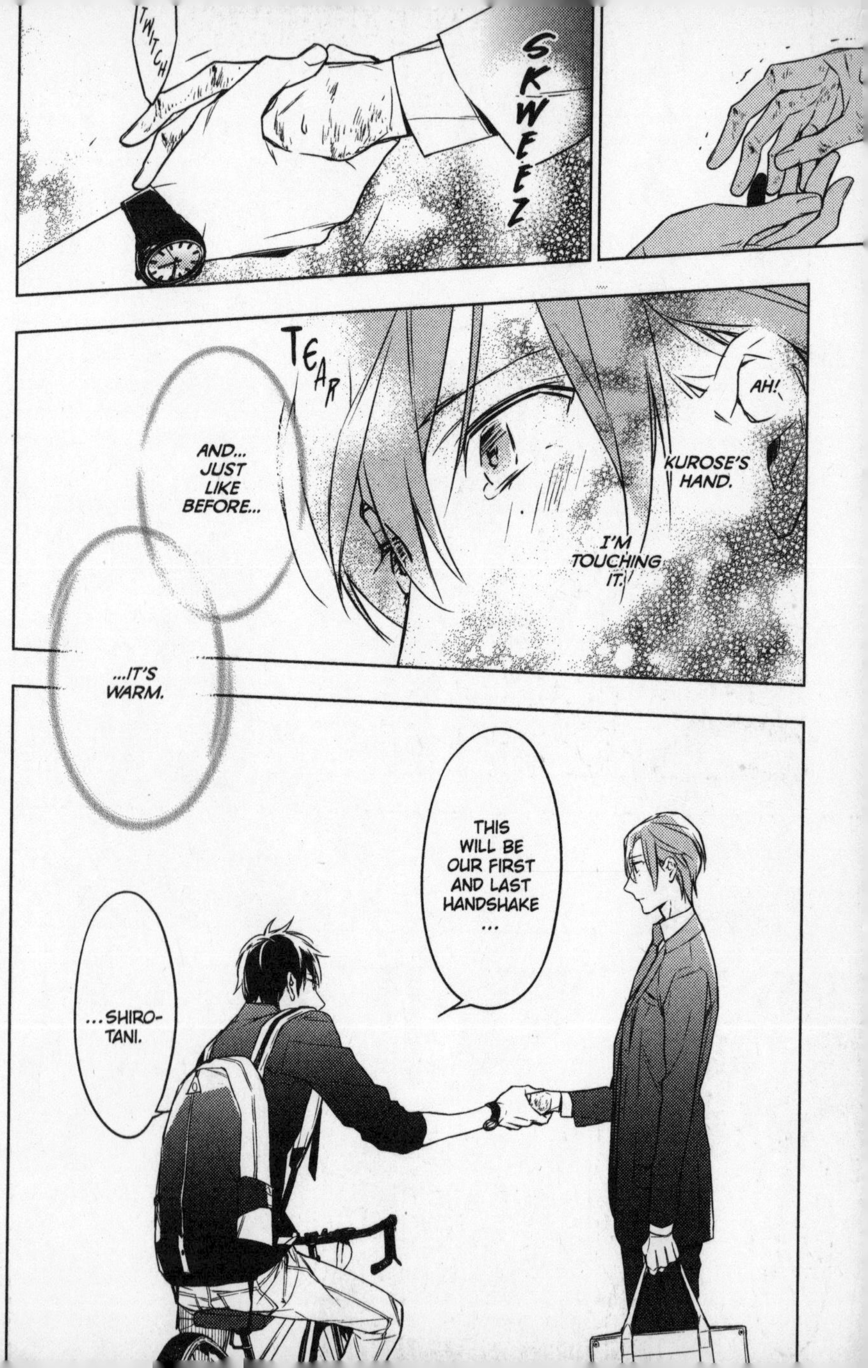
SKWEEZ
TWITCH
AH!
KUROSE'S HAND.
I'M TOUCHING IT.
TEAR
AND... JUST LIKE BEFORE...
...IT'S WARM.
THIS WILL BE OUR FIRST AND LAST HANDSHAKE ...
...SHIRO-TANI.

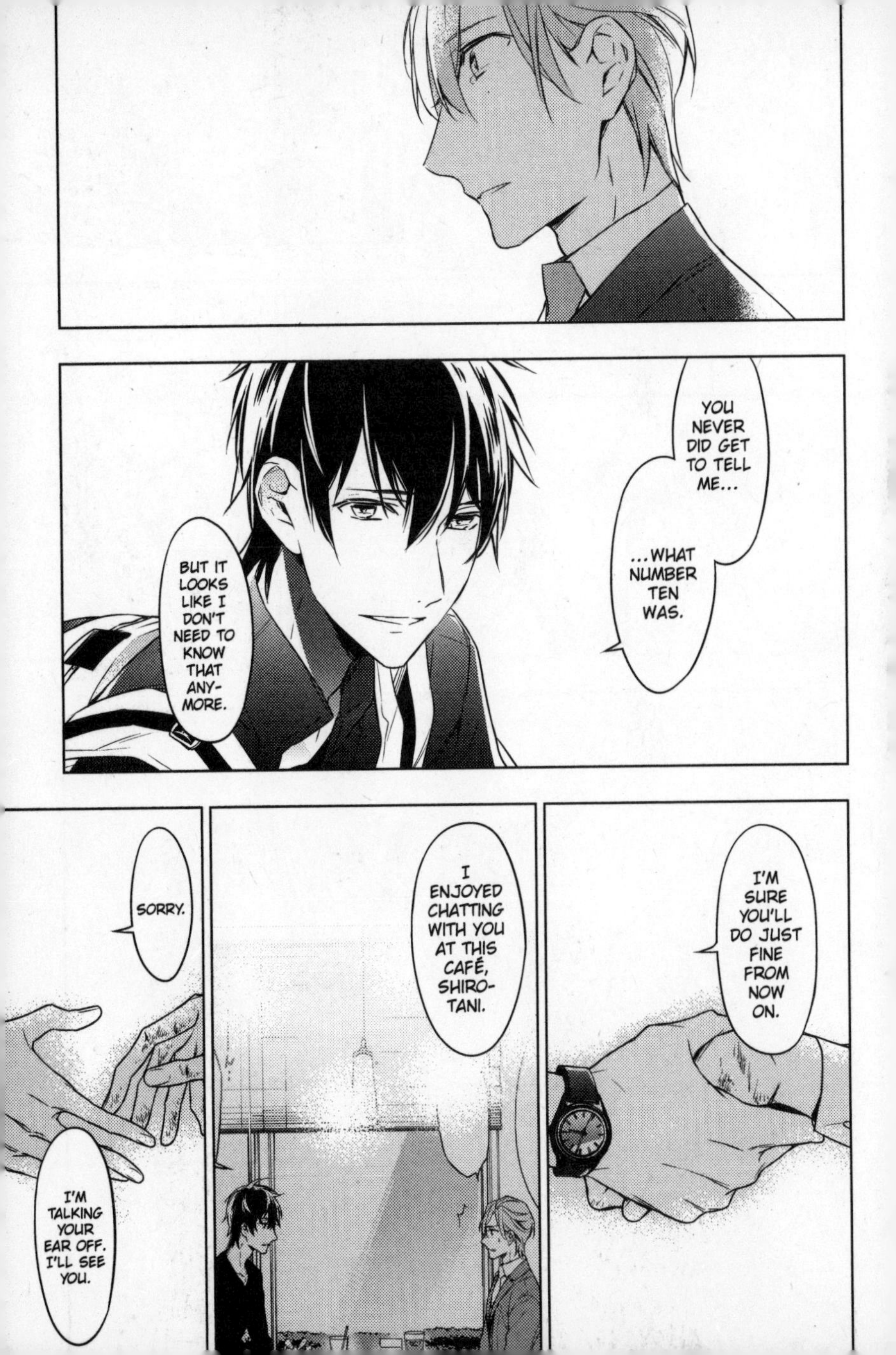
YOU NEVER DID GET TO TELL ME...
...WHAT NUMBER TEN WAS.
BUT IT LOOKS LIKE I DON'T NEED TO KNOW THAT ANYMORE.
I'M SURE YOU'LL DO JUST FINE FROM NOW ON.
I ENJOYED CHATTING WITH YOU AT THIS CAFÉ, SHIRO-TANI.
SORRY.
I'M TALKING YOUR EAR OFF. I'LL SEE YOU.

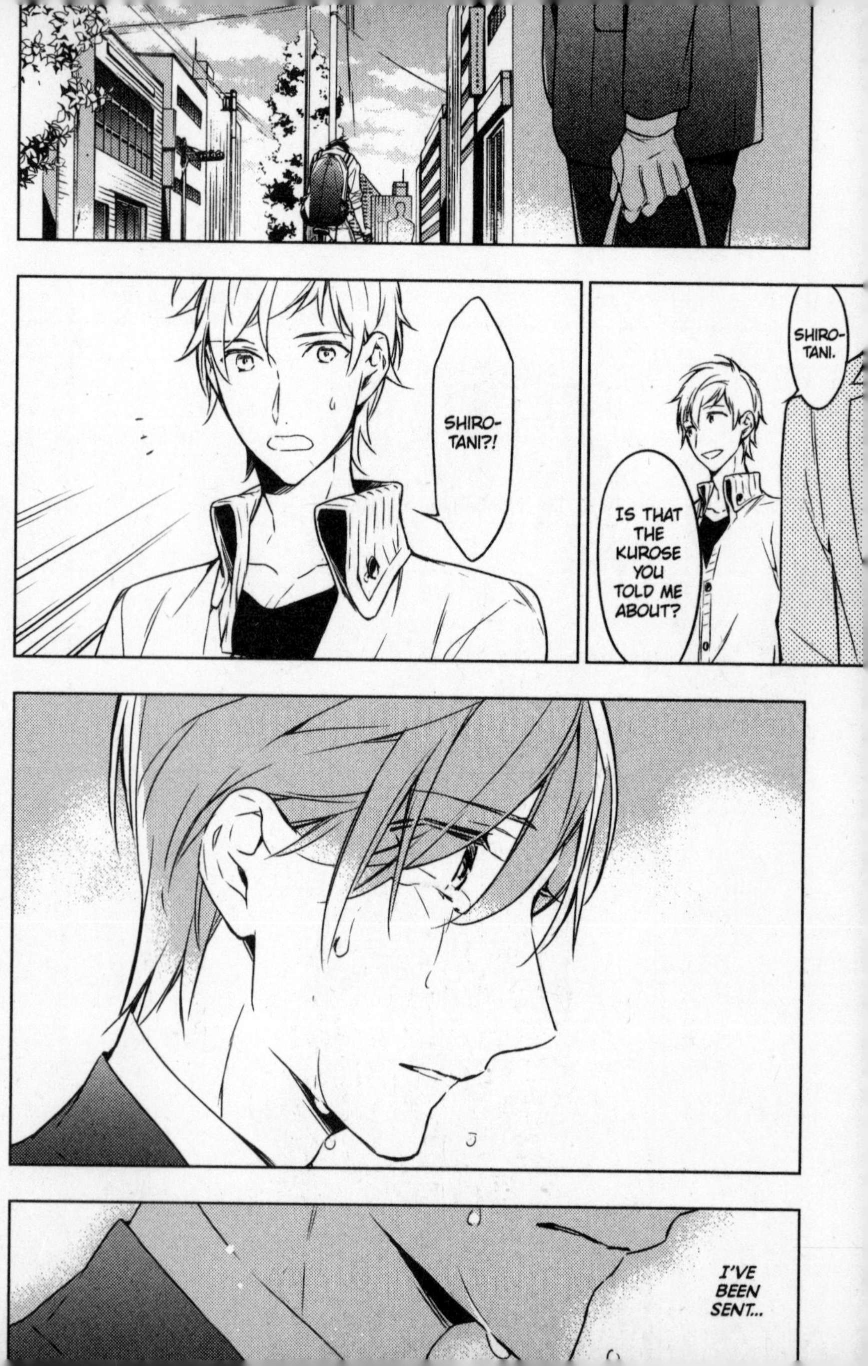
SHIRO-TANI.
IS THAT THE KUROSE YOU TOLD ME ABOUT?
SHIRO-TANI?!
I'VE BEEN SENT...

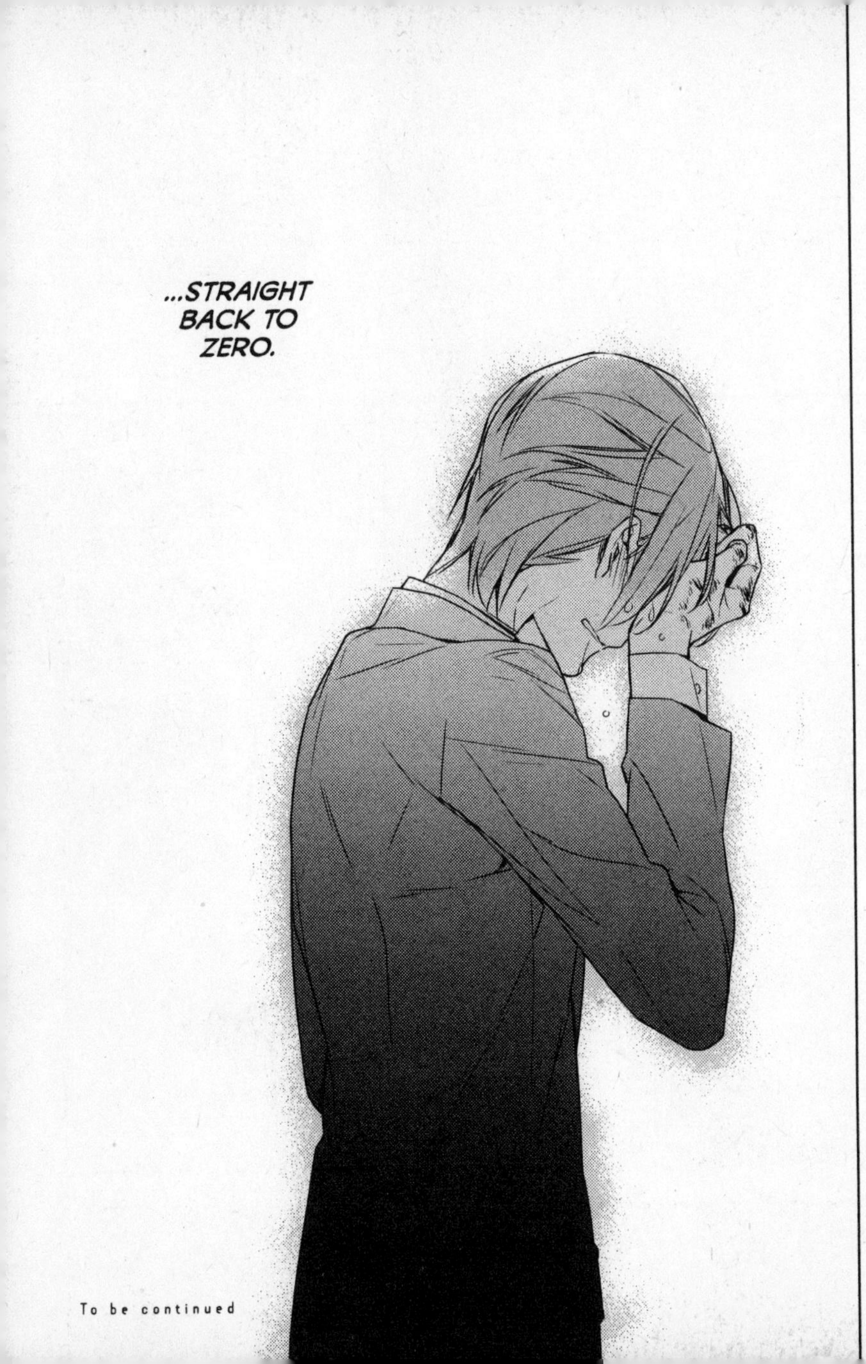
...STRAIGHT BACK TO ZERO.
To be continued

ten count by rihito takarai

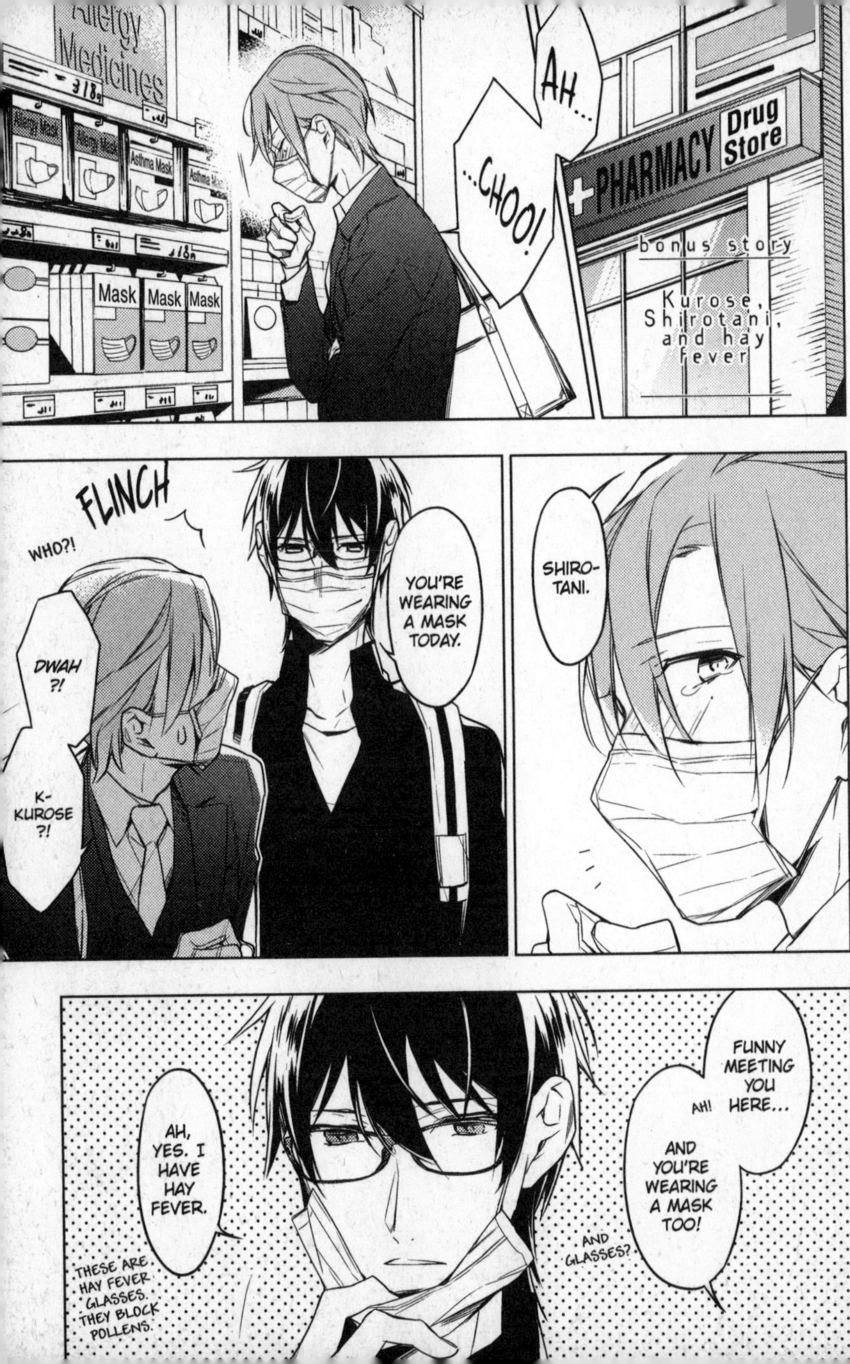
PHARMACY
Drug Store
bonus story
Kurose, Shirotani, and hay fever
AH...
...CHOO!
Allergy Medicines
Allergy Mask
Allergy Mask
Asthma Mask
Asthma Mask
Mask
Mask
Mask
SHIRO-TANI.
YOU'RE WEARING A MASK TODAY.
FLINCH
WHO?!
DWAH?!
K-KUROSE?!
FUNNY MEETING YOU HERE...
AH!
AND YOU'RE WEARING A MASK TOO!
AND GLASSES?
AH, YES. I HAVE HAY FEVER.
THESE ARE HAY FEVER GLASSES. THEY BLOCK POLLENS.

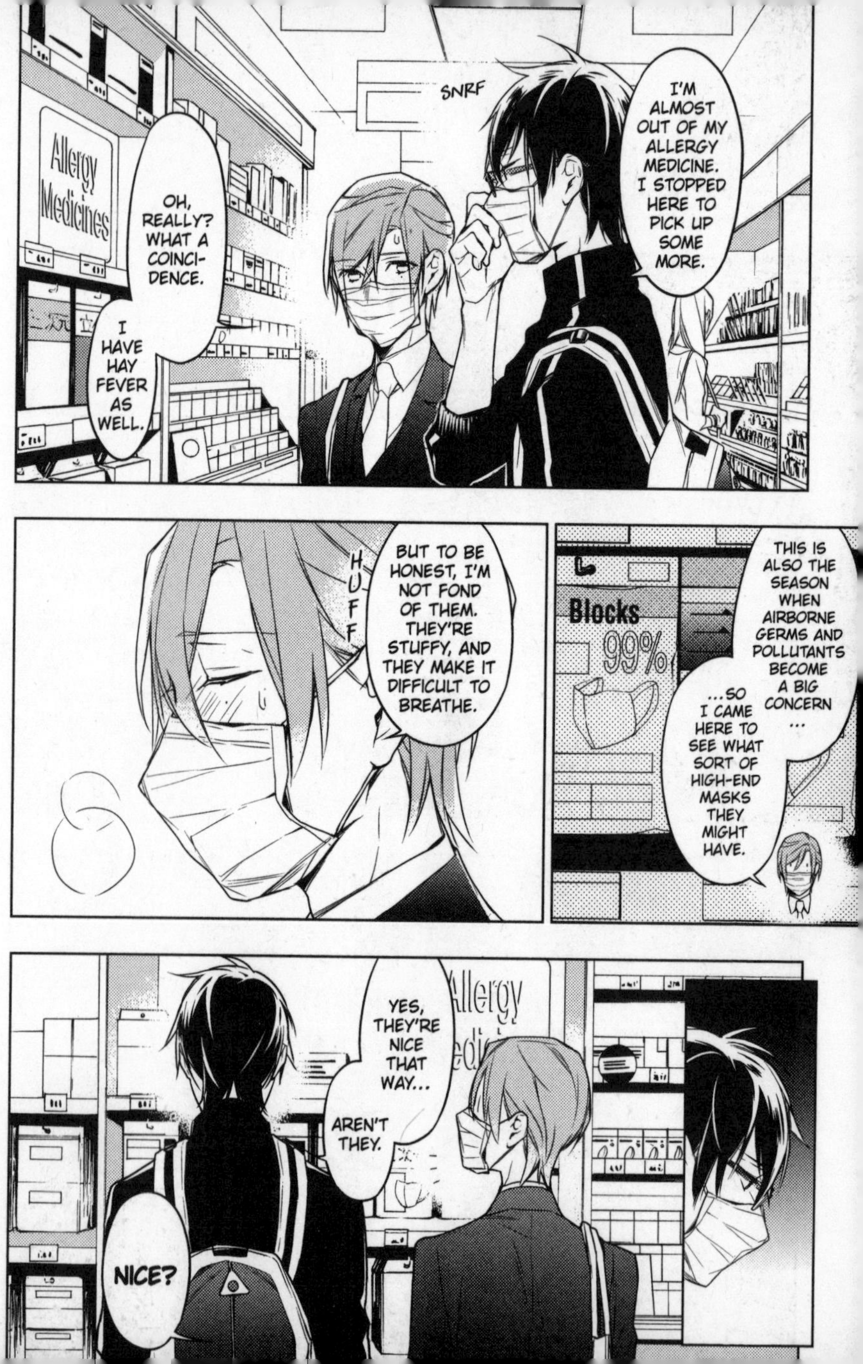
I'M ALMOST OUT OF MY ALLERGY MEDICINE. I STOPPED HERE TO PICK UP SOME MORE.
SNRF
Allergy Medicines
OH, REALLY? WHAT A COINCI-DENCE.
I HAVE HAY FEVER AS WELL.
THIS IS ALSO THE SEASON WHEN AIRBORNE GERMS AND POLLUTANTS BECOME A BIG CONCERN...
...SO I CAME HERE TO SEE WHAT SORT OF HIGH-END MASKS THEY MIGHT HAVE.
Blocks
99%
BUT TO BE HONEST, I'M NOT FOND OF THEM. THEY'RE STUFFY, AND THEY MAKE IT DIFFICULT TO BREATHE.
HUFF
YES, THEY'RE NICE THAT WAY...
AREN'T THEY.
NICE?

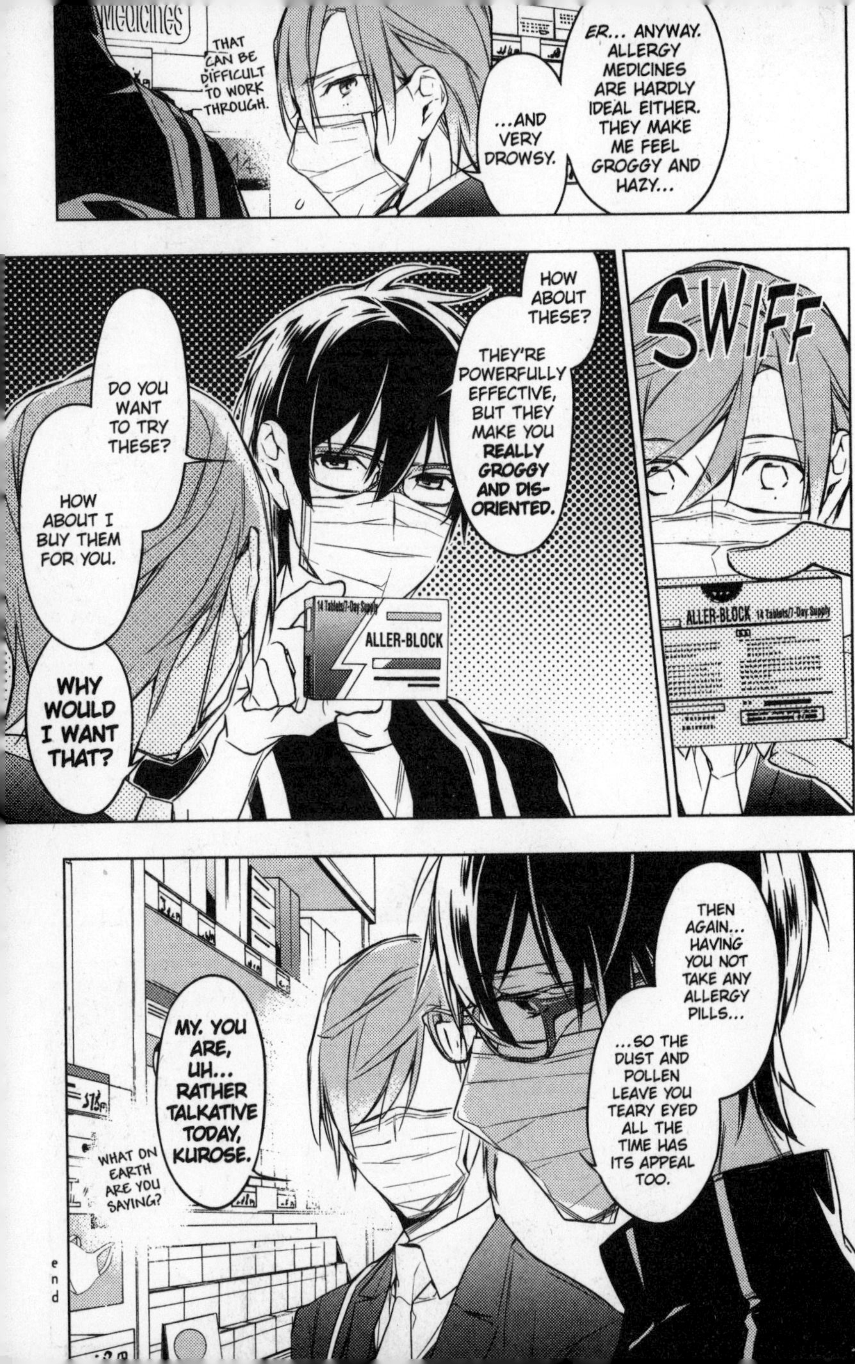
Medicines
ER... ANYWAY. ALLERGY MEDICINES ARE HARDLY IDEAL EITHER. THEY MAKE ME FEEL GROGGY AND HAZY...
...AND VERY DROWSY.
THAT CAN BE DIFFICULT TO WORK THROUGH.
SWIFF
ALLER-BLOCK 14 Tablets/7-Day Supply
HOW ABOUT THESE?
THEY'RE POWERFULLY EFFECTIVE, BUT THEY MAKE YOU REALLY GROGGY AND DIS-ORIENTED.
14 Tablets/7-Day Supply
ALLER-BLOCK
DO YOU WANT TO TRY THESE?
HOW ABOUT I BUY THEM FOR YOU.
WHY WOULD I WANT THAT?
THEN AGAIN... HAVING YOU NOT TAKE ANY ALLERGY PILLS...
...SO THE DUST AND POLLEN LEAVE YOU TEARY EYED ALL THE TIME HAS ITS APPEAL TOO.
MY. YOU ARE, UH... RATHER TALKATIVE TODAY, KUROSE.
WHAT ON EARTH ARE YOU SAYING?

end

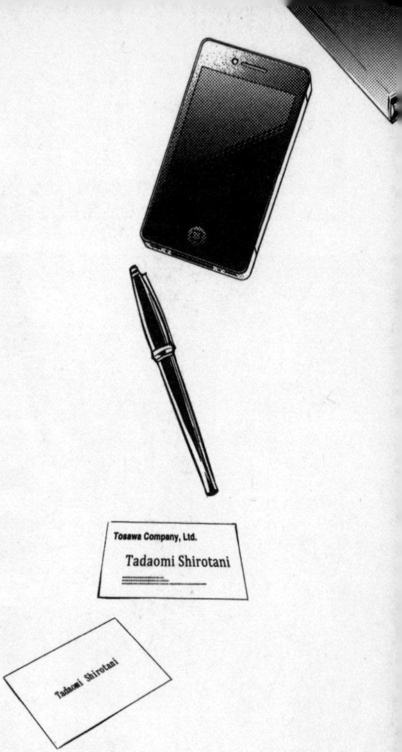
Tosawa Company, Ltd.
Tadaomi Shirotani
Tadaomi Shirotani

Volume 1 turned out to be so leisurely paced that I'm almost worried people will complain the cover was just a tease. Starting with volume 2, the relationship between the two main characters will start to grow and change. I hope you'll stick around to see it.

Thank you very much for reading volume 1.

Rihito Takarai

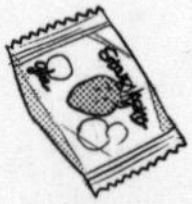